The Appropriation of Religion in Southeast Asia and Beyond

Michel Picard
Editor

The Appropriation of Religion in Southeast Asia and Beyond

palgrave
macmillan

Editor
Michel Picard
Centre Asie du Sud-Est, CNRS EHESS
French National Centre for Scientific
 Research
Paris, France

ISBN 978-3-319-56229-2   ISBN 978-3-319-56230-8 (eBook)
DOI 10.1007/978-3-319-56230-8

Library of Congress Control Number: 2017939077

© The Editor(s) (if applicable) and The Author(s) 2017
This work is subject to copyright. All rights are solely and exclusively licensed by the Publisher, whether the whole or part of the material is concerned, specifically the rights of translation, reprinting, reuse of illustrations, recitation, broadcasting, reproduction on microfilms or in any other physical way, and transmission or information storage and retrieval, electronic adaptation, computer software, or by similar or dissimilar methodology now known or hereafter developed.
The use of general descriptive names, registered names, trademarks, service marks, etc. in this publication does not imply, even in the absence of a specific statement, that such names are exempt from the relevant protective laws and regulations and therefore free for general use.
The publisher, the authors and the editors are safe to assume that the advice and information in this book are believed to be true and accurate at the date of publication. Neither the publisher nor the authors or the editors give a warranty, express or implied, with respect to the material contained herein or for any errors or omissions that may have been made. The publisher remains neutral with regard to jurisdictional claims in published maps and institutional affiliations.

Cover illustration: © Blend Images/Alamy Stock Photo

Printed on acid-free paper

This Palgrave Macmillan imprint is published by Springer Nature
The registered company is Springer International Publishing AG
The registered company address is: Gewerbestrasse 11, 6330 Cham, Switzerland

Acknowledgements

This collection of essays originates in a collaborative research project titled 'Local Traditions and World Religions: The Appropriation of "Religion" in Southeast Asia and Beyond', jointly funded by the French Agence Nationale de la Recherche (ANR) and the German Deutsche Forschungsgemeinschaft (DFG), that ran from January 2011 to June 2014.

Combining anthropological and historical approaches with philology and political science, the participants to this research—placed under the leadership of Bénédicte Brac de la Perrière and Annette Hornbacher—aimed to investigate contemporary religious politics in Southeast Asia and Melanesia by framing it in long-term perspectives. In the course of regular meetings in Paris and Heidelberg, they confronted their analyses of the localization of world religions occurring dialogically with the universalization of local traditions in their respective fields of investigation. While these issues are commonly framed in terms of relations between the 'local' and the 'global', globalization should not be viewed as impacting the local from the outside as it is always localized. Besides, it is inevitably mediated by the state and its religious politics. On the whole, in the name of modernity and progress, Southeast Asian states tend to press their populations to have a 'religion'. On that account, the authors in this volume address religion as a process of 'religionization', implying that adherents of indigenous ritual practices are 'not yet religious' and therefore are due to be 'religionized'.

In this respect, we deem it necessary to problematize the category 'religion', as it is neither a descriptive nor an analytical term but a prescriptive and normative concept, which is too imbued with Christian theology as well as with Western modernity to have a transcultural relevance. However, while religion is not a vernacular category but one projected externally on some aspects of native culture, the fact is that non-Western peoples have appropriated the category religion to define certain practices as differentiated from others. Hence, the issue is to investigate the process whereby such a category has become self-evident even to those for whom it was previously a novelty. That is to say, our aim is to understand what happens when local peoples themselves claim to 'have a religion', whether they want to have a religion or are constrained to demonstrate that they profess one.

In methodological terms, thus, 'religion' is that which is regarded as such by these local actors, which might not correspond to what counts as religion for the observer. Furthermore, local actors do not necessarily concur regarding what their religion is about, as religion is a contentious issue. Indeed, in the course of our research we noticed a tension between proponents of local traditions, who consider them as both self-sufficient and deserving the label 'religion' in their own right, and advocates of a world religion, who deny those local traditions the qualification of 'religion'. What's more, in many cases this tension may coexist within the same actors, who are faced with the predicament of having to integrate both their own indigenous traditions and the locally prevailing world religion(s) into the same socio-cosmic order. In consequence, in each of our case studies, we purpose to elucidate what gets identified and legitimized as 'religion', by whom, for what purpose, and under what political conditions.

For diverse reasons, several of the participants to the initial research project could not be included in this volume, namely Andrée Feillard, Alexandra de Mersan, François Raillon, Susanne Rodemeier, and Gwenaël Njoto-Feillard. On the other hand, the editor would like to express his heartfelt gratitude to Bénédicte Brac de la Perrière and Cécile Barraud for their invaluable assistance in the achievement of this collective enterprise, as well as to Chelsie Yount-André and Richard Fox for having smoothed over the style of some of these chapters. Last but not least, this research project could not have been brought to fruition without the invaluable financial and administrative support of the Centre Asie du Sud-Est.

Michel Picard

CONTENTS

1 Introduction: Local Traditions and World Religions. Encountering 'Religion' in Southeast Asia and Melanesia   1
Michel Picard

2 About Buddhist Burma: *Thathana*, or 'Religion' as Social Space   39
Bénédicte Brac de la Perrière

3 The (Re)configuration of the Buddhist Field in Post-Communist Cambodia   67
Anne Yvonne Guillou

4 Re-connecting the Ancestors. Buddhism and Animism on the Boloven Plateau, Laos   95
Guido Sprenger

5 Balinese Religion in the Making: An Enquiry About the Interpretation of *Agama Hindu* as 'Hinduism'   123
Michel Picard

6 Return to the Source: A Balinese Pilgrimage to India
   and the Re-Enchantment of *Agama Hindu* in Global
   Modernity   153
   Annette Hornbacher

7 A Wall, Even in Those Days! Encounters with Religions
   and What Became of the Tradition   185
   Cécile Barraud

8 Encounters with Christianity in the North Moluccas
   (Sixteenth–Nineteenth Centuries)   217
   Jos. D. M. Platenkamp

9 Continuity and Breaches in Religion and Globalization,
   a Melanesian Point of View   251
   André Iteanu

Index   279

Editor and Contributors

About the Editor

Michel Picard Ph.D. is a retired researcher at the French National Center for Scientific Research (CNRS) and a founding member of the Center for Southeast Asian Studies (CASE, CNRS-EHESS) in Paris. He has published extensively in the field of Balinese studies, specifically on tourism, culture, identity, ethnicity, and religion. He is the author of *Bali: Cultural Tourism and Touristic Culture* (1996) and has co-edited several collective volumes, the latest one being *The Politics of Religion in Indonesia. Syncretism, Orthodoxy, and Religious Contention in Java and Bali* (2011). He has recently published *Kebalian. La construction dialogique de l'identité balinaise* (2017).

Contributors

Cécile Barraud Centre Asie du Sud-Est, CNRS-EHESS, Paris, France

Bénédicte Brac de la Perrière Centre Asie du Sud-Est, CNRS-EHESS, Paris, France

Anne Yvonne Guillou CNRS, IRASEC, Bangkok, Thailand; CNRS, Centre Asie du Sud-Est, Paris, France

Annette Hornbacher Institut für Ethnologie, Heidelberg University, Heidelberg, Germany

André Iteanu Centre Asie du Sud-Est, CNRS-EHESS, Paris, France

Jos. D. M. Platenkamp Westfaelische Wilhelms-Universitaet Muenster, Institut Fuer Ethnologie, Muenster, Germany

Guido Sprenger Institut für Ethnologie, Heidelberg University, Heidelberg, Germany

List of Figures

Fig. 2.1	Monks alms round organized by a local NLD office to prepare Aung San's 100th birthday on the 13th of February 2015	57
Fig. 3.1	Map of Cambodia with the location of the 3 monks involved in this research	70
Fig. 3.2	Part of the *kāt' groḥ* ritual performed by the monks	86
Fig. 6.1	Balinese pilgrims learning how to offer milk to a Shiva Linga in New Delhi, February 2011	161
Fig. 6.2	Kurukshetra, Balinese pilgrims in a temple for the banyan tree where the Bhagavadgita was delivered, February 2011	163
Fig. 6.3	Balinese and Javanese pilgrims during their ritual bath in Haridwar, February 2011	172
Fig. 7.1	The wall (Pleyte 1893)	188
Fig. 7.2	Map of the Kei Archipelago, southeast Moluccas	191
Fig. 7.3	The bay and the remnants of the wall at Tanebar-Evav, July 2009	196
Fig. 8.1	Map of the Moluccas, 1998	219
Fig. 8.2	Map Allain Manesson Mallet, 1683	235
Fig. 9.1	Map of Papua New Guinea	274

CHAPTER 1

Introduction: Local Traditions and World Religions. Encountering 'Religion' in Southeast Asia and Melanesia

Michel Picard

In his influential book *Conceptualizing Religion*, the American anthropologist Benson Saler asserts that 'Religion is a Western folk category that contemporary Western scholars have appropriated' (Saler 2000: IX). As a consequence, anthropologists are liable to use this Western category in order to make sense of what is assumed to be a core identity marker for non-Western peoples. As perplexing as this is, the problem is compounded by the fact that the category 'religion' has been appropriated not only by Western scholars but also by the peoples studied by anthropologists.

Whereas Saler was conceptualizing religion with a view to transforming this Western folk category into an analytical concept suitable for cross-cultural research,[1] our aim is to elucidate what happens when

---

[1] Notwithstanding, as Maurice Bloch reminds us, that 'anthropologists have, after countless fruitless attempts, found it impossible to usefully and convincingly cross-culturally isolate or define a distinct phenomenon that can analytically be labelled "religion"' (Bloch 2008: 2055).

M. Picard (✉)
Centre Asie du Sud-Est, CNRS-EHESS, Paris, France

non-Western peoples themselves claim to 'have a religion.' If indeed it is true that 'to define 'religion' is first and foremost an act,' in the sense that 'to define is to leave out some things and to include others' (Asad 2001: 145), then we will concern ourselves with the very act of asserting that some things are 'religious' and others are not. That is to say that there is no such thing as 'religion' out there, 'only a wide variety of human practices, beliefs, or experiences that may or may not be categorized as such, depending on one's definition' (Hanegraaff 2016: 582). Accordingly, we are not concerned here with establishing what 'religion' ought to mean or what exactly it refers to. Rather, in social constructionist fashion, we are interested in investigating how this category operates for the people who appropriate it and what they do with it. In this respect, for us the relevant question is no longer 'What is religion?' but 'What does and what does not count as religion in a given context' and, above all, 'Who gets to make this decision and why?'

'Religion' is notoriously difficult to define. To this day, there is no scholarly consensus as to 'what religion really is.' The various definitions of religion may be categorized according to a distinction between so-called 'substantive' and 'functional' interpretations. According to the former, religion consists of paying homage to the gods, and their anthropological formulation begins with Edward Tylor's famous minimal definition of religion as 'belief in spiritual beings' and extends to Melford Spiro's 'culturally patterned interaction with culturally postulated superhuman beings' (Spiro 1966). Functional definitions focus on what is of 'ultimate concern' (Paul Tillich), to either an individual or to a social group. The problem with these approaches is that substantive definitions are too narrow to account for situations occurring in cultures that do not conceive of a distinction between religious and secular domains, whereas functional definitions are too broad to establish any empirical boundaries around religion and to thus distinguish it from other sociocultural phenomena. Following Émile Durkheim, religion has been further characterized as concerned with the relationship between man and the 'sacred' (Borgeaud 1994), which was construed as an ontological category manifest in feelings of awe by phenomenologists like Rudolf Otto ('numinous') and Mircea Eliade ('hierophany'), for whom the human being is a *homo religiosus*—thereby substituting a hierocentric definition of religion supposedly found in all cultures for the previous theocentric model.

In any case, such attempts to define religion in transhistorical and transcultural terms necessarily impute upon it a fixed essence, which is precisely what is denounced by scholars who deny the prevalent assumption of the religious studies discourse—the universality of religion as a distinct domain of human societies.² They propose instead to submit religious phenomena, like all other social facts, to the critical analysis of the social sciences, an approach deemed 'reductionist' by their opponents, who claim that religion is a *sui generis* phenomenon. On the contrary, these critics argue that religion is neither natural nor universal, but instead a specifically Christian, Eurocentric, modern category that has been unduly projected on ancient and foreign cultures.

Genealogy of the Category 'Religion'

'Religion' is neither a descriptive nor an analytical term but a prescriptive and normative category and a contentious one at that. Originating in the Roman notion of *religio*, it was appropriated by Christian theologians, who radically shifted its meaning by uprooting it from its 'pagan' framework (Sachot 2007). To the Romans, *religio* was what *traditio* is all about, a set of ancestral practices developed by a people and transmitted over generations.³ Just as there are different peoples, so are there different traditions. As a set of practices, the predicates 'true' and 'false' are not applicable to tradition. By claiming to be the true *religio*, Christianity opposed its doctrines to the prevalent practices, rejected as false beliefs marred by 'superstition.' This distinction between *vera* and *falsa religio* marked a conceptual shift characterized by a scriptural turn, a substitution of dogma for ritual, of orthodoxy for orthopraxy, that introduced a novel kind of truth: a revealed, absolute truth (Assmann 2003). The

---

²See Goody (1961), Smith (1962), Gauchet (1985), Asad (1993), Staal (1996), McCutcheon (1997, 2004), Fitzgerald (1997, 2000, 2007), Smith (1998), Dubuisson (1998, 2007), King (1999a, 2011), Nye (2000), Peterson and Walhof (2002), McKinnon (2002), Balagangadhara (2005), Masuzawa (2005), Bell (2006), Nongbri (2014). For some of these authors at least, the critique of the category religion appears to be part and parcel of the post-colonial denunciation of dominant Western worldviews and epistemologies.

³As is well known, Cicero's etymology related *religio* to *religere*, meaning 'to retrace' or 'to read anew.' In this sense, *religio* involved the scrupulous reiteration of the ritual traditions of one's ancestors. In the early fourth century, the Christian theologian Lactantius rejected Cicero's etymology, arguing instead that *religio* derives from *religare*, meaning 'to bind' or 'to link,' which eventually became the common understanding of religion. On the origin and evolution of the category religion, see Sachot (2003).

Christian appropriation of *religio* thus established the exclusivist monotheism of Christianity as the normative paradigm for understanding what a religion is. Religion became a matter of adherence to a particular doctrine rather than allegiance to customary ritual practices. The religious field, previously embedded in the culture of a particular society, then turned into an autonomous domain that could be taken up by other societies. The question remains as to how this Christian theological category, which issued from a specific polemical context, evolved to the point of becoming the central explanatory category of religious studies.

It is important to note that for most of the history of European Christendom, the word 'religion' (*religio*) meant something very different than it does in contemporary usage (Smith 1962, 1998; Despland 1980). 'Religion' is a secular category, in the sense that its modern understanding as a 'system of beliefs and practices' is a product of secularization, that is, of the differentiation of spheres of life in modern societies (Bourdieu 1971; Asad 2003). Specifically, secularization refers not only to the formal institutional separation of Church and State, but further to an epistemic turn in which a field of beliefs and practices comes to be constituted as 'religion' as such. This religious field emerged during the Renaissance, evolved as a result of the Reformation and was reworked in the Enlightenment, before acquiring its present significance in the course of the nineteenth century.

The Protestant doctrine of salvation focused attention on inner piety and personal faith. With this emphasis on private religious consciousness, institutional forms of liturgy, priesthood and Church were relegated to merely external social phenomena. This shift to belief as the defining characteristic of religion resulted in a change from an institutionally based understanding of exclusive salvation within the Catholic Church to a propositionally based understanding that thereafter conceived of religion as a set of propositions to which believers gave assent (Fitzgerald 2007).

The fragmentation of Christendom following the Reformation resulted not only in confessional disputes and 'Wars of Religion,' but also in critical comparisons of competing forms of Christianity. Polemics and apologetics among Christians prompted the proponents of 'deism' to deal with these disputes by trying to determine the lowest common denominator of the various Christian denominations, an approach that was eventually extended to all creeds. The search for a universal core of religion based on reason instead of revelation produced a substantive definition of what came to be known as 'natural religion'—as distinct from the 'revealed religion' of Christianity—defined as a set of beliefs (which hinged upon the existence of one supreme being), practices (in the form of sanctioned worship) and ethics (a code of conduct based on rewards and punishments after this life), supposed to be common to all peoples (Asad 1993: 40; see Bossy 1985, Byrne 1989, Harrison 1990, Stroumsa 2010).

At the same time that this universal core of religion was being devised, the discovery of the rites and creeds of faraway peoples in the Americas and Asia as well as the rediscovery of antiquity were calling into question the Biblical world of faith. These combined circumstances set the stage for construing the peoples of the world as being divided into different 'religions,' conceived as objectified doctrinal systems, each with their own distinct claims to propositional truth. Thus, from the seventeenth century onward, the conventional ordering for categorizing the peoples of the world in terms of Christians, Jews, Mohammedans and heathens turned into a division between four sorts of religions—Christianity, Judaism, Mohammedanism and heathenism[4]—but with only one 'right' way of worshipping God. In this perspective, Christianity provided the norm to which Judaism and Mohammedanism could be somehow related as competing 'Abrahamic religions',[5] as opposed to heathenism, long perceived as an indiscriminate lump.

As the voyages of exploration and the subsequent rise of colonialism were providing opportunities for European scholars, administrators and missionaries to acquire some first-hand knowledge of heathens' manifold customs, this latter category was progressively disaggregated into distinct religions. In the course of the nineteenth century, the prevalent fourfold division of humanity declined to be replaced by a list of 'world religions' that could be compared with one another as particular instances of the universal genus 'religion' (Masuzawa 2005). The common assumption of

---

[4] In this process, heathenism, or paganism, became a central organizing category governing much of Europe's early relationship to both the new worlds discovered by travelers and missionaries, and the ancient worlds recovered by philologists. See Ryan (1981) and Chidester (1996).

[5] Notwithstanding the fact that each of these 'Abrahamic' religions claims to be the sole rightful heir to Abraham's covenant, they share references, beliefs and practices that distinguish them quite radically from other traditions. On this, see for example Hughes (2012) and Levenson (2012).

Western scholarship was that these world religions shared essential similarities with Christianity—even though, weighed against what was considered to be God's last word, they were necessarily found wanting—in the terms of which they were assessed: namely formal soteriological doctrines resting on canonical authority, enforced by a priestly hierarchy and sustained by congregational worship. From the prevailing evolutionist perspective of the times, world religions were considered advanced religions, as opposed to ethnic religions, regarded as primitive and riddled with superstition.

In sum, the contemporary understanding of 'religion' emerged both out of the encounter of Christendom with other 'religions' during the great march of European discoveries and colonial expansion and of Enlightenment struggles to differentiate between rational knowledge and revealed dogmas to emancipate society from the smothering power of the Church—in such a way that it eventually became conceivable to separate the study of religion from its practice. Thus presented in a secular garb by post-Reformation and post-Enlightenment thinkers, the Christian conception of religion became a scholarly construct with the development of the so-called science of religion (*Religionswissenschaft*) (Sharpe 1986). As a result, at issue is the fact that the category religion is too imbued with Christian theological apologetics, as well as with European colonialism and Western modernity, to have a transcultural or a transhistorical relevance. Consequently, 'religion' ought not be taken for a conceptual tool but, rather, should itself be the object of analysis. That is to say, instead of essentializing religion as if it were a universal and generic category, one needs to historicize and deconstruct it.[6]

Asian Traditions as World Religions

Whereas in the Christian context 'religion' exists as a category to its own participants, outside of this context it is a second-order category, constructed by observers from a variety of phenomena which the actors do not necessarily combine into a coherent institution and for which they

---

[6]One of the first scholars to deconstruct the category religion was Wilfred Cantwell Smith (1962). Yet he too clung to essentialism. In retracing the genealogy of the category religion, Smith separates 'faith' from what he calls 'cumulative tradition.' And in taking faith to be primary and transcendent in opposition to religious traditions, treated as its secondary worldly expressions, he holds to a typically Protestant outlook, which is not surprising coming from a Presbyterian minister.

usually do not possess a corresponding word (Cohn 1969). Now, it appears that the terms under which Christianity defines itself as a religion are comparable to the terms under which Islam and Judaism recognize themselves as religions. Therefore, the category religion is to some extent common to these three Abrahamic traditions, which are related by a similar belief in one exclusive God and divine revelation recorded in a Holy Book. In contrast, there was no corresponding indigenous terminology in Asian traditions prior to the modern period. According to the approach of the contributors to this volume, if there is no equivalent term in another culture, it is not only the word that is missing, but that particular entity 'religion' itself—in the sense of a set of beliefs and practices with some kind of systemic coherence that could be conceptually isolated from other aspects of social life, and to which one could 'convert'—does not exist. In this respect, we concur with Ludwig Wittgenstein that analyzing a concept amounts to analyzing the use of a word. Indeed, it is difficult to conceive of an institutionalized religion in the absence of a vernacular denomination substantiating its existence.

However, the fact that religion is 'a category imposed from the outside on some aspect of native culture' (Smith 1998: 269) does not imply that it is 'solely the creation of the scholar's study,' as Jonathan Smith would have it (1982: XI)—not only because, historically, the concept of 'religion' was not created by scholars but emerged over the centuries as a discursive formation proper to Christian culture, but, more to the point, because members of other cultures have now appropriated the term religion to define some of their practices as differentiated from others. Hence, a distinction has to be made between scholarly analytical definitions of the term religion and its indigenous uses, between its etic and its emic understandings.[7] In other words, the issue is to investigate the historical process whereby the category 'religion' has become self-evident even to those for whom it was previously a novelty (King 2011: 45).

As it happens, it was not enough for missionaries, along with Orientalists and colonial administrators, to impute characteristic features of Christianity to Asian traditions to bring forth such 'religions' as Hinduism, Buddhism, Jainism, Sikhism, Taoism, Confucianism and

---

[7] In this, I must agree with Claude Lévi-Strauss, who argues that 'No common analysis of religion can be given by a believer and a non-believer' (Lévi-Strauss 1972: 188).

Shintoism[8]—as if local people were only passive recipients and had no agency of their own in the matter. Their native interlocutors had to further claim for themselves the privilege of possessing their own religion, construed as a soteriological system on a par with Christianity. To do this, they emphasized the doctrinal features as well as the ethical precepts in their traditions, while condemning blind superstition, mindless priestcraft and backward customs. By conforming orthopraxy to orthodoxy, reformers attempted to discriminate between 'true religion' and 'mere tradition.' Such a replacement of disparate local traditions by a normative and de-territorialized form of religion was marked by rationalization (the formulation of a canonical corpus, its institutionalization and its effective socialization), as well as by secularization (the de-sacralization of the immanent concrete in favor of an abstract and transcendent divine) (Hefner 1993, 1998). In addition, it usually brought about a politicization of religion, which was instrumentalized to articulate ethnic or national identities.

The dialogic construction of 'Hinduism' and 'Buddhism' as world religions is a case in point. Ever since the publication of Edward Said's *Orientalism* (1978), there has been a tendency to see the forms of knowledge produced by colonial scholars, administrators and missionaries as a one-sided imposition of power, tantamount to denying agency to colonial subjects—when in fact, from the very beginning, Asian actors exposed to European representations and criticisms of their 'religion' became active participants in Orientalist discourse. Lest we be suspected of granting colonial power too much credit in this affair, let us declare from the outset with Tomoko Masuzawa that 'the European-initiated ideas of Hinduism and Buddhism [...] could not have acquired such an overwhelming sense of reality had it not been for those who positively and actively identified themselves as Hindus or Buddhists [...] What remains yet to be studied concertedly is the very process of mutually interactive development, on the one hand, of European representations of non-Christian religions and, on the other hand, the native appropriation, reaction, or resistance to such representations' (Masuzawa 2005: 282).

Due to India's long history of exposure to both Islam and Christianity, Hinduism provides an informative paradigm for

---

[8] See Oberoi (1994), Lopez (1995), Jensen (1997), Girardot (1999), Brekke (2002), Mandair (2009), Goossaert and Palmer (2011), Josephson (2012), van der Veer (2014).

understanding the relational process through which a local tradition was turned into a world religion. As is well known, the word 'Hindu'—the Persian form of the Sanskrit word 'Sindhu' (the Indus river)—was originally a geographic and ethnic identifier, used by the Persians to designate the inhabitants of the country they named Hindustan (the land of the Hindus). For the Persians, Hindus were Indians that were not Muslims (Sharma 2002).

Some of those designated as 'Hindus' began to use that word by the sixteenth century in order to distinguish themselves from the 'foreign and barbarous' peoples, the *mleccha*, who were not thought of primarily as 'Muslims' (Sanderson 2015: 156, n. 2). Not before the eighteenth century did Hindus begin to acknowledge that those barbarous foreigners were Muslims (O'Connell 1973). But even when used by indigenous Indians, it is clear that the term 'Hindu' carried no specifically religious denotation, as revealed by the fact that in the early nineteenth century it was still common to refer to natives who had converted to Islam or Christianity as Hindu Muslims and Hindu Christians.

In the course of the eighteenth century, European observers took the term 'Hindu' to designate the followers of a particular Indian religion, after having long wondered whether they comprised one religion or several (Marshall 1970; Sweetman 2003; Gelders 2009). Through a process of reification, the word 'Hindooism' was first coined in 1787 by the Evangelical missionary (and subsequent director of the East India Company) Charles Grant, to name 'the religion of the Hindoos' (Oddie 2006: 71)—an imagined religion that had never existed as a religion in the minds of Hindus themselves. Hitherto, there had been only multiple communities identified by locality, language, caste, lineage, occupation and sectarian affiliation. Indeed, Hindus could not consider themselves to be members of a single religious community, because their idea of *dharma* insisted upon distinctions between heterogeneous groups.

The concept of *dharma* is complex and cannot be reduced to one general principle. Nor is there one single translation that encompasses all its meanings—which span religion, ritual, law, conduct and ethics—all of which are distinct in the Western perspective. *Dharma* is both an account of the cosmos and a norm on which to base social life, which at once describes how things are and prescribes the way they should be. It is an all-encompassing category, whose scope is both considerably broader and much more specific than that of the category religion (Rocher 2003; Holdrege 2004).

Dharma may be defined as that which upholds the world and supports order. In the *Dharmaśāstra*,[9] the word *dharma* refers specifically to the *varṇāśramadharma*, the duties and qualifications of an individual according to his social class (*varṇa*) and stage of life (*āśrama*). That is to say, the differential norms of *varṇāśramadharma* apply only to the *svadharma* of the male members of the 'twice-born' *varṇa* (*brāhmaṇa*, *kṣatriya*, *vaiśya*). *Dharma* is thus an exclusive and personal norm, as attested by the well-known verse from the *Bhagavadgītā* that states: 'It is better to perform one's own *dharma* poorly than to perform another's *dharma* well' (B.G. 3.35).

Now, as a result of the demands of British colonial administration, on the one hand, as well as of the pursuits of Christian missionaries, on the other, the concept of *dharma* has been both fragmented and universalized. In his Judicial Plan of 1772, Warren Hastings, the first British Governor-General of Bengal, decreed that the Hindus should be governed by the laws of the Shastra and the Muslims by the law of the Quran (Rocher 1993: 220). This decision implied that native laws would apply only to 'religious' matters, that is, matters corresponding to that which in Britain fell under the purview of ecclesiastical law. This put the British in a position of having to discriminate the religious from the lay in all subjects relating to the Hindus. Furthermore, the source of law was to be found in the *Dharmaśāstra* rather than in local jurisprudence and other living sources of the law. In consequence, law and religion, which were inextricably enmeshed in the *Dharmaśāstra*, were artificially set apart.

Then, from 1800 onward, when Baptist missionaries in Bengal translated the Bible—which they titled *dharmapustaka* ('the book of *dharma*') in Sanskrit—they chose the term *dharma* as a gloss for the term religion and began to proclaim Christianity as the 'true *dharma*' (*satyādharma*).[10] By thus depriving the Hindus of their *dharma*, which they expounded as a false religion, the missionaries channeled the

---

[9] The *Dharmaśāstra* are ancient Sanskrit treatises of the Brahmanical tradition that refer to the branch of learning (*śāstra*) pertaining to the subject of *dharma*. They are considered part of the *smṛti* ('that which is remembered,' i.e., the 'tradition') and find their source in the transcendent authority of the *Veda*—the *śruti* ('that which is heard,' i.e., the 'revelation').

[10] In contrast, in South India, where Jesuit missionaries had been translating the Bible since the close of the sixteenth century, the category religion was commonly rendered by the terms *veda* and *mata*. Thus, Christianity was dubbed the 'true Veda' (*satyāvedam*) and the Bible was titled *vedapustaka*.

Hindu reaction in two directions (Halbfass 1988: 342). On the one hand, in order to meet the Christian challenge, Hindus themselves started using the word *dharma* in the sense of religion, with the result that the Hindu *dharma* became one religion among others, to be compared and opposed to the Christian *dharma* or the Muslim *dharma*. On the other hand, some Hindus disclaimed the exclusive character of the *varnāshramadharma* and attempted instead to universalize *dharma*, by invoking the inclusive notion of *sanātanadharma* as the 'eternal and universal religion.' In that respect, *dharma* was considered as a principle superior to and, moreover, encompassing all religions.

In 1816, the term 'Hinduism' was first appropriated by a Hindu, the Bengali religious reformer Rammohun Roy, who was also the first Indian to speak of *dharma* in the sense of religion (Killingley 1993: 61). In due course, the name Hinduism was taken up by the Anglicized Indian elites, in their attempt to establish a religion that could compete with Christianity and Islam for equal standing. For the members of this Western-educated intelligentsia, the English language was not just a means of communicating with a foreign culture; it also served as a medium in which they articulated their self-understanding and reinterpreted their own traditions. They initiated reform movements that drew on models from both the contemporary West and an idealized Indian past that was actively been uncovered by British Orientalists (Kopf 1969). Whereas Hindu practices were traditionally localized, sectarian and segregated, reformers formed pan-Indian associations that promoted the idea of a single inclusive religion for all Hindus, now being defined as a national religious community.

In the evolutionary worldview of nineteenth-century Europe, monotheism was seen as the highest form of religion. Embracing the Protestant emphasis on sacred texts as the locus of religion, reformers singled out Vedic and Brahmanical scriptures as canonical, while dismissing popular religious practices. They claimed that Hinduism was originally a monotheistic religion, whose true doctrines were to be found either in the *Veda*, the *Upaniṣad* or the *Bhagavadgītā*, but which had degenerated into polytheism and image worship during the Puranic period. In this, they aligned themselves with the Orientalists, for whom true Hinduism was the pristine religion of bygone India and not that which was commonly observable in modern times.

In response to missionary criticism and for fear of conversion to Christianity, reformers pressed their fellow coreligionists to eradicate what the missionaries described as 'demonic' practices, and they set about drawing a distinction between true Hinduism and mere traditions. This distinction was commonly framed in terms of a contrast between that which belongs to *dharma* and that which pertains to *ācāra*—the established rules of conduct that constitute *varnāśramadharma*, which are thus endorsed by the *Dharmaśāstra* but which the reformers did not consider to be an essential part of Hinduism.

In point of fact, reformers held divergent opinions on the principles of reformed Hinduism.[11] Whatever their particular tenets, all these reform movements met with resistance from Hindu traditionalists, who formed conservative organizations dedicated to the defense of the *sanātana dharma*. Despite their claims that this was the 'eternal religion,' *sanātana dharma* is as modern a construct as Hinduism, in the sense that it emerged as a self-conscious reaction to both Christianity and reform movements (Halbfass 1988: 343–346).

In any case, it was not before the book *Hinduism* was published in 1877 by the famous British Sanskritist Sir Monier Monier-Williams that the term Hinduism gained full currency in English. But even then, it was not universally accepted in India itself. Thus, when the British colonial government introduced a census in 1871, many Indians either did not understand the category or else refused the label Hindu outright (Haan 2005). As there are no criteria for deciding who is and who is not a Hindu, government officials resolved that Hinduism could only be defined residually, that is, Hindus are Indians who are neither Muslims, nor Christians, nor Sikhs, nor Jains, nor Buddhists, and so on. In other

---

[11] One can distinguish three main reform-minded responses to the Christian attack on Hinduism. Rammohun Roy (1772–1833) and the Brāhmo Samāj (founded in 1828) saw Christianity as one instance of universalist religion and combined elements of Sufism, Advaita Vedānta and Christian Unitarianism into a common religion with strong deist tendencies (Kopf 1979; Mitter 1987). A few decades later, Dayananda Sarasvati (1824–1883) and the Ārya Samāj (founded in 1875) adopted a much more radical stance by rejecting Christianity altogether and calling for the Āryas to 'Go back to the Veda' (Jordens 1978; Llewellyn 1993). A third response was developed by Vivekananda (1863-1902), who argued that Christianity was simply a lesser form of the universal spirituality found in all religions, which had reached its highest level in Advaita Vedānta (Radice 1998; Basu 2002).

words, Hindus are those who are left after others have set themselves apart. It was only after the publication in 1923 of the book *Essentials of Hindutva*[12] by V.D. Savarkar—which popularized the neologism *hindutva* ('Hinduness')—that Hinduism became a common denomination in India, and this in a nationalist perspective.

The point here is that defining Hinduism is not only difficult but contentious as well, because 'Hinduism' is an ideological construct.[13] In this respect, the nineteenth-century reform movements did not so much describe what Hinduism was, as prescribe what it should be. Hence, the name 'Neo-Hinduism' commonly given to this idealized Hinduism (Hacker 1995), which in actual fact never concerned more than a tiny minority of those regarded as Hindus, who continued worshipping their gods, singing their songs and telling their stories.

The denomination 'Buddhism' appears to have arisen at around the same time as its sibling 'Hinduism' (King 1999a). According to Philip Almond (1988), the invention of Buddhism as a world religion occurred in two distinct phases. From the late eighteenth century onward, a motley collection of religious phenomena throughout Asia was being classified under the purview of the 'religion of Buddha,' soon to be labeled 'Buddhism.' Thus the word Buddhism appeared several times in the first issue of *The Asiatic Journal and Monthly Register for British India and its Dependencies* in 1816 and was popularized by the Orientalist Edward Upham, whose 1829 volume *The History and Doctrine of Buddhism* was the first book in English to include the name 'Buddhism' in its title.

By the late nineteenth century, fully fledged Orientalist discourse about Buddhism had developed. Early Buddhologists assumed that the original Buddhism was the authentic Buddhism and that its ancient Pāli

---

[12] Reprinted in 1928 under the title *Hindutva: Who is a Hindu?*

[13] Numerous studies have been published on the construction of 'Hinduism' as a 'religion.' See Marshall (1970), Inden (1986), Thapar (1989), Fitzgerald (1990), Frykenberg (1993), Hawley (1991), Dalmia and von Stietencron (1995), Von Stietencron (1997), Lorenzen (1999), King (1999a, b, 2011), Sontheimer and Kulke (2001), Sharma (2002), Sugirtharajah (2003), Sweetman (2003), Balagangadhara (2005), Pennington (2005), Lipner (2006), Jha (2006), Bloch et al. (2010).

canon[14] contained its definitive doctrine. Competence in Pāli, and a corresponding familiarity with the canonical texts, grew progressively, to achieve excellence in the work of Thomas William Rhys Davids, whose book *Buddhism* appeared in 1877 (the very same year that saw the publication of Monier-Williams' *Hinduism*). In 1881, Rhys Davids founded in Ceylon the Pāli Text Society with a view to foster and promote the study of Pāli scriptures. Thereafter, 'originally existing 'out there' in the Oriental present, Buddhism came to be determined as an object the primary location of which was the West, through the progressive collection, translation, and publication of its textual past' (Almond 1988: 13).

By that time, Buddhism had been distinguished from Hinduism and was conceived as having been founded by Gautama in India. The historical Buddha was thought to have challenged Vedic authority presided over by the Brahman priesthood and rejected the inequities of the caste system. He was valued, in consequence, as a rationalist reformer of the evils of Hinduism—just as Luther had reformed the decadent Roman Catholic Church—and Buddhism came to be seen as the Indian Protestantism.[15] Yet, if Buddhism, as it was being construed through the editing and studying of its ancient texts, was viewed somewhat favorably in opposition to Hinduism, it was painfully clear that its contemporary manifestations in the Orient measured unfavorably against their ideal textual exemplifications. Due to this perceived disparity between the canonical Buddhist texts and the actual practices of Buddhists, Buddhism was henceforth seen as being in a general state of decay. This was particularly the case with later Mahāyāna and Vajrayāna Buddhism, as contrasted with Theravāda Buddhism seen as containing the essence of Buddhism.

While Almond referred to the formulation of an Orientalist image of Buddhism in Victorian Britain, he made no attempt to inquire into Buddhist thought and practice in nineteenth-century Asia, denying

---

[14] Pāli is a Prakrit, an ancient vernacular language of India derivative of Sanskrit. Etymologically meaning 'text,' the word Pāli had been used since the eighteenth century to designate the language of the *Tipiṭaka*, the canonical texts of Theravāda Buddhism, the 'Doctrine of the Elders,' dominant in Sri Lanka and in Southeast Asia. On Theravāda Buddhism, see Gombrich (2006), and on the modern genealogy of the terms 'Theravāda' and 'Theravāda Buddhism,' see Perreira (2012).

[15] This is especially the case of Theravāda, as opposed to Mahāyāna (the 'Great Way,' that was taken up in China whence it spread to East Asia) and to Vajrayāna (the 'Diamond Way,' established in Tibet and Mongolia), which have been commonly likened to Roman Catholicism. On this, see Gellner (1990).

any voice to Buddhists in the representation of Buddhism as religion (Hallisey 1995: 31; see Harris 2006). The fact is that the editing and publishing of the Pāli canon by Orientalists made it accessible to a wider range of Buddhists than ever before, at a time when attacks on Buddhism by Christian missionaries were stirring up reactions among both monastic and urban elites in Ceylon and Southeast Asia, initiating a reform movement that has been characterized as 'Buddhist Modernism' by Heinz Bechert (1966; see McMahan 2008) and as 'Protestant Buddhism' by Gananath Obeyesekere (1970; see Gombrich and Obeyesekere 1988). Originally, Buddhist Modernism sought to respond to the negative colonial portrayal of Buddhism by presenting its teachings in modern and positive terms. It was both a protest against Christianity and a confrontation with popular Buddhism. In dealing with Christian proselytism, this reformed Buddhism assumed some of the characteristics of Protestant Christianity and became a challenge to Theravāda Buddhism as actually practiced. It was characterized by an emphasis on scriptures, rationality, meditation, ethics and increased participation of the laity, along with a de-emphasis on ritual, dogma, clerical hierarchy, traditional cosmology and 'superstition.' Although this movement was novel in many ways, its promoters claimed to return to the original teachings of the Buddha himself, prior to the extraneous cultural accretions that had become associated with it over the centuries. Thus it is that, in some respects, 'Buddhism was represented as a "world religion" fully the equal of Christianity in antiquity, geographical expanse, membership, and philosophical profundity, with its own founder, sacred scriptures, and fixed body of doctrine' (Lopez 1998: 185). But, in other respects, Buddhism was not just considered on a par with other religions; it was posited as superior to them—just as the Hindu *dharma* claimed a spiritual heritage superior to that of mere religions.[16]

Colonel Henry Steel Olcott, the co-founder and first president of the Theosophical Society, has been credited with initiating the revival that gave birth to Protestant Buddhism (Prothero 1995). He introduced

---

[16] The similarity between Hindu and Buddhist reform movements went even further, in the sense that in his speeches at the World's Parliament of Religions conducted in 1893 in Chicago the Sinhalese revivalist Anagarika Dharmapala rejected the very term 'Buddhism' as a Western construct, preferring instead 'Ārya Dharma,' just like Dayananda Sarasvati and the Ārya Samāj had attempted to replace the term 'Hinduism' with 'Ārya Dharma,' that is, the system of doctrines and duties held and practiced by the Āryas.

into modern Sinhalese consciousness the notion of Buddhism as a system of beliefs through the publication in 1881 of his *Buddhist Catechism* (Olcott 1881),[17] modeled upon Protestant catechisms, which has gone through numerous editions and been translated into many languages, and is still in use in Sri Lankan schools. The emulation of the Christian model was further manifested in his formulation of fourteen 'Fundamental Buddhist Beliefs' in 1891. Considering Olcott's prominence in Sinhalese Buddhist revival[18]—and taking into account his aspiration to unify the diversity of the Buddhist world beyond Ceylon to Burma, India and Japan—it is tempting to see Buddhist Modernism as a mere product of colonialism, the combined outcome of Victorian Orientalism and Protestant Christianity. Yet we should be aware that the concern with religious renewal on the basis of textual authority is not entirely a modern innovation but was an integral part of Theravāda Buddhism as well. As Charles Hallisey reminds us, developments similar to those which shaped modern Sinhala Buddhism also transformed Thai Buddhism, even without the twofold influences of colonial domination and Christian proselytism (Hallisey 1995: 48).

Nonetheless, if the invention of Buddhism as a world religion was not the exclusive enterprise of colonial outsiders, it remains that for centuries 'Buddhists' had not interpreted what they were doing as practicing 'Buddhism,' as they had no need for such a reified category. Hence, Buddhists had no word that could be glossed as 'Buddhism' or as 'religion' for that matter. The vernacular field of Buddhism as religion was formulated only in the nineteenth century. Previously, it was understood as something one did, not something one believed and one can surmise that it was under the dominance of the Western concept of religion that Buddhism became a commitment to a set of propositions rather than rituals (Josephson 2006). Casting the teachings and practices derived from the word of the Buddha as 'Buddhism,' which was in turn categorized as a 'religion,' allowed the Buddhist faithful to establish themselves as members of an inclusive and unified religious community on equal footing with the adherents of other religions. At the same time, by reducing the

---

[17] It is worth noting that Annie Besant, who would later succeed Olcott as president of the Theosophical Society, published in 1902 a Hindu catechism entitled *Sanātana Dharma Catechism. A Catechism for Boys and Girls in Hindu Religion and Morals* (Besant 1902).

[18] He was instrumental in Anagarika Dharmapala's decision to reform Buddhism with an emphasis on its spirituality and worldwide import.

gap between the monks (*sangha*) and the laity, this new terminology provided a novel vision of a common Buddhist identity. This indigenization of the category religion has been investigated most particularly in Ceylon. The Sinhalese terms used by Buddhists to refer to their religious life originally had very specific and particularistic meanings. Such were *bauddha-samaya* ('Buddhist views,' and by extension 'the Buddhist community') and *buddhasāsana* ('instruction, admonition of the Buddha') (Carter 1977: 264–270; see Southwold 1978, Carter 1993 and Scott 1996). *Sāsana* was the term that Sinhala Buddhists most commonly used to refer to the precepts they followed. It seems that in the course of time it came to designate both an established system of teachings and the institution that promoted it. Sometime in the nineteenth century, the word *āgama*[19] was chosen by Christian missionaries as the vernacular equivalent of religion. Referring to Christianity as *kristiyāni āgama*, they named the 'religion of the Buddha' *buddhāgama*. Later on, this name gained acceptance among the Sinhala Buddhists as a term of self-reference (Malalgoda 1997: 56). As a religion, *buddhāgama* was then commensurable with other religions, while *sāsana* was conceived as *sui generis*—just like *dharma* had been in India before becoming the Hindu equivalent of religion. Henceforth, the Sinhala Buddhists began to consider themselves as having a religion of their own, with clear boundaries marking it off from other religions. Thus, one notices the occurrence of the terms *buddhāgama* and *kristiyāni āgama* in vernacular texts documenting debates that occurred in the 1860s and 1870s between representatives of the Buddhist and the Christian communities. Eventually, in the 1880s, the compound *āgamadharma* became used in the sense of a system of teaching (*dharma*) based on canonical texts (*āgama*).[20]

To summarize, when colonial Orientalists and Christian missionaries began to inquire into the 'religions' they termed 'Hinduism' and 'Buddhism,' they were faced with a perplexing discrepancy between

---

[19] According to Carter (1993: 17), '*Āgama* is an old Sanskrit and Pāli word. Its basic meaning is 'coming, approach, arrival,' and it is used also to mean 'that which has come down to the present' in the sense of tradition preserved in writing. Through this extension the term means also 'religious text,' 'authoritative text' and, further, 'established procedure, discipline.'

[20] If Buddhism shares with Hinduism the notion of *dharma*, its significance is markedly different. As mentioned earlier, Brahman ethics relate specifically to the position of birth, that is, to one's own exclusive *dharma*. On the contrary, Buddhist ethics are supposedly universal and require not only proper behavior but proper motivation as well.

scriptural doctrine and sociological reality. That is to say, a disjuncture existed between what Hindus and Buddhists actually practiced and believed in daily life, on the one hand, and what their 'canonical' scriptures prescribed, on the other. The prevailing Protestant assumptions of these early European observers, which ascribed primacy to textual sources, predisposed them to systematically de-value what local people effectively did and to deny that it had any place in 'true religion.' Regarding Hinduism and Buddhism as systems of beliefs and practices that function according to the model of Christianity, and consequently expecting 'Hindu' and 'Buddhist' to be exclusive identities, they deemed these religions corrupt, forming only a thin veneer over indigenous 'spirit cults.' These views were internalized by indigenous reformers as an encompassing frame of reference within which they reinterpreted their past practices and cosmologies as respective enactments of 'Hinduism' and 'Buddhism.' They endeavored further to make their newly devised 'religion' conform to the Christian conception of what a religion should be by presenting themselves as members of one exclusivist religious community relative to others. As a result, whereas formerly Buddhism had been primarily a soteriology and Hinduism a social system allowing numerous alternative soteriologies, both would henceforth be conceptualized and institutionalized as providing for all the social and soteriological needs of their adherents (Gellner 1999).

The Process of 'Religionization'

Thus, if it is indeed true that 'religion' was not a vernacular category, it has become so as a consequence of the colonial encounter and broader Western political and epistemological domination across the world, which induced the native interlocutors of Orientalists, administrators and missionaries to invent for themselves the idea that they too had a proper religion. In the words of Daniel Dubuisson: 'The West did not only conceive the idea of *religion*, it has constrained other cultures to speak of their own religions by inventing them for them' (2003: 93). As a result, scholars of religion today deal with peoples who consider themselves to 'have a religion.'

What remains thus to be investigated is the dialogic process by which non-Western peoples appropriate that foreign category for their own purposes. How is it that peoples identify themselves in terms of their 'religion,' whether motivated by the active desire to have a religion or constrained to demonstrate that they profess one? How and why has religion become such a prevailing marker of identity? Further, how do people construe what they are doing by converting to a religion, which might range from the strategic use of religious affiliation to a deep adhesion to a revealed faith?

In this respect, one must assess what is lost in the translation of vernacular words like *dharma, sāsana* or *āgama* (not to mention *dīn, mana, tao, shūkyō, bhakti, sampradāya, śraddhā*, etc.) in terms of 'religion'.[21] Hence the importance of delineating the vernacular conception of a religious field, by assessing how the category religion is construed locally and how it operates in relation to other categories. Indeed, far from being autonomous, religion is part of the semantic field it composes with related categories, such as tradition, culture, politics, law, ethics, ritual, superstition, idolatry, magic, and so on. The relationship is one of mutual definition by mutual exclusion. That is to say, as a category, religion is a classificatory device, which involves the construction and maintenance of boundaries. Accordingly, scholars of religion should address the practical work accomplished through the use of religion as a taxonomy, that is, both what it includes and what it excludes.

In methodological terms, 'religion' is thus that which is regarded as such by local actors, which may not correspond to what counts as religion for the observer. Furthermore, these local actors do not necessarily concur regarding what their religion is about, as religion is a contested issue, having to do with institutionalized values and their relation to authority and its legitimation. Consequently, our purpose is not to determine what in truth is the religion of, for example, the Burmese or the Balinese, but rather to elucidate what, in Burma or in Bali, gets—or does not get—identified and legitimized as religion, by whom, in what circumstances, for what purposes and under what political conditions.

The focus of the present research revolves around the appropriation of 'religion' in Southeast Asia and Melanesia, through a dialogic process of localization of 'world religions' and globalization of 'local traditions.' For ages, anthropologists have debated about how one can best grasp that dynamics, whether through the 'great' versus 'little' traditions scheme devised by Robert Redfield and developed by Milton Singer to

---

[21] Conversely, one could ask what might be gained from a reversal of this translation process and the mapping of Western traditions in terms of such vernacular categories (King 2011: 50). See Sharma (1994) for an attempt at addressing religious studies in terms of *dharma* as well as of *dīn*, rather than through the conceptual framework of religion; as well as Turner (2014) for using *sāsana* to question religion as a universal comparative frame.

account for the divide between scripturally consecrated religious doctrine and indigenous ritual practices, or following the controversy which opposed Melford Spiro to Stanley Tambiah regarding the place of 'spirit cults' within Buddhism. While these issues are commonly framed in terms of the relations between the 'local' and the 'global,' globalization should not be viewed as impacting the local from the outside, because it is always localized. Besides, it is inevitably mediated by the state and its religious politics. Thus, we should first identify the prevailing religious politics in the various nation-states in which we work, before we could compare the way local people navigate either their aspirations to have a religion or the obligation for them to exhibit one. This is what Arvind-Pal S. Mandair and Markus Dressler refer to in terms of 'religion-making' from above and from below (2011: 21–22). That is to say, we should distinguish between, on the one hand, the enforcement of certain religious politics by state institutions and, on the other hand, the claims made by particular social or ethnic groups to legitimate their religious identity. Furthermore, if there are negative incentives for people to affiliate with a world religion, such as the threats of proselytizing, there are also positive motivations, as the alignment of a local tradition with a world religion can result in its recognition by the state. In any event, we should investigate the dialogic interplay between the emic significance of the category religion in a given society and the one that is conveyed therein by the state and predominant world religion(s).

On the whole, the contemporary states of Southeast Asia tend to press their populations, including marginal ones, to 'have a religion,' in the name of modernity and progress.[22] In the post-colonial era of independent nations, indigenous spirit cults are looked upon as obsolete remnants of backward customs and mere superstitions, and as such, they are socially discredited when not outlawed altogether.[23] On that account, we ought to address religion as a process—the process of

---

[22] See Howell (1982), Kipp and Rodgers (1987), Stange (1992), Keyes et al. (1994), DuBois (2009).

[23] This does not mean that 'spirits' have disappeared in the enlightened world of modernity, far from it (see Wilford and George 2005, Endres and Lauser 2011, Gottowik 2014).

'religionization'[24]—which implies that adherents of indigenous traditions are 'not yet religious' and must, therefore, be 'religionized.' With this perspective in mind, the working hypothesis proposed in this volume is that, in the different cases investigated, there exists an ongoing and shifting tension between proponents of local traditions, who consider them self-sufficient and deserving the label 'religion' in their own right, and advocates of a world religion, who deny those local traditions the qualification of 'religion.' In fact, in many cases, this tension may coexist within the same actors, who are faced with the predicament of having to integrate both their own indigenous traditions and the locally prevailing world religion into the same sociocosmic order.

In the course of our research, coherence among our respective case studies emerged surrounding questions sparked by the notion of 'encountering religion.' By 'encounter' we are referring to the process through which local societies wherein 'religion'—as a specific field, conceived as distinct from the customary order—did not exist, were confronted with this alien category. The following questions motivate and structure our analysis of these encounters:

(1) Which agencies introduced 'religion' in the societies concerned— missionaries, Orientalists, colonial administrators, government bodies, etc.?
(2) What phenomena do these agents identify as pertaining to the category 'religion' in the local milieu, and what are those which they dismiss as such?
(3) How do local people construe the category 'religion' and how do they fit it into their indigenous sociocosmic order?
(4) What are the overall implications of this 'encounter with religion' for the societies under consideration?

---

[24] We use the term 'religionization' in the sense given to it by Robert Hefner, that is, 'the reconstruction of a local or regional spiritual tradition with reference to religious ideals and practices seen as standardized, textualized, and universally incumbent on believers' (Hefner 2011: 72–73).

The Appropriation of 'Religion' in Southeast Asia and Melanesia

The following chapters investigate various processes of localization and appropriation of the category 'religion' by peoples in Southeast Asia and Melanesia, specifically by contrasting the modes of rationalization and secularization resulting, respectively, from Asian traditions (Buddhism and Hinduism) and from Abrahamic religions (Islam and Christianity). In our analysis of the religious encounters, we came across two main lexemes articulating the local semantic fields of 'religion': *sāsana* and its lexical variations in the Buddhicized societies of the Peninsula and *agama* in the Islamized societies of the Archipelago.

In Buddhicized societies, *sāsana* is diversely construed according to differing localizations of Theravāda Buddhism. Three authors address these issues: Bénédicte Brac de la Perrière in Burma, Anne Guillou in Cambodia and Guido Sprenger in Laos. This allows for comparison between that which the Burmese call *thathana*, the Cambodians *sāsanā* and the Lao *sadsana*.

To begin with, one should bear in mind that *sāsana* amounts neither to 'religion' nor to 'Buddhism.' The Pāli term *sāsana* signifies literally 'teaching, precept, doctrine,' and in the syntagm *buddhasāsana*, it refers to the Buddha's teachings. The Buddha did not teach 'Buddhism;' he taught *dharma* (*dhamma* in Pāli). Indeed, it is significant that *sāsana* is sometimes equated to *dhamma*.

In Burma, these two Pāli loanwords have been used in reference to the Buddha's instructions: *dhamma*—the doctrinal contents of the Buddha's teachings; and *thathana* (*sāsana*)—the dispensation of the Buddha's teachings in Burmese society. Historically, *thathana* referred to Burmese Buddhist kingship with all its institutions aimed at dispensing the teachings of the Buddha, especially the monastic community (*sangha*) that supports the Theravādin tradition. In the nineteenth-century colonial situation, a semantic differentiation occurred when Christian missionaries chose the term *batha* (from the Pāli *bhāsā*, meaning 'language') to convey the conception of religion as a professed denomination. 'Buddhism' was thus introduced into Burmese as *Buddha batha* ('the religion of the Buddha'), making it commensurable with *Kirian batha* (Christianity) and *Muslim batha* (Islam). These new names were adopted by the colonial administration and came to be widely used among Burmese elites in the twentieth century. By introducing the term *batha* into Burmese, Christian missionaries subverted the special position of pre-colonial *thathana* and redefined Buddhist identity in Burma. **Bénédicte Brac de la Perrière** analyzes the evolution of the semantic scope of *thathana*—understood as the Burmese Buddhicized social space—through its differentiation from various other individually professed doctrines (*batha*), as well as from fields of practice defined as 'paths' (*lan*), such as spirit worship, esoteric Buddhism, ritual practices and politics. In particular, the changing balance of power between Buddhist and political institutions explains the impossibility of delineating a definite domain of religious action in the Burmese sociopolitical order. Thus, when the symbiotic relationship between state and *sangha* weakened, as it did during the colonial period (1885–1948) or the military regime of the Ne Win era (1962–1988), defense of the *thathana* tended to represent moral opposition to the government. When, on the contrary, the symbiotic relationship was revived, as was the case under Nu during the post-independence parliamentary era (1948–1962) or under the junta after the 1988 popular uprising, a discourse of *thathana* dispensation prevailed. Today, with the recent opening of the political field, the defense of the *thathana* is asserting its exclusively Buddhist character and takes the form of an aggressive nationalism targeting religious otherness, particularly that of the Muslims, who are excluded from the Burmese definition of national identity. Fundamentally, this analysis demonstrates that *thathana* operates as an endless process of Buddhicization.

While in Burma the categories 'religion' and 'Buddhism' were brought about through the introduction of the word *batha* by Christian missionaries, in Cambodia these categories have been glossed by the terms *sāsanā* and *buddhasāsanā*, respectively. As **Anne Guillou** substantiates in her chapter, this terminology gradually appeared from the mid-nineteenth century onward, under the combined influence of Cambodian monks who traveled to Thailand and, later, of the French colonial administration which organized the *sangha* at a national level and whose Orientalist scholars focused on canonical scriptures and religious literacy. Thus, a process of 'religionization' arose, which asserted the pivotal importance of the *dhamma* as displayed in the Pāli canon, stressed the 'purification' of the behavior of both monks and laypeople and rejected the spirit cults. These developments were violently interrupted by the Pol Pot regime (1975–1979), but have resurfaced anew since the 2000s, alongside a concern for building a national identity founded on Buddhism. In this context, the semantic perimeter of the words *sāsanā* and *buddhasāsanā* is currently shifting. On the one hand, religious specialists are attempting to discriminate between 'true' Buddhism (*buddhasāsanā*) and so-called Brahmanism (*brahmaññasāsanā*), referring to pre-Buddhist ritual practices in Cambodia—typically the cult of land guardian spirits. On the other hand, the conception of what actually constitutes *buddhasāsanā* varies relative to the conflicting views of diverse social groups in Cambodian society that support different religious schools or ideologies. As a case in point, Anne Guillou contrasts three categories of monks according to their definition of *buddhasāsanā* and what they believe their role should be in today's Cambodia, which she describes as 'reformist,' 'traditionalist' and 'activist' monks, according to their respective focus on *dhamma*, 'customs' and 'society.'

In his chapter on Buddhism and animism in Laos, **Guido Sprenger** revisits the issue of the relationship to spirits in Buddhist societies by addressing two questions. The first asks how the impression of dualism between local tradition and world religion originally emerged. This has to do with the contrasting connectivity of different cultural representations and institutions. His second question concerns the ontological status of the beings connected this way. According to the assumption that persons, both human and non-human, are constituted through relationships and communication, a change in the type of communication affects the relational beings constituted therein. In order to deal with these questions, Guido Sprenger juxtaposes the situation in two villages of Jru', an ethnic group on the Boloven Plateau in southern Laos. While in the first case, villagers identify predominantly as adherents of local 'spirit religion' (*sadsana phi*), in the other, they claim to practice both 'spirit religion' and 'Buddhism' (*sadsana phud*). This means that they carry out rituals of both religions in parallel, each with its own experts and practices. The choice between these options is seen as a choice of ethnicity, as Buddhism is associated with the dominant ethnic group, the Lao, while spirit rituals are identified with the Jru'. Yet, this does not mean that the two ritual systems are disconnected, as the combination of the term *sadsana* ('religion') either with their ethnonym or with the Lao term *phi* ('spirit') allows the Jru' to gloss over some of the differences between them. Thus, integration or segregation is a way of describing the confluence or divergence of connections between the representations that make up the different religious systems. In the Jru' case, the symmetric use of *sadsana* produces a dichotomy, in that it implies a constant reversal of hierarchies. On the one hand, Buddhism tends to restrict the operation of Jru' ancestral relations. But, on the other hand, the ancestors are an ultimate relational reality that must be dealt with, either by Buddhism or by Jru' rituals.

The comparison of these three case studies reveals significant variations in the localization of the Pāli concept of *sāsana*, in the context of similar transformations. Whereas the Lao term *sadsana* and the Khmer word *sāsanā* are used to translate the notion of Buddhism as a world religion—and thus apply to Christianity and Islam as well—in Burma it is the word *batha* which is used in that sense, since the term *thathana* refers exclusively to Buddhism as institutionalized in the Burmese society. Besides, in Laos as well as in Cambodia, *sāsana* can, in certain contexts, be extended to indigenous rituals, such as *sadsana phi* and *brahmaññasāsanā*, which refer to pre-Buddhist spirit cults. This comparison demonstrates that the perennial issue of the relationship between the proclaimed universalism of Buddhism and the particularism of local traditions largely depends on the specific situation under observation and, further, that its variations ought to be assessed in a processual fashion.

In the Islamized societies of the Malay Archipelago– like in Sri Lanka, although through a different process—the category 'religion' has been appropriated through the Sanskrit loanword *agama*, which is the peculiar combination of a Christian view of that which constitutes a 'world religion,' with an Islamic understanding of what defines a 'proper religion': that is, a prophet, a holy book and a belief in the one and only God. And just like in Burma *thathana* as 'religion' refers specifically to Buddhism, in Indonesia *agama* as 'religion' referred initially to Islam.

In contemporary Indonesia, *agama* is differently contrasted with indigenous customary practices—subsumed under the generic term *adat*—according to whether the locally predominant *agama* is Islam, Christianity or the so-called Balinese 'Hinduism.' Four studies deal with Indonesian cases: Michel Picard and Annette Hornbacher examine the whys and wherefores of the invention of Balinese religion as 'Hinduism' (*agama Hindu*), while Cécile Barraud and Jos Platenkamp analyze the interrelationship in the Moluccas between indigenous sociocosmic orders and foreign religions.

Unlike in Islamized or Christianized areas of Indonesia, in contemporary Bali *agama* is still not clearly differentiated from *adat*. **Michel Picard** investigates how the word *agama* took on the meaning of 'religion' in Bali, how the Balinese chose to label their own *agama* '*Hindu*' and what resulted from this endeavor. It appears that it was only when they were obliged to defend themselves against Muslim and Christian proselytism, starting in the 1920s, that the Balinese began to use the word *agama* in the sense of 'religion,' so as to define their own religion in opposition to Islam and Christianity. Following Indonesia's independence, the Balinese religion was not recognized by the Ministry of Religion, considered instead to belong to the domain of *adat* rather than *agama*. Consequently, in order to avoid becoming the target of Muslim or Christian proselytizing, the Balinese people's only recourse was to rationalize their religion and redefine it in transcendent and monotheistic terms, in order to make it eligible for the status of *agama*. Stressing the theological import and the ethical implications of religion, Balinese reformers urged their coreligionists to return to the fold of Hinduism, which they presented as the source of their rites. Hence, they attempted to restrain the Balinese ritualistic leanings, while construing their Hindu heritage in line with Islam and Christianity. This move initiated an enduring tension between Balinese who wanted to retain their local traditions and those who aspired to reform them according to what they assume Hinduism, as a 'world religion,' is about. This tension recently resulted in a schism, when an influent faction within the Balinese religious establishment attempted to reverse the ongoing globalization of their religion by relocalizing it. That which began as a struggle on the part of the Balinese for the recognition of their religion ultimately led to the breakup of their religious identity.

For her part, **Annette Hornbacher** explores the dynamics of *agama Hindu* from another perspective: that of a group of Balinese pilgrims she accompanied in 2011 on a voyage to the source of their 'Hindu religion' in India. The pilgrimage (*tirtha yatra*) made the Balinese aware that they were not just a Hindu minority in a Muslim country, but part of a universal Hindu community. However, this perception was not shared by Indian Hindus, who tended to consider the Balinese to be foreigners and refused them entrance to their temples to prevent any risk of ritual pollution. In consequence, the Indian travel agent who organized the tour had to carefully choose religious sites where restrictions for foreigners were not expected, to prevent embarrassing experiences for the Balinese pilgrims. In fact, their only integrative experience happened to be their ritual immersion in the Ganges River in Haridwar, where they found the true 'source' of their religion. Yet, rather than a means for the realization of a transcendent end—the ultimate liberation from the world (*moksa*), held to be the highest goal of *agama Hindu*—this purifying bath was experienced by the Balinese pilgrims as a familiar ritual practice. Indeed, while in Sanskrit the word *tīrtha* designates a 'crossing-place' between the material world and *mokṣa*, in Balinese it refers to the 'holy water' that is essential for each and every ritual. Accordingly, the Balinese pilgrims 'asked for holy water' (*nunas tirtha*) from the Ganges, which they carried back to Bali to mix it in their local rituals with the holy waters from their own island. Thereby, they subverted the political agenda of *tirtha yatra* and for that matter of *agama Hindu*, as they expanded their own immanent animist ontology to India rather than adopting a transcendent and rationalist reform Hindu paradigm of religion.

The Balinese are not the only people in Indonesia concerned with *agama Hindu*. As a matter of fact, its recognition by the Ministry of Religion drove a few ethnic minorities to affiliate with *agama Hindu* in hopes of being allowed to conserve their ancestral rites, inasmuch as it was reputedly more accommodating in this respect than Islam or Christianity. The case of Tanebar-Evav, a small island of the Kei Archipelago, in the Southeast Moluccas, analyzed by **Cécile Barraud**, is a particularly significant example of the ambiguous status held by *agama Hindu* in Indonesia, precariously positioned between 'religion' (*agama*) and 'tradition' (*adat*). The villagers of Tanebar-Evav have, from time immemorial, refused to let *agama*—in this instance, Islam, Protestantism and Catholicism—enter their territory. While over the years villagers have increasingly converted to either Islam or Christianity, the rule was that their places of worship, whether mosque or church, should not penetrate their ancestors' land, for fear of destroying their *adat*. Until the early 2000s, villagers who had not converted were dubbed *masih Hindu* ('still Hindus'), meaning that they had no religion yet (*belum beragama*). The situation began to change when villagers in contact with Balinese workers in the Kei Archipelago came to find some concordance between their own *adat* and *agama Hindu*. With the backing of the Ministry of Religion and the agreement of ritual leaders, they decided to construct a *Hindu* temple (*pura*) on the village territory. Although as a place of worship, the *pura* is assimilated to a mosque or to a church, the rituals therein are not likened to those of Islam or Christianity, and they are referred to as *adat* and not as *agama*. While these new adherents of *agama Hindu* have very little knowledge of its doctrinal contents, they see it both as a shelter for their *adat* and as a way of complying with their obligation as Indonesian citizens to demonstrate their *agama*. Thus, whereas Indonesian authorities view 'religion' as clearly distinguished from 'tradition,' in the eyes of the villagers of Tanebar-Evav *adat* encompasses *agama*.

In his comprehensive chronicle of the introduction of the category 'religion' in the relations between the Iberian, the Dutch and the North Moluccan societies between the sixteenth and the late nineteenth centuries, **Jos Platenkamp** identifies certain long-lasting structural patterns governing the 'foreign' provenance of people and ideas as a constitutive part of overall indigenous sociocosmic orders. He first focuses on the distinct meanings attributed to this category by the Portuguese and Spanish military merchants and Roman Catholic priests entering the region in the sixteenth century and then by the Muslim sultans of Ternate and Tidore. Second, he analyzes the relevance of the Dutch Reformed Protestant creed relative to the ideology of Natural Law and Free Trade and of Islam in the political–economic interactions during the seventeenth and eighteenth centuries between the United East India Company and the Moluccan sultans. He finally examines how the 'religion' propagated by the Dutch Protestant mission from the nineteenth century onward was viewed in the non-Muslim societies of North Halmahera. In all these cases, the local powers perceived the representations of Christianity as signifying relations with foreign sources of authority, which they could draw upon in order to transitively articulate their own position vis-à-vis their local competitors and their dependents alike. This inability to value Christian 'religion' as a system of beliefs and practices in its own right, independent of the diarchic relationship between their own society and the foreign source of political power, frustrated the missionaries, who judged the local people being 'totally indifferent concerning anything resembling religion.' But that which in missionaries' perspective was an inadmissible confusion of 'religion' and political authority, the colonial government perceived as advantageous to the colonial polity as a whole.

Finally, **André Iteanu** examines how—beyond the confines of Southeast Asia—Melanesian societies have managed to thoroughly localize Christianity. Building on ethnographic material primarily gathered with the Orokaiva people in Papua New Guinea, he describes continuity between customary circulating cults that anthropologists call 'Cargo cults,' conventional Christian Churches (Anglican, Catholic and Methodist), Evangelical denominations and emergent local Churches that have characterized Melanesia's religious history for as long as we have knowledge of it. He argues that far from triggering a major disruption in the indigenous sociocosmic order, the advent of Christianity was viewed as another instance of a familiar type of event. Rather than accepting Christianization in its own terms, Melanesians have thus treated it in the way in which they previously dealt with recurring pre-Christian cults. That which missionaries presented as the ultimate and unsurpassable religion was, for them, merely another transient circulating cult to be replaced as soon as its specificity wore off. As such, in line with the way in which these cults worked, following the keen and sweeping adoption of Christianity, a period of disenchantment began, during which Melanesians gradually assimilated Christian elements into their own customary practices—those designated by the Pidgin term *kastom*. Accordingly, even if deeply involved in Christianity, few Melanesians contemplated giving up their previous beliefs and rituals, including those related to their ancestors. The resulting mixture of Christianity and indigenous customs is now so intertwined that it has become difficult, if not impossible, to distinguish one from the other. This means that Melanesians construe their *kastom* as universal, while viewing Christianity as particular.

To conclude, we notice similar tensions between world religions and local traditions on the Buddhicized Peninsula, the Islamized Archipelago and Christianized Papua New Guinea. Buddhism and Hinduism appear to have comparable rationalizing implications as Islam and Christianity in transforming or marginalizing indigenous cultural features. Yet, the relationship between Buddhism and spirit cults, each with their own rituals, seems more compartmentalized than that between *agama* and *adat*, as Muslims are less likely to accept that there could be distinct Islamic and non-Islamic spheres in their daily life.

Whereas in Indonesia the concept of *agama* has been historically pitted against that of *adat*, we see that the emergence of and subsequent official recognition of *agama Hindu* brought forth a mediating category that blurs the boundaries between *agama* and *adat*. The case of Tanebar-Evav is exemplary in this respect, since the rituals of *agama Hindu* are regarded by villagers as *adat*, not as *agama*. This is to say that, for some Indonesian peoples at least, *agama* oscillates between 'religion' and 'tradition.' While *agama* as religion revolves around true belief according to an imported doctrine, *agama* as tradition amounts to correct practices upheld as the way of one's ancestors.

Finally, we see further that with the localization and appropriation of the Indic loan words *sāsana* and *āgama*, fairly identical signifiers do not necessarily entail an identical signified: while the signifier is either Buddhist or Hindu, that which is signified is local. In the dialogic process of vernacularization of the category religion, it appears that local sociocosmic systems and native categories tend to determine the outcome of the religious encounter. This suggests that we should pay more attention to the vernacular usage of the borrowed terminology than to its origins. In other words, the focus should be less on how local peoples adopted Buddhism or Hinduism, Islam or Christianity and more on how they adapted these exogenous beliefs and practices to suit their own needs and values. Indeed, once localized, world religions are filtered through the lens of local traditions and enter into play with indigenous concerns, such as spirit cults, ancestor worship, magic, mediumship, healing and ideas of power. In consequence, we ought to address the appropriation of world religions in such a way as to bring to light local productions of meaning—as a result of indigenous agency, that which one might identify as 'religion' in a given society is an ever-shifting entity.

REFERENCES

Almond, Philip C. 1988. *The British Discovery of Buddhism*. Cambridge: Cambridge University Press.
Asad, Talal. 1993. The Construction of Religion as an Anthropological Category. In *Genealogies of Religion. Discipline and Reasons of Power in Christianity and Islam*, 27–54. Baltimore: The Johns Hopkins University Press.
Asad, Talal. 2001. Reading a modern classic: W.C. Smith's The Meaning and End of Religion. In *Religion and Media*, ed. H. de Vries, and S. Weber, 131–147. Stanford: Stanford University Press.
Asad, Talal. 2003. *Formations of the Secular: Christianity, Islam, Modernity*. Stanford: Stanford University Press.
Assmann, Jan. 2003. *Die Mosaische Unterscheidungoder der Preis des Monotheismus*. München: Carl Hanser Verlag (French translation, *Le Prix du Monothéisme*, Paris, Aubier, 2007).
Balagangadhara, S.N. 2005. *"The Heathen in His Blindness…". Asia, the West and the Dynamic of Religion*. New Delhi: Manohar (1st ed. 1994).
Basu, Shamita. 2002. *Religious Revivalism as Nationalist Discourse: Swami Vivekananda and New Hinduism in Nineteenth Century Bengal*. New Delhi: Oxford University Press.

Bechert, Heinz. 1966. *Buddhismus, Staat und Geselschaft in den Ländern des Theravāda Buddhismus*, vol. 1. Frankfurt & Berlin: Alfred Metzner.
Bell, Catherine. 2006. Paradigms Behind (and Before) the Modern Concept of Religion. *History and Theory* 45: 27–46.
Besant, Annie. 1902. *Sanâtana Dharma Catechism. A Catechism for Boys and Girls in Hindu Religion and Morals.* Benares: The Board of Trustees, Central Hindu College.
Bloch, Esther, Marianne Keppens, and Rajaram Hegde (eds.). 2010. *Rethinking Religion in India. The Colonial Construction of Hinduism.* London & New York: Routledge.
Bloch, Maurice. 2008. Why Religion is Nothing Special but is Central. *Philosophical Transactions of the Royal Society B* 363: 2055–2061.
Borgeaud, Philippe. 1994. Le couple sacré/profane. Genèse et fortune d'un concept 'opératoire' en histoire des religions. *Revue de l'Histoire des Religions* 211 (4): 387–418.
Bossy, John. 1985. *Christianity in the West, 1400–1700.* Oxford & New York: Oxford University Press.
Bourdieu, Pierre. 1971. Genèse et structure du champ religieux. *Revue Française de Sociologie* 12 (3): 295–334.
Brekke, Torkel. 2002. *Makers of Modern Indian Religion in the Late Nineteenth Century.* Oxford & New York: Oxford University Press.
Byrne, Peter. 1989. *Natural Religion and the Nature of Religion. The Legacy of Deism.* London: Routledge.
Carter, John Ross. 1977. A History of 'Early Buddhism'. *Religious Studies* 13 (3): 263–287.
Carter, John Ross. 1993. The Origin and Development of 'Buddhism' and 'Religion' in the Study of the Theravāda Buddhist Tradition. In *On Understanding Buddhists: Essays on the Theravāda Tradition in Sri Lanka*, 9–25. Albany: State University of New York Press.
Chidester, David. 1996. *Savage Systems: Colonialism and Comparative Religion in Southern Africa.* Charlottesville: University Press of Virginia.
Cohn, Werner. 1969. On the Problem of Religion in Non-Western Cultures. *International Yearbook for the Study of Religion* V: 7–19.
Dalmia, Vasudha and Heinrich von Stietencron (eds.). 1995. *Representing Hinduism. The Construction of Religious Traditions and National Identity.* New Delhi & London: Sage Publications.
Despland, Michel. 1980. *La Religion en Occident. Évolution des idées et du vécu.* Paris: Les Éditions du Cerf.
DuBois, Thomas David (ed.). 2009. *Casting Faiths. Imperialism and the Transformation of Religion in East and Southeast Asia.* London & New York: Palgrave Macmillan.

Dubuisson, Daniel. 1998. *L'Occident et la religion. Mythes, science et idéologie*. Bruxelles: Éditions Complexe (English translation, *The Western Construction of Religion. Myths, Knowledge, and Ideology*, Baltimore, The Johns Hopkins University Press, 2003).

Dubuisson, Daniel. 2007. Exporting the Local: Recent Perspectives on 'Religion' as a Cultural Category. *Religion Compass* 1 (6): 787–800.

Endres, Kirsten W., and Andrea Lauser (eds.). 2011. *Engaging the Spirit World. Popular Beliefs and Practices in Modern Southeast Asia*. New York & Oxford: Berghahn Books.

Fitzgerald, Timothy. 1990. Hinduism and the 'World Religion' Fallacy. *Religion* 20 (2): 101–118.

Fitzgerald, Timothy. 1997. A Critique of 'Religion' as a Cross-Cultural Category. *Method & Theory in the Study of Religion* 9 (2): 35–47.

Fitzgerald, Timothy. 2000. *The Ideology of Religious Studies*. Oxford & New York: Oxford University Press.

Fitzgerald, Timothy. 2007. *Discourse on Civility and Barbarity. A Critical History of Religion and Related Categories*. Oxford & New York: Oxford University Press.

Frykenberg, Robert Eric. 1993. Constructions of Hinduism at the Nexus of History and Religion. *Journal of Interdisciplinary History* 23 (3): 523–550.

Gauchet, Marcel. 1985. *Le Désenchantement du monde. Une histoire politique de la religion*. Paris: Gallimard.

Gelders, Raf. 2009. Genealogy of Colonial Discourse: Hindu Traditions and the Limits of European Representation. *Comparative Studies in Society and History* 51 (3): 563–589.

Gellner, David N. 1990. Introduction: What is the Anthropology of Buddhism About? *Journal of the Royal Anthropological Society of Oxford* 21 (2): 95–112.

Gellner, David N. 1999. Religion, Politics, and Ritual. Remarks on Geertz and Bloch. *Social Anthropology* 7 (2): 135–153.

Girardot, N.J. 1999. 'Finding the Way': James Legge and the Victorian Invention of Taoism. *Religion* 29 (2): 107–121.

Gombrich, Richard F. 2006. *Theravāda Buddhism. A Social History from Ancient Benares to Modern Colombo*. Abingdon & New York: Routledge (1st ed. 1988).

Gombrich, Richard F., and Gananath Obeyesekere. 1988. *Buddhism Transformed: Religious Change in Sri Lanka*. Princeton: Princeton University Press.

Goody, Jack. 1961. Religion and Ritual: The Definitional Problem. *The British Journal of Sociology* 12 (2): 142–164.

Goossaert, Vincent, and David A. Palmer. 2011. *The Religious Question in Modern China*. Chicago: The University of Chicago Press.

Gottowik, Volker (ed.). 2014. *Dynamics of Religion in Southeast Asia. Magic and Modernity*. Chicago: The University of Chicago Press and Amsterdam: Amsterdam University Press.

Haan, Michael. 2005. Numbers in Nirvana: How the 1872–1921 Indian Censuses Helped Operationalise 'Hinduism'. *Religion* 35 (1): 13–30.

Hacker, Paul. 1995. Aspects of Neo-Hinduism as Contrasted with Surviving Traditional Hinduism. In *Philology and Confrontation. Paul Hacker on Traditional and Modern Vedanta*, ed. W. Halbfass, 229–255. Albany: State University of New York Press.

Halbfass, Wilhelm. 1988. *India and Europe: An Essay in Understanding*. Albany: State University of New York Press (1st ed. 1981).

Hallisey, Charles. 1995. Roads Taken and Not Taken in the Study of Theravāda Buddhism. In *Curators of the Buddha. The Study of Buddhism under Colonialism*, ed. D.S. Lopez Jr., 31–61. Chicago & London: The University of Chicago Press.

Hanegraaff, Wouter J. 2016. Reconstructing 'Religion' from the Bottom Up. *Numen* 63 (5-6): 577–606.

Harris, Elizabeth J. 2006. *Theravāda Buddhism and the British Encounter. Religious, Missionary and Colonial Experience in Nineteenth Century Sri Lanka*. London & New York: Routledge.

Harrison, Peter. 1990. *'Religion' and the Religions in the English Enlightenment*. Cambridge: Cambridge University Press.

Hawley, John Stratton. 1991. Naming Hinduism. *Wilson Quarterly* 15 (3): 20–34.

Hefner, Robert W. 1993. World Building and the Rationality of Conversion. In *Conversion to Christianity. Historical and Anthropological Perspectives on a Great Transformation*, ed. R.W. Hefner, 3–44. Berkeley: University of California Press.

Hefner, Robert W. 1998. Multiple Modernities: Christianity, Islam, and Hinduism in a Globalizing Age. *Annual Review of Anthropology* 27: 83–104.

Hefner, Robert W. 2011. Where Have all the Abangan Gone? Religionization and the Decline of Non-Standard Islam in Contemporary Indonesia. In *The Politics of Religion in Indonesia. Syncretism, Orthodoxy, and Religious Contention in Java and Bali*, ed. M. Picard and R. Madinier, 71–91. London & New York: Routledge.

Holdrege, Barbara A. 2004. Dharma. In *The Hindu World*, ed. S. Mittal and G. Thursby, 213–248. New York & London: Routledge.

Howell, Julia Day. 1982. Indonesia: Searching for Consensus. In *Religions and Societies: Asia and the Middle East*, ed. C. Caldarola, 497–548. Berlin: Mouton.

Hughes, Aaron W. 2012. *Abrahamic Religions: On the Uses and Abuses of History*. Oxford & New York: Oxford University Press.

Inden, Ronald B. 1986. Orientalist Constructions of India. *Modern Asian Studies* 20 (3): 401–446.
Jensen, Lionel. 1997. *Manufacturing Confucianism*. Durham: Duke University Press.
Jha, Dwijendra Narayan. 2006. Looking for a Hindu Identity, Presidential Address to the 66th Indian History Congress, Shantiniketan, January 28, 2006: http://sacw.insaf.net/India_History/dnj_Jan06.pdf.
Jordens, J.T.F. 1978. *Dayananda Sarasvati. His Life and Ideas*. Delhi: Oxford University Press.
Josephson, Jason Ānanda. 2006. When Buddhism Became a 'Religion'. Religion and Superstition in the Writings of Inoue Enryō. *Japanese Journal of Religious Studies* 33 (1): 143–168.
Josephson, Jason Ānanda. 2012. *The Invention of Religion in Japan*. Chicago & London: The University of Chicago Press.
Keyes, Charles, Laurel Kendall, and Helen Hardacre (eds.). 1994. *Asian Visions of Authority. Religion and the Modern State of East and Southeast Asia*. Honolulu: University of Hawaii Press.
Killingley, Dermot. 1993. *Rammohun Roy in Hindu and Christian Tradition*. Newcastle upon Tyne: Grevatt & Grevatt.
King, Richard. 1999a. *Orientalism and Religion: Postcolonial Theory, India and the 'Mystic East'*. London & New York: Routledge.
King, Richard. 1999b. Orientalism and the Modern Myth of 'Hinduism'. *Numen* 46 (2): 146–185.
King, Richard. 2011. Imagining Religions in India: Colonialism and the Mapping of South Asian History and Culture. In *Secularism and Religion-Making*, ed. M. Dressler and A.-P. S. Mandair, 37–61. Oxford & New York: Oxford University Press.
Kipp, Rita Smith, and Susan Rodgers (eds.). 1987. *Indonesian Religions in Transition*. Tucson: The University of Arizona Press.
Kopf, David. 1969. *British Orientalism and the Bengal Renaissance. The Dynamics of Indian Modernization 1773–1835*. Berkeley & Los Angeles: University of California Press.
Kopf, David. 1979. *The Brahmo Samaj and the Shaping of the Modern Indian Mind*. Princeton: Princeton University Press.
Levenson, Jon D. 2012. *Inheriting Abraham: The Legacy of the Patriarch in Judaism, Christianity, and Islam*. Princeton: Princeton University Press.
Lévi-Strauss, Claude. 1972 (1963). The Bear and the Barber. In *Reader in Comparative Religion: An Anthropological Approach*, ed. W.A. Lessa and E.Z. Vogt, 181–189. New York: Harper.
Lipner, Julius J. 2006. The Rise of 'Hinduism'; or, How to Invent a World Religion with Only Moderate Success. *International Journal of Hindu Studies* 10: 91–104.

Llewellyn, J.E. 1993. *The Arya Samaj as a Fundamentalist Movement. A Study in Comparative Fundamentalism*. New Delhi: Manohar.
Lopez Jr., Donald S. (ed.). 1995. *Curators of the Buddha. The Study of Buddhism under Colonialism*. Chicago & London: The University of Chicago Press.
Lopez Jr., Donald S. 1998. *Prisoners of Shangri-La: Tibetan Buddhism and the West*. Chicago & London: The University of Chicago Press.
Lorenzen, David N. 1999. Who Invented Hinduism? *Comparative Studies in Society and History* 41 (4): 630–659.
Malalgoda, Kitsiri. 1997. Concepts and Confrontations: A Case Study of Agama. In *Sri Lanka: Collective Identities Revisited*, vol. 1, ed. M. Roberts, 55–77. Colombo: Marga Institute.
Mandair, Arvind-Pal S. 2009. *Religion and the Specter of the West: Sikhism, India, Postcoloniality, and the Politics of Translation*. New York: Columbia University Press.
Mandair, Arvind-Pal S., and Markus Dressler. 2011. Introduction: Modernity, Religion-Making, and the Postsecular. In *Secularism and Religion-Making*, ed. M. Dressler and A.-P. S. Mandair, 3–36. Oxford & New York: Oxford University Press.
Marshall, Peter J. 1970. *The British Discovery of Hinduism in the Eighteenth Century*. Cambridge: Cambridge University Press.
Masuzawa, Tomoko. 2005. *The Invention of World Religions. Or How European Universalism Was Preserved in the Language of Pluralism*. Chicago: The University of Chicago Press.
McCutcheon, Russell T. 1997. *Manufacturing Religion. The Discourse on Sui Generis Religion and the Politics of Nostalgia*. Oxford & New York: Oxford University Press.
McCutcheon, Russell T. 2004. Religion, Ire, and Dangerous Things. *Journal of the American Academy of Religion* 72 (1): 173–193.
McKinnon, Andrew M. 2002. Sociological Definitions, Language Games, and the 'Essence' of Religion. *Method & Theory in the Study of Religion* 14 (1): 61–83.
McMahan, David L. 2008. *The Making of Buddhist Modernism*. Oxford & New York: Oxford University Press.
Mitter, Partha. 1987. Rammohun Roy and the New Language of Monotheism. *History and Anthropology* 3 (1): 177–208.
Nongbri, Brent. 2014. *Before Religion. A History of a Modern Concept*. New Haven & London: Yale University Press.
Nye, Malory. 2000. Religion, Post-Religionism, and Religioning: Religious Studies and Contemporary Cultural Debates. *Method & Theory in the Study of Religion* 12 (4): 447–476.

Oberoi, Harjot. 1994. *The Construction of Religious Boundaries: Culture, Identity, and Diversity in the Sikh Tradition.* Chicago & London: The University of Chicago Press.
Obeyesekere, Gananath. 1970. Religious Symbolism and Political Change in Ceylon. *Modern Ceylon Studies* 1 (1): 43–63.
O'Connell, Joseph T. 1973. The Word 'Hindu' in Gaudiya Vaishnava Texts. *Journal of the American Oriental Society* 93 (3): 340–344.
Oddie, Geoffrey A. 2006. *Imagined Hinduism. British Protestant Missionary Constructions of Hinduism, 1793–1900.* New Delhi & London: Sage Publications.
Olcott, Henry S. 1881. *A Buddhist Catechism, According to the Canon of the Southern Church.* Colombo: The Theosophical Society, Buddhist Section.
Pennington, Brian K. 2005. *Was Hinduism Invented? Britons, Indians, and the Colonial Construction of Religion.* Oxford & New York: Oxford University Press.
Perreira, Todd LeRoy. 2012. Whence Theravāda? The Modern Genealogy of an Ancient Term. In *How Theravāda is Theravāda? Exploring Buddhist Identities,* ed. P. Skilling, J.A. Carbine, C. Cicuzza, and S. Pakdeekham, 443–571. Chiang Mai: Silkworm Books.
Peterson, Derek, and Darren Walhof (eds.). 2002. *The Invention of Religion. Rethinking Belief in Politics and History.* New Brunswick: Rutgers University Press.
Prothero, Stephen. 1995. Henry Steel Olcott and 'Protestant Buddhism'. *Journal of the American Academy of Religion* 63 (2): 281–302.
Radice, William (ed.). 1998. *Swami Vivekananda and the Modernisation of Hinduism.* Delhi: Oxford University Press.
Rocher, Ludo. 2003. The Dharmaśāstras. In *The Blackwell Companion to Hinduism,* ed. G. Flood, 102–115. Oxford: Blackwell Publishing.
Rocher, Rosane. 1993. British Orientalism in the Eighteenth Century: The Dialectics of Knowledge and Government. In *Orientalism and the Postcolonial Predicament. Perspectives on South Asia,* ed. C.A. Breckenridge and P. van der Veer, 215–249. Philadelphia: University of Pennsylvania Press.
Ryan, Michael T. 1981. Assimilating New Worlds in the Sixteenth and Seventeenth Centuries. *Comparative Studies in Society and History* 23 (4): 519–538.
Sachot, Maurice. 2003. Objet et trajectoire d'un mot: religion. *Enseignement et Religions.* http://www.formiris2.org/medias/er_236_1.pdf.
Sachot, Maurice. 2007. *Quand le christianisme a changé le monde. La subversion chrétienne du monde antique.* Paris: Odile Jacob.
Said, Edward. 1978. *Orientalism.* New York: Random House.

Saler, Benson. 2000. *Conceptualizing Religion. Immanent Anthropologists, Transcendent Natives, and Unbounded Categories*. New York & Oxford: Berghahn Books (1st ed. 1993).
Sanderson, Alexis. 2015. Tolerance, Exclusivity, Inclusivity, and Persecution in Indian Religion During the Early Mediaeval Period. In *Honoris Causa: Essays in Honour of Aveek Sarkar*, ed. J. Makinson, 155–224. London: Allen Lane.
Scott, David. 1996. Religion in Colonial Civil Society. Buddhism and Modernity in 19th-Century Sri Lanka. *Cultural Dynamics* 8 (1): 7–23.
Sharma, Arvind. 1994. The Bearing of the Different Understandings of the Words *Religion, dharma* and *dīn* on Religious Study and Research. In *The Notion of "Religion" in Comparative Research: Selected Proceedings of the XVI IAHR Congress*, ed. U. Bianchi, 591–602. Rome: Bretshneider.
Sharma, Arvind. 2002. On Hindu, Hindustan, Hinduism and Hindutva. *Numen* 49 (1): 1–36.
Sharpe, Eric J. 1986. *Comparative Religion: A History*. La Salle: Open Court.
Smith, Jonathan Z. 1982. *Imagining Religion: From Babylon to Jonestown*. Chicago & London: The University of Chicago Press.
Smith, Jonathan Z. 1998. Religion, Religions, Religious. In *Critical Terms for Religious Studies*, ed. M.C. Taylor, 275–280. Chicago & London: The University of Chicago Press.
Smith, Wilfred Cantwell. 1962. *The Meaning and End of Religion. A New Approach to the Religious Traditions of Mankind*. New York: The Macmillan Company.
Sontheimer, Günther-Dietz and Hermann Kulke (eds.). 2001. *Hinduism Reconsidered*. New Delhi: Manohar (1st ed. 1989).
Southwold, Martin. 1978. Buddhism and the Definition of Religion. *Man* 13 (3): 362–379.
Spiro, Melford E. 1966. Religion: Problems of Definition and Explanation. In *Anthropological Approaches to the Study of Religion*, ed. M. Banton, 85–126. London: Tavistock Publications.
Staal, Frits. 1996. Religions. In *Ritual and Mantras. Rules Without Meaning*, 387–420. Delhi: Motilal Banarsidass (1st ed. 1990).
Stange, Paul. 1992. Religious Change in Contemporary Southeast Asia. In *The Cambridge History of Southeast Asia, Volume 2: The Nineteenth and Twentieth Centuries*, ed. N. Tarling, 529–584. Cambridge: Cambridge University Press.
Stroumsa, Guy. 2010. *A New Science: The Discovery of Religion in the Age of Reason*. Cambridge: Harvard University Press.
Sugirtharajah, Sharada. 2003. *Imagining Hinduism. A Postcolonial Perspective*. London & New York: Routledge.
Sweetman, Will. 2003. *Mapping Hinduism. 'Hinduism' and the Study of Indian Religions, 1600–1776*. Halle: Franckesche Stiftungen.

Thapar, Romila. 1989. Imagined Religious Communities? Ancient History and the Modern Search for a Hindu Identity. *Modern Asian Studies* 23 (2): 209–231.
Turner, Alicia. 2014. *Saving Buddhism: The Impermanence of Religion in Colonial Burma*. Honolulu: University of Hawai'i Press.
Van der Veer, Peter. 2014. *The Modern Spirit of Asia. The Spiritual and the Secular in China and India*. Princeton & Oxford: Princeton University Press.
Von Stietencron, Heinrich. 1997. *Hindu Religious Traditions and the Concept of 'Religion'*, 1996 Gonda Lecture. Amsterdam: Royal Netherlands Academy of Arts and Sciences.
Wilford, Andrew C., and Kenneth M. George (eds.). 2005. *Spirited Politics: Religion and Public Life in Contemporary Southeast Asia*. Ithaca: Cornell University Press.

Author Biography

Michel Picard Ph.D., is a retired researcher at the French National Center for Scientific Research (CNRS) and a founding member of the Center for Southeast Asian Studies (CASE, CNRS-EHESS) in Paris. He has published extensively in the field of Balinese studies, specifically on tourism, culture, identity, ethnicity and religion. He is the author of *Bali: Cultural Tourism and Touristic Culture* (1996), and has co-edited several collective volumes, the latest one being *The Politics of Religion in Indonesia. Syncretism, Orthodoxy, and Religious Contention in Java and Bali* (2011). He has recently published *Kebalian. La construction dialogique de l'identité balinaise* (2017).

CHAPTER 2

About Buddhist Burma: *Thathana*, or 'Religion' as Social Space

Bénédicte Brac de la Perrière

INTRODUCTION

Amidst my field memories in Burma, I still have very vivid in mind the vision of an energetic woman belonging to the urban lower middle class that had come about in the 1990s. She was telling me with genuine amazement how she became a caretaker of 'religion' (*thathana pyu di*) against all her expectations. After years of economic restriction under the Burmese socialist regime, the new junta[1] had opened business opportunities that together with her husband she had managed to grasp. They

---

[1] Burma gained independence from the British Empire on January 4, 1948, only to experience a very troubled parliamentary era. It ended with Ne Win's coup in 1962, which imposed the rule of the military. A socialist ideology framed by the BSPP (Burmese Socialist Party Program) was soon implemented, and Ne Win stayed at the top of the state until 1988 when massive popular protests led him to withdraw. However, after the lost elections of 1990, the army stepped back into power with a liberalized economic policy while holding tightly the reins of government. SLORC (State Law and Order Council) and SPDC (State Peace and Development Council) are the two military–government organs that exercised power over Burma (Myanmar) from 1990 to 2011.

B. Brac de la Perrière (✉)
Centre Asie du Sud-Est, CNRS-EHESS, Paris, France

© The Author(s) 2017
M. Picard (ed.), *The Appropriation of Religion in Southeast Asia and Beyond*, DOI 10.1007/978-3-319-56230-8_2

started spending their surplus in setting up a pagoda network in the eastern part of Yangon where they had settled as a newlywed couple some 30 years earlier when it was just urbanizing.[2] Since that time, very few significant religious establishments had been set up in the new suburbs. Despite their very simple background, the couple had done so well in society following the change of regime that they were able to reach a status that allowed them to take part in the development of Buddhist institutions in the recently urbanized territories; they could share in the new policies meant to legitimate the junta's power through religious foundations. The dazzling social rise as told by the lady was embedded in a truly Buddhist discourse of karmic determination, which was demonstrated by tangible achievements: the transforming of a suburban space into a Buddhicized landscape of stupas and religious images.

My sensitivity to the specificity of the Burmese notion of *thathana* (Pali, *sāsana*)—as a rendition of 'religion'—dates back to this field encounter. *Thathana* was yet to be identified by Gustaaf Houtman and later on by Alexey Kirichenko—two fine connoisseurs of Burmese semantics—as a key word in Burmese conceptualizations of religion, in two seminal papers that will be commented hereafter.[3] As to my own understanding of *thathana*, I had yet to learn how the uses of the word might be at bewildering variance according to both particular local contexts and the overall socio-political situation.

The Burmese word tentatively translated as 'religion,' *thathana*, encapsulates the ideas of the teachings of the Buddha and their dispensation. Certainly, this word does not correspond with the Western common understanding of 'religion.' Nor is it the only Burmese term that could translate one aspect or another of what is subsumed under the notion of religion in the West. *Batha* (Pali *basha*) is another of those terms. Originally used to mean 'language,' in the mid-nineteenth century *batha* came to be used to signify religion as a professed denomination. *Dhamma*, a Pali word whose general meaning is 'law,' also denotes the doctrinal contents of the Buddha's teachings.

---

[2] See Brac de la Perrière (1995) about the foundation of this network of pagodas.
[3] Regarding the semantic field covered by *thathana*, and its history, see Houtman (1999) and Kirichenko (2009). In reference to the reformulation of *thathana* through the colonial encounter, see also Turner (2014).

Thus, basic notions referring to different aspects of religion, as it is generally understood in the West, have a Pali origin in Burma and other countries in which Buddhist tradition identified as Theravāda refers to the Pali textual corpus.[4] However, Pali concepts have evolved in specific ways in the different vernaculars forming what Gustaaf Houtman has called the 'Pali trap' (1990). Beyond the intrinsic complexities of the semantic field of 'religion' in different countries of the Theravādin tradition, the encounter with Western notions had a distinctive effect on the formation of this field. 'World religions' discourses have been, generally speaking, found to impact the identification of ideas, institutions and practice as religious, in different local exotic contexts, in such a way that these processes have come to be addressed under the label of 'religionization' or of the 'making of religion' (Mandair and Dressler 2011). However, in Burma, these processes have not led to the formation of a clearly differentiated sphere of religious life as I will argue in the following sections.

In Burmese, should one try to find an equivalent for the concept of 'religionization' or the 'making of religion,' one could choose *thathana pyu*. This was the term the woman at the start of this chapter used to give a sense of what was, at the time, 'religion in the making' in Burma, that is, a never-ending process of manifesting the Buddha's teachings in the social world. However, another discourse about the 'defense of *thathana*' has recently developed anew.[5] This discourse is mainly circulated by the Ma Ba Tha association, which was established by a number of abbots in the wake of anti-Muslim violence in 2013, and draws on the exclusively Buddhist character of *thathana* to promote an aggressive Buddhist nationalism.[6] This discourse about the 'defense of religion' suddenly overwhelmed the public sphere, at a time when Burma was experiencing a political transition and a push for acceptance of human rights values, leaving observers in a quandary.

It is my hypothesis that, in the modern context, this move from one discourse of *thathana* to the other has been an effect of the unstable

---

[4] See Perreira (2012) about the genealogy of 'Theravāda' as the category identifying the Pali tradition.

[5] 'Defense of religion,' or *thathana saung shauk yay*, has long been present in Buddhist discourses in Burma as a duty of the political power. See below on the traditional articulation of Buddhist and kingship institutions in Theravādin societies.

[6] Ma Ba Tha is the acronym for *Amyo batha thathana saung shauk yay ahpwe*, which could be translated as: 'Association for the Defense of the National Religion' (Brac de la Perrière 2014).

relationship between Buddhist and political institutions. This instability can only be explained by the impossibility, up to now, of delineating or isolating a definite domain of religious action in the Burmese sociopolitical order. It has also to do with the specificity of the process of 'religionization,' that is, its non-finiteness. In order to address this question, I will attempt to reach a working definition of the moving concept of *thathana* through an analysis of the semantic field of 'religion' and, then, examine how the religious sphere is constructed against other fields of practice conceptualized in Burmese as 'paths' (*lan*).

The Burmese Semantic Field of 'Religion'

In standard use,[7] *thathana* only concerns the Buddha's teachings as they have been spread, materialized, and institutionalized. As such, it cannot be used to refer to any other religious denomination. If translated, it should be through the deictic 'the religion' and would actually mean Buddhism, excluding all other world religions or local beliefs present in the Burmese context.[8] Except in very specific contexts, *thathana* designates Buddhism only. This is a marked difference with the contemporary use of this Pali concept in neighboring Buddhist cultures where *sāsana* may be linked to other denominations, or even to spirit cults in order to denote the 'religion of the spirits,' as in the Lao *sadsana phi*, for instance.[9]

While it excludes all other religious denominations, *thathana* does not necessarily lack pluralistic connotations. Among others, it allows for

---

[7] It is beyond the scope of this chapter to give a detailed analysis of all the uses of *thathana*, be it monastic, administrative, or legal. It is similarly beyond its scope to trace the evolution of its understanding through successive *thathana* reforms. As described by Alicia Turner, historically, the meaning of *thathana* 'was fluid, reinflected, and reinvented with each new instance of sāsana reform' (2014: 136). Therefore, we shall stay at the level of its general understanding and evolution.

[8] I only recently came across one occurrence of *Kirian thathana* (Christian teachings) in a very specific context: a legal claim placed by the Christian authorities in Burma against an offense to their institution. They needed to use the concept of *thathana* because of the formulation of the law involved. Significantly, the newly formed Buddhist nationalist association (Ma Ba Tha) protested vehemently against this use of *thathana* (*Eleven Daily*, December 12, 2014).

[9] See Sprenger, this volume.

the differentiation of various levels of Buddhist practice.[10] These levels are organized hierarchically under an all encompassing whole, which is ultimately linked to the teachings of Gautama Buddha. According to Buddhist cosmology, this dispensation is supposed to last only five thousand years and then to vanish until the coming of a next Buddha.

In Burma, however, *thathana* refers to the Buddha's legacy as grounded in Burmese society. Historically, this refers to Burmese Buddhist kingship with all its institutions aimed at passing on the teachings of the Buddha and, most importantly, the monastic community or Sangha (*thangha*) that bears the Theravādin tradition. In the Buddhist kingship configuration, different levels of *thathana* were encompassed and crisscrossed by one primary division that set monks apart from the laity. Monks ordained in the Sangha stand apart as crucial defenders of Buddhist teachings and providers of spiritual merit.[11] The partition between Sangha and lay Buddhist people was and still is the most striking statutory distinction within the Burmese social world and other Theravādin societies.

In any case, historically, *thathana* allowed for more idiosyncratic delineations than might be suggested by its translation as 'the' exclusive and single 'religion.' Not only did *thathana* imply different levels of practice that could be conceived of as distinctive sets of observances but it also allowed religious pluralism within the Buddhist polity or *thathana-daw*,[12] in which Buddhism and kingship were knitted together in a 'symbiotic' relationship. In this pre-colonial context, people identified themselves or were identified by others as subjects of the Buddhist kingdom, rather than categorized by 'religious' or 'ethnic' denominations (Lieberman 1978).

---

[10] Kirichenko quotes historiographical mentions of differentiated *thathana* according to status, such as the *thathana* of the monks (*yahan-thathana*) and the *thathana* of the laypeople (*lu-thathana*) (Kirichenko 2009). I have come across lists of distinctive *thathana* organized according to monastic practice followed: *pariyatti thathana, patipatti thathana, pativeda thathana.*

[11] This function of providers of merit is the basis of the relationship linking the Sangha to Buddhist lay people, as the latter may mainly acquire spiritual merit (*kutho*) in order to progress on the karmic path via their offerings to the Sangha.

[12] Followed by the suffix *daw*, an honorific qualifying particularly royal things, *thathana-daw* could be translated as Buddhist kingdom.

However, through the development of the colonial situation, religious belonging took on new importance, or so we have to infer from the semantic differentiation occurring in the mid-nineteenth century. In dictionaries of Burmese compiled at that time by Western missionaries, *batha,* the Burmese version of Pali *bhāsā* meaning 'language,' is defined as 'religion' for the first time.[13] At that point, *batha* was mainly found in the reports of the colonial administration—the census or the legal codes (Kirichenko 2009)—that is to say, in colonial efforts to classify populations. Around 1920, however, *batha* was used to mean religious affiliation quite generally. In the meantime, the all-encompassing dimensions of the previous Buddhist royal order (*thathana-daw*) seem to have lost ground to religious pluralism, which was no longer contained within a Buddhist polity and became restricted to more doctrinal connotations than had been previously the case.

As a concept for religion, *batha* is today understood in two main ways. First, it refers to various '-isms' or systems of religious beliefs that are considered independent of the societies in which they are transmitted. In Burmese, one can speak of *Kirian batha*, *Muslim batha* or *Buddha batha*, and this had set the foundation for evaluative comparisons.[14] But, to the best of my knowledge, there are no occurrences of *batha* used to talk about spirit worship, given that the latter does not fit into the Western notion of 'world religions' contained in the newly formed concept. Secondly, *batha* also implies a sense of religion as individually professed and suggests a personal involvement.

To encapsulate the semantic differentiation that occurred through the introduction of the term *batha* between the mid-nineteenth century and the 1920s, one could say that this concept brought about the very categories 'Buddhism' and 'religions.' The difference construed through opposing *batha* to *thathana* in Burma may be understood as mirroring

---

[13]'Religion' is one meaning of the entry *batha* in Judson's *Dictionary* (Houtman 1990), and *botdabatha* is used in the title of the Reverend J. Wade's *Dictionary of Buddhism and Burmese Literature* (Kirichenko 2009). Both dictionaries were originally published in 1852. As *thathana* was embedded in a discourse of true Buddhist views contrasted to false ones, Judson, a Baptist missionary, apparently renounced the extension of its use to Christianity. This would have been the reason for introducing *batha* to designate 'religions' (Houtman 1990).

[14]See the famous *Shin Okkata & Kyauk Kwin A Yaydawbon*, authored by Myat Hsain in 1962, as one example of literary production about this kind of evaluation. But, as early as 1919, the abbot of Ledi produced 'a polemical study of the "four great religions" (*Batha-kyi-le-ba*),' as quoted by Green (2015) through Patrick Pranke.

Western discourses about religion increasingly being replaced by the plural form 'religions,' as opposed to the single form of 'religion' meant to designate Christianity, soon to produce the syntagm 'world religions' (Masuzawa 2005). However, while these discourses evolved alongside the secularization process in the West, this was not quite the case in the Theravādin area, especially in Burma.

Similar genealogies of the way religious terminology coalesced through the colonial encounter could be traced in neighboring Theravādin countries. The case of Sri Lanka is particularly well researched. For instance, elaborating on previous erudition, Kitsiri Malalgoda has shown how *āgama*, a Pali word which had long designated categories of religious texts in the island, was appropriated at the turn of the nineteenth century by Western missionaries to designate Christianity against the prevailing term *sāsana* used for Buddhism as a socio-temporal phenomenon. At the turn of the twentieth century, *āgama* had become the generic term for 'religion' and 'religions' in Sri Lanka (Malalgoda 1997).[15]

This brief comparison of concepts for 'religion' and 'religions' in Burma and Sri Lanka emphasizes their commonalities, particularly similarities in the impact of the encounter with the Western notion of 'religions,' soon to become 'world religions,' conveyed by the Christian missionaries. However, out of this common background, the differentiation of the religious semantic field in these two countries produced definite specificities. An immediately perceptible specificity is the Burmese choice of *batha*, referring to 'languages,' rather than *āgama*, denoting 'scriptures,' to mean 'religions' as doctrinal systems independent of the societies in which they are present, as opposed to *thathana/ sāsana*, or the Buddha's teachings and the institutions ensuring their transmission in a given society. This choice of *batha* is particularly striking if one remembers the well-documented scriptural dimension of the

---

[15] The first author analyzing the semantics of religion in Sri Lanka is the anthropologist Richard Gombrich in his famous *Buddhist Precept and Practice* (1971). He delineated his object of study as 'religion' in that his informants considered themselves a 'religion,' that is to say, *dhamma*. Another main reference about the semantic field of religion in Sri Lanka is Carter (1993). About the way Buddhism was affected by the British encounter in Sri Lanka, see Harris (2006).

Western discovery of Buddhism.[16] However, this Burmese idiosyncrasy speaks for the independent formation of the semantic fields of religion in Theravādin countries facing comparable circumstances.

There is little to no information concerning the rationale behind the Burmese selection of *batha* for 'religions'; Kirichenko (2009) notes that this term was first understood as teachings by one of the main Burmese literati of the turn of the twentieth century, the abbot of Ledi, who highlighted the initial oral dimension of the Buddha's teachings. At first, there was a lack of differentiation between *batha* and *thathana*, the former used only to signify other religions, while the latter retained its value to specify Buddhist teachings and their dispensation. But soon, through the advent of the 1920s nationalist movements, following the formation of lay associations for the defense of the Buddha's teachings, *batha* took its distinctive identity dimension of 'religion' as professed and 'religion' as a doctrinal system. *Thathana*, meanwhile, recovered its unique status of delineating the Burmese socio-religious order as Buddhist. However, these categories evolve depending on context. In the current political transition and release of vocal Buddhist nationalism, *batha* takes on a more encompassing dimension, merging religious, ethnic and national belonging, as exemplified in the name of the new nationalist association Ma Ba Tha (see above note 6).

Thathana came out of these developments as a locally reappropriated concept referring to the Buddha's teachings and their dispensation in the Burmese social order. In other words, *thathana* may be understood as the Burmese Buddhicized *social space*.[17] This is the definition that should be kept in mind while parsing out what counts as 'religion' in this social space.

---

[16] See in particular, Philip Almond's *The British Discovery of Buddhism* (1988). Almond analyzes how Buddhism was identified through Burnouf's discovery of a Buddhist-Sanskrit corpus and invented during the Victorian era as a textual object located mainly in the Pali Text Society, a history that determined the enduring textual bias of the Buddhist studies. See also Lopez (1995).

[17] Regarding the concept of *social space*, see Condominas, who applied this concept to Southeast Asia, defining it as 'the space delineated by the set of relationships systems that characterize the group under consideration' (*l'espace déterminé par l'ensemble des systèmes de relations, caractéristique du groupe considéré*) (1980: 14). Aspects of this concept are useful for our depiction of *thathana* in that it is dynamic and applies to various levels of organization of social groups.

THATHANA AND BUDDHISM AS A 'UNIVERSALISM'

To relate the Burmese concept of *thathana* to the broader context of the Western encounter with Buddhism, it is important to first note how it is inscribed in the locality, far from the universal dimension that the Orientalist discovery found in deciphering the Buddhist textual corpus. From the beginning, whatever ambiguities underlaid the perceptions of its first discoverers in Europe, Buddhism was perceived by them as universal and philosophical. It included the main features of the 'world religion' category, that is, a historical founder (the Buddha) and the recognition of an ancient textual corpus. Masuzawa explains how the vision of Buddhism as 'a historical reform movement' initiated against Vedism and Brahmanism 'by an extraordinary but historically real individual' helped these discoverers to view it as 'a decidedly non-national religion,' even before the distinction between world and national religions had been made (2005: 136–138). When these categories came into use, Buddhism *inevitably* entered the category of 'universalisms' and was thus represented at the World's Parliament of Religions in Chicago in 1893.

However, as suggested by the reformulation of *thathana* in Burmese, there is a gap that needs to be bridged between the notion of Buddhism as a transnational religion and the localized conception of *thathana* as embedded in the presence of a monastic order or Sangha (*thangha*) pertaining to the Burmese society and the nation. The main Buddhist institution in Burma, like in all societies belonging to the Pali tradition, is the Sangha, because in this tradition it is regarded as the main recipient of the Buddha's teachings recorded in the Pali canon known as the *Tipitaka* ('The Three Baskets'), as well as the main provider of merit for the lay Buddhist people.

Through their ordination in the Sangha, men are turned into monks who are mendicant renouncers.[18] As such, they are supposed to follow the Buddhist monastic way of life, consisting of practice (Pali *patipatti*) and study (Pali *pariyatti*), in order to transmit the Buddha's teachings and to get closer to liberation from the cycle of lives (*thanthaya*, Pali *samsarā*). Obedience to the monastic rule, consisting of the 227 precepts recorded in the *Vinaya* book, ensures the monks' renunciation of the

---

[18] In Burma, women may also adopt a monastic way of life by becoming *thilashin*, but their status is lower than that of monks and the question of their belonging to the Sangha is ambiguous (see Kawanami 2013).

world. The effectiveness of their renunciation is, in turn, what entitles them to receive religious donations from lay Buddhist people willing to provide for their material needs. These latter gain merits through their donations to monks, which improve their karmic status. Monks and ordinary Buddhists are thus in a relation of interdependency based on hierarchically defined statuses.

In historical times, the Sangha was under the lay authority of the Burmese Buddhist king, who guaranteed its 'purity,' that is, the effectiveness of its renunciation of the world. The king was the chief donor among his subjects, and his legitimacy was linked to the prosperity of Buddhist institutions that were intended to ensure the proper transmission of the Buddha's teachings. The implication of such a configuration was that Sangha and kingship were also in an interdependent relation in the political-religious order, which as a whole formed the Buddhist polity (*thathana-daw*), that is, an instance of the dispensation of the Buddha's teachings.

In the mid-nineteenth century, while Burmese Buddhists were starting to recognize themselves as Buddhists vis-à-vis other denominations through the concept of *batha* (religion as professed), they also learned that they were part of the southern branch of this newly discovered 'world religion.' This branch was then designated Hīnayāna, meaning 'Little Vehicle,' and distinguished through its Pali canon from the Mahāyāna branch, meaning 'Great Vehicle.' It was not until June 6, 1950, that the World Fellowship of Buddhists decided at its inaugural meeting held in Colombo to name the southern branch of Buddhism Theravāda, the Elders' Path, rejecting the resented Hīnayāna (Perreira 2012). In Burma, The Sixth Buddhist Council held in 1956 in Yangon was decisive in the popularization of the new denomination. Although the genealogy of the differentiation of the two branches (Mahāyāna and Theravāda) has been recently the object of academic debate, Buddhists from Sri Lanka, Burma, Thailand, Cambodia, and Laos, recognize their tradition as pertaining to the Theravāda today.

This brings to light the role of councils as a practice of universality in the Theravādin tradition. In 1956, the 6th council was held in Yangon, at Kaba Aye, a brand new pagoda built for the occasion. The council was a major event for the nascent Burmese nation and for the international community of Theravādin Buddhists. In continuity with previous Buddhist councils, it was a huge gathering of learned monks convened in order to revise the Pali canon (*Tipitaka*). In the case of the previous historical Buddhist councils, Buddhist kings convened the monastic communities in order to 'purify' Buddhist teachings or *sāsana* in their efforts to control the Sangha, as shown by Robert Lingat (1989). Thus, councils aimed at the redefinition of textual orthodoxy were both an expression of the various communities linked by the Pali tradition and an act of political authority exerted upon the monastic order at the polity level, combining a practice of universality with the affirmation of a localized power.

In the same vein, the Kaba Aye council convened by Burmese authorities aimed at producing 'a new and truly international version' of the *Tipitaka* in the context of newly gained independences (Clark 2015: 95).[19] The council was planned by Nu, who was then the Burmese Prime Minister and who, in the post-colonial context, envisioned a program of Buddhist revival as a tool for national consolidation. The newly defined Burmese nation was to be identified as Buddhist, in concert with other new Asian nations. As a result, Theravāda, a new denomination of the common religious identity of the region's states, was to emerge as a reflection of the post-colonial political agenda, with an enduring impact.

Significantly, the call on universality to reaffirm lay power in a *sāsana* appears to have been implemented through textual practice. The common reference to the Theravādin denomination is indeed the Pali canon or *Tipitaka*, which purports to be an exclusive list of Buddhist scriptures. Steven Collins suggested in his seminal paper, 'On the Very Idea of the Pali Canon,' that 'the actual importance of what we know as the Pali Canon has not lain in the specific texts collected in that list, but rather in the very idea of such a collection' (Collins 1990). Recent studies on religious textual cultures in Theravādin countries have led some scholars to question the permanence of this reference and to show how, in fact, it has mainly percolated in these societies through oral teaching of monks

---

[19] In his recent paper on the 6th Buddhist council, Chris Clark shows particularly that Burmese authorities spared no effort to make the result of this impressive editorial undertaking recognized by the whole Theravāda Buddhist world, although only but a few monks from other Theravādin countries did participate in the work. However, the new edited *Tipitaka* does not exclusively represent a Burmese version but makes liberal use of all the sources and has become a major reference.

and predicators using vernacular commentaries of Pali texts as sources.[20] Monks, without having to prove the authenticity of their teachings, are considered the legitimate interpreters of the Buddha's words. In this respect, monks are active agents of transmission for an evolving canon. Thus, whereas the effectiveness of secular powers on Buddhist polities depends on their preserving the supposedly original canon, practices of transmission in the communities reveal that the nature of the Pali canon is in reality much more fluid and elusive.

In local communities, the Pali canon exists mainly as an idea of the 'universal,' orally transmitted, negotiated, and appropriated by monastics seen as the depositaries of the Buddha's teachings. Secular powers have the responsibility to import and preserve the universal canonic corpus and to materialize it through revision, copy, and editing by the most learned monks gathering in councils. Councils are thus politico-religious events enabling the localization of the universal, a transformation that is also, partly, that of the written form into the oral. In 1956, at the Kaba Aye council, the Burmese invented for themselves a national identity partly defined as a return to traditional forms of order conveyed by the concept of *thathana*, in which secular power and Buddhist institutions appear intrinsically related.

SYMBIOTIC VARIATIONS: FROM THE DISPENSATION TO THE DEFENSE OF *THATHANA*

The ideas conveyed through *thathana* belong to their respective times and to evolving configurations of power, as exemplified in the various discourses of dispensation[21] and the recently renewed theme of national Buddhist identity, suggesting to defend the *thathana* against the presence of other religions. Both also result from the difficulty to differentiate political and Buddhist action in a Theravādin society like Burma. In such society, the relationship between secular power and Buddhist establishment is so intricate that Tambiah (1976) characterized it as a 'symbiosis.' In this regard, determining what counts for 'religion' in Buddhist Burma depends largely on the balance of power between these

---

[20] For two brilliant examples of the recent study of textual practices in a Theravādin context, see Blackburn (2001) and McDaniel (2008), both of whom were largely inspired by the analysis of Collins (1990 and 1998).

[21] *Thathana pyu* means literally taking care of the Buddha's teachings, as seen earlier.

institutions in a particular situation and at a given time. That is why, in order to understand the process of religionization in Burma, one must examine the history of power relationships between political and Buddhist institutions.

As explained above, in former times the main Buddhist institution was the Sangha, linked to the Burmese kingship in an embedding *thathana*, which was one manifestation of the Buddha's dispensation.[22] The fall of Burmese kingship in the last phase of the British colonial conquest (1885) was decisive in reformulating the Burmese Buddhicized social space. The new situation caused major social and political crisis.[23] The fall of the monarchy suddenly deprived the Buddhist institutions of their main protection and destabilized the socio-religious order. Since that time, the delineation of the *thathana* has evolved according to the balance of power between political and Buddhist institutions.

Alicia Turner (2014) has described the colonial scene at the turn of the twentieth century, in which Burmese managed to negotiate a space free of colonial subordination by making use of the changing definition of 'religion.' Under the colonial administration, the defense of the *thathana* became a lay cause in Burma, because of the British avoidance of involvement in religious matters. The laity began to assume royal duties of protecting the *thathana* and expanded the lay donation path with involvement in practices that were previously reserved to monastics, such as the study of Buddhist writings and meditation.[24] A number of lay Buddhist associations flourished at the turn of the twentieth century, engaging in the support of the Sangha. Some of them were formed with the purpose of organizing collective donations to the Sangha, on a community base, creating a new sense of identity. Others began financing Pali examinations to promote *pariyatti*, the study of Buddhist teachings,

---

[22] On the history of the Sangha in Burma, see Mendelson (1975).

[23] The formal colonization of Burma occurred in three stages during the nineteenth century. The first war ended with the takeover of Arakan and Tenasserim by the Company in 1824, the second was concluded by the seizure of Lower Burma that became a province of India in 1852, and the third ended with the complete surrendering of Burma to the British Empire in 1885.

[24] This period saw the abbot of Ledi, the famous Burmese cleric, actively promoting among laity the practice of insight meditation (P. *vipāssana*, B. *wipathena*), the most elevated kind of meditation, which was previously only a monastic practice (Houtman 1999; Jordt 2007).

whereas the preservation of Buddhist manuscripts and the supply of copied versions had previously been the prerogative of court monasticism.

As explained by Turner, the first discourses by lay Buddhist associations in defense of the *thathana* made Buddhism public, but they were not explicitly political. 'Religion' was simply the only sphere left by the colonial administration in which the Burmese could act upon their lives. However, with the nascent sense of collective identity, new nationalist associations would soon emerge and the whole process was later reinterpreted in the context of the independence struggle. Defense of the *thathana* came to be intermingled with proto-nationalist political discourse that recalled the pre-colonial 'symbiosis' of Buddhist institutions and political power, in spite of its anti-colonial stance. This worked as a strong precedent for the contemporary reformulation of Buddhist nationalism.

The defense of the *thathana* has thus evolved into a moral discourse of opposition to political orders—contra the discourse of dispensation—in which members of the Sangha have been vocal on several occasions. This was the case during the colonial era when young monks began to promote the emerging nationalist cause by preaching. Among them, the best known were Ottama and Wisara,[25] who were deprived of their monastic status by the colonial authorities under the pretext that political activism was an infringement on monastic rule. This was again the case more recently, in September 2007, when members of the Sangha decided to demonstrate against the junta, in a movement known as the 'Saffron revolution.' The leaders of the monks' peaceful demonstrations were also defrocked and arrested by the Burmese junta on account of their political involvement, which paradoxically aligned the military with the colonial authorities. However, the relationship between the government and the Sangha was no longer the same as in the 1920s. At the time, the British administration was resuming the role of controlling the Sangha—which was previously the kings' responsibility—without depending on it for its legitimacy. The military, meanwhile, depended on

---

[25] Ottama (1879–1939) and Wisara (1888–1929). Wisara died in jail in 1929 following a hunger strike of 166 days intended to defend monks' right to wear their robes in jail, in other words, while trying to recognize the monks' rights to act politically without losing their religious status. Regarding these monks, see in particular Smith (1965) and Sarkisyanz (1965).

the monks to gain merits and reinforce their legitimacy as patrons of the monastic order on a national scale.

To summarize the evolution of the *thathana* in relation to the balance of powers, one can say that when the symbiotic relationship between state and Sangha weakened, as it did during the colonial period (1885–1948) or the first military regime (Ne Win era, 1962–1988), defense of the *thathana* and Buddhist practice tended to represent moral opposition to the government. When, on the contrary, the symbiotic relationship was revived, as under Nu during the post-independence parliamentary era (1948–1962) or under the junta after the 1988 events, the politics of the *thathana* tended to invade the public life. Today, however, the defense of the *thathana* has become a discourse that has taken possession of the whole of public life under the motto of a reformulated Buddhist nationalism. The latter has been represented by the tentacular association known as Ma Ba Tha, which was founded by a large, independently convened meeting of monks in May 2013, following anti-Muslim violence, as mentioned above (note 6). No longer expressing a contestation of the authorities, this discourse spread at the expense of the nascent political sphere.

The 2007 so-called Saffron revolution was a monastic protest after decades of containment under military rule. It can shed light on the articulation of politics and Buddhism in Burma, revealing the evolving relations between state and Sangha. In the 1950s, the issue of religion held increasing importance, which led the Prime Minister Nu to put forth an amendment to the Constitution, adopted in August 1961, to establish Buddhism as the state religion (*naingnan daw thathana*). Nu's government was also under pressure from certain monastics to introduce Buddhist teachings in public schools. In this context, Ne Win led military men seized power in March 1962 in order to maintain the precarious national balance concerning the place of ethnic and religious minorities (Smith 1965). Ne Win set up a military regime based on a socialist ideology that advocated secular principles.

Although Ne Win kept a distance from Buddhism and monks, in May 1980 he was forced to hold a national monastic convention and launch a 'purification' program in order to reassert the government's control over the Sangha. This led to a reform and to the unification of various segments under one single administration, the Sangha Maha Nayaka Ahpwe, a body of forty-seven senior abbots nominated by the Department of

Religious Affairs (*thathana yay usitana*) and placed under its authority.[26] The Sangha Maha Nayaka Ahpwe exerts disciplinary authority over the Sangha according to the monastic rule (*Vinaya*). It is an irony of history that one of the most important administrative reforms of the Sangha, still in use today, was implemented by the most outwardly secularist regime of independent Burma.[27]

After the 1988 popular uprising, the army regained power through a coup. Although general elections were organized in 1990, which were overwhelmingly won by the candidates from the National League for Democracy (NLD), the main opposition party, military men did not relinquish power. Instead, the new junta called itself the State Law and Order Restoration Council (SLORC). Lacking the legitimacy of the popular vote, the SLORC sought to establish itself through, among other measures, a systematic policy of funding and supporting Buddhist institutions, which represented a clear break from the political approach of the previous regime. As Juliane Schober writes, the 'military regime's patronage of Buddhism provided an alternative source of legitimation and transformed a national community into a ritual network' (Schober 2011: 86).[28]

However, in 2007 the monks' protest signaled a return of monastics (some of them at least) to the political arena as a force equipped with a certain degree of autonomy, ready to challenge the powers-that-be. In order to show his opposition to the political power, a monk can only act by refusing donations, that is, by turning his alms bowl upside down (*thabeik hmauk*). This amounts to a break in the ritual relationship with laypeople, which involves a concerted decision of the Sangha. In September 2007, following a series of incidents that prompted the monks' action, the ritual link with the military regime was broken. Because the regime had used the national economy of merit as the

---

[26] In 1962, under Ne Win's rule, Home and Religious Affairs were merged into one ministry. It is only in 1992 that a Ministry of Religious Affairs (*thathana yay wongyi tana*) was again formed, under which the Sangha Maha Nayaka Ahpwe operates. First constituted of thirty-three senior abbots, today this body has forty-seven members.

[27] In 1988, Tin Maung Maung Than published one of the few analyses of Ne Win's religious policy, assessing very favorably the 1980s' reform of the Sangha (Tin Maung Maung Than 1988). To be noted, parts of the Sangha are, on the contrary, very critical of this reform today, blaming it for having 'enslaved' the monks to political power (See Brac de la Perrière 2014).

[28] See also Houtman (1999) for one of the most comprehensive analyses of the cultural outcome of SLORC policies.

cornerstone for its legitimacy and control over the monks, the break resounded with an astounding strength.

The situation provoked a flow of conflicting comments regarding the effectiveness of the renunciation of the world of those monks involved in the protest movement. For the government and its affiliates, the protest movement amounted to a breach in the renouncer status, which authorized them to question the participants' religious status as monks, by labeling their action 'political.' But many civilians interpreted the act of defrocking monks, to arrest and interrogate them, as an insult to monkhood. The government proceeded to arrest monks according to a decree passed in October 1990 that allowed them to defrock monks involved in anti-governmental action without going through the Sangha Maha Nayaka Ahpwe. Consequently, under the Burmese junta as well as the colonial regime, the label 'political' was negatively used to question monks' action in the secular world whenever they targeted the powers-that-be. Moreover, the term 'governmental' was similarly used to question the authority of those segments of the Sangha deemed corrupted by the political power. Critiques of 'government' monks circulated undercover, alleging that these monks were deprived of 'true' intentions and accusing them of straying from the monkhood world renouncement ideal.

Thus, under military regimes, both sides have used labels of 'political' and 'governmental' to question the authenticity of monkhood renunciation of the world—that is to say, to question the monks' 'religious' status. In other words, these labels have been an integral part of the Burmese debates about what counts for 'religion.' This raises questions of the encroachment of politics on *thathana* in a situation where neither domain is properly delineated. The defense of *thathana* has been mapped onto the moral position of contesting the repressive government. Ultimately, in this eminently political game, no position can be considered exclusively religious or political, due to the renewed symbiotic relationship between state and Buddhist institutions.

However, in March 2011, a new political situation was established by introducing electoral legitimacy and democratic values that contribute to separate political and religious orders in a phase of democratic transition. One can already postulate that regime change and the opening of a legal field of action for politics—legitimized by popular vote—creates a new situation, since the legitimation of power no longer directly depends on the function of monks as providers of merit. Arguably, the opening created by democratic transition in the political arena is contributing to the weakening of the symbiotic link between state and Sangha, putting monks at risk of being dismissed from public affairs.

This is all the more true, given that political action has now been authorized for civilians within the constitutional framework, but is not allowed for members of the Sangha, who (like in Thailand) are even excluded from voting due to their status as renouncers.[29] The issue of the place of *thathana* under a democratic regime is therefore a true cause of concern for the monks, who view their current situation as precarious. This is why, far from withdrawing into their monasteries, members of a new generation of monks are paradoxically attempting to define their role in this new game, weighing the extent of their influence on current issues.

Under the juntas, the defense of *thathana* took the form of a moral stance against the powers-that-be, while discourse on the dispensation of *thathana* was based on the symbiotic relationship between religious establishments and political class. Today, the defense discourse takes the form of a strident nationalism targeting religious otherness, particularly Muslims. Buddhist nationalism is displayed in the association known as Ma Ba Tha, bringing together, in an unheard of way, three overlapping concepts of identity: ethnic identity or nationality (*a myo*), religious denomination (*batha*), and Burmese Buddhicized social space (*thathana*). Religious otherness is excluded from the Burmese delineation of national identity through this conflation of signifiers, as if *thathana* in asserting itself in front of an emerging political field of action had to discard all pluralistic potential once contained in this concept, under the aegis of Burmese Buddhist kingship (Fig. 2.1).

THATHANA AND RITUAL

However, Buddhism does not account for all Burmese practices that could be considered religious from an etic perspective. Specifically, Burmese Buddhists do not consider the spirit worship they practice to be a part of their religion (*batha*), but it is nonetheless a part of the Burmese Buddhicized social space (*thathana*). This worship is addressed

---

[29] Regarding this constitutional law issue, cf. Larsson (2015). Buddhist monks were also banned from voting in the pre-communist Constitution of Cambodia.

2 ABOUT BUDDHIST BURMA: *THATHANA*, OR 'RELIGION' AS SOCIAL SPACE

Fig. 2.1 Monks alms round organized by a local NLD office to prepare Aung San's 100th birthday on the 13th of February 2015

to spirits of the Burmese pantheon of spirit possession, known as the 'Thirty-seven Lords' (*thonze hkunit min*), which includes a number of individual tutelary spirits worshiped in local communities.[30] The emergence of this pantheon may be seen as the legacy of the kings' ritual policy of recognizing and paying homage to the main local spirits. It survived the collapse of kingship as an impressive ritual complex that underpins huge annual public festivals, celebrating each member of the pantheon in its specific domain, as well as private ceremonies in which all the spirits of the pantheon are called on to be embodied by mediums. In short, it articulates local rituals commemorating tutelary spirits with spirit possession ceremonies focused on a pantheon of spirits whose specialists are spirit mediums.

---

[30] Concerning the worship of the Thirty-Seven Lords, see Brac de la Perrière (1989) and Spiro (1967).

These practices of the Burmese Buddhists could be considered religious, if only because they fit the substantive definition of religion in relation to supernatural beings.[31] But are we then obliged to conclude that the Burmese have 'two religions'? This was the thesis of Melford Spiro, who produced the first anthropological interpretation of religion in Burma in two renowned books, *Buddhism and Society* (1970) and *Burmese Supernaturalism* (1967). Stanley Tambiah criticized this thesis of 'two distinct religions' on the grounds that Spiro failed to account for the overall structuration of Burmese religion. Spiro in turn defended his position, highlighting the fact that the Burmese exclude spirit worshipping from their Buddhist *batha*. On the one hand, Burmese do not consider their 'supernaturalism' to be a *batha* at all, which negates the 'two religions' thesis. On the other hand, some Burmese rationalize practices dedicated to spirits on the grounds of Buddhist cosmology. This position was exemplified in a paper by former Prime Minister Nu (1989), but is rather exceptional.

In fact, the acceptance of spirit possession in a context of Buddhism-based morality is a matter of debate among Burmese. While belief in spirits is not necessarily questioned, choosing to worship them or not does denote different standards of practice in the Burmese Buddhicized social space (*thathana*). The 'two religions' thesis seems unable to account for the intricacies of the Burmese religious field, particularly the historical development of the Thirty-Seven Lords cult under the aegis of Buddhist kingship. In this regard, the words used or avoided are indicative of hierarchies. Putting the label of religion (*batha*) on a field of practices implicitly serves to deny this status to other practices and is thus a gesture of power.

Now, if spirit possession is only religious from an etic perspective, it surely pertains to ritual, a realm of action whose articulation with *thathana* must be examined. However, defining ritual is no easier than defining religion. Scholars' positions on this matter have varied from those founded on the opposition of sacred and profane (Durkheim) to those who refuse the relevance of the sacred, focusing instead on the meaning of ritual (Leach), and from those who claim ritual as the

---

[31] Interestingly, Melford Spiro has authored one well-known formulation of this kind of definition (Spiro 1966).

root of religion to those who locate ritual as the core of all social life.³² Catherine Bell (1992) drew attention to processes of differentiation that produce 'ritual,' or in other words 'ritualization.' This implies that ritualization is what produces the sacred in any given society, which is to take the other way around Durkheim's definition of religion and ritual as that which deals with the sacred.

Aside from these variations, the concept of ritual has been looked down since its inception in early modern Europe (sixteenth century) as the practices of 'others.' As phrased by Edward Muir (1997: 9): 'What I do was ordained by God and is "true religion"; what you do is "mere ritual" at best useless, at worst profoundly evil.' This low esteem is still prevalent in the common use of the word to designate a formal practice without any meaning.³³ In some cultural contexts, rituals may be altogether dismissed on the grounds that they do not belong to the sphere of religious activity.³⁴ Looking at how the Burmese conceptualize the category of ritual—if they do it at all—through an examination of the main words used in Burmese to qualify the kind of events that we would consider rituals will bring forth similar rejection of ritual on a religious basis.

Most ritual events are actually referred to in Burmese by adding the word *pwe* to specific descriptive terms. *Pwe*, however, is a word with a large semantic field. When qualified with specific descriptive terms, *pwe* appears to be a very inclusive category, bringing together various events pertaining to all spheres of social life: the public sphere, the private one, the Buddhist one, or the one connected to the spirit cult. Although this includes the events most vital for the maintenance of *thathana*, *pwe* does

---

³²One may recall Durkheim's famous definition of ritual and religion as domains of social life which deal with the sacred. However, criticisms of 'ritual' were raised later on by Jack Goody and Edmund Leach, first due to shortcomings of definitions based on dichotomous criteria of ritual actions, such as religious/secular, sacred/profane, or non-rational/rational, for these criteria come mainly from the observer's own categorization (Goody 1977; Leach 1968). See also Coppet (1992), in which he states that 'the domain of rituals resists efforts to theorize about and to define it.'

³³This use of the category of ritual is underlying some critics, as that of Goody in his famous 'Against ritual' (1977).

³⁴The Jains, for instance, would make a radical distinction between the practices that we recognize as rituals, dividing those that they perceive as religious, which are therefore, not ritual, from those that are ritual, challenging most theories of ritual (Humphrey and Laidlaw 1994).

not convey the sense that they are related to the Buddha's teachings. It rather indicates a quality of action that these events share with other rituals. This term includes most Burmese rituals, except those dealing with death (*athoba*), because they are categorized as *a-mingala*, meaning that they are 'inauspicious.' By contrast, *pwe* appears to be imbued with a sense of festiveness.

Other words belong to the semantic field of ritual. The term *yoya* covers a range of social practices legitimated by being handed down by the predecessors, a process that suggests invariance and formality, characteristics recognized as specific to ritual actions. It is often translated as 'tradition' and associated with words such as *dale* and *thonzan*, meaning 'customs' or 'habits,' and with *pwe* as well. *Yoya*, in the sense of repetitive action, is indeed very close to the common sense meaning of ritual as a 'habitual action.' Among practitioners of the spirit cult, one often hears the sentence *yoya hpyek de*, meaning that any initiative in this context, perceived as an interaction with the spirits, will become a ritual obligation.

Yoya, however, also has more specific meanings. It refers to the worship of a particular spirit among the thirty-seven figures of the Burmese pantheon. This practice, transmitted in the family (through women or men), apparently comes from the worship of the tutelary spirit of the place where the family had its origins and is also known as *mi hsain hpa hsain*. In this sense, *yoya* means a particular form of cult practice that is transmitted rather than legitimated by spirit possession. Thus, *yoya* is specific in two ways, first because it qualifies a general characteristic of ritual action, and second because it designates a kind of ritual legitimated by this characteristic as opposed to other rituals in the spirit possession frame.

Another expression belonging to the semantic field of ritual is *a hkan a na*, which may designate the ceremonial or ostentatious aspects of a number of rituals. Among the rituals that could have ceremonial elements, called *a hkan a na*, civil rituals through which a change in the social status is effected, such as wedding rituals, are particularly preeminent.[35] The ceremonial part is performed by professional ritualists, called

---

[35] The proper ritual through which an engaged couple is married is the gesture of putting their right hands upon each other, *lek htap de*, after having paid their respect to the Buddha, the spirits protecting the house, and their parents. This ritual could be performed with formal entertainment, in which case it becomes *mingala hsaung a hkan a na*.

beitheik hsaya, whose presence refers to the Indian ritual of *abhiseka*, or unction, particularly as connected with the kings' consecration, which thus appears as the prototype of all transitional rituals.[36] The implicit technical reference to the presence of *beitheik hsaya* in transitional rites such as novicehood or marriage is the royal model of rituals, a model borrowed from India.

The fact that these rituals are connected with ceremonial entertainment, as suggested by the expression *a hkan a na*, is in itself revealing of particular aspects of Burmese rituals. One important aspect of these rituals is that they disclose the change that is effected through representation of the missing kingship. In other words, changes of position in the life cycle need to be performed in the context of representation of a royal social order to be effective. Not surprisingly, kingship rituals themselves were construed as a show of the kingship's social order. Nowadays, novicehood, marriages, and other rituals like those of the spirit cults, always display the aesthetics of kingship. The main forms of performing arts are also representations of kingship. Altogether we have an intricate network of links connecting representations of kingship, rituals, and performances, through which the social order is reproduced and changes of position are enacted by means of representing kingship.

Most interestingly, the rituals involved—royal consecration, marriage, novicehood—are included in the same category as other rituals referred to as *beitheik pwe*. Through a technical term rooted in Indian cultural heritage emerges the possibility of gathering, in the same category, rituals from various contexts that all imply a change of status. However, if at the conceptual level, this opens the possibility of considering side-by-side rituals from diverse contexts that have similar functions, such as the consecration of images, at the level of practice, we see a differentiation that tends to separate and distinguish rituals connected closely to the *thathana*, such as the consecration of the Buddha's images (*anekaza tin*), from others like the consecration of spirits' images (*leippya theik*).[37]

I will not go into further detail here, but will try to reach a tentative conclusion regarding the way the notion of ritual is construed in Burmese, relative to the semantic field of religion. Thus far, we have seen

---

[36] As the inheritors of the Indian ritual specialists who once performed these rituals for Burmese kings, *beitheik hsaya* are nowadays quite Buddhicized and Burmanized.

[37] See Brac de la Perrière (2006) for a comparative analysis of these two kinds of rituals.

a ritual sphere coalescing around the notion of *pwe*, whose moving limits stretch from a quality of action shared by types of ceremonial events to the transmissibility of practice, as in tradition. As such, it does not set 'religion' apart but is so inclusive as to gather events from the whole of social life. In so doing, it creates a unified field of practice whose events share characteristics of regularity and formality, and whose main elements may be found in different ritual contexts. This allows for the establishment of a universal sense of convention or ritual obligation in all the spheres of social life.

However, the specific order in which ritual elements are arranged, in cases like the consecration of images, allows for the differentiation of events pertaining to the *thathana* from those belonging to the ritual sphere. Conversely, those events of civil life calling for *a hkan a na* and mirroring kingship protocol, through which action on the world is possible, are plainly 'ritual' in the Burmese sense. Contrary to the notion of *pwe*, this allows for the examination of the ritual sphere delineated through contrast with the soteriological orientation of Buddhism toward the renunciation of the world. In the same way, spirit worship contrasts with the renouncement orientation of Buddhism because it allows for action on this world. In this sense, it truly belongs to ritual sphere, as it is segregated from 'religion' conceptualized through the individualistic and universalistic notion of *batha*. Significantly, the Burmese make use of the notion of *batha*—the concept for religion that has emerged from the Western encounter—to emphasize the 'religiosity' of the Buddha's teachings relative to ritual practice in their Buddhicized social space.

Conclusion

During military rule, politics of *thathana* have varied from the dispensation of Buddha's teachings to their defense, depending on the balance of power between state administration and the Sangha, and according to the position of various stakeholders. As the political field opens, unleashing new anxieties, the defense of the *thathana* has become a virulent discourse of Buddhist nationalism conveyed by particularly vocal monks pursuing various agendas. For parts of the Sangha, this political transition represents an opportunity to restore their agency as leaders of the Buddhist 'nation,' a function that had been monopolized by the military for decades. The recent conflation of overlapping concepts of identities in the name of Ma Ba Tha, the main association advocating the defense of *thathana*, is in the process of reframing the once pluralist Buddhicized social space of the Burmese Buddhist kingship into an increasingly exclusive one. Finally, in Burma, religionization is the process of producing a Burmese Buddhicized social space through differentiation from various other individually professed doctrines (*batha*) or of fields of practice defined as 'paths' (*lan*), such as spirit worshiping, esoteric Buddhism, or, pertaining to a more general level, politics, rituals, or exchange. All these domains represent potential infringements on the *thathana*, which in turn reveals itself to be a never-ending process of Buddhicization. This is all the more true given that the Buddha's teachings are in a constant need of affirmation against adversaries, due to their intrinsic degenerative tendency.

References

Almond, Philip. 1988. *The British Discovery of Buddhism*. Cambridge: Cambridge University Press.
Bell, Catherine. 1992. *Ritual Theory. Ritual Practice*. Oxford: Oxford University Press.
Blackburn, Anne. 2001. *Buddhist Learning and Textual Practice in Eighteenth Century Lankan Monastic Culture*. Princeton: Princeton University Press.
Brac de la Perrière, Bénédicte. 1989. *Les rituels de possession en Birmanie. Du culte d'État aux cérémonies privées*. Paris: Éditions Recherches sur les Civilisations, ADPF.
Brac de la Perrière, Bénédicte. 1995. Urbanisation et légendes d'introduction du bouddhisme au Myanmar (Birmanie). *Journal des Anthropologues* 61–62: 41–66.
Brac de la Perrière, Bénédicte. 2006. Les consécrations des statues de Bouddha et des statues de nat en Birmanie. Adaptation de rituels indiens?. In *Les rituels hindous. Transformations et transferts*, ed. G. Colas and G. Tarabout, 201–236. Paris: EHESS, Purushartha.
Brac de la Perrière, Bénédicte. 2014. Ma Ba Tha. Les trois syllabes du nationalisme bouddhique birman. In *L'Asie du Sud-Est 2015. Bilan, enjeux et perspectives*, ed. A. Pesses and F. Robinne, 31–45. Bangkok: IRASEC.
Carter, John Ross. 1993. *On Understanding Buddhists: Essays on the Theravāda Tradition in Sri Lanka*. Albany: State University of New York Press.
Clark, Chris. 2015. The Sixth Buddhist Council: Its Purpose, Presentation, and Product. *The Journal of Burma Studies* 19 (1): 79–115.
Collins, Steven. 1990. On the Very Idea of the Pali Canon. *Journal of the Pali Text Society* XV: 89–126 (Re-published in Collins, Steven. 2013. *Self &*

Society. Essays on Pali Literature and Social Theory 1988–2010. Bangkok: Silkworm Press).
Collins, Steven. 1998. Nirvana and Other Buddhist Felicities. Utopia of the Pali Imaginaire. Cambridge: Cambridge University Press.
Condominas, Georges. 1980. L'espace social à propos de l'Asie du Sud-Est. Paris: Flammarion.
Coppet, Daniel de. 1992. Introduction. In Understanding Rituals, ed. D. De Coppet, 1–10. London: Routledge, European Association of Social Anthropologists.
Gombrich, Richard. 1971. Precept and Practice: Traditional Buddhism in the Rural Highlands of Ceylon. Oxford: Oxford University Press.
Goody, Jack. 1977. Against Ritual: Loosely Structured Thoughts on a Loosely Defined Topic. In Secular Ritual, ed. S.F. Moore and B.G. Myerhoff, 25–35. Assen: Van Gorcum.
Green, Nile. 2015. Buddhism, Islam and the Religious Economy of Colonial Burma. Journal of Southeast Asian Studies 46 (2): 175–204.
Harris, Elizabeth J. 2006. Theravāda Buddhism and the British Encounter. Religious, Missionary and Colonial Experience in Nineteenth-Century Sri Lanka. London: Routledge.
Houtman, Gustaaf. 1990. How a Foreigner Invented Buddhendom in Burmese: From Tha-tha-na to Bok-da' ba-tha. Journal of the Royal Anthropological Society of Oxford 21 (2): 113–128.
Houtman, Gustaaf. 1999. Mental Culture in Burmese Crisis Politics: Aung San Suu Kyi and the National League for Democracy, 33. Tokyo: Institute for the Study of Languages and Cultures of Asia and Africa.
Humprey, Carolyn, and James Laidlaw. 1994. The Archetypal Actions of Ritual: A Theory of Ritual Illustrated by the Jain Rite of Worship. Oxford: Clarendon Press.
Jordt, Ingrid. 2007. Burma's Lay Meditation Movement. Buddhism and the Cultural Construction of Power. Athens: Ohio University Press.
Kawanami, Hiroko. 2013. Renunciation and Empowerment of Buddhist Nuns in Myanmar-Burma. Brill: Leiden.
Kirichenko, Alexey. 2009. From Thathanadaw to Theravāda Buddhism: Constructions of Religion and Religious Identity in Nineteenth- and Early Twentieth-Century Myanmar. In Casting Faiths. Imperialism and the Transformation of Religion in East and Southeast Asia, ed. Th. DuBois, 23–45. New York: Palgrave Macmillan.
Larsson, Thomas. 2015. Monkish Politics in Southeast Asia: Religious Disenfranchisement in Comparative and Theoretical Perspective. Modern Asian Studies 49 (1): 40–82.
Leach, Edmund. 1968. Ritual. In International Encyclopedia of the Social Sciences, vol. 13, ed. D.L. Sills, 520–526. New York: Macmillan.

Lieberman, Victor B. 1978. Ethnic Politics in Eighteenth-Century Burma. *Modern Asian Studies* 12 (3): 455–482.
Lingat, Robert. 1989. *Royautés bouddhiques. Asoka. La fonction royale à Ceylan.* Paris: École des Hautes Études en Sciences Sociales.
Lopez Jr., Donald S. (ed.). 1995. *Curators of the Buddha. The Study of Buddhism under Colonialism.* Chicago: University of Chicago Press.
McDaniel, Justin Thomas. 2008. *Gathering Leaves & Lifting Words. Histories of Buddhist Monastic Education in Laos and Thailand.* Seattle: University of Washington Press.
Malalgoda, Kitsiri. 1997. Concepts and Confrontations. A Case Study of *Agama.* In *Sri Lanka: Collective Identity Revisited*, vol. 1, ed. M. Roberts, 55–77. Colombo: Marga Institute.
Mandair, Arvind-Pal S., and Markus Dressler. 2011. Introduction: Modernity, Religion-Making, and the Postsecular. In *Secularism and Religion-Making*, ed. M. Dressler and A.-P.S. Mandair, 3–36. Oxford: Oxford University Press.
Masuzawa, Tomoko. 2005. *The Invention of World Religions. Or How European Universalism Was Preserved in the Language of Pluralism.* Chicago: University of Chicago Press.
Mendelson, Michael E. 1975. *Sangha and State in Burma: A Study of Monastic Sectarianism and Leadership*, ed. J.P. Ferguson. Ithaca: Cornell University Press.
Muir, Edward. 1997. *Ritual in Early Modern Europe.* Cambridge: Cambridge University Press.
Nu, U. 1989. Nats. *Crossroads* 4 (1): 1–12.
Perreira, Todd LeRoy. 2012. Whence Theravāda? The Modern Genealogy of an Ancient Term. In *How Theravāda is Theravāda? Exploring Buddhist Identities*, ed. P. Skilling, J.A. Carbine, C. Cicuzza, and S. Pakdeekham, 443–571. Chiang Mai: Silkworm Books.
Sarkisyanz, Emmanuel. 1965. *Buddhist Backgrounds of the Burmese Revolution.* The Hague: Martinus Nijhoff.
Schober, Juliane. 2011. *Modern Buddhist Conjunctures in Myanmar. Cultural Narratives, Colonial Legacies and Civil Society.* Honolulu: University of Hawai'i Press.
Smith, Donald Eugene. 1965. *Religion and Politics in Burma.* Princeton: Princeton University Press.
Spiro, Melford E. 1966. Religion: Problems of Definition and Explanation. In *Anthropological Approaches to the Study of Religion*, ed. M. Banton, 85–126. London: Tavistock Publications.
Spiro, Melford E. 1967. *Burmese Supernaturalism. An Explanation on Suffering Reduction.* Philadelphia: Institute for the Study of Human Issues.
Spiro, Melford E. 1970. *Buddhism and Society. A Great Tradition and Its Burmese Vicissitudes.* London: George Allen & Unwin.

Tambiah, Stanley J. 1976. *World Conqueror and World Renouncer. A Study of Buddhism and Polity in Thailand Against a Historical Background.* Cambridge: Cambridge University Press.

Tin Maung Maung Than. 1988. The Sangha and Sasana in Socialist Burma. *Sojourn* 3 (1): 26–61.

Turner, Alicia M. 2014. *Saving Buddhism. The Impermanence of Religion in Colonial Burma.* Honolulu: The University of Hawai'i Press.

Author Biography

Bénédicte Brac de la Perrière Ph.D., is a senior researcher and a member of the Center for Southeast Asian Studies (CASE, CNRS-EHESS) in Paris. She is an anthropologist specializing on Burma where she has regularly conducted field research since the 1980s. She is the author of *Les rituels de possession en Birmanie: du culte d'État aux cérémonies privées* (1989), and has co-edited several collective volumes. Among the latest are: *Power, Authority and Contested Hegemony in Burmese-Myanmar Religion* (with H. Kawanami, *Asian Ethnology*, 2009), and *Champions of Buddhism. Weikza Cults in Contemporary Burma* (with G. Rozenberg and A. Turner, 2014).

CHAPTER 3

The (Re)configuration of the Buddhist Field in Post-Communist Cambodia

Anne Yvonne Guillou

In this article,[1] I document the current process of categorization of religious practices in Cambodia in the global context of a small post-genocide society brutally hit by economic globalization in the 2000s, following decades of relative isolation (circa 1975–1998). Cambodian people are very much concerned about building a sense of a common destiny and national identity (asking what does it mean to be Khmer[2] today?). As in many other Theravādin societies like Myanmar and Laos, Khmer national identity is closely linked to people's affiliation with Buddhism. Hence, one observes the extensive use of words like 'national

---

[1] I am indebted to Michel Picard and Jos Platenkamp for their insightful and demanding comments on earlier drafts of this chapter. My thanks also to Cécile Barraud, Bénédicte Brac de la Perrière, and Michel Antelme for their comments.
[2] Khmers make up around 85% of the population of Cambodia, referred to as a whole as Cambodian citizens.

A.Y. Guillou (✉)
CNRS, IRASEC, Bangkok, Thailand

A.Y. Guillou
CNRS, Centre Asie du Sud-Est, Paris, France

© The Author(s) 2017
M. Picard (ed.), *The Appropriation of Religion in Southeast Asia and Beyond*, DOI 10.1007/978-3-319-56230-8_3

culture,' 'national tradition,' and particularly 'national religion' (i.e., Buddhism) in the media, politicians' discourses, and private discussions.

I will first analyze the 'semantic perimeter' (Paul Ricoeur) of *buddhasāsanā*.[3] The definitions of the Khmer words *sāsanā* and *buddhasāsanā* are currently shifting in Cambodia. *Sāsanā* has come to mean 'religion' in Khmer, and *buddh* is the Khmer spelling of Buddha. Other religious practices and social milieus are defined as *sāsanā* today, like *sasanā īslām* which is the religion of the Cham Muslim minority; *grist sāsanā* which is traditionally associated with the Vietnamese ethnic minority—although ethnic Khmer have increasingly converted to Christianity since the 1990s. *Sāsanā* is also used to mean 'Brahmanism' (*brahmaññasāsanā*[4]) when Cambodians refer to pre-Buddhist religious practices in Cambodia—typically the cult of spirits.[5] As it is clearly shown in these examples, *sāsanā* refers to world religions.[6] But this is not the end of the story. The perimeter of *buddhasāsanā*, that is to say, what is included in this word and excluded from it, is not fixed and stable. Indeed, it varies according to the conflicting views of social groups in Cambodian society that support different religious schools or ideologies. The debate around what constitutes 'true *buddhasāsanā*' and what is true Buddhism is not new and has sometimes sparked open conflict. This

---

[3] The transliteration of the Khmer words follows the Saveros Lewitz's system (1969), except when they are commonly written otherwise.

[4] I follow here one of the spellings given by Michel Rethy Antelme and Hélène Suppya Bru-Nut (2013: 270). Other spellings are also in use as we shall see below (Antelme and Bru-Nut 2013).

[5] This is probably a long-lasting French orientalist influence, which viewed the land guardian spirits as reminiscent of old Hindu gods worshipped in Cambodia in the Angkorean era. 'Many *nak ta* are materialized by linga or statues of Hindu deities (...),' writes Eveline Porée-Maspero (1962: 8. My translation). But this sentence looks like an orientalist *doxa* which is contradicted by another sentence on the same page, based this time on field research: 'The house of the *nak ta* is usually a small wooden hut under a tree; it is sometimes empty but it often contains some strangely shaped roots, some ancient sculptures, sometimes only one small piece. This is the "form," *rub*, of the spirit' (fn. 4, 8). Some land guardian spirits, like Grand-Father Neck Red (sic), have been identified as a reminiscence of Shiva, but this is by no means true of the thousands of *anak tā*, which have been worshipped in Cambodia since the pre-Buddhist time (Theravāda has been broadly introduced in Cambodia around the fourteenth century).

[6] Although the cult to various spirits can certainly not been labeled a world religion, its assimilation to a vanishing worship of Hindu deities (see footnote *supra*) may explain why it is called *sāsanā*.

debate dates back to the colonial period and even earlier. It has resumed since the early 2000s in a different manner with the emergence of young influential monks in their thirties and forties who want to transform the boundaries of which practices and beliefs should be included in *buddhasāsanā*. These ideas hold increasing importance in Cambodia (linked to its diaspora through the invitations sent by members of the Cambodian faith living abroad to monks in Cambodia, requesting that they address sermons in the diaspora), since all Cambodian radio stations now air Buddhist broadcasts (sermons, questions from the listeners, lessons about particular texts of the *Tipiṭaka*) early in the morning and at night. The government—and particularly the Prime Minister Hun Sen—has encouraged Buddhist broadcasts since the 2000s, in its desire to present itself as a protector of Buddhism in continuity with the traditional function of the monarchy.

I will first look at history to show that the syntagm *buddhasāsanā* is new in the Khmer language. Then I will contrast three proposed categories of monks according to their definitions of *buddhasāsanā*, and what they believe monks' role should be therein. These representations involve notions of *dhamma*,[7] 'customs' (*daṃnīem damlāp'*), and 'society' (*saṅgam*). My analysis is primarily based on ethnographic work that I have carried out in the province of Pursat (a rural area in Western Cambodia, dependent on rain-fed paddy fields for sustenance) since 2007.[8] During this long-term research, I have been able to identify two of the three emblematic figures of monks described in this chapter. The last one (which I label 'socially engaged') is typical of a different branch of monks, which is more widely present in urban contexts (although it supports peasants' protest movements). I met the monk I describe here to characterize this type of monastic approach and other supporters of this movement in his monastery in the outskirts of Phnom Penh after I discovered his videos on YouTube.[9] For the purpose of this specific research, I have focused on different monks' discourses (during sermons in monasteries or through radio and Internet broadcasts and interviews) as well as on various social and ritual practices they performed during private and public ceremonies I have attended (see Fig. 3.1).

---

[7] Also currently spelled in Cambodia in its Sanskrit form *dharma*.
[8] This field work, funded by the Centre Asie du Sud-Est, takes place in a personal research program on the construction of memory in post-genocide rural Cambodia.
[9] I am grateful to Michel Antelme who made me aware of these videos.

Fig. 3.1 Map of Cambodia with the location of the 3 monks involved in this research

BUDDHASĀSANĀ, A NEW AND UNSTABLE NOTION

The Words Sāsanā and Buddhasāsanā in Cambodian Dictionaries in the 1930–1960s

The Khmer word *sāsanā* comes from the Pali word *sāsana*, which means 'order, message, teaching' (Rhys Davids and Stele 1966: 707). In two 1930s Khmer–French dictionaries (Guesdon, Tandart), I found *sāsanā* (with the spellings *sāsa* or *sāsa(na)*) translated as 'religion, nationality, order, command, message, precept, discipline, religion, race or ethnic group, caste.' The well-known Khmer–Khmer dictionary of the Buddhist Institute (*Vacananukram khmaer bhāg dī 2 Ya-A* 1968), published during the first part of the twentieth century, reflects the same diversity of meaning when it comes to the word *sāsana* (displayed in its Pali spelling). Interestingly enough, although the word *sāsanā* (displayed in its Khmer spelling) also appears in the dictionary, no definition is given. Instead, two examples of its use are provided, namely 'Buddhism' (*sāsanā brah buddha*) and 'Brahmanism' (*brahma(ṇa) sāsanā*). Until today, *sāsanā* (in its *sāsa(na)* form) also designates 'race' or 'ethnic group' (Antelme and Bru-Nut 2013), in other words, social communities which recognized themselves and are recognized by others as having common origin, language, and traditions, insofar as each of these groups had (and the great majority still have) distinctive religious practices.

This suggests that the Khmers have only recently begun to label the categories 'religion' and 'Buddhism' as *sāsanā* and *buddhasāsanā*, respectively. This is in accordance with new research in the history of Cambodian Buddhism, which shows that the ideas and practices of Cambodian scholar monks have evolved substantially, from the reign of King Aṅg Ḍuoṅ in the second half of the nineteenth century onward, in response to drastic social changes and subsequent anxieties related to the colonial encounter. In her brilliant research of the changing Khmer Buddhism in colonial Cambodia, Hansen (2006–2007: 31) argues that it would be a mistake to simply consider 'the modernized Buddhism that began to emerge in Cambodia in the early twentieth century a colonial creation. [It was also] the outgrowth of nearly a century of indigenous reforms, regional movements and forces reflecting wider pan-Asian trends in the Buddhist world during this period…'.

The Invention of Buddhism as a National Religion During the Nineteenth Century

This analysis is in line with former post-colonial studies in the religious field that challenge the orientalist model of an Indian religious center surrounded by its Southeast Asian peripheries. In the orientalist model, India and Sri Lanka are perceived as the places where Buddhism originally developed, while Asian religions in outlying areas could only develop vernacularized versions of this 'pure' Buddhism. The Pali Text Society was created in 1881, and scholars like Rhys Davids devoted themselves to defining the canonical texts of Theravāda Buddhism It was decided that those texts would be the *Tipitaka* or the 'Three Baskets.' The texts defined as canonical were those supposed to reproduce the

Buddha's teaching. They had been written in Pali in Sri Lanka in the first centuries A.D. by the Buddhist king Vattagamini (Edwards 2007: 95–124).

In fact, the Khmer 'practical canon' began to change in the 1860s, when the 'Khmer Buddhist approach to modernity [...] combined elements of a critique of contemporary moral degeneration with an "authentic" Buddhist vision of how to live a purified life, even amid the temptations and confusions of the modern world' (Hansen 2007: 148). Texts like the widely read cosmological treatise called *Three Worlds* (*Trai bhūm*), which displays a perception of the cosmos as morally constructed and submitted to cycles of destruction, development, and regeneration, depending on kammic forces, became of less interest than before, while literature drawn from the *Tipitaka* and its commentaries, offering prescription for purifying one's conduct, were favored.[10]

The Mahanikaya sect, which was, until the 1850s, the only one in Cambodia, has long been under the Siamese influence. At least one of its leaders at that time was ordained in Bangkok. After Siamese King Mongkut founded a new order in 1829, the Dhammayuttika intended to 'purify' the Sangha's mores in his own country, and Cambodian King Aṅg Ḍuoṅ called for the introduction of this order in Cambodia and requested a copy of the *Tipitaka* some twenty years later. Indeed, at that time, the canonical volumes were mainly unknown as texts but were present as a symbol and given specific esoteric interpretation (Bizot 1981: 2–44).

The French influence during the Protectorate (1863–1953) was also crucial in bringing a 'national religion' to life, on at least three levels: the influence of erudite specialists of Indian Buddhism focusing on sacred texts and religious literacy, the rising feeling of national identity and authentic Khmerness, and the administrative organization of the Sangha at a national level. What the historian Edwards (2007:103) calls 'the scriptural bias of Buddhist studies' and the 'textual reification of Buddhism' were introduced in Cambodia partly by French specialists of Sanskrit, Pali, and Indian Buddhist texts like Louis Finot and Eugène Burnouf. They carried with them a Western religious *imaginaire*. This

---

[10] Texts from the *Tipitaka*, such as the *maṅgaladīpanī*, *samantapāsādikā*, and *visuddhimagga*. The commentaries called *Way of the World* (*Gatilok*), written by the scholar monk Suttantaprījā, also became famous. It introduced secularized interpretations of key concepts such as moral discernment and virtuous friendship (Hansen 2007: 162).

was combined with their interest regarding philosophical background and literary corpus of Buddhism by reference to classical India. A few monks, among others the most brilliant Chuon Nath (1883–1969) and Huot Tat (1891–1975), took major roles in forging the so-called new *dhamma* (*dhamma thmī*) doctrine.

This evolution went in parallel with the creation of new institutions of teaching Buddhism, also motivated by the French efforts to control Cambodian intellectual life and to diminish the Siamese influence on Khmer monks. An École de Pali du Cambodge was created in 1915, followed by an École Supérieure de Pali in 1922. A Commission d'Étude du Tipitaka was launched in 1929 with the task of translating the Three Baskets into Khmer from texts gathered in Ceylon, Burma, and even the London-based Pali Text Society. The following year, scholar Suzanne Karpelès became the first director of the new Buddhist Institute in Phnom Penh. In order to help in the propagation of the Three Baskets, primary Pali schools were opened all over the country in 1933.

National identity and a sense of 'Khmerness'[11] grew in Cambodia at the same time, when 'contradictions between French conceptions of past glory and present decay led to a crisis of identity among educated Khmers in the 1930 and 1940s and so catalysed Cambodian nationalism' (Edwards 2007: 8), leading to 'a narrative of authenticity [emerging] as an hegemonic discourse' (ibid.: 2). The new focus on canonical scriptures was perceived as an effort of revival. Buddhism was now viewed as an element of national culture among others, like architecture and art. Indeed, the words *sāsanā* and *jāti*, which had very similar meanings before the nineteenth century, referring to a group with common origin, customs, and language, were conceptually separated into two fields of understanding. This transformation was influenced by the Siamese linguistic evolution of *chat* (Khmer equivalent of *jāti*) as a 'nation conceived in terms of both territory and people' and the promotion of the national motto of *chat, satsana* (the specifically religious dimension, identified primarily with Buddhism) and *mahakesat* (king, monarchy) (ibid.: 118)—a motto later adopted by the Cambodian monarchy.

---

[11] 'Khmerness' (*bhāb jā khmaer*) is not a usual word in Khmer language. It is better translated by the common expression 'We Khmer' (*khmaer yoeñ*) when one speaks about collective customs, habits, tastes, or even flaws.

Moreover, the 'nationalization' of Buddhism was given an administrative basis. The restructuring of the 'multitude of sanghas' (Harris 2005: 111–112), constituted of largely independent appanages given to abbots, was prompted by the introduction of new bureaucratic policies from Siam in the 1850s, which were then intensified by the French. In 1904, a royal ordinance bound the construction of new monasteries to an official registration process. In 1916, ordination certificates were issued to the monks. The appanages were suppressed in 1919, and a pyramidal ecclesiastical structure from the capital to the provinces down to the monasteries was put in place under the supervision of the national patriarchs of the Mahanikaya and the Dhammayuttika sects, in consultation with the ministry in charge of the religious affairs.[12]

The older Khmer religious ideas and ritual practices based on esoteric interpretations of the *dhamma* and shaped by the global symbolic framework of rebirth, written on hundreds of palm-leaf manuscripts kept in monasteries, became subject to criticism and were less frequently implemented. As Bizot (1981: 16) vividly puts it, the monks who belonged to the rural part of the Mahanikaya sect, less subject to transformation, soon came to be perceived as old-fashioned, with their particular way of wearing the monastic robe and their dark complexion, similar to peasants.

In sum, the modernization movement that began by mid-nineteenth century in Cambodia changed the existing practices in three major ways:

1. it asserted the pivotal importance of the *dhamma* as it is displayed in the *Tipitaka*;
2. it focused on the 'purification' of both monks' and lay people's behavior;
3. it rejected the spirit cults and all practices which were not focused on the effort to learn the *dhamma* and to elevate one's own spiritual level (for example, by the cultivation of the awareness of non-self, the theory of impermanence, benevolence toward all beings,

---

[12] No research has been carried out until now on the history of the Ministry of Cults and Religious Affairs. Until the beginning of the twentieth century (probably as late as in the 1930s) it was contained within the Ministry of Interior and Cults. This strongly suggests that the administrative organization of Buddhism was modeled on the global administrative scheme (personal information from historians Gabrielle Abbe and Mathieu Guérin).

etc.).[13] It therefore promoted an intellectual and individualistic model of the Buddhist faithful.

The dynamic of 'religionization' of Khmer ritual practices was underway—despite strong resistance movements at work—when it was brutally interrupted by the Maoist Khmer Rouge regime (1975–1979), which destroyed all the monasteries and forced all monks to defrock. After the Pol Pot regime, in the 1980s, Cambodia was under the Vietnamese communist control and religion was hardly tolerated. The head of the Sangha was (and still is) a member of the communist party and a former anti-French, nationalist activist. Political and economic liberalization in the 1990s allowed for the reorganization of the Sangha, and debates surrounding what constitutes the *buddhasāsanā* resumed far beyond the monk community.

In particular, many lay specialists of religious rituals (*ācārya*) and learned believers spontaneously chose to express themselves within the conceptual framework of delineation between 'Buddhism' and 'Brahmanism' (*brahmaññasāsanā*) when they interacted regarding specific rituals and ceremonies. I will give an example of this effort of delineation drawn from my recent ethnographic work.

An Ethnographic Account of the Effort of Delineation Between 'Buddhism' and 'Brahmanism'

Grandfather Khleang Muang (spelled *ghlāṃ mīoeṅ*) is an important land guardian spirit (*anak tā*) whose shrine is located in the Western part of Cambodia (province of Pursat). Like certain other land guardian spirits (but not all), Khleang Muang is a former human being. His story—which we know through local legends, toponymy, and royal chronicles—claims that he was a sixteenth-century war chief faithful to the Khmer King Aṅg Cǎnd the 1st[14] in his fight against the Siamese army. As the Khmer Royal Army was defeated by the Siamese, Khleang Muang decided to commit suicide in order to go to the world of the dead and levy an army of ghosts. With his dead soldiers he was able to defeat the Siamese who caught cholera (according to certain versions). Khleang Muang is in many ways a singular character in the Khmer ritual

---

[13] On the Buddhization of cults to land guardian spirits, see Forest (2012).

[14] Aṅg Cǎnd Rājā is the most important and best known of the post-Angkorean kings and a great supporter of Buddhism.

landscape. He is venerated nation-wide as a patriotic hero (at least since Prince Sihanouk's post-independence government in the 1950–1960s), and at the village level he remains a powerful land guardian spirit. An annual tribute is paid to Khleang Muang during the solar–lunar month of *bisākh* (May–June). It is a political cult insofar as villagers, monks, and high-ranking civil servants—including the provincial governor himself— are invited to participate. This is not the case for less important land guardian spirits, which are only worshipped by the neighboring villagers. Until recently, the two-day-long ceremony symbolized the annual revitalization of the social ties between the three major components of the rural Khmer society (Forest 1992). This ritual is undergoing gradual but nonetheless drastic changes following the personal interpretations of Khleang Muang's history by the charismatic chief of the provincial Department of Culture.

When I attended the ceremony in May 2008 and May 2014, I was struck by the way this lay director of the ritual announced in his microphone the different phases of the performance, specifying which part was 'Brahmanist' and which one was 'Buddhist.' My own presence might, of course, have accentuated this effort, conceived—I think—as an educational activity directed toward both the peasants and the only foreigner and researcher, all perceived to be uninformed.

The opening tribute to *kruṅ Bālī* (King Bālī[15]) was labeled 'Brahmanist.' It was followed by a reminder of the respect due to the *sīla* (observance of the Buddhist precepts) and a recitation of the *paritta* (protection recitation) by nine monks from surrounding monasteries. They were offered food by the officials. This portion of the ceremony was characterized as 'Buddhist.' Then a short tribute, labeled 'Brahmanist,' was paid to Grandfather Khleang Muang and his wife. The next morning, the ritual consisted of a speech by the lay director

---

[15] King Bālī is loosely associated in the Khmer minds with deities related to the earth, like Preah Thorni (*braḥ dharaṇī*), the goddess of the earth, and Preah Phum (*braḥ bhūmi*), a spirit protecting the land in each home, among others. Its cult is performed only during weddings and when moving into a new house. *Kruṅ Bālī* is also seen as the giant snake that supports the earth in the Khmer mythology (Porée-Maspero 1961). Offerings to *Kruṅ Bālī* have been integrated only recently in the annual tribute to Khleang Muang for reasons that I cannot develop here.

of the ritual reporting the annual amount of money offered to the shrine (30,000 US dollars), followed by a speech made by the governor. The director of the ceremony avoided labeling the moment when the monks entered the ritual stage. This was the only time when they had direct contact with the land guardian spirit. The monks, standing around the grave where Khleang Muang was said to have committed suicide by throwing himself on lances and swords, performed a *paṅsukūl* prayer consisting of sending (*uddis*) Buddhist merits to the land guardian spirit. In Cambodia, this is the most common way a relationship with the dead is created. In this respect, Khleang Muang is considered as a dead person (more than a land guardian spirit) in this section of the ritual. It is important to remember here that reformist monks are perceived as opposed to *paṅsukūl*. The final parts of the ceremony were labeled, respectively, 'Buddhist' and 'Brahmanist,' namely the offering of food to monks (one hundred and one monks in the case of this sumptuous festival) and the offerings (of food, drink, clothes, and cigarettes) to Khleang Muang and his wife. This linguistic process of labeling echoes many discussions I had with educated Cambodians about the spirit cults, all labeled 'Brahmanist.'

The practical organization of the ceremony reflects two ideas: first, the intention to keep 'Buddhist' and 'Brahmanist' sections unified (by alternating between them in a single program, whereas they could have been quite easily organized as two separate performances) and secondly the intention to separate them ritually. Indeed, the monks stay on a north–south axis outside the shrine,[16] while the shrine is oriented along an east–west axis, with Khleang Muang's statues and grave at the west end and King Bali's shrine at the east end. The part of the offering made of alcohol and meat (pork and chicken) is removed when the monks take an active part in the ceremony and possibly have to enter the 'Brahmanist' axis. There is no mention of such a linguistically and ritually organized separation in the account of this ceremony in June 1948.[17] I think that the reformist movement toward a more textualist approach to

---

[16] There is one exception: the monks enter the Khleang Muang's shrine when they communicate with him *as a dead person* and send him Buddhist merits produced by offerings from the faithful.

[17] The Commission des Moeurs et Coutumes du Cambodge commissioned a description of the ceremony in 1948. It is translated from Khmer and reprinted *in* Forest (1992: 237–241).

Buddhism was underway at that time but had yet to transform local rituals. Although currently undergoing strong pressure to take the reformist ideas into account, this local cult is attempting to adapt itself in order to survive.

What can be concluded from this short account? There is a revival (after the interruption of this process during the political and military turmoil in Cambodia in the 1970s and 1980s) of the process of defining a field of practices labeled as *sāsanā*, where *buddhasāsanā* and *brahmaññasāsanā* are delineated in a cosmological diarchy reflecting separate domains of authority that are hierarchically linked and unequally valued, thus challenging any reformist Buddhist claim to absolute authority.[18]

The efforts at structuring a field of practice known as *buddhasāsanā* find other expressions among the Sangha. I will now depict three young monks who have contrasting perceptions of what *buddhasāsanā* is/should be and what their duties as monks are/should be in present Cambodia.

THREE YOUNG MONKS IN PRESENT-DAY CAMBODIA AND THEIR RESPECTIVE FOCUS ON *DHAMMA*, CUSTOMS, AND SOCIETY

Venerable Sok Sakun[19]: *Buddhasāsanā as a World Doctrine*

I will begin with the presentation of Venerable Sok Sakun, who represents a small but influential trend among the Sangha. I heard about Venerable Sok Sakun for the first time in 2011, when an old Cambodian friend of mine, living in Phnom Penh, told me how much she appreciated and admired this 34-year-old monk. My friend is an urban science teacher in her early sixties, and she has never taken much interest in religion. Over the past twenty years I have often heard her criticize monks' misbehavior, among her other criticisms of current Cambodian society. But as she aged, she had become closer to Sok Sakun and appreciates his teaching skills (he is amusing and at the same time knowledgeable, as a graduate of the Phnom Penh Pedagogy Institute of Pali). He makes

---

[18] Thanks to Jos Platenkamp for his valuable help in formulating this analysis.
[19] Pseudonyms have been used for each of the three monks that I take as examples in this chapter.

Buddhism—even what is perceived as the most technical and arduous part of the Three Baskets, namely the Abhidhamma—understandable to lay people. In his mouth, she says, Buddhism is presented like a rational doctrine in line with scientific knowledge rather than a corpus of ancient beliefs.

He is a successful monk gaining more and more followers every year, and my own estimation is that around two thousand believers came to his monastery (250 km away from Phnom Penh) from all over the country during the 2012 *kathina* ceremony.[20] He is invited to many private and public Buddhist ceremonies and collective sermons all around the country, as well as abroad by the Cambodian diaspora in Australia, the USA, and France.

Intellectual Affiliation and Ideology
Sok Sakun is the heir of the reformist monks from the colonial period mentioned above, who promoted the definition of Buddhism as a world religion. He belongs to a social and intellectual milieu that can be contrasted with other Buddhist milieus in Cambodia, especially those I label as 'traditionalist.'[21]

This monk preaches that the most important task of the Buddhist faithful is to learn and understand the *dhamma*, whether in Khmer (for lay people) or—much better—in Pali (for monks and advanced students of Buddhism). Indeed, learning Pali is the only way to gain direct access to the Three Baskets. In his biography published in Khmer, Sok Sakun focuses on his personal study, giving details about the monasteries where he studied, his teachers, and the texts he examined. He has specialized himself in the Abhidhamma commentary[22] and has also learned the Thai language in order to gain access to books unavailable in Khmer. At the same time, he does not neglect more mundane training, like that provided by NGOs and other institutions (training in information technology, human rights, English, etc.). This proclivity for the rational study

---

[20] The ceremony of offering new robes to monks at the end of the rainy season.

[21] All of those contrasting trends in contemporary Cambodian Buddhism belong to the Mahanikaya sect. Although the Dhammayuttika sect is still the sect of the Cambodian royal family, today it holds a weak position and has lost the challenger status it held before the Pol Pot regime. It should be made clear that what is called 'traditionalism' here was already transformed during the French Protectorate.

[22] Particularly the *Aṭṭakathā ṭīka* and *yojanā*.

of texts in Pali, attraction to Thailand, perceived as more advanced in terms of the Buddhist academic environment, and receptiveness to modern knowledge already existed among colonial reformist monks.

Indeed, in his biography, Sok Sakun gives a list of the eight masters most influential on his education. Among them, we find without surprise the two main chiefs of the Sangha (*sangharāja*), Chuon Nath and Huot Tat mentioned above. The other notable master Sok Sakun mentioned in his biography is Buth Savong, one of the first monks,[23] in the post-Pol Pot years, who brought the reformist legacy to life again and emerged as a well-known *dhamma* teacher on radio in the 1990s (Marston 2012).[24]

Teaching the Dhamma
In his sermons, Sok Sakun first defines Buddhism as a 'theory' (*dṛṣṭī*) similar to other theories, which is one of the features of a world religion. In line with his ideas that the teaching and the learning of the *dhamma* are at the core of the monks' duties, he opened a Buddhist school for adults in the vicinity of his monastery in the province of Pursat and teaches annually in two religious schools in other provinces (Kompong Thom and Kompong Cham). By 2010, he had authored sixteen books in Khmer,[25] which aim at popularizing key Buddhist notions for lay people. The books were published using money his followers offered and were distributed for free during the ceremonies he presided over. He gives radio and Internet broadcasts of sermons which are listened to both inside and outside of Cambodia. In the sermons I have listened to, he deliberately used simple and unsophisticated words so that anyone could understand him. He is sensitive to the 'show' dimension of his sermons while keeping the performance authentic. In one case, he began a sermon given to students by chanting a poem, making clear his self-described taste for music and poetry. Although the use of printed materials is no longer controversial (during the French Protectorate,

---

[23] Buth Savong was a monk for many years and afterward remained close to the monastic way of life. He is well respected for his asceticism.

[24] Sok Sakun, like Buth Savong, gives importance to relics and relic stupas.

[25] Some are on the Dhammapada (Sutta Piṭaka), others on Abhidhamma Piṭaka (including one volume on the Dhamma Saṅgaṇi Book). Other publications have more general topics, like (my translation) *The course of life*; *Life explained* [literally: *Life translated*]; *A true life needs the Dharma*; *Does hell really exist?*, among others.

conservative monks fought to preserve manuscripts for their religious potency), in using simple words in Khmer, encouraging his followers to ask questions and give their own opinions, etc., he implicitly takes a position in the current debates regarding the sacred power of the Pali scripture and prayers and the use of Pali by monks who do not understand the meaning of their prayers. The underlying message is that *dhamma* can be learned by anyone in any language, in an individual spiritual quest. This is in line with Sok Sakun's strong anti-ritualistic commitment.

The Anti-ritualistic Approach
Sok Sakun's opinion that *sāsanā* is first of all *dhamma* is consistent with his rejection of *dāna* (donations) as the core Khmer Buddhist practices. What he is opposed to, he says, is the lack of religious education, which encourages monks and other pious people to use all their energy to search for offerings of money to build more religious buildings. This is indeed a central activity of Khmer religious practices. His reluctance to accept offerings from the lay people—or rather, his insistence that offerings are far from compulsory—is quite revolutionary in Cambodia today. In the Khmer non-reformed Mahanikaya sect, for example, offerings are the most important way to gain Buddhist merits and, moreover, donations at all levels are the very thread of the social fabric, inside and outside monasteries. Sok Sakun's refusal of offerings is a tacit criticism of monks who become rich, flouting the monks' discipline code (*Vinaya*), which stipulates that the monks should remain poor beggars (Theravādin monks, for example, are expected to beg for their food barefoot every morning[26]). However, this is a general stance aimed at positioning Sok Sakun in the Buddhist field rather than a statement of his own commitment. Indeed, although he comes from a poor peasant background, he is now quite well off and his reformist philosophy has gained the sympathy of at least one rich and generous sponsor from the USA, who is helping him build a huge stupa that costs hundreds of thousands of dollars to shelter a Buddhist relic brought from India. Monks like Sok Sakun gain support from rich businessmen because of their disgust of thirst for wealth.

---

[26] Buth Savong requires this basic rule from his monks (Marston 2012). In recent years, it has become less commonly observed by Mahanikaya monks—particularly in towns—where it seems that a dispensation has been given to them for security reasons.

Sok Sakun criticizes many other core aspects of the traditional Khmer Buddhism, such as the *paṅsukūl*, the prayers used to send merits to the ancestors[27]—a ritual which can be analyzed as a Buddhicized version of the cult of ancestors (see Sect. "An Ethnographic Account of the Effort of Delineation Between 'Buddhism' and 'Brahmanism'"). In his sermons, Sok Sakun also mocks monks who sprinkle holy water on the faithful. 'This is just a way to have a glance at undressed pretty girls,' he claims. He also criticizes monks who act as soothsayers. He explained why he rejected soothsayers by telling me an amusing anecdote of a soothsayer who had predicted some years ago that Sok Sakun would be appointed to a higher position. 'Then I refused the appointment,' he said, 'in order to be stronger than the soothsayer.' The soothsayer's prediction is not carried by the same 'stream' as the strong power of *kamma*.

Sok Sakun's opinion of the spirit cults, particularly those of the land guardian spirits called *anak tā*, is also of critical importance in order to understand what is included and what is excluded from *buddhasāsanā*. Spirit cults are indeed a large part of the Khmer religious system and are usually part of the rituals performed in the Buddhist monasteries. Sok Sakun told me that there are no *anak tā* in Buddhism. People just confuse *anak tā* with the Buddhist category of non-human (Khmer: *amanussa*; from Pali: *amānusa*). Sok Sakun adopts a rather Durkheimian way of thinking when he says that the *anak tā* have an influence on people because people give them too much importance by worshipping them. He told me that Buddha has acknowledged all the non-humans (i.e., spirits like *anak tā* and other categories of beings), but they keep a very low spiritual level and are therefore placed in a low position within the Buddhist hierarchy of values, while the *dhamma* is higher and stronger. He does not allow any practice of worship of *anak tā* in his monastery, and this issue is now becoming a clear-cut line of delineation between 'reformist' and 'traditionalist' monasteries.

Position Vis-a-Vis the Political Power and National Community
The faithful are aware that Sok Sakun's opinion on the *dāna* expresses a potentially critical view toward political power. Indeed, since its

---

[27] *Paṅsukūl* has another meaning in the non-reformed Mahanikaya ritual. See Bizot (1981).

progressive abandonment of the communist ideology in the early 1990s, the Cambodian People's Party (CPP) has endeavored to support the Sangha and to present itself as a great supporter of Buddhism, like in Burma and other post-socialist countries. But instead of backing reformist movements, like kings have done since the mid-nineteenth century (by welcoming Dhammayuttika and so on), the post-communist government has favored the pragmatic individual patronage of traditionalist monasteries. This patronage is shown in particular through the mushrooming of huge, brand new, and often ostentatious religious buildings and statues. This is the reason Sok Sakun's rejection of *dāna* (donations) as a central practice is potentially politically problematic.

As we shall see when I present the last category of monks, 'patriotism' has become another major social issue shaping contentious debates about the Vietnamese immigrants. This issue clearly divides two major political camps: the Cambodian People's Party, backed by Vietnam since its arrival to power, and the opposition, which is increasingly violently anti-Vietnamese and 'patriotic.' As far as I know, Sok Sakun has never taken an explicit position on this matter. Always adopting the same philosophy and avoiding any allusions to a specific political stance, Sok Sakun has said that 'patriotism' (*snehā jāti*) is explicitly linked to love of Buddhism. It is in this sense that he suggests that '*sāsanā khmaer*' must be promoted. The path Sok Sakun proposes to follow to achieve the promotion of a *sāsanā khmaer* is paradoxically to separate Buddhism from Cambodian society at all levels, politically (by avoiding big men's patronage) and at the village level (by forbidding apotropaic rituals, etc.).

While the pre-colonial concept of *sāsanā* was designed to separate communities and cement distinct socioreligious identities, reformist monks offer an alternative vision of a *sāsanā* based on individual cultivation of awareness (through learning the *dhamma*) to purify the self, bringing in turn the spiritual purification of the Khmer community (Hansen 2007: 149). It is in this sense that one must understand Sok Sakun's praise of Chuon Nath as the greatest figure of Khmer Buddhism in a sermon broadcast by radio: 'No monk today is able to get a position in Cambodia like that of Chuon Nath, who had power (*aṃṇāca*), morality (*sīladharma*) and knowledge (*caṃṇeh dịṅ*).'[28] 'Knowledge' can be seen in this discourse as referring to the learning of the *dhamma*, 'morality' as the implementation of the *Vinaya*, and 'power' as the strength of a Sangha independent from the political power.

---

[28] My translation from Khmer.

Venerable Rong Veasna: Buddhasāsanā as Local Practices Based on Khmer Customs

The field of *buddhasāsanā* is becoming increasingly homogenized under the pressure from the intellectual conception of Buddhism as the study of the *dhamma*. But traditional practices of Khmer Buddhism still represent the most common practices. Venerable Rong Veasna is the abbot of a monastery situated just twelve kilometers from Sok Sakun's. I first met him in 2010 when I came to his monastery with a young woman from a neighboring village whose family knew of the abbot's reputation for religious potency and attended the Buddhist ceremonies he organized. She hoped to ask the monk for protection prayers and astrological advice for help with her personal troubles.

Local Implantation

Rong Veasna is not at all an intellectual like Sok Sakun. He did not learn Pali but was a student in the pagoda where he is now the abbot, before taking the robe and becoming a monk at the age of twenty-four in 1989. His father was a monk here before him[29] and taught his son many secrets. He is very modest, friendly, and plump, always smiling and joking. He chews betel—which is becoming less common among monks of his age[30]—sitting in a relaxed attitude as he receives visitors throughout the day. Rong Veasna was born in a village near his monastery and has not travelled extensively like Sok Sakun. He has almost never left his village. He says with a laugh that the farthest point he ever reached in his life was Angkor, some one hundred kilometers from the monastery.

He is nonetheless very much respected by the villagers and well known in his district. His influence can be observed through his ability to raise funds for construction work. Contrary to Sok Sakun, he is proud to show that his monastery is embellished every year with the help of supporters in the US Khmer diaspora as well as certain local leaders in the ruling party.

However, his positive reputation locally is based on skills that Sok Sakun would not favor. Indeed, Rong Veasna is believed to have strong powers and gifts. He has a *grū* (immaterial master, personal spirit taking care of him) who helps him. He knows when he will die and when his parents will. He is well known as a healer, a soothsayer, and an astrologer. He is still in possession of a handwritten book transmitted by his father.

---

[29] It goes without saying that his father quit the monastic robe and then got married.
[30] Taking intoxicating substances is forbidden by the monks' discipline.

An Apotropaic Approach

During my visits, Rong Veasna was always very busy—albeit smiling and joking—receiving dozens of people and phone calls asking for help. For example, one day one of his followers called him asking for advice about a land plot that he wanted to sell. He was not confident in his Chinese business partner and asked Rong Veasna for advice. The monk answered that today was not a good day for selling the land and that the Chinese man was not a good partner because his astrological birth sign did not correspond with his follower's sign. The monk recommended that the man waits until the next full moon (a holy day according to Theravāda Buddhism). The man was encouraged to offer incense to the land guardian spirit (*anak tā*), which was the 'master of the land,' and ask the spirit for the permission to sell the land. He should wait two more years before selling the land in order to make a ten thousand-dollar profit.

A family came after him with a young woman who had fallen ill and also had a car accident. It was obvious to everyone that she had *groḥ*, meaning that her birth planet was not in accordance with the planet of the current year. The Khmer dictionary of the Buddhist Institute (whose latest editions were directed by the prominent reformist monk of colonial times Chuon Nath) gives an orthodox definition of the word *groḥ*, defined as 'events occurring in one's life according to one's positive or negative actions.' In this definition, *groḥ* is assimilated with the individual *kamma*. But in Rong Veasna's monastery, the monks and the lay master of ritual (*ācārya*) do not agree with this kammatic view, their beliefs being closer to an apotropaic perspective (Spiro 1982).[31] They usually perform a ritual called 'cutting the (wrong) planet' (*kāt' groḥ*), to prevent people from further car accidents, illness, or bad business[32] (see Fig. 3.2). This monastery is one of the most famous in the district for this ritual.

---

[31] Spiro contrasts various types of Theravāda Buddhism, including nibbanic, kammatic, and apotropaic views. The first trend refers to the learning of the *dhamma*, its revelation of the cause of suffering, and the way of its extinction. The second refers to the adaptation of the nibbanic view in a more mundane way: Buddhism provides the path toward a better future life. The third one refers to the ritualistic approach, where rituals help in changing human's current lives. Spiro's framework can be applied easily to the Khmer context.

[32] This ceremony is in fact a ritual of rebirth—rebirth being a central issue for the non-reformed Mahanikaya adepts of whom Rong Veasna is the heir. François Bizot has extensively published on many aspects of the question of rebirth (see for example Bizot 1976, 1992).

Fig. 3.2 Part of the *kāt' groḥ* ritual performed by the monks

All this of course has nothing to do with the teaching of the *dhamma*, defined by Sok Sakun as the main aim of teaching novices and laypeople. Nevertheless, Rong Veasna is convinced that he also 'follows the religion.' During our talks, he told me that the spirit cults were not *buddhasāsanā* but 'customs' or 'habits' (*daṃnīem damlāp*). However, he said, monks must accept and respect these customs. Rong Veasna himself shelters a land guardian spirit in his monastery. He believes that the spirit cults are necessary and complementary to *buddhasāsanā*, because '*buddhasāsanā* is not able to relieve people from their ailments and sufferings in their daily life.'

However, he feels obliged to position himself in relation to reformist pressures and claims. For example, he claims that he refuses to make predictions or sprinkle holy water during the four Buddhist holy days each month. In reality, this is nearly impossible due to the pressures exerted by an unending flow of faithful waiting impatiently for his astrological advice and potent prayers.

Instead of a stupa sheltering Buddha's relics, like in Sok Sakun's monastery, he has built an equally huge Buddha Sakyamuni statue designed in a somewhat naive artistic style. But the most striking symbol of his idea of Buddhism as made firstly of inner-world practices is that of Maitreya, represented by a 4-m-high statue made of cement. Maitreya plays a major role in Khmer Buddhism and is venerated in Cambodia since the middle period (sixteenth century) (Thompson 1999). He represents (in a Buddhist idiom) the old Khmer tradition and possibly displays a millenarist message of hope: better times are coming after the recent decadence of Cambodia. Indeed, he is not yet enlightened (and therefore not yet a Buddha) but is still present among human beings.[33] It could mean that this Future Buddha—as he is often called—like all land spirits inhabiting Cambodia, is closer to human beings than the Buddha Sakyamuni who already attained extinction (*nibbāna*). This statue might have been placed there as a symbol of resistance to intellectual, purely nibbanic forms of Buddhism.

Venerable Lan Sokhan and Socially Engaged Buddhism

The third (etic) category of monks is even smaller than the reformist one. It belongs to the *buddhasāsanā saṅgam* ('social Buddhism') ideological line.[34] I first came to know Lan Sokhan through his Internet postings on YouTube and his connections with human rights workers I know in Phnom Penh. Indeed, Venerable Lan Sokhan was briefly arrested in 2012 and there were rumors that he would be defrocked by the Ministry of Cults and Religions because of his political and social activities. When I met him in 2014, he was sheltered in a monastery in a suburb of Phnom Penh known for its political opposition to the ruling party. I was introduced to him by his young 'personal secretary,' who had apparently adopted the style of the foreign NGOs personnel. He immediately took our photograph for their Facebook page. It was obvious that Lan Sokhan hoped to meet as many foreigners as possible in order to feel protected against possible intimidation from the government. None of the usual formal rules of interaction between a lay

---

[33] Maitreya is often presented by scholars as the only bodhisattva of the Theravāda way.
[34] *Saṅgam* means 'society.'

person—especially a woman—and a monk were used: the monk insisted that I sit close to him on a bench and we stayed alone together in this closed room for almost three hours. His cell phone rang frequently and Lan Sokhan compulsively used his iPad (he told me later in a joke that he was almost addicted to it and found it difficult to travel to rural places in Cambodia where there is no Internet connection). The room resembled an NGO's office more than a monk's cell, with computers and cameras everywhere and an absence of religious images. In order to go beyond this well-oiled meeting designed to please foreign human rights activists, I initiated the interview in Khmer, even though Lan Sokhan is fluent in English, probably the only English speaker among the three monks taken here as examples.

Ideological Affiliation
Like Sok Sakun, Lan Sokhan is concerned about the purification of Buddhism in Cambodia, but he acts on this concern in a very different way. Indeed, he explained to me how Buddhism developed in a satisfactory way under the aegis of Chuon Nath, after Cambodian independence (here again, Chuon Nath is associated with national independence and Khmer culture rather than with his intellectual affiliation to French scholars and specialists of religion). In Lan Sokhan's narrative, Buddhism was destroyed during the Khmer Rouge regime and has never recovered since. Such that what is called 'Buddhism' today no longer has anything to do with 'true Buddhism,' but has instead become a toy in the hands of the authoritarian ruling party. He himself took the monastic robe in 1990 when he was twelve years old, as a way to escape conscription. However, he continues, the situation improved after 1993 when free and fair elections were organized under United Nations supervision.

In a very casual way, he exposes his political point of view in two directions, his strong anti-Vietnamese feelings and his commitment to social justice and support of protest movements. The anti-Vietnamese discourse is not new in Cambodia and is linked to the irredentist movement of the Downstream Kampuchea (Kampuchea Krom, a former Khmer territory in the Mekong delta, progressively colonized by the Vietnamese after the seventeenth century). The monastery where Lan Sokhan lives was built by Khmer Krom (Vietnamese nationals of Khmer ethnic background) monks in 1997. His abbot and other resident monks strongly oppose what they see as the historical desire of the Vietnamese to take over the Khmer land and natural resources, as well as the weak immigrant policy of the government, which is still a 'Vietnamese puppet' and allows hundreds of thousands of Vietnamese to settle in Cambodia. Lan Sokhan calls those monks the 'patriotic monks' (*lok saṅgha snehā jāti*).

In the minds of these 'patriotic monks,' social justice is related to this anti-Vietnamese opinion: land grabbing and illegal mass logging are, in their discourse, mainly organized by the Vietnamese.[35] In May 2014, the monastery had been sheltering more than four hundred families[36] for one month, most of whom came from the province of Kratie, where their land had been grabbed by a commercial company which had been given a 99-year commercial land concession. They had come to Phnom Penh in order to have their protest heard by the authorities. In the monastery, they benefitted from the neighbors' solidarity as well as from donations of rice and money from the main opposition party, the Cambodian National Rescue Party.

Lan Sokhan claims no direct connections with Heng Monychenda, a former monk who gained some popularity in Cambodia, in the wake of the United Nations organized elections in 1993, as a knowledgeable person and one of the first who introduced the notion of 'social Buddhism' (*buddhasāsanā saṅgam*). He was very much supported by NGOs and worked for the NGO Buddhism for Development, funded by the German-based Konrad Adenauer organization in refugee camps at the Thai-Cambodian border. Heng Monychenda has written several books in Khmer, the most renowned of which is *Braḥ pād dhammik*. This title refers to a millenarist theme stipulating that a Buddhist king (*cakkavattin*) will come to earth and rule following the *dhamma*. In his book, Heng Monychenda developed the idea that 'dharmism' (*dharmmadhipateyya*) and 'democracy' (*prajādhipateyya*) are based on the same principle. The rulers who do not rule following the *dhamma* disrupt the social and cosmic orders. Much in the same way, Lan Sokhan sees his opposition activities as perfectly in accordance with the *dhamma*: he knows what justice is because he knows what compassion is. The Buddha's teaching of relief from suffering (*dukkha*) is also linked to more social concerns. Indeed, he says that the Buddha reformed the

---

[35] In fact, as far as figures are available, Vietnamese enterprises have land concessions in Cambodia just like any other foreign enterprises from Southeast Asian countries and elsewhere.

[36] Number provided by the abbot. The monastery was full of these internal refugees when I visited it.

caste system so that people could have equal statuses. In this respect, the Buddha's teaching is also a message of social reformism.

Lan Sokhan's adversaries, including religious leaders, blame him for not having behaved like a 'true monk' when he took part in demonstrations, but in fact, he argues political involvement of monks is not new in Cambodia.

Activism

He has become an 'activist' (*sakammajana*), a new word in the Khmer NGO vocabulary. He describes in detail his self-training and expertise in the field of communication technologies, which are now both his most efficient protection against political harassment ('As soon as somebody comes and tries to intimidate me, I record and upload the recording on Facebook, YouTube, Twitter and Line') and a major means of political struggle. He recognizes that human rights activism in Cambodia has become a competing market for funds coming from opposition parties (rooted in the diaspora) and foreign institutions. 'I am a model for many monks and lay people who praise my courage. As a Buddhist, I know that I will die (i.e. I am deeply aware that death is a normal end of life). But everybody in our networks knows who is a sincere activist and who is not.' Lan Sokhan has travelled even more extensively than Sok Sakun abroad. He has been invited to the USA, Canada, Australia, France, Germany, and Ireland, and has won two human rights awards.

Conclusion: Society, Extra Mundane Orientation, and Political Power

Buddhasāsanā has not gained a single, unrivaled definition in Cambodia today, despite the growing influence of the reformist monks who attract the faithful from upper social strata and endeavor to insert *buddhasāsanā* within the conceptual framework of a world religion. These efforts resumed after years of political and military breakdown between the 1970 and 1990s that put an end to a trend that began in the mid-nineteenth century as an echo of the intellectual work of inventing 'religions'—including Buddhism—in other parts of the world. The effort of delineation between so-called Brahmanism and Buddhism inside the Khmer ritual landscape appears to be an effort to 'religionize' ritual practices (first, undertaken under the influence of French orientalists). This is still at work, as shown in my description of the land guardian spirit Khleang Muang's annual tribute. However, other lines of delineation are now appearing in public and private debates regarding what monks' role should be in today's Cambodian society and what kind of *buddhasāsanā* is embodied by those monks. At first glance, the three major trends that I have discussed in this chapter focus on key notions like '*dhamma*,' 'customs,' and 'society,' each of them put forth by the different (etic) categories of monks—the reformists, the traditionalists, and the activists, respectively. They imply contrasting perceptions of Buddhism in Cambodia in reference to a community of pious individuals, or the traditions, or a fair society.

At a deeper level, though, the ethnographic data presented in this chapter draw other lines of distinction[37] between the focus on the secular social order versus world-renunciatory ambitions; ritualistic versus scripturalist approaches; emphasis on individual versus collective achievement; kammatic versus apotropaic practices; and relationship with political power.

It is easy to replace this Cambodian ethnography in Spiro's framework of kammatic versus apotropaic practices. First, the emphasis reformist monks place on the learning and teaching of the *dhamma* as a way to improve one's own *kamma* definitely places the core efforts of *buddhasāsanā*'s followers outside the world, with the hope of eventually reaching the (non-)state of *nibbāna*.[38] The other monks, on the contrary, perceive *buddhasāsanā* as primarily embedded in social ties and everyday actions—although these social ties and actions are each hierarchically structured (rhetorically, the *dhamma* has the highest authority relative to all other practices). Second, according to the reformist perception, building a national community can be achieved only through each Buddhist follower's individual efforts to improve one's own spiritual awareness. These monks are neither more nor less than particularly learned teachers. Traditionalist and activist monks, on the contrary, put religious practices at the center of their collective forces, at the core of which stay the monks. As sacred individuals (more or less) full of the

---

[37] Analysis in terms of delineation inside the religious field has been inspired by the thoroughly theoretical approach of Brac de la Perrière (2009).

[38] This hope is actually rarely explicitly expressed by the believers I have met. They insist instead on the necessity of carrying out positive actions. Meditation practices, although unknown by the average believer, have dramatically increased in recent years.

Buddha's spiritual potency, they are perceived as being able to transform those forces into one category or another, be they magical, social, financial, or even kammatic. For example, monks who have reached a high spiritual level—expressed in terms of one's amount of *kamma*—are believed to be the most successful in attracting powerful patrons to their monasteries. This can be immediately assessed though the embellishment of their religious buildings. Similarly, kammatic achievement can be 'converted' into magical healing powers which are in turn 'convertible,' for example, into the currency of the realm. Monks are also able to transform gifts into merits. In the terms of Bourdieu's notion of capital, one would say that traditionalist (and to a lesser extent, activist) monks are the agents of transformation of one form of capital into another.

The relative authority of the Sangha vis-à-vis political powers is also very differently comprehended by each category of monks. Traditionalists as well as activists (although in opposite ways) perceive political power as deeply linked to the Sangha—be it through big men's patronage, in line with King Asoka's scheme of a Buddhist monarchy, or through the governance of a Righteous King following the *cakkavattin* model of a Buddhist king ruling according to the *dhamma*. The reformists, on the contrary, claim to create an independent religious field in which the monks gain their moral authority from this very neutrality.[39]

References

Antelme, M.A., and H.S. Bru-Nut. 2013. *Dictionnaire français-khmer*. Paris: L'Asiathèque.
Bizot, F. 1976. *Le figuier à cinq branches. Recherches sur le bouddhisme khmer*. Paris: Publications de l'EFEO.
Bizot, F. 1981. *Le don de soi-même. Recherches sur le bouddhisme khmer III*. Paris: Publications de l'EFEO.
Bizot, F. 1992. *Le chemin de Laṅkā*. Paris, Chiang Mai, Phnom Penh: École Française d'Extrême-Orient.
Brac de la Perrière, B. 2009. An Overview of the Field of Religion in Burmese Studies. *Asian Ethnology* 68 (2): 185–210.
Edwards, P. 2007. *Cambodia. The Cultivation of a Nation*. Honolulu: University of Hawai'i Press.

---

[39] It is difficult to implement, as any attempt to position oneself as neutral is always interpreted by the ruling power as an assertion of opposition.

Forest, A. 1992. *Le culte des génies protecteurs au Cambodge*. Paris: L'Harmattan.
Forest, A. 2012. *Histoire religieuse du Cambodge. Un royaume d'enchantement*. Paris: Les Indes Savantes.
Hansen, A.-R. 2006–2007. Modernist Reform in Khmer Buddhist History. *Siksācakr, Journal of the Center for Khmer Studies* 8–9: 31–44.
Hansen, A.-R. 2007. *How to Behave. Buddhism and Modernity in Colonial Cambodia, 1860–1930*. Honolulu: University of Hawai'i Press.
Harris, I. 2005. *Cambodian Buddhism. History and Practice*. Honolulu: University of Hawai'i Press.
Lewitz, S. 1969. Note sur la translittération du cambodgien. *Bulletin de l'École française d'Extrême-Orient* 55: 163–169.
Marston, J. 2012. Buth Savong and the new proliferation of relics in Cambodia. Paper presented at the Siem Reap Conference on Special Topic in Khmer Studies, Religious Studies in Cambodia: Understand the old and trace the new, Siem Reap, June 9–11 (Published in Spanish: Marston, J. 2015. "Buth Savong y la nueva proliferación de reliquias en Camboya". *Estudios de Asia y África* 50 (2): 265–284).
Porée-Maspero, E. 1961. Kroṅ Pali et rites de la maison. *Anthropos* 56 (1–2, 3–4 and 5–6).
Porée-Maspero, E. 1962. *Étude sur les rites agraires des Cambodgiens*, vol. I. Paris: Mouton and Co.
Rhys Davids, T.W., and W. Stele (eds.). 1966. *The Pali Text Society's Pali-English Dictionary*. London: Luzac.
Spiro, M.E. 1982. *Buddhism and Society. A Great Tradition and Its Burmese Vicissitudes*. Berkeley: University of California Press (1970).
Thompson, A. 1999. Mémoires du Cambodge. Ph.D. dissertation, Paris VIII University.
Vacananukram khmaer bhāg dī 2 Ya-A. 1968. 5th ed. Phnom Penh: Édition de l'Institut Bouddhique.

Author Biography

Anne Yvonne Guillou Ph.D. is a tenured researcher at the French National Center for Scientific Research and is currently assigned in Cambodia by the French Research Institute on Contemporary Southeast Asia (IRASEC). Her research interests are in social and ritual resilience and memories in postgenocide Cambodia; Khmer religious system; and medical anthropology. Her publications include a book on Cambodian healers (*Cambodge, soigner dans les fracas de l'histoire. Médecins et sociétés*, 2009). She has co-guest edited (with S. Vignato) a double special issue on mass destruction in Southeast Asia (*Southeast Asia Research*, "Life after collective death in South East Asia", 2012 and 2013).

CHAPTER 4

Re-connecting the Ancestors. Buddhism and Animism on the Boloven Plateau, Laos

Guido Sprenger

Local traditions and world religions are prominent among a series of related dualisms which are employed to analyze Southeast Asian religious practices and discourses. Others are indigenous and non-indigenous (Kirsch 1977), animism and world religion (Sparkes 2005), philosophy and practice (Leach 1968), syncretic and compartmentalized (Terwiel 2012), and so on. These dualisms are used experimentally and often only to be interrogated, relativized or entirely discarded. This is complemented by the different relationships between the terms, which have been variously described as two complementary systems (Spiro 1967), one system with different fields (Tambiah 1970), harmonious symbiosis (Zago 1972: 383), transformative dialectic (Holt 2009: 233), etc. In addition, there are tripartite models (Kirsch 1977) or monistic ones (Van Esterik 1982; Tannenbaum 1987).

The following chapter situates itself within these debates. It makes the obvious point that both the terms and the relationships between them largely depend on the data, that is, on the local situation. The

G. Sprenger (✉)
Institut für Ethnologie, Heidelberg University, Heidelberg, Germany

© The Author(s) 2017
M. Picard (ed.), *The Appropriation of Religion in Southeast Asia and Beyond*, DOI 10.1007/978-3-319-56230-8_4

relationship between Buddhism and 'spirit religion' among Jru' on the Boloven Plateau appears as structurally tense and contrastive, not because this is a general feature of Southeast Asian religious practices, but because of the specific conditions of this place.

However, I also address some more general questions. The first asks how the impression of dualism arises in the first place. This has, I propose, to do with the contrasting connectivity of different cultural representations and institutions. A second question concerns the ontological status of the beings that are connected this way. I assume that persons, both human and non-human, are constituted through relationships and communication (Sprenger 2017a). A change in the type of communication, that is, a shift in the way communications connect to each other, affects the relational beings that are constituted through them. Such shifts differentiate contexts or historical phases in which the beings involved have divergent ranges of action or impact on the networks they exist in. Thus, the divergent connectivities of different representations point toward different socio-cosmic fields, which in turn suggests generalizations in dualist terms. This model should make clearer the ambiguous position of spirits in a multi-religious field.

The first question, about the contrastive tendencies toward local and global forms of religion, relates to the connectivity of the representations in question. Cultural representations are made of communication. Each representation, when realized in communication, has a certain potential to relate to other representations or communications, some past, some successive to it. Regarding the latter, the use of a particular representation prepares the ground for future communications. This potential of producing and linking communications is the representation's connectivity (*Anschlussfähigkeit*), a notion that I adapt from the theory of autopoietic social systems (Luhmann 1984: Chap. 1, II, Chap. 8, IX). Thus, what the representation 'makes present anew,' in Coppet's words (Coppet 1992: 65), is its own connectivity, that is, the communications that employ it, in particular the successive ones which the representation makes possible. Connectivity thus does not only denote the actual interactions in which a specific representation features, but also the potential interactions it suggests, a horizon of possibilities. Representations thus differ by their connectivity.

There are two dimensions of this difference that are particularly helpful in the present context—the social range of a representation and its value. The social range is that aspect of connectivity that references a particular social field or rather opens a way toward it. I will illustrate this by introducing politics and religion in Laos below. Also, in order for representations to be employed in communication in the first place, they need to be valorized in relationship to other representations. Connectivity is an important aspect of valorization, as it indicates which social or cosmological domains a particular representation allows access to, insofar as these domains are valorized. The value of a representation is therefore a matter of the recognition of its connectivity to such domains (see Dumont 1991). For example, ownership of a domestic animal is connective to markets, insofar as the animal can be sold, but also connective to the spirit world, insofar as it can be sacrificed. These are mutually exclusive connectivities—the market and the spirit world are differentially valorized. If the spirit world is contextually assigned a higher value than the market, and the animal is sacrificed instead of sold, the connectivity toward the spirit domain is elaborated, while the one to the market is curtailed. Assigning a higher or lower value to a particular representation in a particular context equals the expansion or the trimming of its connectivity.

This brings me back to the question why dualisms of the sort listed at the beginning are so debated. On the micro-level, there is often no contradiction or no dualism; therefore, dualism is hard to grasp (e.g., Rehbein 2011: 103; Brac de la Perrière, this volume). As Tambiah has suggested, the coherence of community-based religion and practice provides a level on which contrasting connectivities cannot be meaningfully separated (Tambiah 1970: 369–371). This foreshadows Bruno Latour's observation that there is no threshold between the local and the global, only a series of small connective steps making up a network (Latour 2008: 161).

When moving toward generalizations, however, the divergence of connectivities often assumes the form of dualisms. These usually emerge from academic, highly Europeanized discourses, thus producing a friction between local and academic terms. At the same time, Southeast Asians themselves often employ dualisms to describe their own situation, and the import of a European concept of doctrinal and pure 'religion,' as this volume suggests, has significantly contributed to such self-descriptions. This is why dualisms are a real and often considerable discursive force on the level of generalization, but seem to dissolve when examined at the micro-level.

There is a second factor undermining the application of dualisms. Dualisms would be easy to apply if there was a match between the range of connectivities and the value of the representations. If wide-ranging connectivity—say, of Buddhist ritual to the state—would automatically provide a representation with a higher value than one with lesser connectivity, 'high' and 'low,' local and global could be neatly disentangled. However, this is not the case. As I am going to demonstrate, in many contexts the more restricted connectivity of certain representations of ancestors or local spirits contrasts with the high value assigned to them in local socio-cosmic reproduction. This, however, is embedded in a national framework of differentially valorized representations of 'religion.'

THE POLITICS OF RELIGION IN LAOS

In Laos, Buddhism (L: *sadsana phud*)[1] is closely associated with the state and the dominant ethnic group, the Lao. Historically, the various kingdoms in Laos built their legitimacy through Buddhism, as protectors of the faith and the monkhood (Sangha) (Stuart-Fox 1999). Even the communist movement, which came to power in 1975, never attempted to eradicate Buddhism, as in Cambodia, but rather co-opted it into the socialist project. The current one-party state is not as explicitly Buddhist as Thailand, but most attempts to establish a common national culture involve representations of Buddhism. In particular, after the initial phase of the revolution was over, Buddhism once again moved to the center of national identity (Evans 1998: 49–71; Ladwig 2009; Tappe 2008). Any Buddhist representation—monks, temples, sacred texts, etc.—thus is connective to the state and to a reified 'national culture.' Buddhism in a socialist state, however, implies a purification of the faith that is at once related to purifications in the past as well as to modern notions of science and rationality (Evans 1998: 62, 65). Laotian monks are supposed to refrain from 'superstitious' practices like driving away harmful spirits (ibid.: 72–73). Thus, the connectivity between Buddhism and spirits has been curtailed by the state, as part of the modern religionization of Buddhism.

---

[1] For the origin and range of meaning of the term *sadsana*, see Brac de la Perrière, this volume.

Yet, ethnic Lao are only a slight majority in a country composed of 49 recognized ethnic groups, most of whom adhere to local ritual systems. According to the 2015 census, about 31.4% of the population register as 'no religion.' This number mostly consists of people practicing 'animism' (L: *sadsana phi*), which is explicitly 'not regarded as a religion' (Steering Committee 2006: 8; Lao Statistics Bureau 2016: 36, 123).[2] In the official English-language publication *Religious Affairs in the Lao P.D.R.*, this section of the population is awkwardly described as 'animism share with Buddhism' [sic] (Vannasopha 2005: 103). The following parentheses, 'non-believers are rare,' reveals the contradictory policy of religion in Laos. It implies that animism does not equal non-believing and thus is indeed a kind of religion.

Such contradictions run through the entire politics of religion in Laos. On the one hand, the Laotian state explicitly identifies as multi-ethnic, the constitution allows for freedom of religion, and official nationalism aims at integrating ethnic plurality (Tappe 2008: 83). On the other, animist practices are consistently denigrated and labeled 'superstition' (*ngom ngai*) in official rhetoric. Not practicing 'superstition' is thus one criterion for elevating a village to the status of 'culture village' (*ban wadthanatham*), an official recognition of its civilized status. Thus, 'animist' practices restrict desirable connections with the state. Being denied any recognition as religion or culture, animism remains almost anomic on the state level. The notion of 'tradition' (*hidgong*, also *hiid* or *riid*) is positively valorized and provides a largely undefined umbrella term that occasionally covers local religious practices. However, it is mostly restricted to staged representations of ethnicity, like costume and dancing (ibid.: 151).[3]

---

[2] Given the low regard 'animism' is held in, some people register as Buddhist, even though they hardly practice Buddhism—e.g., non-Buddhists living in Buddhist villages. The 2005 census registers 30.9% as 'no religion,' implying animism. The slight increase is probably due to the fact that population is growing faster in rural areas where most non-Buddhists live.

[3] Like in Indonesia, to have a proper religion in Laos is to be civilized, making religion an attribute of citizenship. However, the relation between *hidgong* and *sadsana* is certainly less articulated and debated as that between *adat* and *agama* in Indonesia, but requires further research. See Picard's chapter in this volume.

This creates a close association of ethnic Lao lifestyle and culture and the nation-state with prosperity and high status.[4] Thus, a Buddhist representation, a ritual for example, connects to the state, to the dominant ethnicity, and to a network of temples and monks stretching from centers to peripheries and from Laos to other countries like Thailand. The range of a Buddhist ritual's connectivity thus is markedly different from a local *hidgong* ritual that addresses territorial spirits. For the same reason, the connectivity of Lao representations like the wrist-tying ritual closely resembles that of Buddhist ones, even though they are not specifically Buddhist. Therefore, some animists adopt them alongside Buddhism for their connective potentials.

The connectivity of representations also encompasses non-humans and cosmological forces, and in this respect, ethnic Lao non-Buddhist representations differ from Buddhist ones. The wrist-tying rituals address the *khwan*, life souls of which every person has 32, while the Buddhist rituals address the *vinyan*, the soul that departs to the afterworld after death. These two concepts are variously identified with each other or differentiated. The differences between Buddhist and 'animist' representations are even more pronounced.

The Setting

Fieldwork was conducted in two villages whose inhabitants predominantly identified as Jru' (also spelled Jruq or Yrou and called Loven or Laven by the Lao), a Mon-Khmer-speaking ethnicity numbering about 56,000 persons.[5] One of the two villages, Lak Sip Ha, according to its inhabitants, follows 'spirit religion' and is known among its Jru' neighbors for its 'old traditions' (L: *hiid kao*). In the other village, Huaisan, villagers claim to practice both religions, Buddhism (L: *sadsana phud*) and 'spirit religion' (L: *sadsana phi*). This claim as such is remarkable, as I will elaborate below.

---

[4] Young people on the Boloven Plateau, for example, see government jobs as ideal future opportunities (Portilla 2015).

[5] The following findings come with a number of caveats. Fieldwork was restricted to only five months, in the years 2012–2016. Time did not suffice to learn the local language, Jru', so most data were collected in Lao. I used crucial Jru' terms, in particular regarding kinship, ritual and cosmology, in my interviews.

Both villages are situated in Paksong district, in the province of Champassak, in southern Laos. Lak Sip Ha (literally Km 15) is, as its name says, situated 15 km east of the district capital, Paksong, on a road to Vietnam that has been upgraded within the last few years. A chain of villages skirts the road, most of them populated by Jru', but also including some dominated by Lao and Ta Oy, as well as mixed ones. Huaisan is situated about 7 km north of Paksong and also has Jru' and Lao villages in its neighborhood.

Before the end of the civil war in 1975, the Boloven Plateau, a high plateau with an elevation of about 1100 m above sea level, was almost exclusively populated by Mon-Khmer-speaking ethnicities, predominantly Jru', but also Ta Oy, Alak and Nya Hön. The Jru' differ from many other upland ethnicities in Laos for having almost entirely shifted from swidden agriculture to cash cropping within the last few decades. The plateau's climate, together with comparatively easy accessibility, allows cultivation of coffee, which has expanded continuously since the 1930s (Ducourtieux 1994: 62–64; Ducourtieux and Songsamayvong 2003: 15–16; Sallée and Tulet 2010). Today, virtually all Jru' villagers I know are primarily coffee farmers. The Boloven Plateau is currently the most important coffee production area in Laos, coffee being among the most important agricultural exports of the country. The area is therefore wealthier than many other rural areas in Laos (Ducourtieux and Songsamayvong 2003: 12, 36; Portilla 2015; Schönweger et al. 2012: 58) and has attracted numerous Lao and other migrants.[6]

Coffee is also an important factor in the tensions of cosmology and religion that I am going to document. All clues indicate that coffee cultivation started earlier in the area north of Paksong, where the Buddhist village Huaisan is situated, which consequently has seen a stronger immigration of lowland Lao. As many villagers in Huaisan argued, Buddhism arrived with the Lao immigrants, many of whom married into the Jru'

---

[6]Despite this, anthropological research on the plateau is scarce. The Jru' have not been subject to a full anthropological study. Diane Alexander ceased her research in 1973 after a few months, due to civil war (Alexander 1978). A few other studies, some of them by colonial administrators and surveyors, have briefly touched upon the Jru' (Dauplay 1929; Fraisse 1951; Harmand 1997 [1878–1879]; Lavallée 1901; see also Hours 1973). The most in-depth study of the Jru' was conducted by linguists Pascale Jacq and Paul Sidwell. In particular, Jacq's master thesis on Jru' language is admirably comprehensive, despite some ethnographic shortcomings (Jacq 2001; Jacq and Sidwell 1999).

villages. This led to the ethnicization of the difference between world religion and local tradition.

LOCAL RELIGION AND LOCALIZED 'RELIGION'

A dualist approach that distinguishes Buddhist world religion (*sadsana phud*) and 'spirit religion' (*sadsana phi*) as local tradition is highly suggestive, as the Jru' themselves use it to frame their discourse. In contrast to studies like those of Spiro (1967), Tambiah (1970), Kirsch (1977) or, more recently, Platenkamp (2010) or Sparkes (2005), my data suggest little mutual reinforcement of the two sets of ritual practices. In addition to distinguishing between Buddhism and spirit relations, as many other Southeast Asians do, the Jru' also ethnicize the difference. Buddhism is marked as Lao culture, while spirit relationships are identified with Jru'—notwithstanding the fact that the Lao see a similar distinction within their own practices. Yet, this does not mean that the two ritual complexes are isolated. Their interaction led to changes even within the period of fieldwork. These changes testify to re-evaluations of certain relations regarding their connectivity. In some cases, people expressed clear choices regarding such potentials to relate.

Like *agama* in Indonesia (see Picard, this volume), the Lao word *sadsana* currently denotes the so-called world religions, in particular Buddhism, Christianity and Islam. As mentioned above, *sadsana phi*, however, is not an officially recognized category and cannot be used in official forms recording a person's religion. The term is presumably not older than the revolutionary struggle that started in the 1950s and promised to treat uplanders and lowlanders as equals.[7] Still, Jru' in Lak Sip Ha say that they are *sadsana Jru'* or *sadsana phi*. Others, however, state that they *thue phi*, 'believe in or venerate spirits.' *Thue* is also used in the expression *thue sadsana*, to adhere to a religion, or *thue bapeni*, to observe tradition. The notion *thue* thus places spirits in a semantic field that encompasses religion without being confined to it, similar to Burmese *pwe* (see Brac de la Perrière, this volume). While some people stress the difference between *sadsana* and *thue*, the terms indicate a similar kind of relationship for others.

---

[7] I thank Vanina Bouté for suggesting this possibility.

The term *sadsana phi* is actually widespread, and even government officials use it in conversation. However, most Buddhists make a difference between *sadsana* (*phud*), which for them is exclusively Buddhism, and *thue phi*. Therefore, the notion that Buddhism and animism both count as religion and can be practiced in parallel is quite unusual in the Lao context. Similar to Cambodia (see Guillou, this volume), non-Buddhist practices in the Buddhist ritual system are sometimes identified as *sadsana pham* (Brahmanism).

My two field sites differ in respect to the avenues of communication that their religious practices offer, including communication with non-human beings like ancestors.[8] Lak Sip Ha, a village of about 634 people, is neighbored by another Jru' village and Chansavang, a Lao village. Chansavang has a Buddhist temple (*wad*) which is, like most village temples in the area, staffed with a single fully ordained monk and a small number of novices.

Most rituals in Lak Sip Ha, including life-cycle rituals such as marriages, healing rituals and those for the village spirit, are performed or supervised by a specialist called *griang*. Most Jru' villages have two or three *griang*, who have volunteered for this position after learning from an older expert over an extended period of time. The most active *griang* in Lak Sip Ha was my main informant and a well-regarded man, holding several other official functions in the village. He professed a comprehensive view of the ritual system that was obviously not shared, but respected by many other villagers.

Regarding ritual, the *griang* have considerable authority. In principle, any Jru' ritual should be performed with a *griang* present, and very often they would give detailed instructions to ritual performers. While some villagers knew the proceedings well and the *griang* mostly acted as a witness, performers often gladly submitted to his authority. Therefore, people were quick in referring me to the *griang* when I asked questions about ritual details. Ritual knowledge is thus unevenly distributed, and accordingly, my data were clearly shaped through this channel—sometimes conveniently, sometimes restrictively.

Ritual specialists with such a broad field of expertise and authority are not typical for many of the Mon-Khmer-speaking, non-Buddhist

---

[8] In the present case, there is no difference between ancestors and the spirits of the dead.

societies of Laos. A corresponding role seems to be absent among the Jru's immediate neighbors, the culturally and linguistically closely related Nya Hön (Wall 1975). However, the Jru' stand out for their long-lasting relationships with lowland Lao and their higher rank in relation to surrounding uplanders (ibid.: 6–7). In fact, an early explorer described them in 1877 as 'not really *kha*' (i.e., barbarian mountain dwellers) (Harmand 1997: 91). If I am allowed some speculation, it is conceivable that the elaboration of an authoritative ritual specialist role reflects proximity to similar models, especially the monk, among Lao. At least, Jru' villagers explicitly equate the function of the two roles.

The ritual system of Lak Sip Ha Jru' is based on the provision of spirits, in particular those of the ancestors of individual households. The connectivity of the ancestors follows a clear genealogical grid. Kinship is bilateral, and circumscribed kin groups are lacking. Both terminology and much of ritual practice indicate gender symmetry, although there is a matrilineal bias in kinship arrangements and a patriarchal one in politics. Couples tend to build their houses close to the wife's parents' home, resulting in matrilineal compounds, similar to Lao and Northern Thai (Condominas 1970: 13; Sparkes 2005: 21; Turton 1972). During the Second Indochina War, Lak Sip Ha was relocated in the mid-1970s, and interlocutors stressed the decrease of the matrilineal clusters as the major feature of the resulting rearrangement. However, a majority of households are still situated beside relatives connected through the mother, especially on the village periphery, where more land is available.

The rituals acknowledge the nexus of residence and the genealogical connectivity of ancestors, which, like in some house societies (e.g., Waterson 1995), are linked to the inhabited buildings. The majority of houses in Lak Sip Ha are classified as *hnom riid*, 'house of ritual/tradition.'[9] These consecrated houses feature a window pointing east, through which food offerings for the dead are thrown out during ritual. If a person gets ill, a diviner and shaman (*yaamuan*) is called, and regularly he reveals 'mother and father who want to eat' as the cause of the illness—that is, ancestors demanding a sacrifice. Each *hnom riid* is specified regarding the ancestors that can be addressed within it. A matrilocal household 'has the *riid* of the wife's side.' This means, the wife's

---

[9] Like in Tanebar-Evav (Barraud, this volume), loanwords with an abstract, general meaning are used here to denote something rather concrete like a spirit or a ritual status.

ancestors are fed inside the house, while the husband's ancestors are attended for on the ground outside or in his parent's house. If a building is not a *hnom riid*, the rituals are performed in the house of the parents of the respective spouse.

The establishment of a *hnom riid* on the husband's side, i.e., patrilocal residence, demands a ritual of transfer. Of 59 houses surveyed, 48 related to the dead of the wife's side, six to the husband's side and five were not *hnom riid*. This implies that the relationship between a woman and her parents is higher valued in relation to the dead than the relation between a man and his parents. The orientation toward the respective dead supports the establishment of matrilocal compounds, with patrilocal and bilateral options. Addressing the ancestors thus entails the creation of residence groups and healthy bodies. The connectivity of these ritual communications also points at the village level, insofar as the *griang*, who represents the village as a whole, supervises the proceedings.[10] Also, ritual detail often varies between villages, a well-known fact reinforcing village identity.

This network also used to encompass the graveyard, where gender symmetry and matrilineal bias are similarly present. This, however, has changed with the replacement of Jru' mortuary rituals with Buddhist cremations, involving monks from Lao villages, in Lak Sip Ha in the period between 2004 and 2012, approximately. This replacement was slow and occurred by household.[11] Still, some Jru' mortuary practices, which I will not deal with here, are retained. As the transition to Buddhist cremation is only recent, other rituals relating to the dead remain unchanged. Therefore, I detail here the earlier burial rituals, as they shed light on the way the dead are linked to the living.

The dead were normatively buried close to their consanguines, preferably near the parent who died last. However, if both parents were still alive, a child was buried near its mother's relatives. Spouses were not

---

[10] In Huaisan, each larger ritual begins with a brief address, in the form of libations, to the village spirit.

[11] Some neighboring villages pioneered this move away from Jru' style burials in earlier years. Still, Jru' villagers did not say they were Buddhists. There is also no prohibition against Jru' mortuary rituals. However, it seems that most households prefer Buddhist over Jru' rituals, as they are said to be more hygienic and shorter. They are also more expensive and thus more prestigious.

buried side by side of each other. Here, the relationship between husband and wife was subordinated to the one between consanguines.

Like *hnom riid*, houses on the graveyard materialized relations with the forebears. In Lak Sip Ha, coffins were placed inside individual wooden houses.[12] According to the wealth of the family, these ranged in size from a building a bit larger than the coffin to constructions of about 3 m height and length. These houses featured small windows for ritual offerings, enabling the dead to venerate their forebears in the same way as the living do. Thus, a relationship with earlier generations is constitutive of houses, even when its occupants are dead. In this particular mode of connectivity, the difference between life and death is subordinated to the difference between earlier and later generations.

The houses of the dead enabled a kind of automated secondary burial. The coffin lies on three crossbeams spanning a pit. After the flesh has rotten away, the beams and the coffin become brittle and crash down into the pit, releasing the bones into the ground. Only then, the deceased turns from a 'dead human being' (*pnux ket*) into an ancestor (*kshok*, the term used in rituals for the dead).[13]

The houses are sites of offerings, including the personal items of the dead placed inside or besides the building, cigarettes given on the day of the burial, and finally cigarettes offered during the rare visits of the living on the graveyard. All these practices established each singular dead as a separate person.

This is also stressed in the most important means for choosing a gravesite or a cremation site. Before the burial, a close relative of the dead throws a raw egg on the graveyard. The place where the egg breaks is the site chosen by the dead her-/himself. Due to undergrowth, only several attempts, some near the dead person's consanguines and some elsewhere, will reveal the chosen spot. This method stresses the dead person's intentionality and the flexibility of the kinship system, as it ultimately overrides the norms of choosing a site mentioned above.

---

[12] Harmand (1997: 88, 90) in 1877 found Jru' burial sites consisting of low rectangular fences decorated with flags and household utensils. Lavallée (1901: 293) observed large wooden constructions on top of the graves.

[13] Buddhists in this region also practice secondary burial. After cremation, the relatives of the dead collect the bones and place them in a stupa on the temple grounds. This retains the separation of bones and flesh, but speeds it up.

Thus, the spatial arrangement of the buildings, both for the living and the dead, enabled a sociality of kinship relations, with the village as an encompassing level. These relationships also reach out into the upcoming generations. Occasionally, a child turns out to be the rebirth of one of his or her forebears. Usually, these reborn ancestors reveal themselves through an illness that afflicts the child during the first year of its life. After the ancestor has been identified as a specific relative, the child's parents perform a ritual with food offerings, in which he or she figures as recipient. From then on, relatives of the dead address the child with the kin terms they used for the deceased person. This is quite different from Buddhism, where every soul is being reborn, but without its individual identity.

While cremations are the most prominent case in which Jru' rituals have been replaced with Lao ones, others demonstrate a flexible combination of elements from both systems. Weddings are now performed as a mixture of Jru' and Lao usages in all villages I know. Among the Jru' elements are the drinking of rice wine and the symmetry of ritual procedures in the husband's and the wife's parent's houses. Dancing the *lambong* has, however, become a general element of the feast that is acknowledged to be Lao. In some instances, the dress of the newlyweds, in particular of the bride, and the wrist-tying ceremony (*baci sukhwan*) were also adopted from the Lao.

Probably most significant is the introduction of the Lao bride price. Before that, mutual feasting marked marriage exchanges, as well as divorce payments. As bride price is transferred publicly, it is a measure of the respective families' prestige and wealth. It provides a means to compare status through money and gold jewelry and to communicate with the dominant ethnicity of the country. Status then can be expressed in an idiom that transcends ethnic boundaries. Thus, both mortuary and wedding rituals nowadays encompass relations with the Lao and therefore with a nationalized cultural standard for establishing relationships with the dead and among affines.

Another innovation is the introduction of *baci sukhwan*. These rituals focus on the tying of strings around the recipients' wrists on the occasion of any kind of transition: arrivals from and departures to long journeys, weddings, the reception of respected guests, etc. (see Tambiah 1970; Ngaosyvathn 1990). The ritual is often described as pan-Laotian, being shared by numerous non-Lao and non-Buddhist groups as well (Singh 2014). However, Lak Sip Ha Jru' do not perform it as part of

'Jru' tradition' (*riid jru'*) but clearly perceive it as Lao. Other than cremations, this and the additions to the wedding rituals are not Buddhist as such, but demonstrate the association between Buddhism and ethnic Lao.

Since 2012, a few households have performed the Buddhist *sia kho*, a ritual aiming at driving away bad luck, indicated by accidents and other mishaps. At its core is also a *baci sukhwan*, but furthermore the ritual involves monks chanting *suttha* as well as a big communal meal. It is quite costly and thus another occasion for demonstrating wealth. Still, the households organizing them did not identify as Buddhist. Rather, the ritual enables comparisons of status and binds Jru' personhood into a wider network of forces that foster prosperity, fortune and health. Thus, it is wealthy households seeking connections beyond the village that act as agents in the introduction of Buddhism.

In 2013 and 2014, for the first time, two boys from Lak Sip Ha entered the *wad* of Chansavang as novices. Once again, this indicated not so much a replacement of one cosmology by another, but rather a reorientation toward different, but co-existing socio-cosmic horizons, motivated by local reasoning (e.g., Kammerer 1990; Tooker 1992). Both boys were not sent as agents of conversion, but for reasons of health and education. Like in the past, the monkhood provides a network of schools as education opportunities for young men from poor families, some of them not Buddhists (High 2014: 119; Holt 2009: 202). Thus, Buddhism is valorized for its communicative horizons.

It is therefore significant that, in the 2015 census, numerous Lak Sip Ha villagers registered as Buddhists, even though many of them continue to think of themselves as *sadsana Jru'*, which the census registers as 'no religion.' Here, the state and Buddhism are closely associated. An animist village with an openness to Buddhist connections appears as Buddhist under the gaze of the state. Thus, the introduction of 'religion' (*sadsana*) had two effects—the designation of a local ritual system as something comparable to Buddhism and other world religions and a bias for identifying with the dominant religion of the state.

The People of Two Religions

The second village, Huaisan, which contains about 210 families, has a temple since 1995, but before that shared one with the adjacent village of Sethapung, from which Huaisan had split off. This temple had been founded, according to conflicting information, in the late 1950s or early 1970s, the earliest ordinations of villagers probably occurring in the early 1960s. The transition to Buddhism had thus been an extended, gradual process, making statements about it incongruous. Even the appropriation of Buddhist ritual by non-Buddhists, as in Lak Sip Ha, may in hindsight qualify as taking up the religion. In any case, the building of a temple is usually taken as an important transition in village history—some interlocutors said that before the temple there was only *sadsana phi* in the village.

Huaisan villagers identify as Buddhists, but also say that they have both, *sadsana phud* and *sadsana phi*. They practice rituals of both religions in parallel, each with its own experts and practices. While I did not find Buddhist and non-Buddhist factions in the village, not a single practice or role from one system depends on representations from the other in any direct manner. Huaisan Jru' spirit rituals hardly employ Lao verses, and *griang* need no connection with Buddhism in order to perform their rituals properly. The roles are not exclusive either—one old man who had been ordained as a monk for almost a decade from the 1960s to the 1970s now performs as a *griang*, thus providing spiritual services of both kinds to his community. While some ritual occasions are exclusively Buddhist, others demand a choice between Lao or Jru' style. This is thus seen as a choice of ethnicity.

The term *phi* functions as a relay point between the two ritual systems and allows glossing over some of their differences. Jru' from both Lak Sip Ha and Huaisan sometimes seek help from neighboring Lao diviners when searching for the cause of an illness. On a level that is less specific than the elaborate system of ancestors and houses found in Lak Sip Ha, the notion of illness-causing ancestors connects communications produced within two fairly different systems—systems whose difference is carefully elaborated, possibly even exaggerated, when Jru' ethnicize the two *sadsana*.

Huaisan has two *griang*, but although they are respected members of the community, they are not as central as the *griang* of Lak Sip Ha. While the latter felt it to be his duty to attend all kinds of rituals, even those performed by the single Vietnamese husband in the village, the *griang* of Huaisan clearly stated that their expertise only applies to 'Jru' tradition' (*riid jruq*). Huaisan *griang* join Buddhist rituals, but have no distinguished role in them. The latter are performed by monks and *salawad*, former monks who act as mediators between laymen and monks.

All three *salawad* in Huaisan are Lao and had married Jru' women after leaving the order. Although Jru' from Huaisan and its neighboring villages are or have been monks, the Huaisan temple had been staffed exclusively with Lao until April 2016, when a novice from another Jru' village was ordained as a full monk.

The relationships with and rituals for the ancestors are less elaborate than in Lak Sip Ha, although I am not sure if this results from Buddhist influence or is due to local variation. Consecrated houses (*hnom riid*) are absent, but the principle of gender symmetry with a matrilineal bias is maintained in different form. Like in Lak Sip Ha, each house is oriented toward either the wife's or the husband's ancestors, determining where the 'feeding of the ancestors' (*ciam kshok*) can be performed. This is usually determined by a sequence of two rituals for ancestor-induced illnesses, 'buffalo eating' (*ca kopou*) and 'rice spirit' (*brah ceh*). The sequence is first addressed to the wife's ancestors, and until it is completed, the 'feeding' is only performed for her side in the house. The second round of the sequence addresses the husband's ancestors, including 'feeding' rituals for his side during that period. This alternation usually takes decades to occur, but in principle would be reversed after each sequence (Sprenger 2017b). However, the nexus of residence and kinship seems to be lacking in Huaisan. Although my data are incomplete, it seems that kin clusters are mostly absent or, when they exist, tend to be bilateral.

The diverging connectivity of the Buddhist and the animist ritual system became obvious in two healing rituals, which I observed in the span of two days. One was a Jru'-style chicken sacrifice for the spirits of the dead and the other an elaborate Lao-style *sia kho* ritual. The latter requires the help of a large group of relatives, expensive gifts for the monks, as well as food. Both households were Jru' and both transferred gifts to the ancestors who demanded them through illness, but the latter was clearly wealthier. The rituals also implied different connections with the market. The Lao-style ritual necessitated the purchase of standardized sets of gifts (L: *khueang boun*): two beds with canopies, ritual fans, toiletries and household products for monks, coming pre-packaged in plastic wrap, and money. Certain ritual and food items were made by the household and its relatives, but the most conspicuous objects were bought on the market, all shiny and brimming with color. In the Jru' ritual, in contrast, the spirits received miniature replicas of dishes, food and other consumables on a rack of about 50 cm^2. The shreds of meat presented to them were tiny. Almost everything was made from perishable everyday materials, produced at home. Nothing necessarily connected the ritual to markets or socialites beyond a Jru' village.

This difference does not only mark the respective households as poor and wealthy, respectively. The rituals also pursue different types of relationships. The Jru' ritual does what many rituals for capricious spirits in the region do—keep the spirits, both ancestral and environmental, at bay. This is mirrored in the diminution of the gifts to the spirits and their perishability.

In contrast, the gifts to the monks aim at expanding and strengthening a relationship, in which the monks represent the protective and encompassing force of the Buddhist cosmos. The rejection of various types of harmful spirits formed an important part of this ritual as well, represented by a tray of perishable offerings that the household head unceremoniously dumped at the village boundary. However, the reinforcement of relationships with the monks was a much more visible aspect of the ritual. This also concerns their stability over time, as the durable parts of these gifts, like the bed and the ritual paraphernalia, are stored in the temple when they are in excess.

Mortuary rituals in Huaisan are the occasions in which the uneasy relationship between the two systems emerges most clearly. Both the *griang* and the monks play prominent roles in them, but they neither overlap nor complement each other. Each ritual specialist operates as if the other was not involved. Still, there is an attempt to integrate them, albeit without overcoming their difference.

This shows, among others, in the temporal sequence of rituals. Auspicious days for Buddhist cremations are Thursdays (L: *wan pahad*) and Sundays (L: *wan thid*), following a layperson's death. But Jru' mortuary rituals demand a series of seven chicken sacrifices, one per day. Bloody sacrifices, even though they exist among Lao (e.g., Sparkes 2005: 193; Archaimbault 1956), mark a major difference between ethnicized Buddhism and *sadsana phi* in local perception (Sprenger 2009). Buddhism forbids killing animals, while spirit religion demands it, as one of Huaisan's *salawad* stressed in discussion. As Buddhism is dominant among the two religions, it restricts the other in its operations. Each mortuary ritual requires the *griang* to adapt the sacrifices to the time frame of cremation, either by cutting the sequence short or by performing two sacrifices a day. There seems to be no widely shared way to integrate the two sequences.

There are also conspicuous differences regarding the funeral itself. The graveyard of Huaisan features three kinds of graves. Houses are built for persons who were too young to be cremated or died a bad death. The second type represents a compromise between Buddhist and Jru' rituals. Cremation sites are of little importance to the Lao, as the relatives put the remaining bones in a stupa on the temple grounds two days after cremation. However, a significant number of Huaisan villagers placed a small house on top of the heap of ashes, miniature versions of the earlier grave houses said to house the soul of the dead. The third type is a plain cremation with no house placed on the cremation site later.

However, in all three varieties, the *griang* erects a small house on a post about two meters away from the burial or cremation site. This shrine (L/J: *ho*) is also found at house burials in Lak Sip Ha, but not on cremation sites of Lao villagers in this area. Before the cremation, the *griang* connects the shrine and the pyre with a white thread. The *vinyan* (soul) of the dead passes into the shrine, where small offerings are laid in place.

This observation raises questions about the nature of the dead and their connectivity.

The Ontology of the Dead

I now turn to the second question raised in the introduction: when beings are created through communication and the connectivity of communication changes, how do these beings change? In general, spirits, like living human persons, are communicated into being through sets of actions, concepts, discourses, etc., in rituals and everyday communication. Like the dividual Strathern (1988) has posited for Melanesia, Southeast Asian personhood is often a matter of relationships. As I have argued elsewhere (Sprenger 2017a), the notion that personhood emerges from communication might account better for how spirits, as more or less complete persons, gradually come into being. But if communication and the rituals that establish these beings include new representations, the spirits change as well. This poses a problem regarding the positioning of the ancestors within the networks of human and non-human beings. The spirits of the dead play a rather different role in Buddhism than in Jru' cosmology, and the connectivity of the dead becomes incongruent.

The contradiction can be elicited by the question where the soul is actually located. Hardly any other question I asked in Huaisan produced such a plethora of different answers. Some said that the soul only rests in the shrine temporarily and moves to the stupa after the bones have been placed there. Others said the soul usually stays in the shrine and moves to the stupa during Buddhist festivals. A third answer accorded no significance whatsoever to the shrine, because the souls go to heaven or hell, according to Buddhist cosmology. A fourth variety simply identified both shrine and stupa with heaven.

The variety of answers might be due to the fact that for the people I talked to the coherence of generalized ideas is less important than the maintenance of relationships in practice. However, their answers demonstrate tensions similar to the ritual procedures; therefore, I consider them as valuable data for the issues at hand. If each of these positions constitutes its own strand of communication, the discursive field lacks a mainstream. The friction between the Buddhist conception, in which anonymous souls move to a remote domain, and the animist one provides ritual and everyday communication with a certain dynamic that keeps producing variance. This is characteristic of the interaction of Buddhism with local animism in general; however, it is enhanced in the present case.

The consequences this has for the ontology of the dead were sometimes made explicit by my interlocutors. I received different answers to my questions why Buddhism had been adopted in the first place, the most common I have mentioned before. An increasing number of Lao immigrants married Jru', people said, thus marking the distinction between the *sadsana* as an ethnic difference. Yet, interlocutors also said that the temple of Sethapung was founded when only a few Lao were living in the village, but entirely with local funding. Therefore, as far as I see it, the 'pioneer temples' which Goudineau (2008) identified as agents of Buddhification were not present.

However, some interlocutors framed the process in terms of the relationships with the ancestors and other spirits. In the past, one Huaisan *griang* explained, 'father and mother' (the dead) stayed in the houses, so the Jru' got ill all the time and had to sacrifice animals. Nowadays, 'father and mother' go to the temple to eat. Thus, it seems Buddhism is also regarded as a smarter way to deal with the dead. In this sense, ancestral relations are primary, as they motivate the adoption of Buddhism in the first place. In these contexts, the value of the relationships with local ancestors is higher than the more far-reaching connectivity of Buddhism. Paradoxically, the dead were resituated in the process and in many respects anonymized and 'silenced.'[14]

The genealogical identity of the Jru' ancestors is reproduced in the sacrificial rituals for the patrilateral or matrilateral ancestors, but is denied in the Buddhist context. The major Buddhist festivals for the dead in the annual cycle are directed to an anonymous multitude of souls in hell (Ladwig 2012a), and this is how Huaisan villagers perceive these rituals as well. Jru' ritual also connects to the ancestors immediately. Elaborate gifts to one's own forebears do occur during *sia kho* and some other rituals, but it is the monks who transfer them to the dead—they are their physical recipients (Ladwig 2012b).

In both villages, the shift from Jru' mortuary rituals to Buddhist cremation has not (yet?) affected the treatment of ancestors during Jru' rituals in the houses. Matrilateral and patrilateral spirits are still ritually differentiated, almost as if the mortuary rituals had no effect on the nature of the spirits. What is more, Lak Sip Ha villagers keep identifying as *sadsana phi* privately, but increasingly as Buddhists in face of the state.

This gives another dimension to connectivities. When Buddhism means a different kind of relation to the state, the Lao majority, etc., then this relationship is not merely political. The relationship with the state implies redefinitions of the ontological status of some of the actors within the collective. The communications by which the ancestors come into being are redirected and reshaped, with the result that the means of communication with the ancestors are altered as well. In the Buddhist context, there is much less opportunity to receive messages from the dead, as they are different beings now.

I asked only a few people, including *griang*, if they were about to shed their ritual system entirely. The response was quite unequivocal: father and mother will not like it. The dead are Jru' and thus would reject forms of addressing them other than Jru' rituals. This reasoning might look circular at first. The Jru' rituals provide a particular relationship to a specific type of dead, which exists primarily through this relationship. That is, rituals exist because of ancestors, and ancestors exist because of rituals. The circularity gains a different edge when

---

[14]This is so even though monks may participate in the creation of more personalized ancestors, e.g., in the Lao-speaking parts of Thailand (Sparkes 2005: 146).

the hierarchies of the ideas are considered. Mortuary rituals transform the relationships constituting a living person into those of the dead. Thus, the relationships have been established during their lifetime. Not addressing the ancestors does not make them disappear. It just transforms them from protectors to malevolent beings that make people ill. In this sense, the refusal of ritual has a similar effect as its performance—it creates particular beings, that are, in this case, antagonistic to the lives of living people.

But this is not to deny that Buddhist relations come with their own potentials and their own communicative ways of creating and situating beings. The diversity of answers regarding the nature of the ancestors and the spirits that I received in Huaisan indicates the unresolved question which set of relations, Buddhist or non-Buddhist, plays a superior role in the respective contexts of communication. But even without the anthropologist provoking theological speculation, it is quite obvious that the various rituals address very different beings. Jru' mortuary ritual consists of a series of sacrifices that transfer the dead to a new home on the graveyard. Buddhist ritual is supposed to transform the dead into remote and de-individualized beings set on their way to rebirth. Even though people keep relationships with their dead ongoing, via gifts channeled through monks or offerings of food to the stupas, the close relationship between houses and the dead has disappeared. A family house in a Buddhist context is much less a community made up of the living and the dead as it is in the Jru' animist context.

Both types of dead are thus fundamentally different, but both are equally produced through ritual procedures. The *griang* were maybe pessimistic about the prospect of being badgered by one's forebears forever, but at the same time they were clearly optimistic in the sense that their way of making beings as members of their collectives would not disappear.

Yet, this was balanced by a clear sense of irretrievable loss of language and ethnic identity that numerous interlocutors expressed to me. This attitude was particularly pronounced in Huaisan, but clearly present in Lak Sip Ha as well. I see this as a function of the ethnicization of the difference between Buddhism and spirit relations. The gradual adoption of Buddhism raises the question how the boundaries between Lao and Jru' can be maintained. Rituals for the dead reproduce this difference, managing connectivities to state, education, markets and nationalized Lao culture on the one hand, and those to locality, matriline and health on the other. The unclear status of the ancestors is thus charged with more significance, the difference between the systems being less well integrated than in the Lao or Thai systems.

Conclusion

The differentiation of connectivity does not necessarily classify and thereby separate representations. Pali verses, for example, are used among Lao or Thai both for rituals by monks in temples and by healers who relate to spirits—they are part of different chains of communications. The notion of connectivity makes it possible to situate a single event or representation within such chains and at the same time address the relationships between different chains—if they overlap, contradict each other, run parallel, etc. The emergence of cultural boundaries is just one form which the chains of communication produce as a function of their differentiation. Within such an analytical framework, the variations of dualisms in religious studies in Southeast Asia can be located. The introduction of the notion of 'religion' (*sadsana*) supports this differentiating process.

At first glance, there are two possible models to analyze the Jru' situation in terms of its dualisms, both being more or less local and analytical at the same time. The first model would stress the ethnicization of the dualism of Buddhism and Jru', as suggested by the Jru' themselves. In this view, relations to ancestral spirits are Jru' and relations to Buddhist forces and persons Lao. This would take account of the strong divergence of connectivities of the two *sadsana*. Analytically, however, it reiterates the idea of trait-bound cultural boundaries which anthropology has shed in the past decades. Still, this idea is sometimes employed locally as a self-description that feeds back into the differentiation of ethnicities. Using the notion of *sadsana* as an ethnic marker adds another semantic level to this difference.

The second model would identify the situation as one variation of a pattern common to Southeast Asia, in which spirits and world religions are somehow integrated. Harmony or dichotomy, dialectic or integration are ways of describing the confluence or divergence of connections between the representations that make up the different ritual systems. In these terms, the Jru' case is one, albeit not of hostility, but of pronounced dichotomy, in which Buddhism limits Jru' ancestral relations. These connectivities mostly point into different directions, as the case of the two healing rituals demonstrates. The social domains implied by the Jru' ancestral ritual and the *sia kho* are largely separate, in particular their relationship to the monkhood (Sangha) and to the market. However, the fact that both rituals were performed in a single community demonstrates that the range of connectivities of representations and their respective value do not always match. One of the households assigned a higher value to Jru' ancestors than the other.

The ethnicization of the difference is an important semantic device to elaborate this dichotomy—one might even argue that it exaggerates differences where a stress on commonalities, e.g., between Jru' and Lao spirit relations or the pragmatic use of Buddhism among both, is an option. However, ancestral relations, with their dimensions of kinship and village, are by necessity 'local.' Insofar as Jru' ethnicity is seen as local and particular by my interlocutors, in contrast to Lao general national culture, the equation of ancestral with local supports the ethnicization of ritual systems by *sadsana*.

At the same time, the mixture of ritual systems, which is always a potential of non-doctrinal, flexible and adaptable practices like *sadsana phi*, produces narratives of loss and degeneration of local identity. The form of reproduction that Jru' ancestral relations take is one that allows for variation. Differences in ritual practice between villages are known and unproblematic, as relations are localized and personalized. This contrasts with the (seeming) standardization and repetition characterizing Buddhism. In Buddhism, local variation is smaller and, it seems to me, less tolerated (see Rehbein and Sprenger 2016). Thus, in the relationship between normative and non-normative *sadsana*, the 'original' *sadsana*, Buddhism, turns out to be superior.

The dichotomy of the two connective sets is enhanced through ethnicization, the notion of 'religion,' and the frictions between the ontological definitions of ancestral spirits that emerge from them. While such frictions potentially occur in many cases where beings are produced through differentially connected representations—the world religion and local tradition issue—they appear as less integrated and more pronounced in the Jru' case.

In particular, the symmetric use of *sadsana* for both complexes is productive of the dichotomy, as it implies a constant reversal of hierarchies. On the one hand, Buddhism limits Jru' ritual, up to the point that, from some actors' perspective, Jru' rituals do not constitute a religion at all. On the other hand, as the argument of the Huaisan *griang* suggests, the ancestors are an ultimate relational reality that has to be dealt with, either by Buddhism or by Jru' rituals. Thus, on this encompassing level, the ancestors constitute a constitutive element. At the same time, through their differentiated treatment, they oscillate between seemingly incompatible modes of being. 'Religion' thus appears as a notion that supports an asymmetric differentiation of practices and cultural belonging.

References

Alexander, D. 1978. The introduction of modern medicine into a tribal village: The Loven of DakTrang, Laos. In *Aspects of tribal life in South Asia: Part. I. Strategy and survival, Proceedings of an international seminar, Berne, 1977*, ed. R. Moser and M.K. Gautam, 209–226. Berne.
Archaimbault, C. 1956. Le sacrifice du buffle à Vat Ph'u (Sud Laos). *France-Asie* XII (118, 119, 120): 841–845.
Condominas, G. 1970. The Lao. In *Laos: War and revolution*, ed. N. Adams, and A. McCoy, 9–27. New York: Harper and Row.
Coppet, D. de. 1992. Comparison, a universal for anthropology: From 're-presentation' to the comparison of hierarchies of value. In *Conceptualizing Society*, ed. Adam Kuper, 59–74. London: Routledge.
Dauplay, J.-J. 1929. *Les terres rouges du plateau des Bolovens*. Saigon: Chambre d'Agriculture de la Cochinchine.
Ducourtieux, O. 1994. *L'Agriculture du Plateau des Bolovens: Évolution du système agraire de la région de Paksong – Sud-Laos*. Rome: FAO.
Ducourtieux, O., and K. Songsamayvong. 2003. *Étude de faisabilité du programme de la capitalisation en appui à la politique de développement rural: point d'application Bolovens*. Paris & Montpellier: IRAM.
Dumont, L. 1991 [1983]. *Individualismus: zur Ideologie der Moderne*. Frankfurt & New York: Campus (1st edition: *Essais sur l'individualisme. Une perspective anthropologique sur l'idéologie moderne*. Paris: Seuil).
Esterik, P. van. 1982. Interpreting a cosmology: Guardian spirits in Thai Buddhism. *Anthropos* 77 (1): 1–15.
Evans, G. 1998. *The Politics of Ritual and Remembrance: Laos since 1975*. Chiang Mai: Silkworm Press.
Fraisse, A. 1951. Les Villages du plateau de Bolovens. *Bulletin de la Societé des Études Indochinoises* 26: 52–72.
Goudineau, Y. 2008. L'anthropologie du Sud-Laos et l'origine de la question Kantou. In *Nouvelles recherches sur le Laos*, ed. Y. Goudineau and M. Lorrillard, 639–663. Paris & Vientiane: EFEO.
Harmand, F.J. 1997. *Laos and the Hilltribes of Indochina: Journeys to the Boloven Plateau, from Bassac to Hué through Laos, and to the Origins of the Thai*, trans.

W.J. Tips. Bangkok: White Lotus (1st edition: *Le Laos et les populations sauvages de l'Indochine*, 1878–1879).

High, H. 2014. *Fields of Desire: Poverty and Policy in Laos*. Singapore: National University of Singapore Press.

Holt, J. 2009. *Spirits of the Place: Buddhism and Lao Religious Culture*. Honolulu: University of Hawai'i Press.

Hours, B. 1973. *Rapports inter-ethniques dans le Sud-Laos: Changements sociaux et régression rituelle chez les Lavè*. Paris: École Pratique des Hautes Études, VIe section. http://tel.archives-ouvertes.fr/docs/00/12/65/91/PDF/Rapports_Inter_-Ethniques.pdf.

Jacq, P. 2001. *A description of Jruq (Loven) grammar: A Mon-Khmer language of the Lao PDR*. Canberra: MA-Thesis, ANU.

Jacq, P., and P. Sidwell. 1999. *Loven (Jruq) consolidated lexicon*. Munich: Lincom.

Kammerer, C.A. 1990. Customs and Christian conversion among Akha highlanders of Burma and Thailand. *American Ethnologist* 17(2): 277–291.

Kirsch, A.T. 1977. Complexity in the Thai religious system: An interpretation. *The Journal of Asian Studies* 36 (2): 241–266.

Ladwig, P. 2009. Prediger der Revolution: Der buddhistische Klerus und seine Verbindungen zur Kommunistischen Bewegung in Laos (1957–1975). *Jahrbuch für Historische Kommunismusforschung* 15: 181–197.

Ladwig, P. 2012a. Visitors from hell: Transformative hospitality to ghosts in a Lao Buddhist festival. *Journal of the Royal Anthropological Institute* 18: 90–102.

Ladwig, P. 2012b. Can things reach the dead? The ontological status of objects and the study of Lao Buddhist ghost festivals. In *Engaging the Spirit World in Modern Southeast Asia*, ed. K. Endres and A. Lauser, 19–41. Oxford & New York: Berghahn.

Lao Statistics Bureau. 2016. *Results of population and housing census 2016*. Vientiane: Lao Statistics Bureau.

Latour, B. 2008 [1991]. *Wir sind nie modern gewesen: Versuch einer symmetrischen Anthropologie*. Frankfurt am Main: Suhrkamp (1st edition: *Nous n'avons jamais été modernes*. Paris: La Découverte).

Lavallée, M.A. 1901. Notes ethnographiques sur diverses tribus du Sud-Est de l'Indochine. *Bulletin de l'École française d'Extrême-Orient* 1: 291–311.

Leach, E.R. 1968. Introduction. In *Dialectic in Practical Religion*, ed. E.R. Leach, 1–6. Cambridge: Cambridge University Press.

Luhmann, N. 1984. *Soziale Systeme: Grundriß einer allgemeinen Theorie*. Frankfurt am Main: Suhrkamp.

Ngaosyvathn, M. 1990. Individual soul, national identity: The *Baci-Sou Khouan* of the Lao. *Sojourn* 5 (2): 283–307.

Platenkamp, J.D.M. 2010. Political change and ritual tenacity: The New Year's ritual of Luang Prabang, Laos. In *La cohérence des sociétés: Mélanges en hommage à Daniel de Coppet*, ed. A. Iteanu, 193–233. Paris: Maison des Sciences de l'Homme.

Portilla, G.S. 2015. Land concessions and rural youth in Southern Laos. In *Land-grabbing, conflict and agrarian-environmental transformations: International Conference*, Chiang Mai, 5–6 June 2015, Conference Paper 9.

Rehbein, B. 2011. Monks and magic revisited. In *Southeast Asian Historiography—Unravelling the Myths: Essays in Honour of Barend Jan Terwiel*, ed. V. Grabowsky, 100–111. Bangkok: River Books.

Rehbein, B., and G. Sprenger. 2016. Religion and differentiation: Three Southeast Asian configurations. In *Configurations of Religion—A Debate. A DORISEA network discussion opened by Boike Rehbein and Guido Sprenger. DORISEA Working Paper series*, ed. P.J. Bräunlein, M. Dickhardt, and A. Lauser, 7–19, 24 (special issue).

Sallée, B., and J.-C. Tulet. 2010. Développement de la caféiculture paysanne et concessions de terres sur le plateau des Bolovens (Sud Laos): synergie ou antagonisme? *Les Cahiers d'Outre-Mer* 249: 93–120.

Schönweger, O., A. Heinimann, M. Epprecht, J. Lu, and P. Thalongsengchanh. 2012. *Concessions and leases in the Lao PDR: Taking stock of land investments*. Centre for Development and Environment (CDE), University of Bern. Bern & Vientiane: Geographica Bernensia.

Singh, S. 2014. Religious resurgence, authoritarianism, and 'ritual governance': Baci rituals, village meetings, and the developmental state in rural Laos. *The Journal of Asian Studies* 73 (4): 1059–1079.

Sparkes, S. 2005. *Spirits and Souls: Gender and Cosmology in an Isan Village in Northeast Thailand*. Bangkok: White Lotus.

Spiro, M. 1967. *Burmese Supernaturalism: A Study in the Explanation and Reduction of Suffering*. Englewood Cliff: Prentice Hall.

Sprenger, G. 2009. Invisible blood: Self-censorship and the public in uplander ritual, Laos. *Asian Journal of Social Science* 37 (6): 935–951.

Sprenger, G. 2017a. Communicated into being: Systems theory and the shifting of ontological status. *Anthropological Theory* 17 (1): 108–132. doi:10.1177/1463499617699330.

Sprenger, G. 2017b. Piglets are buffaloes: Buddhification and the reduction of sacrifice on the Boloven Plateau. In *Changing Lives in Laos: Society, Politics, and Culture in a Post-Socialist State*, ed. V. Pholsena and V. Bouté, 281–300. Singapore: National University of Singapore Press.

Steering Committee for Census of Population and Housing. 2006. *Results from the population and housing census 2005*. Vientiane: Government of Lao P.D.R.

Strathern, M. 1988. *The Gender of the Gift: Problems with Women and Problems with Society in Melanesia*. Berkeley: University of California Press.

Stuart-Fox, M. 1999. Laos: From Buddhist kingdom to Marxist state. In *Buddhism and Politics in Twentieth-Century Asia*, ed. I. Harris, 153–172. London: Continuum.
Tambiah, S. 1970. *Buddhism and the Spirit Cults in North-East Thailand*. Cambridge: Cambridge University Press.
Tannenbaum, N. 1987. Tattoos: Invulnerability and power in Shan cosmology. *American Ethnologist* 14 (4): 693–711.
Tappe, O. 2008. *Geschichte, Nationsbildung und Legitimationspolitik in Laos: Untersuchungen zur laotischen nationalen Historiographie und Ikonographie*. Münster & Berlin: Lit.
Terwiel, B.J. 2012. *Monks and Magic: Revisiting a classic study of religious ceremonies in Thailand*. Copenhagen: NIAS Press.
Tooker, D. 1992. Identity systems of highland Burma: 'Belief', Akha zang, and a critique of interiorized notions of ethno-religious identity. *Man N.S.* 27: 799–819.
Turton, A. 1972. Matrilineal descent groups and spirit cults of the Thai-Yuan in Northern Thailand. *Journal of the Siam Society* 60 (2): 217–256.
Vannasopha, M.K. 2005. *Religious Affairs in the Lao P.D.R.: Policies and Tasks*. Vientiane: National Front of Construction.
Wall, B. 1975. *Les NyaHön: Étude ethnographique d'une population du Plateau des Bolovens (Sud-Laos)*. Vientiane: Vithagna.
Waterson, R. 1995. Houses and hierarchies in island Southeast Asia. In *About the House: Lévi-Strauss and Beyond*, ed. J. Carsten and S. Hugh-Jones, 47–68. Cambridge: Cambridge University Press.
Zago, M. 1972. *Rites et Cérémonies en Milieu Bouddhique Lao*. Rome: Universitas Gregoriana.

AUTHOR BIOGRAPHY

Guido Sprenger is Professor of Social Anthropology at the Institute of Anthropology, University of Heidelberg, since 2010, after positions at the Academia Sinica, Taipei, and the University of Münster, Germany. He has done research on ritual, cosmology and transculturality in the uplands of Laos since 2000. Among his publications are *Die Männer, die den Geldbaum fällten (The Men who cut the Money Tree: Concepts of Exchange and Society among Rmeet of Takheung, Laos)* (2006), and *Animism in Southeast Asia* (co-edited with Kaj Århem, 2016). His research interests include exchange, kinship and social morphology, human-environment relations, animism, cultural identity, gender and sexuality.

CHAPTER 5

Balinese Religion in the Making: An Enquiry About the Interpretation of *Agama Hindu* as 'Hinduism'

Michel Picard

Bali is commonly depicted as an island of Hinduism in a sea of Islam. Such a pervasive cliché is misleading, inasmuch as it assumes that, unlike their Javanese neighbours, the Balinese people have just managed to preserve their Hindu heritage against the encroachment of Islam. Yet, the fact that the island of Bali had been exposed to Indic influences does not imply that the Balinese are Hindus. Indeed, facts are not sufficient to establish that a group is of a particular 'religion', in the sense that a religious identity is relationally constructed; it does not simply exist.

Over the last hundred years, Balinese have increasingly been subjected to the perspectives of powerful outsiders, with whom they had to engage—European Orientalists, colonial administrators, Christian missionaries, Muslim school teachers, Indian gurus, artists, anthropologists and tourists, not to forget Indonesian government officials. Under the intrusive gaze of these significant others, some Balinese—especially social elites, urban intelligentsia and religious leaders—were forced to reflect

---

M. Picard (✉)
Centre Asie du Sud-Est, CNRS-EHESS, Paris, France

on their past practices, which they then formulated as enactments of 'Hinduism', in addition to whatever local meaning they already had. This is not simply a case or 'religious modernization', as it involved constructing the separate existence of 'religion' as an objectified frame of reference for the interpretation of practices (Johnsen 2007). Thus, far from being a return to their Indian roots as claimed by its initiators, this process amounts to the outright invention of Balinese 'religion' as 'Hinduism'—or *agama Hindu* in official parlance.

My purpose in this chapter is not to assess whether the Balinese people are Hindus—neither whether they have been Hindus, nor even whether they are becoming Hindus—but to question the conceptual categories of '*agama*' and '*Hindu*', in order to investigate both how educated Balinese elites construed the project of Balinese religion as *agama Hindu* and what resulted from their endeavour.

AGAMA

In contemporary Indonesia, the category 'religion' has been appropriated by way of the word *agama*, which does not have any equivalent in Austronesian languages. Most Indonesianists appear to take for granted that *agama* is a straightforward translation of the word religion. And indeed, this is the meaning one finds in bilingual Indonesian dictionaries. However, this translation is not as straightforward as it might seem, because *agama* encompasses a much more restricted semantic field than does the common understanding of the word religion, for which Indonesians draw on the Dutch loanword *religi*. In fact, *agama* is the peculiar combination in Sanskrit guise of a Christian view of what counts as a 'world religion', with an Islamic understanding of what defines a 'proper religion'[1]—namely a prophet, a holy book and a belief in the one and only God. Accordingly, Indonesian religious politics can be labelled 'religionization' (*agamanisasi*), implying that followers of local traditions 'do not yet have religion' (*belum beragama*), and therefore are due to be

---

[1] Inasmuch as the Indonesian notion of *agama* is congruent with the Islamic acceptation of 'religion', it is commonly equated with the Arabic word *dīn* as used in the Quran. In this respect, it is important to note that, before being glossed as 'religion', the word *dīn*—which signifies 'practice, custom, law'—referred to 'the body of obligatory prescriptions to which one must submit', according to the *Encyclopaedia of Islam*.

'*agama*nized'—meaning that they could, and should, be a target of proselytizing. For Indonesian authorities, to 'have a religion' is to be civilized and, therefore, it is an attribute of good citizenship. On that account, *agama* is the object of competing claims between, on the one hand, proponents of indigenous cosmological frameworks and customary ritual practices, who consider them as both self-sufficient and deserving of the label *agama* in their own right, and, on the other, advocates of a world religion of foreign origin, who deny those local traditions the qualification of *agama*.

Agama has not always meant 'religion' in Indonesia. In order to assess how this word came to acquire such a meaning, it is necessary to examine its significance in Sanskrit. Etymologically derived from the verb root /*gam*/, meaning 'to go', and the preposition /*ā-*/, meaning 'towards', the word *āgama* signifies 'that which has come down to the present', and it refers to 'anything handed down as fixed by tradition', according to Indologist Jan Gonda in his study of *Sanskrit in Indonesia*.[2] As such, *āgama* is one of the sources of knowledge—the *pramāṇa*—which vary according to the different 'points of view' (*darśana*) that comprise Hindu philosophy. *Āgama-pramāṇa* refers to authoritative scripture as a means of valid cognition and is usually considered equivalent to *śabda-pramāṇa* (revealed knowledge). Additionally, *āgama* is the name of a genre of non-Vedic scriptures regarded as revelation by specific Hindu sects, which became prominent during the early mediaeval period. This genre includes the Shaiva *āgama*, the Vaishnava *samhitā* and the Shakta *tantra* centred on the cult of the Goddess. More specifically,

---

[2] This is how Gonda accounts for the appropriation of *agama* in the Archipelago: 'In Sanskrit *āgama*, apart from other use, designates "a traditional precept, doctrine, body of precepts, collection of such doctrines"; in short, "anything handed down as fixed by tradition"; it is, moreover, the name of a class of works inculcating the so-called tantric worship of Śiva and Śakti. In Old Javanese it could apply to a body of customary law or a Dharma-book, and to religious or moral traditions, and the words *sang hyang* "the divine, holy" often preceding it emphasize its superhuman character. The term is, moreover, used to signify the religious knowledge of a brahman [...], and also that of a high Buddhist functionary. Islam, in the spread of which many compatriots of Shivaists and Buddhists who had led the way into the Archipelago took an important part, adopted the term, and so did, in the course of time, Christianity. Nowadays *agama* [...] is in Javanese, Malay etc. "religion"' (Gonda 1973: 499–500).

the term *āgama* applies in particular to the canonical texts of the Śaiva-Siddhānta order.[3]

Surprisingly, few Indonesianists appear to have wondered how this Sanskrit loanword, laden with Indic references, could have come to designate an Islamic conception of what 'religion' is about. One notable exception is Jane Atkinson, who attempted to trace the historical development of the term *agama* into what she called the 'Indonesian civil religion' (Atkinson 1987: 174–178). However, she did not specify why it was precisely the word *agama* that came to stand for religion in Indonesia. Judith Becker attributed this to the paramount importance of the Shaivite agamic texts in Java and Bali (Becker 2004: 16).[4] Yet, this leaves many questions unanswered, since in Śaiva-Siddhānta *āgama* does not signify religion, a notion that was actually unknown to the Indian world before the nineteenth century.

Although we do not know when the word *agama* came to mean 'religion' in Indonesia, we know that in Javanese and Balinese literary traditions the generic title *Agama* is 'used to refer to a range of texts dealing with moral, religious and legal sanctions and practices' (Creese 2009a: 242, n. 2; see also Hoadley and Hooker 1981, 1986). These texts were mainly drawn from the Sanskrit *Mānava Dharmaśāstra*, or *Manu-Smṛti*—the 'Laws of Manu'—the oldest and most prominent of the *Dharmaśāstra*[5] (Rocher 2003). According to textual and epigraphic evidence, from as early as the twelfth century, law codes in use in the Indic courts of Java and Bali were modelled on Sanskrit legal thought, thoroughly adapted and contextualized to suit indigenous needs.

In her study of Old Javanese legal traditions in pre-colonial Bali, Helen Creese informs us that the titles of some of the main legal texts—namely the *Agama*, *Adhigama* and *Dewāgama*—were also generic

---

[3] Śaiva-Siddhānta, 'the final truth of Shiva', is the most important of all the Shaiva schools, predominantly in Tamil Nadu. The primary sources of Śaiva-Siddhānta are the 28 *Śaivāgama*, a body of Sanskrit texts that are treated as authoritative because they claim to have been revealed by Shiva to his *śakti* Parvati. They usually consist of four parts: theology (*jñāna*), concentration (*yoga*), ritual (*kriya*) and rules (*carya*). On Śaiva-Siddhānta and the *Śaivāgama*, see Davis (1991).

[4] This is also the conclusion reached by Hooykaas (1966), Brunner (1967: 416) and Staal (1995: 45), who investigated the connections between the Shaiva *āgama* and Balinese ritual.

[5] The *Dharmaśāstra* are ancient Sanskrit treatises on the subject of *dharma*. See the introduction to this volume for the meaning and scope of *dharma*.

terms for particular kinds of judicial knowledge and practice that were hierarchically ordered: '[...] *agama* refers to texts and social practices in which the teachings of Manu are invoked, that is the written texts; *adhigama* reflects the legal jurisdiction of the ruler in cases brought before the council of priests and the application of the *agama*; while *dewāgama* refers to the administration of sacred oaths as an integral part of the judicial process, but one which drew its authority not from human princes or priests but from the gods (*dewa*) themselves' (Creese 2009a: 283). Furthermore, *agama* texts overlap with didactic texts—the *sasana*—which also draw on *Dharmaśāstra* and *Nītiśāstra*[6] traditions, that prescribe appropriate behaviour for particular social groups, especially for members of the nobility (ibid.: 249).

This is also how the Bengali historian Himansu Bhusan Sarkar interpreted the word *agama* in his study of *Indian Influences on the Literature of Java and Bali*, published by the Greater India Society (Sarkar 1934). His chapter on 'The Āgama or Dharmaśāstras of Indonesia' is divided into two sections: (1) the *Nīti* literature, which expounds moral precepts and maxims—e.g. the *Sārasamuccaya*, the *Kuñjarakarna* and the *Navaruci*; and (2) the legal literature, or jurisprudence—e.g. the *Śivaśāsana* or *Pūrvādhigama*, the *Āgama* or *Kutāramānava* and the *Ādigama*. He deemed it significant that the Sanskrit term *āgama*, which refers to a *śāstra* handed down by the gods, has been retained in the Javanese and Balinese law codes, which are predicated on a divinely ordained set of rules drawing their legitimacy from Shiva's supreme authority. Sarkar's interpretation is substantiated by Lévi (1933: XI), who explains that in Bali the *Āgama* comprises the *Dharmaśāstra*, the *Śāsana* and the *Nīti* literature, that is, legal and political texts corresponding to the Indian *Dharmaśāstra* and *Nītiśāstra*.

If *agama* is thus equated with *dharma* in Old Javanese and Balinese legal texts from the twelfth century onward, we know moreover that in Malay chronicles dating back to the fourteenth century the term *agama* is systematically associated with Islam and used in a sense equivalent to that of *dīn*. Therefore, one has to conclude that for centuries the word *agama* had two distinct denotations in the Archipelago, that of *dharma* as well as that of *dīn*, according to the context and language

---

[6] *Nītiśāstra* refers to a class of didactic texts on political ethics.

of its occurrence.[7] By appropriating the word *agama*, Indonesian Muslims endowed it with new meaning, namely the exclusive worship of one supreme God and the requirement of conversion to a foreign doctrine whose teachings are contained in a Holy Book propounded by an inspired Prophet. Later on, through its adoption by Christian missionaries, *agama* became associated with an ideal of social progress, while 'pagan' beliefs were scorned as bygone superstitions and viewed as a cause for shame.

As *agama* came to mean 'religion'—in a process similar to that which occurred with the concept of *dharma* in India[8]—the term was not only dissociated from 'law' but also from 'tradition', which was previously one of its senses in Sanskrit. In contemporary Indonesia, this notion is rendered by the Arabic loanword *adat*, commonly translated by 'custom'. But this translation does not do justice to the importance of *adat* for traditional Indonesian societies, which Hans Schärer aptly conveyed regarding the Ngaju in Borneo: '[*Adat*] certainly means more than simply usage, custom, habit [...] the notion has a double meaning. Firstly, that of divine cosmic order and harmony, and secondly, that of life and actions in agreement with this order' (Schärer 1963: 74). Like *dharma*, *adat* refers thus to the cosmic order and to social life abiding by that order—at once describing the ideal order and prescribing the behaviour required to achieve that order.

This comprehensive scope of *adat* was fragmented through a series of reductions: first by Islamic proselytizers—followed suit by Christian missionaries—who strove to curtail the religious import of *adat* by confining its significance to the habits and customs of a people (*adat kebiasaan*).[9] By thus qualifying as *adat* those customs that do not have an explicit religious legitimation, they could be neutralized: no longer

---

[7] This is not unlike what happened in nineteenth-century colonial India where, once the word *dharma* had acquired the sense of 'religion', there was a convergence between *dharma* and *dīn* as two distinct embodiments of that same category (Pernau 2011: 37).

[8] See the introduction to this volume for an outline of the process through which the concept of *dharma* became fragmented in colonial India.

[9] Here again, one notices a certain similarity with the situation prevailing in nineteenth-century India, where Hindu reformers disparaged *ācāra*, the customary rules of conduct governing the correct performance of social and ritual duties constitutive of the *varṇāśramadharma*, that are thus endorsed by the *Dharmaśāstra* but which they claimed was not part of true Hinduism. On this question, see the introduction to this volume.

considered as challenges to *agama*, they were reduced to superstition and old-fashioned ways. In particular, the word *adat* entered the language of Islamized populations in the Indonesian Archipelago to refer to indigenous 'customary law' as opposed to Islamic 'religious law' (*hukum*). Subsequently, Dutch jurists codified the indigenous customary law (*adatrecht*, that is, '*adat* with legal consequences', translated as *hukum adat* in Malay) of the various peoples on whom they had imposed their colonial empire (Van Vollenhoven 1928; Korn 1932). By thus attributing to each ethnic group its own *adatrecht*, the Dutch colonial policy widened the divide between *adat* and Islam.

Such a dissociation between *agama* and *adat* entailed certain consequences that are worth considering. Whereas in *adat* practices are followed inasmuch as they have been handed down from generation to generation, in *agama* they are held to be motivated on the basis of prior belief. And while different *agama* make exclusive claims about being the truth, attributing the predicates 'true' and 'false' to *adat* would be a category mistake. Lastly, *adat* as a fixed set of practices inherited from one's ancestors is tied to a particular ethnic group, contrary to *agama*, which explicitly aims at transcending ethnic and national boundaries.

This is, in short, how *agama*, *hukum* and *adat* have come to mutually define each other in Indonesia, each category being continually redefined through the process of their interaction. Whereas in the past the semantic field of the word *agama* encompassed that which Indonesians characterize, respectively, as *hukum* and *adat*, today 'religion' is dissociated from both 'law' and 'tradition', particularly in Islamized and Christianized societies (Abdullah 1966; Benda-Beckmann 1988). The emergence of the category *agama* in the sense of 'religion' thus amounts to its differentiation from the categories *hukum* and *adat*. This is to say that, instead of assuming the autonomy of these concepts, it is only by addressing their interrelationships that their respective semantic fields can be appropriately circumscribed and analysed.

However, in contrast to Islamized or Christianized areas of Indonesia, in Bali the word *agama* has retained its original polysemy, as attested by Balinese–Indonesian dictionaries, which translate *agama* as (1) *agama*, (2) *hukum* and (3) *adat*.[10]

---

[10] On the other hand, the Balinese religious scholar Sri Reshi Anandakusuma translated *agama* as *dharma* in his Indonesian–Balinese dictionary (Anandakusuma 1986: 234).

AGAMA HINDU

Admittedly, we do not know when Balinese started using the word *agama* in the sense of 'religion'—nor when they actually chose to label their own *agama* as *Hindu*. But we do know that long before they began defining themselves as Hindus, the Balinese had already been 'Hinduized' by Orientalists, at a time when they had yet to learn the word 'Hindu' (Guermonprez 2001: 272). As it happens, before Dutch colonial administrators began to engage with Balinese society, it had been imagined by Orientalists as a 'living museum' of Indo-Javanese civilization, the one and only surviving heir to the Hindu heritage swept away from Java by the coming of Islam. In their view, Hinduism had been brought to Bali in the fourteenth century by Javanese conquerors from the kingdom of Majapahit, who had also imposed the division of society into four 'castes', in accordance with the Indian model of the *varna*. When Majapahit fell to Islam at the turn of the sixteenth century, the Javanese nobility who refused to embrace the new faith were said to have found refuge at the courts of their coreligionists on Bali, where they nurtured the Indo-Javanese civilization in splendid isolation.[11]

The first Orientalists to visit Bali were agents of the British East India Company sent out from Calcutta in 1811 to prevent Java from falling into the hands of the French, who occupied the Netherlands. There they transferred the assumptions they had formed in India regarding 'Hinduism'. Thus, in his report titled *On the existence of the Hindu religion in the island of Bali*, which recorded his brief stay on the island in 1814, British administrator-cum-Orientalist John Crawfurd took it for granted that the Balinese were Hindus and, moreover, he used the word *agama* in the sense of religion: 'When interrogated respecting their religion, the natives of Bali say that they are of the religion of Siva (*agama Siva*) or of the religion of Buddha (*agama Buddha*)' (Crawfurd 1820: 129). He specified further that *agama Siva* was the 'national religion of Bali'. Crawfurd obtained his information from *brahmana* priests (*pedanda*),[12]

---

[11] For an informed assessment of such a prevalent assumption, which dates back to the eighteenth century, see Hinzler (1986), Schulte Nordholt (1986: 11–14), Creese (2000).

[12] *Pedanda* are the literate and initiated high priests, originating from Majapahit, whose position is the exclusive prerogative of the *brahmana*. Their role was initially similar to that of court Indian and Javanese Brahmans (*purohita*). Today their main function is to prepare the holy water (*tirtha*) that plays a major role in Balinese rites. There exist two categories

who provided him with manuscripts in *kawi*[13]—'the language of learning, of religion, and of the law' (ibid.: 144). Most of these manuscripts bore the word *agama* in their title—'a generic term in Sanskrit for any composition treating of those sciences which are considered by the Hindus as sacred' (ibid.: 147).

In 1817, Sir Thomas Stamford Raffles, Lieutenant-Governor of British Java (1811–1815), published his monumental *History of Java*, in which an appendix presented an account of Bali, depicting the island as the last living vestige of the lost Hindu civilization of Java: 'On Java we find Hinduism only amid the ruins of temples, images, and inscriptions; on Bali, in the laws, ideas, and worship of the people. On Java this singular and interesting system of religion is classed among the antiquities of the island. Here it is a living source of action, and a universal rule of conduct' (Raffles 1817, vol. 2: ccxxxv–ccxxxvi; see Aljunied 2004).

The Dutch pursued these Orientalist conjectures after they had regained possession of their territories in the East Indies. In 1846, as they were about to launch their first military expedition against the northern Balinese kingdom of Buleleng, Wolter Robert Baron van Hoëvell, the president of the Royal Batavian Society of Arts and Sciences (Koninklijk Bataviaasch Genootschap van Kunsten en Wetenschappen), sent the German Sanskritist Rudolf Friederich to collect manuscripts and document Bali's Hindu religion and culture (Van Hoëvell 1848).[14] After a 2-year stay on the island, Friederich wrote an extensive report, which is the first erudite study on Bali (Friederich 1849–1850). Like Crawfurd before him, he confirmed that Hinduism and Buddhism coexisted in Bali, even if most Balinese were Shaivite and Buddhism was vestigial. Regarding manuscripts bearing the title *Agama*, he stated: 'In the

---

Footnote 12 (continued)

of *pedanda*, the *pedanda Siwa* and the *pedanda Buda*, whose differences reside mostly in ritual paraphernalia and divinities invoked in their *mantra*—and who are, in any case, both considered '*Hindu*' at present. According to the nature of the rites over which they officiate, they can be either interchangeable or complementary.

[13] Literally, the 'language of poets', that is, the language of religion and scholarship in Bali, which encompasses a variety of interrelated language registers, including Old Javanese, Middle Javanese and various forms of literary Balinese.

[14] '[...] it is necessary that all Kawi and other manuscripts which can be heard of should be collected, because these are of the utmost importance for the illustration of the social and religious condition not alone of Bali itself, but also of the still more important ancient Java' (Van Hoëvell 1848: 154).

Malayan and common Balinese language *agama* signifies religion; in the names *Agama*, *Adigama*, *Devāgama*, it has evidently more the old Indian meaning, and especially that of law-book' (Friederich 1959: 30, n. 21).

It is noteworthy that these early Orientalists held divergent opinions as to how far the religion actually practised on the island adhered to its Indic model. Thus, Crawfurd and Raffles considered that, unlike that of the *brahmana* priests, the worship of the people was mere superstition, which could not be called Hindu. This was disputed by Friederich, who deemed that the popular religion was itself also truly Hindu. Be that as it may, Crawfurd's and Friederich's accounts still beg the question whether the word *agama* did actually mean 'religion' for Balinese in the nineteenth century, as this would have required that they had already been secularized, so as to be able to discriminate clearly between the respective senses of *agama* as 'religion', 'law' and 'tradition'. I think this is unlikely, as *agama* still retained the meaning of *dharma* in Bali during the Dutch colonial period.

Thus, the *Agama* texts continued to be used for the administration of justice in the Balinese courts of law, which were presided over by a council of *brahmana* priests called the *kerta*. When the Dutch established their authority on the northern part of the island in 1882, they took over the Balinese legal system and adapted it to their colonial needs by setting up courts of law which they renamed Raad Kerta (Korn 1932: 42; Robinson 1995: 33; Creese 2009b: 525). Then, after they had imposed their colonial rule over the entire island, in 1908, Dutch government officials had the main *Agama* law codes edited and translated, first into Balinese (1909) and later into Malay (1918), as they deemed that the *pedanda* sitting at the Raad Kerta were unable to adequately understand these *kawi* texts. By thus homogenizing and fixing the *Agama* codes in printed editions, the very essence of Balinese judicial practice, based on exegetical textual traditions open to flexible interpretation, was fatally undermined (Creese 2009b: 545).

Further evidence that *agama* still had the common denotation of *dharma* in Bali during the late colonial period is provided by the Kirtya Liefrinck-Van der Tuuk, the library the Dutch administration had set up in 1928 to preserve traditional manuscripts. In the library catalogue established by Balinese scholars, the entry *agama* refers not to 'religion' but to *Dharmasastra*, *Nitisastra* (ethical and didactic precepts) and *Sasana* (rules of life). There is no entry corresponding to the category 'religion',[15] whose semantic field is divided up between two headings: one—termed *Weda*—which included *Stuti* and *Stawa* (songs of praise), *Mantra* and *Kalpasastra* (rituals); and the other—called *Wariga*—composed of *Wariga* proper (astrology), *Tutur* (cosmology, mysticism), *Kanda* (technical manuals of grammar, metrics, mythology and sorcery) and *Usada* (medicine) (Kadjeng 1929).[16]

The Kirtya library was an essential feature of the Dutch colonial policy, inspired by the Orientalist vision of Bali as the depositary of the great Indo-Javanese civilization of Majapahit. Such a vision was informed by several assumptions: first that the present situation of Bali reflected that of Java prior to its Islamization, second that the Balinese religion was located in texts of Indian provenance on which the indigenous social and judicial order had been modelled, and third that the *brahmana* priests were the depositaries of these sacred texts and the custodians of the Balinese religion. The task set for Orientalists was then to compare Balinese texts to their Indic models and to remove indigenous 'corruptions' in order to recover their 'authentic source'.

In any case, Orientalists held Hinduism to be the core of Balinese society and the warrant of its cultural identity. As such, it had to be protected through the enlightened paternalism of colonial tutelage from both the intrusion of Islam, which had strengthened its grip on the better part of the Indonesian Archipelago, and from Christian missionaries, eager to set foot on the island (Korn 1925; Goris 1933). This conservative colonial policy was to have long-lasting consequences. For one thing, by looking for the singularity of Bali in its Hindu heritage, while conceiving of Balinese identity as formed through an opposition to Islam and Christianity, the Dutch established the frame of reference within which the Balinese would define themselves. Furthermore, by attempting to preserve Bali's singularity from the rest of the Indies, they ended up emphasizing it far more than they had ever envisioned, all the while turning it into a challenge for the Balinese.

---

[15] There is no entry for *adat* either nor for *hukum*.

[16] On the other hand, in *Bhāwanāgara*, the journal published by the Kirtya from 1931 to 1935, we find both meanings of the term *agama*, the legal one as well as the religious one; the latter is glossed as *Kesewasogatan*, from *Sewa*, Siwa's devotees and *Sogata*, Buddha's disciples, in reference to the two categories of *brahmana* priests, the *pedanda Siwa* and the *pedanda Buda*.

AGAMA HINDU BALI VERSUS *AGAMA BALI HINDU*

Despite the Dutch attempt to insulate Balinese society from disturbing foreign influences, Bali actually underwent rapid and profound changes as a result of the colonial encounter. In particular, the requirements of a modern administration were instrumental in the emergence of a Balinese intelligentsia, since the colonial state needed educated natives to mediate between the local population and their European masters. These Dutch-educated Balinese strove to make sense of the situation brought about by the opening up of their world to the advent of 'modern times' (*zaman modern*).

Not only did the emerging Balinese intelligentsia have to face the disruption of the familiar references which ordered and gave meaning to their lives, they were confronted with foreign discourses telling them who they were and how they should conduct themselves. As the upheaval inflicted by the colonial occupation of their island compelled the Balinese to reassess the foundations of their identity, the inquisitive gaze of foreigners in their midst demanded that they explicitly define what it meant to be Balinese in terms comprehensible to non-Balinese.

In the 1920s, the first generation of Balinese educated in colonial schools founded modern organizations and started publishing periodicals, a novelty in Bali. These publications, devoted chiefly to socio-religious issues, were written in Malay, the lingua franca of trade and Islam in the Archipelago, which was adopted by the Dutch as the language of education and administration, and would soon become the language of Indonesian nationalism. The use of Malay, rather than Balinese, to address thoroughly Balinese topics destined to an exclusively Balinese readership, indicates that the intelligentsia were conscious of being an integral part of a larger entity, as a result of the incorporation of their island into the colonial state. Thus, the same process which prompted the Balinese to question their identity dispossessed them of their own words, by inducing them to think about themselves in a language that was not their own, but the language used by their fellow countrymen and by their colonial masters. Such a linguistic substitution marked a reflexive distancing from the Balinese universe of reference, which was decontextualized, relativized and homogenized in the process.

In these publications, for the first time, the Balinese began to view themselves as a singular entity—as a 'people' (*bangsa*).[17] Formerly, their identities were particularistic: Balinese identified themselves as members of a village, a kinship group or a temple network, rather than as 'Balinese'. Their collective identity, based on an awareness of shared characteristics and adherence to unifying symbols, took shape during the colonial period, when they attempted to define themselves as different from both the foreign colonizers and the other peoples in the Indies (Howe 2001).

As a specific people, the Balinese defined themselves as a religious minority threatened by the aggressive expansionism of Islam and Christianity, as well as a particular ethnic group characterized by their own customs. More precisely, they construed their identity—which they called their 'Balineseness' (*Kebalian*)—as being based on *agama* and on *adat*. The very fact that Balinese resorted to these terms to define their identity is a testament to the conceptual shift occurring on the island after its takeover by a foreign power.

Introduced to Bali by the Dutch, the word *adat* replaced diverse terms for locally variable customs that governed the relationships between social groups and sanctioned the sense of communal solidarity in the villages (Warren 1993). The advent of this word in Bali entailed a twofold consequence. First, it created a new conceptual category, that of 'tradition', which initially was not contrasted with the category of 'religion' but with 'administration' (*dinas*, from the Dutch *dienst* meaning 'service'), referring to that which came under the authority of the colonial state. Second, the incorporation of a miscellaneous assortment of local customs into this generic term altered their meaning for the Balinese. That which had been, hitherto, an interplay of significant differences deliberately fostered between villages, became the locus of Balinese ethnic identity, in the sense of a customary body of inherited values, norms and institutions governing the lives of the Balinese people.

It is no coincidence that it was also in these publications in Malay that Balinese started using the word *agama* to mean 'religion', as they set out to portray their own religion as being on par with Islam and Christianity, in an attempt to resist proselytism. For the Balinese, Islam and Christianity were seen not only as a threat, but also as a model of

---

[17] The Malay word *bangsa*, derived from the Sanskrit *vaṃśa* meaning 'lineage', conveys the idea of a people sharing a common ethnic origin and similar customs.

what a true religion should be. Confronted with Muslim schoolteachers and Christian missionaries, they were challenged to formulate what exactly their religion was about. This proved to be a highly contentious issue, which triggered a protracted conflict between the Balinese intending to retain their local traditions and those who strove to reform them in accordance with what they assumed Hinduism—as a 'world religion'—was about. This conflict set the rising elite of educated commoners (*jaba*) against the conservative nobility (*triwangsa*)[18]—with the periodicals *Surya Kanta* (1925–1927) and *Bali Adnjana* (1924–1930) as their respective mouthpieces—in their attempts to hold sway over the religious life of the Balinese people (Picard 2004).

If both commoners and nobility shared a common reference to *agama* and *adat* as the foundations of *Kebalian*, their opinions diverged concerning their respective domains. While the *triwangsa* were determined to reinforce both tradition and religion, the *jaba* wanted to reform *agama* while ridding *adat* of all the customs they deemed obsolete. Thus, for the former, Balinese religion was based on the customary social order, within which *agama* was inseparable from *adat*. Whereas for the latter, religion could and should be dissociated from a traditional order seen not only as unfair but also as a hindrance to progress. Yet, they proved unable to differentiate between that which belongs to *agama* and that which pertains to *adat*.

This should come as no surprise given that, despite the presence of Sanskrit words and ritual elements of Indic origin, Balinese religious life is highly localized, consisting of rites that connect specific groups of people to one another, their ancestors and their territory. Participation in these rites is a customary obligation for the Balinese, which sanctions membership in a village, a kinship group and a temple network. Accordingly, the Balinese are far more concerned with appropriate behaviour (orthopraxy) than with right beliefs (orthodoxy). Rather than something to be believed in, Balinese 'religion' is something to be carried out. Such evidence led Indologist Frits Staal to conclude that 'Balinese ritual is a classic case of ritual without religion' (Staal 1995: 31).

---

[18]The Balinese nobility is composed of the *triwangsa* (literally, the 'three peoples': *brahmana*, *satria* and *wesia*), as opposed to the *jaba* (literally the 'outsiders', that is, those who are outside the sphere of the courts), who make up the bulk of the population. According to their myth of origin, the *triwangsa* claim to be the descendants of the Javanese conquerors from the kingdom of Majapahit who subjugated the island of Bali in the fourteenth century.

Hence, *agama* could not become a boundary marker for the Balinese people until they began to view Islam and Christianity as a threat (Vickers 1987; Couteau 1999; Hauser-Schäublin 2004). Up to that point, the Balinese had yet to single out and distinguish a system of beliefs and practices that could be demarcated from other aspects of their life and labelled 'religion'.[19] In this respect, we should pay attention to the controversy that has divided the Balinese intelligentsia over the proper name of their religion, because it reveals serious contention regarding the main points in debate, that is, how is *agama* related to *adat* on the one hand, and how is Balinese religion connected to Indian Hinduism on the other.

In the past, the Balinese had no generic name to designate that which would later become their 'religion'. Once they adopted the word *agama* for that purpose, they referred to their religion simply as *agama Bali*. Afterwards, Balinese started using a variety of names for their religion, such as *Tirtha, Siwa, Buda, Siwa-Buda, Trimurti, Bali Hindu, Hindu Bali* and *Hindu*.[20]

In 1925, a dispute erupted between commoners and the nobility over the name of the Balinese religion. The *triwangsa* proposed to call their religion *agama Hindu Bali*, stressing the fact that the Balinese people had appropriated and reinterpreted *agama Hindu* to such an extent that it had become indigenous to their island. In this way, they were clearly trying to preserve the established socio-religious order of yore, by endorsing the religion actually practised by the Balinese, whereas, in defending the name *agama Bali Hindu*, the *jaba* claimed

---

[19] Margaret Wiener substantiates this assertion in a most convincing manner: 'Balinese praxis and discourse blur the lines between sacred and secular, for almost everything Balinese do involves seeking the aid of auspicious forces or asking for protection against inauspicious ones. In precolonial Bali there was no clear demarcated domain of action that could be termed "religion", since all power was understood to derive from relationships to invisible forces' (Wiener 1995: 73–74).

[20] *Agama Tirtha* refers to the holy water required for most religious rites. *Agama Siwa* and *agama Buda* pertain to the two categories of initiated *brahmana* priests—the *pedanda Siwa* and the *pedanda Buda*—while *agama Siwa-Buda* points more specifically to the Tantric fusion of Shaivism and Buddhism that originated in East Java in the thirteenth century. The name *agama Trimurti* designates the Hindu triad Brahma, Wisnu and Iswara. Finally, one finds *agama Bali Hindu*, *agama Hindu Bali* and *agama Hindu*. In this respect, one should be aware that it is only through the work of Dutch Orientalists that educated Balinese elites became acquainted with the word '*Hindu*' in the early twentieth century.

that the Balinese were truly Hindus, even if their religious practices were corrupt, owing to their ignorance of the true nature of their religion. Consequently, in order to become the true Hindus they were supposed to be, the Balinese should discard all indigenous accretions that contaminated their religious practices. Hence, the *triwangsa* accused the *jaba* of attempting to promote a form of Hinduism similar to that found in India. This, they claimed, amounted to inventing a new religion, which was alien to the Balinese, because their religion originated not in India but in Majapahit. It was therefore the duty of the Balinese to remain faithful to the religion their ancestors had brought to Bali at the peril of losing their lives, when they were fleeing the propagation of Islam in Java after the fall of Majapahit.

While in the 1920s the context of religious debates had remained essentially Balinese, during the 1930s it was becoming increasingly Indonesian. The questions regarding the Balinese religion were re-emerging, more pressing than ever, in a new periodical, *Djatajoe* (1936–1941). By then the Balinese were clearly on the defensive, as the controversy was due no longer solely to disagreement among themselves, but to the fact that they were at a loss as to how to reply to accusations of paganism by foreigners—not only Indonesian Muslims but also Dutch administrators.[21] This was particularly the case of young Balinese studying outside Bali, who felt embarrassed whenever they were asked about their religion and who, for some of them, converted to Islam or Christianity, for fear of being branded as 'idolatrous' or 'animists' by their schoolmates. The problem was that most Balinese did not know their religion, and thus, reformers urged their fellow coreligionists to investigate the meaning of their religion so as to be able to refute the charges held against it by foreigners (Picard 2004).

---

[21] The following quotation neatly epitomizes the Balinese defensiveness: 'Before the boys and girls of Bali started going to school, and before there were any newspapers on the island, the Balinese were already practicing this religion (*agama*), and there was no one who criticized and blamed them; what we heard were only comments like "the custom (*adat*) in this village is like this, whereas in that village it is like that" [...] Furthermore, one did not speak of religious ceremonies (*upacara agama*), but rather of village customs (*adat desa*). Thus, in short, a proper religion (*agama yang sebenarnya*) was something unknown; what we knew about were only village customs (*adat desa*) and Balinese religion (*agama Bali*), and one did not hear of people who felt ashamed or angry because they had been criticized by Mister... so and so' (Goebah 1937: 131).

Although the first generation of Balinese intellectuals fell short of coming to an agreement on the question of how *agama Bali* was related to *adat* on the one hand, and to *agama Hindu* on the other, their debates had nonetheless prepared the Balinese to confront the pressures imposed upon their religious identity once their island had become part of the Republic of Indonesia. Contrary to what has been asserted by some foreign analysts, in my opinion, what happened during the colonial period is not simply that the former unity of *agama* and *adat* had started to disintegrate due to the colonial confrontation, as these categories were alien and had to be appropriated by the Balinese for their own purpose. It is not even that the Balinese had taken refuge in their religion, after having been threatened by Muslim and Christian proselytism. Rather, it was the conjunction of two distinct processes of differentiation which ended up in the formation of the categories of *agama* and *adat*—on the one hand, the Dutch-enforced separation between religious tradition and colonial administration, and on the other, the growing urge to dissociate religion from tradition on the part of reform-minded educated Balinese.

This conceptual separation of *agama* and *adat* had in fact actually started when Balinese reformers were attempting to find a name for their religion, thereby initiating a process of objectification of religion as a separate field of beliefs and practices. Yet, if the Dutch had de-politicized *adat* by dissociating political power from customary authority, religion remained merged with tradition in the colonial period. Once they had become Indonesian citizens, the Balinese would be compelled to distinguish explicitly between religion and tradition. In order for their rites to accede to the status of *agama*, they had to be detached from what was considered as belonging to the domain of *adat*.

After Indonesia's proclamation of independence, in 1945, the question of the foundation of the new state came rapidly to a head, pitting the 'Islamic group' (*golongan Islam*) against the 'nationalist group' (*golongan kebangsaan*). The former, confident that they represented an overwhelming majority of the Indonesian people, wanted to establish an Islamic state, whereas their opponents, concerned that such a decision would alienate Christians and other religious minorities, argued in favour of a state in which religious and secular affairs would be kept separate. This confrontation resulted in a compromise: the Indonesian state placed 'Belief in the One and Only God' (*Ke-Tuhanan Yang Maha Esa*) first among its founding principles (*Pancasila*), without making Islam an official or even privileged religion. As a concession to the Islamic group, however, a Ministry of Religion (Kementerian Agama) was set up in 1946. Initially designed to promote Muslim interests, it was soon expanded to include separate sections for Protestantism and Roman Catholicism, thereby acknowledging Christianity as a legitimate 'religion of the Book'.

Whereas the 1945 Constitution guaranteed Indonesian citizens the freedom to profess and practise their own religion, the Ministry of Religion endeavoured to restrict the legal acceptance of acknowledged religions in conformity with the Islamic view of what qualifies as a legitimate *agama*—that is, an understanding of religion as exclusivist, congregational, scripturalist and universalist. So much so that, even if Islam failed to establish itself as the official religion of Indonesia, its proponents succeeded in imposing their own conception of the relations between religion and the state, by framing and shaping all the debates about religion. Thus, in 1952, the Ministry of Religion stipulated the following conditions for a religion to be recognized: it must be revealed by God, possess a prophet and a holy book, have a codified system of law for its followers, enjoy international recognition and, further, its congregation should not be limited to a single ethnic group.

According to these conditions, the Balinese did not have a proper 'religion' (*agama*) but possessed only 'beliefs' (*kepercayaan*), which not only were limited to their island, but furthermore failed to form a coherent and unified ensemble valid for the island as a whole. In this sense, Balinese religion was considered to belong to the domain of *adat* and not to that of *agama*. As a result, like other ethnic minorities who still practised their traditional religion, the Balinese were classified as 'people who do not yet have a religion' (*orang yang belum beragama*), a label associated with primitive backwardness and parochialism. Consequently, if the Balinese people did not want to become the target of Muslim or Christian proselytizing, their only recourse was to rationalize their religion and redefine it in transcendent and monotheistic terms, in order to make it eligible for the status of *agama*.

From *Agama Hindu Bali* to *Agama Hindu*

The first question to be settled was for the Balinese to agree on the name of their religion. After lengthy debates, they resolved in 1952 to call it *agama Hindu Bali*—the name championed by the *triwangsa* in the

1920s.²² It appears that it is only after Balinese had started to convert to Islam or Christianity that the name *agama Hindu Bali* became customary, in order to differentiate *Hindu Bali* from *Islam Bali* or *Kristen Bali*. However, even if the Balinese had finally reached an agreement among themselves, they still had to convince the Ministry of Religion of the legitimacy of the *agama Hindu Bali*. Consequently, during the following years, they continued pressing the ministry to recognize their religion. While some religious leaders were looking for the seeds of regeneration in their own indigenous traditions, young Balinese who were studying in India urged their coreligionists to return to the fold of Hinduism, which they presented as the source of their rites. Stressing the theological import and the ethical implications of religion, they attempted to restrain the Balinese ritualistic leanings, while construing their Hindu heritage in accordance with Islam and Christianity.

In 1958, after years of lobbying, a *Hindu Bali* section was finally established within the Ministry of Religion, a few weeks after Bali had become a full-fledged province of the Republic of Indonesia (Picard 2011a). The next step was to decide who should be in charge of the *agama Hindu Bali*, now that the former kings, who had previously been the patrons of the religious ceremonies on the island, had been replaced by the Republican government. For that purpose, a council was set up in 1959 to coordinate the religious activities of the Hindu Balinese—the Parisada Dharma Hindu Bali (PDHB, Hindu Bali Dharma Council) (Bakker 1993: 225–291; see also Ramstedt 2004).²³

With the backing and subsidies of the provincial government, the Parisada undertook to translate Indian sacred scriptures, compile a theological canon (*Panca Çraddha*) (Punyatmadja 1970), publish a Hindu

---

²²Although they had no lack of names to refer to their supreme deity, the Balinese appeared to have concurred rather easily on the name *Sang Hyang Widhi*, popularized in the 1920s as an equivalent to the Malay word *Tuhan*, meaning 'Lord', and chosen by Christian missionaries in the 1930s as the Balinese 'one God'. They had more trouble agreeing on their holy book, wavering between the *Mahabharata* and the *Veda*, the latter of which were ultimately retained—despite the fact that the *Veda* were not known in Bali before the twentieth century. As for their prophet, after some attempt to choose Bagawan Biasa—the mythical compiler of the *Veda* and the *Mahabharata*—Balinese reformers appear to have thought that Hinduism neither had a prophet nor needed one.

²³One notices that instead of the word *agama*, rejected on account of its Islamic connotation, it is the word *dharma* which was retained by former Balinese students from Indian universities, to convey the normative idea of 'religion'.

catechism (*Upadeśa*) (Mantra 1967), standardize religious rites, formalize the priesthood and provide religious instruction to the population. This endeavour amounted to a 'scripturalization' of Balinese religion, a shift in focus from ritual to text. Unlike the kings and the priests, who merely interceded on behalf of their subjects and clients, the Parisada was now instructing the Balinese on what to believe and how to practise their religion.

During the 1960s, the growing presence of Balinese communities outside their own island enabled the Parisada to extend its influence across the Archipelago. Cut off from their temple networks as well as from their deified ancestors, these Balinese migrants needed a delocalized and scriptural religion which they could carry with them. In these circumstances, the Parisada leaders who had studied in India advocated giving up the exclusive ethnic flavour of the label *Hindu Bali* in favour of the more inclusive *Hindu Dharma*, in order to strengthen the position of their religion vis-à-vis Islam and Christianity. As a result, during its first congress, in 1964, the Parisada Dharma Hindu Bali changed its name to Parisada Hindu Dharma (PHD, Hindu Dharma Council), forsaking any reference to its Balinese origins. And when, the following year, President Sukarno specified the religions that would qualify for official recognition, it was *agama Hindu* and not *agama Hindu Bali* that was retained.[24]

Thus it is that, through their struggle to obtain the recognition of their religion, the Balinese came to define their ethnic identity in terms of *agama Hindu*. But it is precisely from the moment they began to identify themselves most explicitly as a Hindu island in a sea of Islam that one can date the premises of the disjunction between the Balinese religious and ethnic identities. This is because their identification of ethnicity and religion would soon be foiled by a twofold process of Indonesianization-cum-Indianization: on the one hand, the affiliation of other Indonesian ethnic groups with *agama Hindu* dissociated it from the Balinese, while on the other hand, the growing influence of Indian Neo-Hinduism on *agama Hindu* rendered the link between religion and ethnicity ever more problematic for the Balinese.

Indeed, once expressly detached from any ethnic reference, *agama Hindu* was no longer the sole property of the Balinese people, who had

---

[24] *Penetapan Presiden n° 1/1965 tentang Pencegahan Penyalahgunaan dan/atau Penodaan Agama.*

to open it up to other Indonesian ethnic groups. Its official recognition brought new recruits in the wake of the anti-communist massacres of 1965–1966, which provoked the 'conversion' to *agama Hindu* of Javanese nominal Muslims (*abangan*) for fear of being branded 'atheists', an accusation synonymous with 'communists' in Indonesia. In the following years, several ethnic minorities took refuge in the '*Hindu*' fold hoping to be allowed to conserve their ancestral rites, *agama Hindu* being reputedly more accommodating in this respect than Islam or Christianity.[25] To integrate the newcomers, the Parisada devised a rite of conversion to *agama Hindu* named *Śuddhi Wadāni* (Titib 1991), adapted from the rite of reconversion invented by the Ārya Samāj in the nineteenth century to bring back into the fold of Hinduism those Indians who had converted to Islam or Christianity (Jordens 1991).

The diffusion of *agama Hindu* outside Bali continued to such an extent that it seemed that the Balinese might lose the control of the religion that they had themselves established.[26] But what appeared to some Balinese as the dispossession of their own religion was perceived by other Indonesian Hindus as Balinese 'colonization'. Hence, a tension, affecting the Balinese themselves, between the Balinization of the religious practices of various ethnic groups affiliated with *agama Hindu* and the Indonesianization of the Balinese religion aimed at detaching it from its ethnic origins.

It did not take long for this tension to concern the Parisada itself. After having established branches in every province of the country, at the time of its fifth congress in 1986, the Parisada Hindu Dharma became the Parisada Hindu Dharma Indonesia (PHDI, Hindu Dharma Council

---

[25] See the chapter by Cécile Barraud for an illustration of the ambiguities surrounding the 'conversion' of an ethnic minority to *agama Hindu* and the difficulty in differentiating it from their own *adat*.

[26] It is rather difficult to know with any precision the number of adherents to *agama Hindu* in Indonesia, inasmuch as the religious composition of the population is a politically contentious matter. According to the 2010 census, there are around 4 million Hindus in Indonesia, a figure disputed by the Directorate of Hinduism at the Ministry of Religion, which puts the number at roughly 10 million, while the Parisada claims that they are 18 million. According to the census, Hindus composed 1.69% of the Indonesian population and 83.5% of the population of Bali. In the opinion of most Balinese religious leaders, the proportion of Hindus is deliberately underestimated at the national level, whereas it is overestimated for Bali so as to prevent the Balinese people from knowing the true weight of the Muslim population on their island.

of Indonesia). By the same token, a regional branch was opened in Bali, the Parisada Hindu Dharma Indonesia Propinsi Bali. Eventually, in 1996, at the time of the seventh congress, the Parisada headquarters were relocated from Bali to Jakarta, leaving only the Balinese branch on the island.

During the 1990s, the Islamic resurgence in Indonesia aroused Balinese apprehension over their religious identity and triggered in mimetic fashion a 'Hindu revival' (*Kebangkitan Hindu*) (Setia 1993). This revival resulted in the fragmentation of the Balinese religious identity. It appears that, from then on, neither the traditional religion, attached to the correct execution of rites, nor its official version, concerned with ethics and theology, was able to satisfy a growing fraction of the Balinese middle class, in quest of religious devotion and personal conviction as well as universalism. At the same time, the Parisada was criticized for being a pressure group of conservative members of the Balinese nobility more than a genuine religious body and for promoting a traditionalist conception of *agama Hindu*, still very much affected by its original Balinese parochialism (Bagus 2004). Such criticism came from two socio-religious movements which pursued distinct aims but whose actors originated from the same milieu—the *warga* and the *sampradaya*.

The *warga* movement resumed the struggle of the commoners against the privileges of the nobility, initiated in the 1920s (Kerepun 2007). After Indonesia's independence, the main *jaba* title groups (Bhujangga Waisnawa, Pasek and Pande) had set up formal organizations (*warga*), uniting all members of a kinship group (*soroh*) who considered themselves the descendants of a common ancestor (*kawitan*). Their aim was to have their rights acknowledged against the *triwangsa*'s privileges and specifically to abrogate the *brahmana*'s monopoly on the initiated priesthood (Pitana 1999).[27] Under the pressure of the *warga*, the Parisada

---

[27] The question of priesthood in Bali is complex, all the more so because it is controversial, due to its link to the hierarchy of the title groups. One can distinguish two categories of priests, according to the conditions on their access. The first one—the *pinandita*, according to the Parisada's terminology—which requires only a purification ceremony (*pawintenan*), is comprised mostly of priests attached to the service of a particular temple (*pemangku*), specific classes of puppeteers (*mangku dalang*), as well as mediums and healers (*balian*). The second category—called *pandita* by the Parisada—which is reserved to those who undergo an initiation (*padiksan*) and are authorized by the Parisada, is monopolized by *brahmana* priests (*pedanda*). It is precisely this privilege that was challenged by the *warga*, whose leaders attempted to impose the use of their own priests—*bhujangga, resi, bhagawan, empu* and *dukuh*—next to that of the *pedanda*.

decreed in 1968, during its second congress, that all the Hindus were entitled to undergo the ordination rite to the initiated priesthood and furthermore, that all duly initiated priests had the same status and were thus equally qualified to officiate at all ceremonies. This decree, however, did not settle the matter as, despite the Parisada's official position, some of its leaders continued to defend the exclusive privileges of the *pedanda*.

While supporting the demand of the *warga* that their priests be allowed to officiate on par with the *pedanda*, Balinese reformers were no longer satisfied with a nationally recognized religion. Instead, they aspired to universalize their religious identity by fully embracing Hinduism as a 'world religion'. They initiated a renewed turn towards India, marked by the promotion of Indian concepts and practices, such as vegetarianism or the performance of the revived Vedic ritual *Agnihotra*. Pilgrimages (*tirtha yatra*) were organized to the holy sites of India, where the Indonesian Hindus were urged to look for their religious sources, in the manner of Muslims going on the *hajj* to Mecca.[28] Furthermore, they introduced the motto 'Back to Veda',[29] in the fashion of Dayananda Sarasvati, the founder of the Ārya Samāj. Most Balinese quoting this rallying cry, however, did not appear to be aware of its origin and clearly had very little notion of what the *Veda* really are. Most of all, this rapprochement with India in the 1990s was marked by the progressive establishment in Indonesia of Neo-Hindu devotional movements (*sampradaya*), such as Sai Baba and Hare Krishna, the most popular among them (Jendra 2007). The propagation of these movements in Indonesia was met with some opposition from the Ministry of Religion as well as from the Parisada, who feared the rise of conflicts between rival

---

[28] On pilgrimages to India, see Annette Hornbacher's chapter.

[29] The motto 'Back to Veda' is based on the presupposition that the *Veda* had been transmitted to Bali, where they fell into disuse, like in India. This illusion, long held by Orientalists, goes back to the report published by Friederich (1849–1850). Had he been allowed to examine the manuscripts that the *pedanda* called *Weda*, Friederich would have discovered that these were not the Indian *Veda*, but were for the most part prescriptions for rituals, interspersed with *mantra* and hymns. In the Balinese language, the word *Weda* refers to liturgical manuscripts composed of ritual prescriptions (*Kalpasastra*), *Mantra* and hymns (*Stuti* and *Stawa*), used by the *pedanda* during their office (*maweda*) (Goudriaan 1970).

sects that could undermine a Hindu community already weakened by the diversity of its ethnic origins.

BACK TO *AGAMA HINDU BALI*

The spate of ethnic and religious identity politics, as well as the radicalization of Islam, unleashed by the fall of President Suharto in 1998 led to strife within the Parisada, on the occasion of its eighth national congress, in September 2001. The Balinese branch of the Parisada objected to some of the decisions adopted by the congress, namely the nomination of a layman to the Parisada's chairmanship, which had so far been monopolized by the *pedanda*, not to mention the massive presence in its direction of *jaba* and non-Balinese, as well as prominent members of the *warga* and the *sampradaya*. In November of the same year, the Balinese Parisada convened its own congress at Campuan, near Ubud. This site was not chosen at random. It was there that forty years earlier the Campuan Charter had been signed, which stipulated that the Parisada would be presided by a *pedanda*. Accusing the national leadership of undermining Balinese identity by unduly Indianizing *agama Hindu*, the Campuan congress refused the admission of the *sampradaya* into the Parisada and demanded the nomination of a *pedanda* at its chairmanship.

Soon afterwards, the central Parisada disowned the Parisada Campuan and convened a competing regional congress in March 2002 at Besakih. This is another site with a highly symbolic value, as it is the main sanctuary on the island, representing the community of Indonesian Hindus in its entirety. After the Parisada Besakih had duly ratified the decisions of the eighth national congress, it was acknowledged as the official Balinese branch of the Parisada. In the years that followed, each of the two Balinese Parisada claimed to be the legitimate representative of the Balinese Hindu community. While the Parisada Besakih had the support of the middle-class urban intelligentsia and those Balinese living outside of the island, the Parisada Campuan appeared to be more aligned with the village population.

In 2007, the Parisada Campuan convened its congress, which decided to return to the 'true self' (*jati diri*) of the Balinese religion—that is, to *agama Hindu Bali*. By the same token, the congress resolved to revert to the name originally chosen by their founding fathers, Parisada

Dharma Hindu Bali, thus reversing the globalization of the Balinese religion by relocalizing it. In this respect, the return to *agama Hindu Bali* reveals itself to be much more than a withdrawal into Balinese parochialism on the part of a group of die-hard reactionaries, as contended by their opponents. Its promoters attempted to put an end to the dispossession of their religion by winning back the direction of the Parisada, which they had lost since the 1990s. The crux of the matter is the challenge to Balinese control over *agama Hindu* in Indonesia, demonstrated by the displacement of the Parisada's centre from Bali to Jakarta, the increasing ascendancy of non-Balinese and non-*brahmana* over its leadership and its inclusion of the Neo-Hindu devotional movements aimed at 'purifying' traditional Balinese religious practices (Picard 2011b).

In recent years, the conflict between the two Balinese factions appears to have faded somewhat, although the reasons for its initial outbreak have yet to be properly addressed. Be that as it may, the comeback of *agama Hindu Bali* might be regarded in retrospect as a return to a signification of *agama* untainted by its Islamic and Christian interpretations, when *agama* had not yet been separated from *adat*. One could say that the Parisada Dharma Hindu Bali reappropriated the power to identify as *agama* that which pertained to *adat* for the Parisada Hindu Dharma Indonesia, just as the latter had claimed the power to designate as *agama* that which the Ministry of Religion had classified as *adat*.

Epilogue

After the Balinese had successfully managed to convince the Ministry of Religion to acknowledge *agama Hindu* as a proper monotheistic religion—even though in the eyes of some of the hard line Islamic organizations the Balinese people are still no better than downright idolaters—they sought to convince Indian Hindus that they truly represented a local branch of Hinduism. From the 1990s onward, Balinese religious leaders endeavoured by various means to demonstrate a firm connection to Indian Hinduism—from embracing Neo-Hindu devotional movements to organizing pilgrimages to the holy sites of India. They have not been entirely successful, as can be seen by the reluctance of Indian Hindus to accept the Balinese pilgrims as fellow coreligionists,[30] not to mention their aborted attempt to build Balinese temples in India.

Nevertheless, the Parisada Hindu Dharma Indonesia succeeded in affiliating itself with the World Hindu Federation (WHF), established in 1981 in Nepal under the patronage of King Birendra. One of the founding fathers of the Parisada was even vice-president of the WHF from 1988 to 1992, the year of its third international conference held in Bali.

The World Hindu Federation was seriously compromised by the abolition of the Nepalese monarchy in 2008. Its leaders have been trying to revive their organization ever since. Following the Parisada's tenth national congress in 2011, its chairman seized the opportunity to meet with the WHF's leadership and they decided to convene a World Hindu Summit in 2012 in Bali. Launched under the aegis of the Parisada, the meeting gathered dozens of delegates from various Hindu organizations. They issued the Bali Charter, which resolved to set up a World Hindu Centre in Bali in charge of implementing a World Hindu Parisad, an umbrella organization bringing together all Hindu organizations in the world with the aim of promoting Hindu Dharma globally. A second World Hindu Summit was convened in 2013 to carry through the decisions adopted the previous year, followed by a so-called World Hindu Wisdom Meet in 2014, 2015 and then again in 2016.

From interviews with its promoters, it emerged that the setting of the World Hindu Parisad in Bali aimed at providing the Balinese with a much needed international backing against the growing pressure of Islam in Indonesia by furthering institutional ties with powerful global Hindu networks. However, it is rather doubtful whether the Balinese are up to the task. Indeed, it is painfully clear that the initial fervour that brought about the World Hindu Parisad has faded rapidly, while most Balinese appear either unaware of or just unconcerned with the lofty endeavour. Furthermore, numerous critics have pointed out that the Parisada is not even able to properly manage *agama Hindu* in Balinese villages, asking in turn, how then, can it hope to successfully champion Hinduism worldwide?

---

[30] See Annette Hornbacher's chapter.

References

Abdullah, Taufik. 1966. *Adat* and Islam: An examination of conflict in Minangkabau. *Indonesia* 2: 1–24.
Aljunied, Syed Muhd Khairudin. 2004. *Raffles and Religion. A Study of Sir Thomas Stamford Raffles' Discourse on Religions Amongst Malays*. Kuala Lumpur: The Other Press.
Anandakusuma, Sri Reshi. 1986. *Kamus Bahasa Bali* [Dictionary of the Balinese Language]. Denpasar: C.V. Kayumas.
Atkinson, Jane M. 1987. Religions in dialogue: The construction of an Indonesian minority religion. In *Indonesian Religions in Transition*, ed. R.S. Kipp, and S. Rodgers, 171–186. Tucson: University of Arizona Press.
Bagus, I Gusti Ngurah. 2004. The Parisada Hindu Dharma Indonesia in a society in transformation. In *Hinduism in Modern Indonesia. A minority religion between local, national, and global interests*, ed. M. Ramstedt, 84–92. London: RoutledgeCurzon.
Bakker, Frederik Lambertus. 1993. *The Struggle of the Hindu Balinese Intellectuals. Developments in Modern Hindu Thinking in Independent Indonesia*. Amsterdam: VU University Press.
Becker, Judith. 2004. *Gamelan Stories. Tantrism, Islam, and Aesthetics in Central Java*. Tempe: Arizona State University (1st edition, 1993).
Benda-Beckmann, Franz von, and Keebet von Benda-Beckmann. 1988. Adat and religion in Minangkabau and Ambon. In *Time Past, Time Present, Time Future. Perspectives on Indonesian Culture. Essays in Honour of Prof. P.E. De Josselin De Jong*, ed. H.J.M. Claessen and D.S. Moyer, 195–212. Dordrecht: Foris.
Brunner, Hélène. 1967. À propos d'un rituel balinais. *Journal Asiatique* 255 (3–4): 409–422.
Couteau, Jean. 1999. Bali et l'islam: 1. Rencontre historique. *Archipel* 58: 159–188.
Crawfurd, John. 1820. On the existence of the Hindu religion in the island of Bali. *Asiatick Researches* 13: 128–170.
Creese, Helen. 2000. In Search of Majapahit. The Transformation of Balinese Identities. In *To Change Bali. Essays in Honour of I Gusti Ngurah Bagus*, ed. A. Vickers and Ny. Darma Putra, 15–46. Denpasar: Bali Post.
Creese, Helen. 2009a. Old Javanese legal traditions in pre-colonial Bali. *Bijdragen tot de Taal-, Land- en Volkenkunde* 165 (2–3): 241–290.
Creese, Helen. 2009b. Judicial processes and legal authority in pre-colonial Bali. *Bijdragen tot de Taal-, Land- en Volkenkunde* 165 (4): 515–550.
Davis, Richard H. 1991. *Ritual in an Oscillating Universe: Worshipping Śiva in Medieval India*. Princeton: Princeton University Press.

Friederich, Rudolf H.Th. 1849–1850. Voorlopig verslag van het eiland Bali [Provisional report on the Island of Bali]. *Verhandelingen van het Bataviaasch Genootschap voor Kunsten en Wetenschappen* 22: 1–63, 23: 1–57.

Friederich, Rudolf H.Th. 1959. *The Civilization and Culture of Bali*. Calcutta: Susil Gupta.

Goebah. 1937. Kebingoengan kita tentang agama [Our confusion about religion]. *Djatajoe* 2 (5): 130–132.

Gonda, Jan. 1973. *Sanskrit in Indonesia*. New Delhi: International Academy of Indian Culture (1st edition, 1952).

Goris, Roelof. 1933. 'De strijd over Bali en de Zending'. De waarde van Dr. Kraemer's boek ['The controversy regarding Bali and the missions'. The worth of Dr. Kraemer's book]. Batavia: Minerva.

Goudriaan, Teun. 1970. Sanskrit texts and Indian religion in Bali. In *India's Contribution to World Thought and Culture*, ed. L. Chandra, 555–564. Madras: Vivekananda Commemoration Volume.

Guermonprez, Jean-François. 2001. La religion balinaise dans le miroir de l'hindouisme. *Bulletin de l'École française d'Extrême-Orient* 88: 271–293.

Hauser-Schäublin, Brigitta. 2004. 'Bali Aga' and Islam: Ethnicity, ritual practice, and 'Old-Balinese' as an anthropological construct. *Indonesia* 77: 1–28.

Hinzler, Hedi. 1986. Facts, myths, legitimation and time in Balinese historiography. In *International Workshop on Indonesian Studies N°1, Balinese State and Society*. Leiden: Royal Institute of Linguistics and Anthropology.

Hoadley, Mason C., and M.B. Hooker. 1981. *An Introduction to Javanese Law. A Translation of and Commentary on the Agama*. Tucson: The University of Arizona Press.

Hoadley, Mason C., and M.B. Hooker. 1986. The Law Texts of Java and Bali. In *The Laws of South-East Asia*. Volume 1: *The pre-modern texts*, ed. M.B. Hooker, 241–346. Singapore: Butterworths.

Hooykaas, Christiaan. 1966. *Sūrya-Sevana: The Way to God of a Balinese Śiva Priest*. Amsterdam: N.V. Noord-Hollandsche Uitgevers Maatschappij.

Howe, Leo. 2001. *Hinduism and Hierarchy in Bali*. Oxford: James Currey.

Jendra, Wayan. 2007. *Sampradaya. Kelompok Belajar Weda, Aliran dalam Agama Hindu dan Budaya Bali* [Sampradaya. Veda study groups, a current in Hindu religion and Balinese culture]. Denpasar: Panakom.

Johnsen, Scott A. 2007. From Royal House to Nation: The Construction of Hinduism and Balinese Ethnicity in Indonesia. Ph.D. Dissertation, Department of Anthropology, University of Virginia, Charlottesville.

Jordens, J.F.T. 1991. Reconversion to Hinduism: The Shuddhi of the Arya Samaj. In *Religion in South Asia. Religious Conversion and Revival Movements in South Asia in Medieval and Modern Times*, ed. G.A. Oddie, 215–230. New Delhi: Manohar.

Kadjeng, Njoman. 1929. Voorloopig overzicht der op Bali aanwezige literatuurschat [Provisional overview of existing literary collections on Bali]. *Mededeelingen van de Kirtya Liefrinck – van der Tuuk*, Aflevering 1: 19–40.
Kerepun, Made Kembar. 2007. *Mengurai Benang Kusut Kasta. Membedah Kiat Pengajegan Kasta di Bali* [Disentangling the mix-up of castes. Dissecting the defense of castes in Bali]. Denpasar: Panakom.
Korn, Victor Emanuel. 1925. Bali is apart... is fijner bezenuwd dan eenig ander deel van Indië [Bali is unique... of a finer grain than any other part of the Indies]. *Koloniaal Tijdschrift* 14: 44–53.
Korn, Victor Emanuel. 1932. *Het Adatrecht van Bali* [The customary law of Bali]. 's-Gravenhage: Naeff (1st edition, 1924).
Lévi, Sylvain. 1933. *Sanskrit Texts from Bali*. Baroda: Oriental Institute.
Pernau, Margrit. 2011. Maulawi Muhammad Zaka Ullah. Reflections of a Muslim moralist on the compatibility of Islam, Hinduism and Christianity. In *Convictions religieuses et engagement en Asie du Sud depuis 1850*, ed. C. Clémentin-Ojha, 31–47. Paris: École française d'Extrême-Orient.
Mantra, Ida Bagus et al. 1967. *Upadeśa Tentang Adjaran-Adjaran Agama Hindu* [Instructions regarding the teachings of the Hindu religion]. Denpasar: Parisada Hindu Dharma.
Picard, Michel. 2004. What's in a name? Agama Hindu Bali in the making. In *Hinduism in Modern Indonesia. A minority religion between local, national, and global interests*, ed. M. Ramstedt, 56–75. London: RoutledgeCurzon.
Picard, Michel. 2011a. Balinese religion in search of recognition: From *agama Hindu Bali* to *agama Hindu* (1945–1965). *Bijdragen tot de Taal-, Land- en Volkenkunde* 167 (4): 482–510.
Picard, Michel. 2011b. From *agama Hindu Bali* to *agama Hindu* and back. Toward a relocalization of the Balinese Religion? In *The Politics of Religion in Indonesia. Syncretism, Orthodoxy, and Religious Contention in Java and Bali*, ed. M. Picard and R. Madinier, 117–141. London: Routledge.
Pitana, I Gde. 1999. Status struggles and the priesthood in contemporary Bali. In *Staying Local in the Global Village. Bali in the Twentieth Century*, ed. R. Rubinstein and L.H. Connor, 181–201. Honolulu: University of Hawai'i Press.
Punyatmadja, Ida Bagus Oka. 1970. *Panca Çraddha* [The five articles of faith]. Denpasar: Parisada Hindu Dharma Pusat.
Raffles, Thomas Stamford. 1817. *The History of Java*. London: Black, Parbury & Allen.
Ramstedt, Martin. 2004. Introduction: Negotiating identities—Indonesian 'Hindus' between local, national, and global interests. In *Hinduism in*

Modern Indonesia. A minority religion between local, national, and global interests, ed. M. Ramstedt, 1–34. London: RoutledgeCurzon.

Robinson, Geoffrey. 1995. *The Dark Side of Paradise. Political Violence in Bali*. Ithaca: Cornell University Press.

Rocher, Ludo. 2003. The Dharmaśāstras. In *The Blackwell Companion to Hinduism*, ed. G. Flood, 102–115. Oxford: Blackwell.

Sarkar, Himansu Bhusan. 1934. *Indian Influences on the Literature of Java and Bali*. Calcutta: Greater India Society.

Schärer, Hans. 1963. *Ngaju Religion. The Conception of God Among a South Borneo People*. The Hague: Martinus Nijhoff.

Schulte Nordholt, Henk. 1986. *Bali: Colonial Conceptions and Political Change, 1700–1940. From shifting hierarchies to 'fixed order'*. Rotterdam: Erasmus University.

Setia, Putu. 1993. *Kebangkitan Hindu Menyongsong Abad ke-21* [The Hindu revival faces the 21st century]. Jakarta: Pustaka Manikgeni.

Staal, Frits. 1995. *Mantras Between Fire and Water. Reflections on a Balinese Rite*. Amsterdam: Koninklijke Nederlandse Akademie van Wetenshappen.

Titib, Made. 1991. *Pedoman Upacara Śuddhi Wadāni* [Guide to the ceremony Śuddhi Wadāni]. Denpasar: Upada Sastra.

Van Hoëvell, Wolter Robert Baron. 1848. Recent scientific researches on the islands of Bali and Lombok. *The Journal of the Indian Archipelago and Eastern Asia* 2: 151–159.

Van Vollenhoven, Cornelis. 1928. *De Ontdekking van het Adatrecht* [The discovery of customary law]. Leiden: E.J. Brill.

Vickers, Adrian. 1987. Hinduism and Islam in Indonesia: Bali and the Pasisir world. *Indonesia* 44: 31–58.

Warren, Carol. 1993. *Adat and Dinas. Balinese Communities in the Indonesian State*. Kuala Lumpur: Oxford University Press.

Wiener, Margaret J. 1995. *Visible and Invisible Realms. Power, Magic, and Colonial Conquest in Bali*. Chicago: The University of Chicago Press.

Author Biography

Michel Picard Ph.D., is a retired researcher at the French National Center for Scientific Research (CNRS) and a founding member of the Center for Southeast Asian Studies (CASE, CNRS-EHESS) in Paris. He has published extensively in the field of Balinese studies, specifically on tourism, culture, identity, ethnicity and religion. He is the author of *Bali: Cultural Tourism and Touristic Culture* (1996), and has co-edited several collective volumes, the latest one being *The Politics of Religion in Indonesia. Syncretism, Orthodoxy, and Religious Contention in Java and Bali* (2011). He has recently published *Kebalian. La construction dialogique de l'identité balinaise* (2017).

CHAPTER 6

Return to the Source: A Balinese Pilgrimage to India and the Re-Enchantment of *Agama Hindu* in Global Modernity

Annette Hornbacher

Modernization has been described as a process of pervasive rationalization and disenchantment that reshapes every aspect of human life—not least the field of religion, as Max Weber (1988) famously argued. While this theory was developed with specific reference to European history, it seems that a similar dynamic may be seen in more recent developments in other parts of the world. This would notably include Indonesia, where local cosmologies and ritual traditions of nature and ancestor worship have been reframed in terms of a modern and normative paradigm of 'religion' (*agama*). In Indonesian politics, *agama* engenders a consistent belief system grounded in a transcendent and universal truth, which is set in opposition to local forms of immanent worship that are dismissed as little more than 'backward' animist traditions (Kipp and Rodgers 1987). In this respect, the idea of religion, under the rubric of *agama*, has become a powerful tool of normalization for the Indonesian nation-state in its drive for modernization. This is particularly evident with regard to Bali, long known for its unique

---

A. Hornbacher (✉)
Institut für Ethnologie, Heidelberg University, Heidelberg, Germany

© The Author(s) 2017
M. Picard (ed.), *The Appropriation of Religion in Southeast Asia and Beyond*, DOI 10.1007/978-3-319-56230-8_6

blend of animist and ancestor rituals, on the one hand, and its sophisticated philosophical and artistic traditions of Buddhist and Śaiva origin, on the other.

The political imposition of 'religion' on the Balinese has been described as a shift from ritual orthopraxy to orthodoxy and from local traditions to a universal or transnational paradigm of religion (Geertz 1964; Kipp and Rodgers 1987; Bakker 1993; Howe 2004; Picard 2004, 2011a and b; Ramstedt 2004; Reuter 2008). I wish to argue that this shift of emphasis from ritual engagement with the world to a doctrinal and more 'rationalized' form of belief has implications of not only an epistemological and theological nature, but ontological as well. It presumes to replace the immanent worship of particular places in the environment with a personal belief system, thus 'disenchanting' Bali's engagement with the world in favor of a modern 'religion'—namely *agama Hindu*.

In this chapter, I will explore the dynamics of, and resistance against, this politics of religion, by investigating the ideas and practices of a social group who ostensibly adopted the paradigm of *agama Hindu*: Balinese pilgrims on their way to the 'source' (*sumber*) of their—purportedly universal—'Hindu religion' (*agama Hindu*) in India. In the course of this pilgrimage, which I joined during ten days of bus trips together with fifty-five Indonesian pilgrims to different Indian sanctuaries, I had the opportunity to explore what the pilgrims were explicitly looking for, what they actually did and found in India, and how their own ideas and practices relate to the national paradigm of a modern religion. I realized that, notwithstanding their explicit compliance with the program of *agama Hindu*, the Balinese were not just passively adopting a political agenda. Instead, they were critically reflecting on, and creatively transforming, the modern paradigm of 'religion,' along with its ontological implications. I therefore regard the pilgrimage (*tirtha yatra*) as a paradigmatic laboratory situation, in which Balinese Hindus have reconsidered and modulated not only their *Hindu* identity *vis-à-vis* an imagined transnational community of Hindus, but also their very ideas about religion and the world, in view of a global modernity.

Disenchanting Bali: The Politics of *Agama Hindu* and Its Ontological Implications

While resisting political pressure to make the majority religion of the world's largest Islamic country a state religion, Indonesia guarantees religious freedom and pluralism only according to the national *Pancasila* doctrine—which declares as its highest principle that there is only one God, but different religions for worshipping Him. According to its formal political definition, every proper religion (*agama*) is grounded in a monotheistic creed, a revealed transcendent truth and a coherent doctrine that is written in a holy book and can be adopted independently of social traditions and local forms of worship. Thus, even though the Indonesian word *agama* derives ultimately from Sanskrit traditions, its current meaning matches the modern concept of religion.[1]

By laying a claim to a universal doctrine and thus disconnecting worship from place and ancestral obligations, this paradigm of a modern, politically accepted '*agama*' differs fundamentally from the ancestor rituals and animist worship which are always tied to specific places and social groups as local custom or tradition (*adat*). This modernizing concept of *agama* has thus been a powerful political instrument—not merely in aid of social normalization and doctrinal rationalization, but also for the desacralization of human–environment relations. For the paradigm of a transcendent and universal religious truth implies the devaluation of immanent worship along with a materialistic and instrumentalized concept of nature.

This is particularly evident with regard to Bali. When the island became part of the Indonesian nation-state, Balinese were forced to specify their *agama*. This was difficult, for among other reasons, because everyday life on the island—from birth to death, and including the wet rice economy as well as market relations—was structured by myriad rituals addressing ancestors, trees, springs, daggers, cattle, dance masks, music instruments and more recently even cars and computers—to say nothing of temples and their gods. Thus, the experience of powerful non-human agents had been an important aspect of Balinese life, and this made it difficult to draw a clear line differentiating between 'religion' and 'non-religion.'

Accordingly, from a Balinese perspective, the worship of particular places and objects is not a matter of belief, or of religious doctrine. It

---

[1] For details see Picard, this volume.

is rather a matter of situational perception, and a particular engagement with the world. Not only do Balinese perform their traditional temple rituals on this basis; they also make offerings to places where they have experienced an extraordinary agency or power. This corresponds to an idea of reality in which the material or visible world (*sekala*) is nothing but the surface of a dimension of invisible actors and powers (*niskala*). The notion of *niskala* encompasses the human intellect and feelings as much as it does gods, ancestors and demons that inhabit specific places of the world, and interact in unpredictable ways and places with humans. I describe this dynamic relation between *niskala* agents and *sekala* effects as a Balinese 'animist ontology' that informs situational perceptions of, and ideas about, a landscape of sacred places[2] and immanent gods, that require ritual engagement rather than personal belief.

In the case of Bali, this ritual engagement with immanent divine presence is combined with Buddhist and Śaiva ideas that reached the Archipelago during the first millennium CE along the maritime trade routes between India and China. However, while Buddhist and Śaiva teachings from India have deeply influenced Bali, Balinese did not regard themselves as 'Hindus,' a term of which they were hardly aware, as Paul Wirz (1928: 9) observed in his early ethnographic research between 1918 and 1926. Similarly, even though the word *agama* was obviously a local term at that time, it had a different meaning. Wirz observes that *agama* was combined with *tirtha*, 'holy water,' and thus *agama tirtha*— the 'religion of holy water'—did not refer to a doctrine but rather to a ritual practice for which holy water is a central ingredient. It is therefore not surprising that decades later, the council of Balinese priests declared that their religion was '*agama tirtha*,' even though other organizations agreed upon the name 'Balinese Hindu religion' (*agama Hindu Bali*)—a

---

[2] I find the term 'sacred' a better fit than 'holy,' because places of worship are in Bali often regarded as imbued with ambiguous and potentially dangerous powers (*tenget*). This applies also to the word '*sacer*' (Lat.) that is not only the opposite of the 'profane' but implies a semantic ambiguity that differs from other terms for 'the holy,' as for example '*sanctus*' (Lat.) or '*hosios*' (Gr.). Agamben (1998) explains this ambiguity with reference to the '*homo sacer*,' the 'cursed man,' a figure of Roman law that stands beyond divine and human law and can be killed but not sacrificed, which would require pureness or sanctity. Similarly, Dihle has shown that 'the sacred' is manifest in specific places within the world, whereas holy ('*sanctus*') is a qualification of the human being, or the circumstances of communion with an unambiguously pure divinity (Dihle 1988; cf. Assmann 2000: 154).

designation that was more in line with the modern national paradigm of a world religion.[3]

Balinese religion was officially recognized as *agama Hindu* only when the Balinese complied with the pressure from the Indonesian government by reinterpreting their flexible and highly integrative ritual traditions as local expressions of a systematic Hindu religion that is based on holy books, in this case the *Veda* and the *Bhagavadgita*. *Agama Hindu* emphasizes a consistent moral doctrine based upon five official articles of belief, the *Panca Sraddha*, which form an ethical system. This includes belief in an eternal soul (*atman*) that returns to God after death (*brahman*), depending on the character of one's deeds during life (*karmaphala*), which determines one's reincarnation (*samsara*) or ultimate liberation from the world (*moksa*). The systematic, moralistic and ultimately transcendent character of these principles emerges if *moksa* is regarded as the highest and ultimate goal of *agama Hindu*.

The immanent forms of ancestor and nature worship, which are crucial for Balinese interactions with their environment, have no place in this transcendent system of belief. Nor does the fact that, even today—after years of indoctrination through state education and television programming—most Balinese are not aiming at ultimate liberation from an illusory world. On the contrary, most Balinese tend to regard ultimate liberation as the prerogative of a small number of religious specialists. Meanwhile, they perform their costly death rituals in order to guarantee that their ancestors can be reborn within the same family, or become tutelary divinities on the holy mountain, providing protection and bliss for their offspring (Hornbacher 2014).

The reinterpretation of Bali's ritual and cosmological traditions in terms of *agama Hindu* can thus be regarded as a specific case of a more general problem that has emerged in tandem with the idea of 'Hinduism.' Given the great variety of local rituals, on the one hand, and general philosophical systems, on the other, the term 'Hinduism' ultimately matches neither the rich Indian traditions nor the ritual practices of Bali (Smith 1962; von Stietencron and Dalmia 1995; Fitzgerald 2000).

But instead of dismissing the concept of 'religion' altogether as a Eurocentric projection, we should recognize that today the question for

---

[3] For details concerning the complex history of *agama Hindu* in Indonesia, see Picard 2011a and 2011b and this volume.

Balinese is no longer whether their religion is *agama Hindu* or not, but rather what this means in practice. It seems more interesting to approach the problem in terms, first, of the ways in which the concept of *agama* is currently used by different actors for different ends and, second, to analyze the normative implications and ontological consequences of *agama Hindu*. As a political instrument, *agama* is directed to something like what Geertz (1964) described as 'internal' conversion—that is, from a ritual practice to a religious doctrine. But it also affects the human–environment relationship, as I argue. Once *agama* is a matter of transcendent belief, personal morality and ultimate liberation from a profane or illusionary world, the worship of particular places, objects and ancestors in the human environment is within the field neither of reality nor of religion. Instead, it can be dismissed as little more than a false or backward tradition, or *adat*. This political conception of *agama* as a world religion implies therefore not only doctrinal standardization or orthodoxy, in contrast to ritual orthopraxy, but moreover a 'disenchantment' of human–environment relations.

This is evident with regard to several environmental conflicts between the Indonesian government and Balinese society: although *agama Hindu* is supposedly a religion of the Book with a transcendent goal, the Balinese fought for the protection of inherently 'sacred' places and landscapes—for example in the environs of the famous sea temple Tanah Lot (Warren 1998)—thus demonstrating that their religious confession did not involve the dismissal of their 'animist ontology.' But it seems that after the resignation of the Indonesian dictator Suharto, Balinese started an increasingly self-confident reinterpretation of *agama Hindu* in terms of immanent worship. Since then, religious and intellectual elites in Bali promoted the idea that Bali's religion is based on a cosmology of harmony between humans, nature and gods (*Tri Hita Karana*). While *Tri Hita Karana* is obviously an invented tradition or ideology, dating back to the 1960s (Roth and Sedana 2015), it is interesting that it is increasingly used to support the reinterpretation of *agama Hindu* as an immanent ecological form of worship rather than as a purified and transcendent Hindu doctrine. This has also a political dimension: during the authoritarian New Order regime, claims to protect inherently sacred land were politically rejected because modern Hinduism was seen as a universal doctrine rather than a human–environment relation. However, since *Reformasi* has triggered a revitalization—and so a 're-invention'—of *adat* as a political instrument for the reclamation of land rights in many parts of Indonesia (Davidson and Henley 2007), it seems that the scope of the term *agama* is changing accordingly in Bali. For example, not only have villages around Lake Buyan defended a particular landscape and its lakes as sacred—and not merely as 'symbols' of an ultimately transcendent *Hindu* religion—this engagement was moreover launched as a 'religious discourse' (*bahasa agama*) (Strauss 2015). The fact that it was politically successful suggests that Balinese traditions of immanent worship could now be defended in terms of *agama*, which had thereby become a means for the defense of the local ontology, rather than for its marginalization.[4]

Tirtha Yatra to India, Between Ideology and Reality

This implies that the relation of *agama* and *adat*, and more interestingly of world religion, modernization and disenchantment, is currently being renegotiated. It is, in other words, not as determinate as the agenda of religious politics would suggest. In Bali, this affects not merely the relation between universal *agama Hindu* and local *adat*. But, moreover, it impinges on the political rearticulation of a local animist ontology, which is related to traditional human–environment practices—not least including *adat* rituals, which in many ways contradict the modern disenchanted paradigm of nature as an object of scientific calculation.

A similar process of renegotiation and appropriation of Balinese animist ontology in terms of global *agama Hindu* became apparent during the Balinese pilgrimage tour to India, to which I now turn. Like other Indonesian pilgrimage tours to India, the *tirtha yatra* that I joined in February 2011 was clearly informed by the agenda of reform Hinduism. Moreover, my Balinese fellow pilgrims regarded themselves without exception as representatives of a modern world religion called '*agama Hindu*.' And they had all accepted the ideology of the official Council of Indonesian Hindus (Parisada Hindu Dharma Indonesia, PHDI) regarding the authority of the *Veda* and the *Bhagavadgita* as the holy books

---

[4] This matches the fact that *Tri Hita Karana* (THK) is promoted by the UNESCO as the traditional 'philosophy' behind Bali's unique rice terrace landscape and 'Cultural Heritage.' See: http://whc.unesco.org/en/list/1194; last checked 31.1.2017. It is used to promote sustainable tourism (Pitana 2010), and it was even recommended by the former Indonesian president Susilo Bambang Yudhoyono in his address to the International Conference on Sustainable Development in Bali, 2013.

of *agama Hindu* originating in India. This was, after all, the reason for traveling to the 'source' of *agama Hindu*, which was—as they told me—the origin of their culture, as Balinese culture was based on the Hindu religion.

However, I realized during the journey, and in my interviews after their return to Bali, that their explicit compliance with *agama Hindu*, and thus with a national paradigm of modernity and internationalization, does not mean that the pilgrims adopted the political agenda of *agama Hindu* as a transcendent book religion. Rather they were actively recalibrating their understanding of Hinduism. This included their sense of belonging to an international community of Hindus and at the same time their engagement with a world that was no longer limited to the island of Bali, but nevertheless 'enchanted,' as we will see.

Pilgrimage tours to India must be seen in the broader context of a global reorientation, which represents the active *Balinese* aspect of the internationalization effected by the island's growing tourism industry, which itself affects ideas about modern lifestyles. The interest in India as a preferred destination of Balinese tourism also displays the historical awareness of Bali's centuries-old exchange with South Asia that is currently being revitalized by the Balinese under conditions of a globalized modernity. This growing interest is not limited to the field of *agama*. Balinese are enthusiastic about daily Indian TV series, and particularly Indian versions of the classical epics, the *Mahabharata* and *Ramayana*. They watch Indian soap operas, buy Ayurvedic medicine, Indian prints with pictures of gods, as well as statues of Ganesha or other gods in Indian style—all of which are absent from the largely aniconic worship characteristic of Balinese rituals, but increasingly available as mass products of Balinese consumer culture.

This fascination is also the result of a religious politics that encourages Balinese to think of *agama Hindu* as a world religion of Indian origin. Pilgrimages to India are therefore recently invented modern rituals for a Balinese middle class, or more precisely for the more wealthy Indonesian Hindus in Bali and elsewhere. Such *tirtha yatra* have an educational aspect, which is evident from their beginning—that is, having been developed after initial attempts to send some Balinese students to Indian universities for Vedic studies (Fig. 6.1).

The idea of encouraging larger groups of Balinese to visit India for pilgrimages to the holy places of *agama Hindu* was first developed by one of these returning students, I Made Titib. Titib was a former head of the Balinese branch of the PHDI, who had studied at the Vedic

Fig. 6.1 Balinese pilgrims learning how to offer milk to a Shiva Linga in New Delhi, February 2011

Department of the Gurukul Kangri University of Haridwar. He subsequently became rector of the Balinese State College for Hindu Religion (Institut Hindu Dharma Negeri, IHDN) and has written many books about *agama Hindu*. He is arguably one of the most influential mediators between Balinese traditions and Indian philosophy. He developed the idea of an Indonesian *tirtha yatra* to India in 1990, and this format of pilgrimage became even more popular when Air India offered a special economy package for Balinese in 1999. Today, several travel agencies have specialized in the organization of *tirtha yatra* to India (Somvir 2004: 261). And, in the meantime, there have also been a number of *tirtha yatra* organized to visit the historically significant sanctuaries of the Hindu–Buddhist past in Java.

Thus, *tirtha yatra* were originally inaugurated as a means of introducing a consistent *agama Hindu*, and at the same time as a Hindu complement to the Hajj, the Islamic pilgrimage to Mecca that is flourishing among Indonesian Muslims across the country. Both forms of pilgrimage tours have an ideological aspect and *tirtha yatra* are supposed to inform Indonesians about the theological essence of Hindu traditions that were once brought from India, but had decayed after being combined with local ideas and practices in Java and Bali.

The educational agenda is evident from the strict program of every *tirtha yatra*, to which the pilgrims must in many respects surrender. They have very limited free time and are largely dependent on the tour guide, who stores their passports and holds a monetary deposit from all pilgrims for the duration of their trip. The usual *tirtha yatra* follow a strict itinerary, and most of the 8- to 12-day tours focus on North India as the heartland of Aryan history—and especially Haridwar as a place of Vedic learning and *moksa*. The historically important connection between South India and Indonesia is usually left out because *tirtha yatra* tend to emphasize a Vedic history and classical literature, including the *Bhagavadgita*—which is also politically important, as it is regarded as one of the holy books of *agama Hindu*.[5] On the other hand, locations with a particular connection to Śaiva traditions, which were influential for Bali's soteriological esoteric literature (*tutur*) and its *tantric* traditions, are ignored in *tirtha yatra*, as are local Indian ritual traditions.

Tirtha yatra begin in New Delhi, and most tours proceed to Mathura and Vrindavan as places of Krishna *bhakti*, before moving on to Haridwar as a center of Vishnu worship, vegetarianism, Vedic learning, pilgrimage and meditation on the riverbanks of the Ganges. Nearby Rishikesh is visited as the capital of yogis; on the way back to New Delhi they stop at Kurukshetra, as the battle field of the *Mahabharata*. Bhishma Kund is also visited, where the hero Bhishma's mother, Ganga, appeared miraculously when he lied down to die. But, above all, Jyotishar is visited, a temple complex in Kurukshetra built around a banyan tree, where it is believed that the *Bhagavadgita* was recited by Krishna to Arjuna. Thus, the itinerary emphasizes the importance of the *Bhagavadgita*, along with the worship of Krishna as its author; it connects the origin of *agama Hindu* as a book religion with the well-known stories of the *Mahabharata* (Fig. 6.2).

The 10-day pilgrimage tour that I joined was generally informed by the same Hindu reformist agenda, with a few significant exceptions, and with some interesting differences that reflect the particular ideas of the

---

[5] The Gita was propagated by Hindu reformers such as Rabindranath Tagore, who visited Bali in the 1920s, and who was also important for the Theosophical Movement. Theosophy was a significant influence for the first Indonesian president, Sukarno, who also appreciated the *Bhagavadgita* (Ramstedt 2004: 11).

Fig. 6.2 Kurukshetra, Balinese pilgrims in a temple for the banyan tree where the Bhagavadgita was delivered, February 2011

man who had founded and advertised the tour. This particular tour had been established by the Bali-based native Indian yogi, Sanskrit scholar and politician, Dr. Yadav Somvir, who is also the founder and director of the Bali-India Foundation in Denpasar. The lead guide for our *tirtha yatra* was a Balinese, Pak Putu[6], who was hired by Somvir as an experienced tour guide for pilgrimages in India.

Somvir himself is a Hindu reformer who came to Indonesia in the early 1990s as a member of Arya Samaj, a Hindu reform movement that aims '(to propagate) Hindu religion and philosophy,' as he said in a published interview in 2003.[7] He taught Sanskrit at the University of Denpasar and planned to establish a reformist Hindu boarding school (*gurukul*) in Bali, including cow worship. However, it would seem that

---

[6] Pseudonym.
[7] http://wwrn.org/articles/13655/, last accessed: 10.10.2015

Somvir's plans have changed substantially since then. During the *tirtha yatra* he was no longer interested in religion (*agama*), as he said, but rather in the propagation of yoga as a pre-and transreligious spiritual practice that realizes his ideal of universality and is able, on his account, to integrate followers of different religions and cultures without proselytization. To this end, he runs a yoga school in Denpasar where he trains local yoga teachers, has established yoga at Balinese schools and has a weekly yoga TV show. At the same time, Somvir teaches yoga for Muslim and Christian disciples in Java, for Buddhist disciples from Japan and for tourists from all over the world. His vision is the implementation of global spiritual tourism in Bali, which is supposed to supersede Bali's former cultural tourism. For this purpose, Somvir has purchased a large plot of land where he is building Markandeya Yoga City in northern Bali (Bedugul), which he promotes as the largest yoga center in Southeast Asia. The location is meant to become a center for classical Patanjali yoga and Ayurveda, but also for international and transreligious spiritual exchange. It seems that the realization of this ambitious plan requires more entrepreneurial and political qualities than a detached yoga guru can possibly offer, and consequently Yadav Somvir has recently become involved in local politics.

It must be emphasized that, in an Indonesian context, Somvir's vision of yoga as a transreligious form of spirituality is a political issue in itself. In January 2009, the Council of Indonesian Muslims (Majelis Ulama Indonesia, MUI) had issued a *fatwa* against all spiritual aspects of yoga. These aspects were deemed unfitting and potentially dangerous for Muslims because they tainted *agama Islam* with *agama Hindu*—an argument that demonstrates quite clearly the dialectical relation between interreligious conflict and the modern concept of religions as mutually exclusive belief systems. Yoga was therefore only accepted as a purely physical health practice, but not as a spiritual exercise involving Hindu *mantra* and sun salutation—which are nevertheless practiced by Dr. Somvir.

In view of the political implications of *agama*, Dr. Somvir avoided the term carefully. He inaugurated and organized the *tirtha yatra* together with a public celebration of his yoga festival that was simultaneously an 'International Bali-India Interfaith Conference' in Delhi. On this occasion, Somvir presented himself simply as a yogi and no longer as a missionary of Hinduism. He denied any interest in religion (*agama*), claiming as his only goal the propagation of yoga as a powerful practice of a pre- and transreligious character, which was able to integrate followers of different religions and cultures, thus fitting the Indonesian Constitution. The conference started with a series of influential keynote speakers, ranging from the Indonesian ambassador in Delhi to yoga sponsors from Japan and India. It included popular Indian yogis as well as a Balinese dancer from the royal family of Badung, who was also there as a pilgrim. As special guests, there were two officials from the conservative Council of Indonesian Muslims (MUI), the organization that had issued the *fatwa* against yoga. Muhyiddin Junaidi, the organization's chairman for international cooperation, presented an ardent speech praising the tolerance of Indonesian Islam and concluding with a commitment to yoga as a kind of exercise acceptable to all religions.

While Somvir may not have liked the idea of yoga as merely a form of sport, Junaidi, who sat to my left side, was shocked to hear Somvir claiming that yoga was more fundamental than any religion (*agama*). But neither of them articulated their irritation publicly, and neither did my Balinese copilgrims. They remained unconvinced by Junaidi's speech about tolerant Indonesian Islam, which is not surprising since they had been the victims of two Islamist terror attacks. And, shortly before the meeting, a mob of radicalized Javanese Muslims had publicly killed members of the heterodox Islamic Ahmadiyya group while smiling policemen watched the scene without attempting to intervene.

After such a diplomatically challenging beginning, it was clear that the pilgrimage had a 'double agenda'—as my roommate, a Balinese woman and factory owner, put it. Nevertheless, it was still seen as a *tirtha yatra* by the Balinese pilgrims. And, while Somvir avoided the term *agama* deliberately, the Balinese tour guide Putu taught the modernist and doctrinal form of *agama Hindu* during our hours on the bus. He acted as a mediator between the Indonesian paradigm of *agama Hindu*, Indian ritual practices and Balinese expectations. Accompanying the group during the entire trip, he explained how to behave in Indian temples and used the time on the bus to elucidate the universal doctrine of Hinduism to the Balinese pilgrims whom he encouraged to ask questions. In this way, he offered *dharma wacana*, a new format of religious education or indoctrination introduced by the PHDI as a complement to religious sermons. Even though he took his academic degree in geography, he considered himself a religious teacher, because he had received some religious training at the Balinese State College for Hindu Religion (IHDN), whose rector, I Made Titib, had inaugurated the practice of *tirtha yatra*. Beyond that, he also recommended himself as a spiritual guru, who had studied yoga in India for many years, suggesting that he was on a par with Dr. Somvir.

Both leading persons tried to realize their respective agendas with regard to modern Hinduism. On the one hand, Somvir wished to combine the program of a *tirtha yatra* with the promotion of yoga and spiritual tourism, for which he visited ashrams, invited international sponsors, politicians and Indian yogis for future collaborations. On the other, the Balinese tour guide used the additional conference day in Delhi to visit more sanctuaries, which were not only Hindu temples, but also sanctuaries with an agenda of religious pluralism—such as the Lotus temple of Baha'i, which claims the oneness of all religions and humankind, an ideal consonant with the Indonesian state doctrine of religious 'Unity in Diversity.'

It seems, however, that in the end the itinerary of this particular *tirtha yatra* was most powerfully informed by ideas of Arya Samaj, which is based on Vedic teachings, asceticism and the rejection of idol worship. Sites of Krishna *bhakti*, such as Mathura and Vrindavan for example, were skipped. And Yadav Somvir did not join the group when it visited temples with idol worship, even though we visited emblematic places and sanctuaries of Vedic history—above all Kurukshetra, Bhishma Kund and the sanctuary of Jyotishar. The focus of this tour was on Haridwar and Rishikesh, where we stayed for about 5 days. In Haridwar, Somvir joined the entire group again for yoga lessons at the Ganges riverbanks and for trips to several yoga ashrams and centers of Ayurvedic healing.

After a very brief touristic intermezzo in Jaipur, the tour ended again in New Delhi, with a visit to a modern temple complex with a decidedly reformist agenda—namely the impressive Akshardham Mandir. This so-called temple is actually a combination of temple and modern cultural center that celebrates, in multimedia shows, the saint and social reformer yogi Swaminarayan, who is deemed to be an *avatar* of Vishnu. When the Akshardham complex opened in 2005, it was promoted as the world's largest temple complex, representing in all its grandeur a socially integrative universal Hinduism. Simultaneously, it celebrates India as a source and global center of spirituality, enlightenment and humanism, thus emphasizing the ideology of Hinduism as a modern—and in this case also national—religion of international significance, if not superiority.

Tirtha Yatra Between 'Imagined Community' and 'Communitas': The Pilgrim's Experiences

I have elucidated so far some of the ideological, political and economic aspects of *tirtha yatra* in general and the double agenda of the *tirtha yatra* that I attended in particular. In what follows, I will contrast this official program with the bottom-up perspective of the pilgrims, whose lives and thoughts I shared night and day, as we slept in two-and three-bed rooms. The ultimate question was, of course, did they actually feel they had found the 'source' of their religion? And, if so, where did they find it?

Through the course of the bus trip, the pilgrims discussed their impressions. One of the first and most exciting experiences they cited was the feeling that, for once in their lives, they were not just a religious minority in the most populous Muslim country of the world. But, rather, they were part of a majority—the world's oldest world religious community. To them, the pilgrimage to the places of Vedic history was not a trip to the past, but instead a way of relocating themselves as Hindus and thus as members of a modern, global community.

We might wish to speculate that the Balinese pilgrims experienced some kind of international Hindu 'communitas' during temple visits, thus substantiating Victor Turner's (1967) classic theory regarding the anti-structural aspects of pilgrimages. This could be connected with Leo Howe's observation that new devotional sects from India, like Sai Baba or Hare Krishna groups, attract Balinese not least because they allow them to combine anti-structural aspects—which are absent from their traditional rituals—such as personal emotional surrender and pastoral care, with a sense of international inclusiveness (Howe 2004).

However, whereas feelings of devotion and international 'communitas' may apply to Sai Baba and Hare Krishna devotees in Bali and India, both were irrelevant for this pilgrimage.[8] The Balinese were not attracted

---

[8] Turner's theory was also contested to some degree with regard to Indian *tirtha yatra* by van der Veer's (1981) distinction between two types of Indian pilgrimage: a ritual-based pilgrimage that emphasizes caste differences rather than a communitas experience and a 'spiritual' pilgrimage to places of *bhakti* worship that ignores structural differences in favor of the personal and ultimately collective surrender to the *ishta-devata*, the personally chosen deity. However, neither of these two Indian paradigms fit the Balinese conception of pilgrimage, which was based neither on traditional ritual and social structures nor on personal devotion.

by devotional forms of worship. And, more importantly, they did not share any significant ritual or religious experience with Indian Hindus. Their sense of inclusion was not based on a transnational 'communitas' experience, but rather on a community that was, as we might say following Anderson, 'imagined' because it was mediatized in many ways by Indonesian *agama* politics, and with the help of the organizers of the *tirtha yatra*.

Behind the Balinese's joy at finally being part of an integrative global Hindu community stood an Indian travel agent who has co-organized *tirtha yatra* with Bali for more than twenty-five years, and who told me how difficult it was to satisfy his Indonesian customers. He had long experience working not only with Balinese pilgrims, but also with students of *agama Hindu* since the 1990s. And he had come to believe that the Balinese were the most pious people he had ever met—certainly much more so than his fellow Indians, whom he felt to be materialistic in comparison with the Balinese pilgrims, who, as he put it, were solely interested in religion.

Nevertheless, he added that it was a real challenge for him to avoid disappointing the Balinese. This was because there was a risk that Balinese would be refused entry by Indian villagers, who were unlikely to accept them as 'Hindus,' but rather classify them as polluting foreigners. Since this would be a shock to the Balinese, he had to choose very carefully only those Indian temples at pilgrimage places, or with a reformist agenda, where caste differences and restrictions for foreigners were not expected. None of the Balinese pilgrims could even imagine that such a problem could arise, as it would contradict the very idea of Indonesian *agama Hindu* as a universal world religion—and, even worse, it contradicts the Balinese ideal of an inherently integrative and harmonious Hinduism understood in opposition to Islam.

This self-image has important political implications and is frequently reaffirmed by Indonesian Hindus, who have come to understand their adherence to Hinduism in opposition to what they perceive as increasingly radical tendencies in Indonesian Islam, as exemplified by recent incidents of Islamist terror and violence. In contrast to such potentially threatening tendencies of Islam, Balinese proudly represent their religion, both on the national and international level, as inherently peaceful, integrative and universal. Their goal is not only to confirm the Indonesian ideal of 'Unity in Diversity,' but also to represent a paradigm of religious integration and peace for the entire world. This is the benchmark of Balinese identity discourse, both within the largest Muslim country and as an island that is living on international tourism, with roughly as many foreign tourists per year as local inhabitants.

Balinese thus regard themselves and their *agama* not only in competitive relation to Islam, but also to the centers of a global—and mostly secular—modern world. One example for this constant reaffirmation is a speech held by the Balinese governor, I Made Mangku Pastika, on the 2014 anniversary of the Islamist terror attack in Kuta, in which he emphasized interreligious harmony and peace, and where he admonished the Balinese: 'Bali is small, but the world is looking at us.'

The deliberate effort to represent *agama Hindu* as an integrative religion, in contrast to Islam and Christianity, offers some insight into how Balinese deal with the many foreigners living in their midst. Instead of excluding them from their temples, Balinese invite everyone to pray and to join rituals, under one condition—namely that foreigners adapt to the local ritual dress (*pakaian adat*) and form of prayer, which includes several items, such as flowers and incense. In other words, they must adapt to Balinese *adat*. Probably the Balinese pilgrims expected that they would be similarly integrated into Indian rituals, even more so because they were Hindus.

They were irritated, therefore, when an Indian priest criticized them for not praying correctly instead of simply showing them the Indian '*adat*.' Another disorienting experience was when the Balinese, who share their equipment for prayers, especially flowers and incense, with everyone who wants to pray, were required to give money to a *pujari*, rather than being invited to pray directly to the gods. Things became even worse when they were invited to pray by an Indian, who offered them flowers, but then asked for a large amount of money as payment. Such experiences did not support feelings of a borderless, transnational Hindu 'communitas,' but rather triggered a reflexive comparison of Bali and India. Over the course of the pilgrimage this gave rise to a wide range of sentiments, from critical differentiation to selective enthusiasm.

Not only did differentiation—rather than identification—inform the relation between Balinese and Indian Hinduism, but criticism and even conflict became an issue within the Indonesian group. And this was partly because of its double agenda. The pilgrims were much more heterogeneous than I had expected. I learned, to my surprise, that they were by no means all Balinese Hindus, but rather a miscellaneous gathering of Balinese Hindu pilgrims and Somvir's yoga disciples. They came both from Java and Bali, with differing backgrounds as to *agama*, ancestry and social status. There were Balinese Brahmin intellectuals, who held academic degrees in philosophy from Indian universities. But there were also casteless north Balinese villagers, who had collected all of their money for a once-in-a-lifetime visit to the holy places of Hinduism. A teacher for *agama Hindu* took part, as well as Muslim and Christian yoga teachers from Java. There were Balinese scientists and managers, who had spent most of their life in the capital city of Jakarta, and even members of the royal family of Badung, many of them supporters of Somvir's vision of a 'Yoga City' and 'spiritual tourism.' Some participants were relatively impoverished shop vendors; others were lawyers, professors, managers and regional politicians from North Bali. Some of the 'expat' Balinese practiced a form of Balinese ritualism (*adat*), while others had abandoned religion altogether, declaring they were 'atheists,' though still engaged with 'spirituality'—ranging from yoga and Transcendental Meditation to what they described as scientifically proven mystical experiences. And finally, there were some Balinese lay temple priests (*pemangku*) from Besakih, the island's most important mountain sanctuary, and the dwelling place of gods and divine ancestors; there was also a priestess, who turned out to be a trance medium, who regularly became possessed during our visits to Indian temples.

This assemblage of pilgrims was not only heterogeneous in terms of 'religion,' ancestry, education and ethnic identity, but also with respect to motivations, which began to clash. Most Balinese, and above all the *pemangku*, insisted that they were on a *tirtha yatra* to the holy places of their religion. Another group, consisting of the atheist Balinese and the Javanese Muslim and Christian yoga practitioners, but also of some of the Balinese yoga disciples and academics, saw themselves either exclusively—or additionally—on a trip to the historical origin places of Hinduism and, above all, of yoga.

Things became complicated when the Muslim and Christian yoga teachers from Java refused to enter local temples around Haridwar. For, besides colorful idol worship, these sites were of no historical significance for them on account of their adherence to a different religion (*agama*). Meanwhile, the urban atheists of Balinese origin refused to pray because they had abandoned *agama* completely. At this point, the non-Hindu pilgrims objected to the official program of the *tirtha yatra*, claiming that they were promised yoga lessons in different ashrams. When, in addition to this, the Balinese tour guide blamed a Muslim yoga teacher from Java for not being properly 'spiritual,' because she was not versed in the teachings of *agama Hindu*, the Javanese lady broke out in tears. Serious conflict was only averted with the timely intervention of Yadav Somvir. From this moment on, the group acknowledged their respective interests by continuing the pilgrimage in two busses, pursuing separate goals. Somvir led the Javano-atheist-yoga section to several ashrams in Rishikesh, avoiding temples with idol worship, which was also at odds with the ideas of Arya Samaj. I joined the Balinese group on their *tirtha yatra*, which was guided by the Balinese tour guide, who was now able to deliver hours of *dharma wacana* during the bus ride.

It is not my aim here to analyze this situation in all of its complexity. What I wish to emphasize is that the conflict which led to a split between the two groups arose only when the term *agama* was used—for once during the entire trip—in its modern sense, that is, as an exclusivist creed and doctrine, and thus in contrast to the Balinese self-perception and inclusivist understanding of *agama Hindu*. The Balinese pilgrims with whom I spoke emphasized not only that everybody could pray at a Hindu temple, and this because there was only one God, but they also distanced themselves from the tour guide's rude behavior. Their only complaint was that Somvir had not sufficiently informed his Javanese disciples that this was in fact a Hindu ritual, a *tirtha yatra*, and not simply a sightseeing trip to the historical sites of yoga. Beyond this, either side avoided discussing their respective religions, which were set aside as a personal matter.

Given this heterogeneous gathering of people with clashing interests, and a potentially exclusivist concept of religion, it is remarkable that there were nevertheless significant moments where the entire group joined in an atmosphere of solidarity—a shared spiritual experience, where their conflicts and differences became meaningless. This happened during what was, according to all the pilgrims, the highlight of the entire trip—a visit to the banks of the holy Ganges River in Haridwar, a place that was significant to both groups because it was a center of yoga as well as an important place of Vedic learning and Hindu pilgrimage. However, the ultimately integrative experience was neither yoga nor was it the visit to the Hindu university. Rather, it was the return to an immanent form of worship: the purifying bath in the Ganges River, in which all the pilgrims immersed themselves several times a day—and this notwithstanding the fact that the water was still icy cold from the melting snow of the

Fig. 6.3 Balinese and Javanese pilgrims during their ritual bath in Haridwar, February 2011

Himalayas. This experience was combined with a prayer by the Balinese and with yoga by many pilgrims (Fig. 6.3).

When asked at the end of the journey for their most important experience, all of them described the Ganges River bath as their central spiritual experience, no matter to which religion (if any) they subscribed. We can thus regard the bath as a trans- or multi-religious ritual integration reviving a common feature of old Indonesian rituals. Historical precedents include the Hindu-Buddha rituals of the rulers of Majapahit. But similar ritual integrations apply to ancestor rituals in Sumatra, performed by Christians and Muslims together, or to Chinese Confucian shrines in Balinese Hindu temples of the Batur region, and on Nusa Penida. And even Muslims who resist the purification of their religion travel from Lombok to Bali to pray at a Śiva Lingga, from which holy water emerges.[9] Or they celebrate together in Hindu Balinese rituals at the old multi-religious temple of Lingsar in Lombok, which is also associated with water (Gottowik 2008; Harnish 2014).

Thus, the Ganges became a 'dominant symbol' (Turner 1967) of this spontaneous multi-religious ritual integration. For, despite its varying theological ascriptions, holy water connects religions as different as Islam, Catholicism and Hinduism. And the collective engagement with water helped to mediate a shared experience, while doctrinal—and for that matter structural—aspects of the respective religions became meaningless.

BACK TO THE SOURCE? BALINESE IDEAS ABOUT HOLY WATER AND PILGRIMAGE

This brings me back to my initial question. If the ritual Ganges bath was an example of multi-religious integration in the face of politically imposed religious purification and polarization, what did this mean to the Balinese pilgrims? Did they find what they had been looking for—namely the 'source' of *agama Hindu*? And if so, where was it located?

We have seen that institutionalized *tirtha yatra* to India supported the political agenda of reform Hinduism, thus imposing a paradigm of transcendent book religion along with a disenchanted world. But the practical realization of this paradigm on the side of the pilgrims differs markedly both from the top-down program of Indonesian politics and from Indian practice. The Balinese way to the 'source' of *agama Hindu* thus had unexpected, or even paradoxical, results, which I would like to illustrate in light of three examples.

The pilgrims' reaction to Indian sanctuaries was split. On the one hand, they were truly impressed and not only by the artistically refined Indian architecture. They were also interested to learn that the narratives of their shadow theater plays were no mere fantasies, but rather had been historically substantiated—as for example, in Kurukshetra. On the other

---

[9] The pair of huge rocks was recently found in the sea of East Bali, but they could not even be lifted by a crane until a priest decided that they were a manifestation of divine presence and should be venerated. Currently, the rocks are in a temporary sanctuary where the *yoni* produces miraculously holy water (*tirtha*), but a new temple is in the making in Ujung. The officiating priest explained to me that many Muslims from Lombok would come to pray at the Lingga Yoni, asking for its holy water as a remedy for all kinds of problems.

hand, they found the extreme poverty, in general, and the great numbers of beggars around temples as disturbing as the commoditized ritual services inside temples. This was particularly the case at pilgrimage centers and in the modern reform Hindu Akshardham Mandir (which some of them even refused to regard as a temple).

But there was one feature that truly intrigued several pilgrims, and this was the naturalistic idols of gods—especially in the more rural temples around Haridwar. Most Balinese *puja* are aniconic, which makes them easily congruent with the program of *agama Hindu* as a monotheist religion with an animist ontology. Balinese share a common understanding that gods, ancestors and demons are invisible beings that can only be 'felt' (*terasa*) as a powerful non-human agency in specific situations and places. Consequently, they regard the mostly abstract effigies of their rituals not as visual representations of gods, but instead as their sitting places (*pelinggih*). Virtually everything can become a sitting place: a rock as well as a piece of coral, or a small piece of wood with a gold-plated face. The visual form says nothing about the power, or nature of the deity, that dwells invisibly on its sitting place during rituals.

It was therefore surprising to me that some of the pilgrims loved the naturalistic and anthropomorphic idols in India and said they felt somehow closer to them. This is all the more interesting because, in recent years, the mass production of statues—especially of Ganesha and the Buddha—has begun in Bali. In particular, Ganesha statues of all sizes are bought for private households, either for decoration or, increasingly, as new objects of worship. In some cases, even new Indian *puja* are introduced. And, since Balinese have learned that Ganesha likes milk (which is absent from traditional Balinese nutrition patterns and rituals), they purchase it from the supermarket and offer it to their Ganesha statues. Thus, it would appear that Indian idol worship is becoming increasingly attractive to many Balinese. And it has also begun to influence Balinese temple rituals—for example in a recent temple foundation in Ujung—where the two huge natural rocks representing Yoni and Linga have been decorated with Indian-style flower garlands and combined with a new Ganesha statue, following the orders of a high ranking priest in Denpasar. This fascination with idol worship is obviously a new aspect of ritual related to the intensified contact with India. But it is nevertheless at odds with the reformist paradigm of *agama Hindu* that criticizes idol worship and emphasizes monotheism and *moksa*.

A second and even more surprising and paradoxical finding for the Balinese pilgrims themselves was the fact that local deities in India, and even their ancestors, possessed them in a foreign land. During the pilgrimage, some important incidents at Indian sanctuaries forced the Balinese pilgrims to reconsider the official agenda of *agama Hindu* in terms of their own framework of interpretation and world perception. This was the case when the priestess (*pemangku*) became unexpectedly possessed at Bhishma Kund. When she returned from the sanctuary, which contained a naturalistic statue of Bhishma lying on the ground and pierced with arrows, she lost consciousness, started wailing and had to be carried to a chair, stammering unintelligible words until the tour guide sprinkled some of the water from the *kund* on her. It was obvious to the entire group that she was undergoing a possession (*kerauhan*), which is a common feature of Balinese ritual, where it indicates that either a local deity or an ancestor—but never one of the Hindu gods—has arrived (*rauh*) and has entered a human body as a vessel for his manifestation. He may just want to join the ritual or share food, but in most cases complains that something with the ritual went wrong. It cannot be predicted who will be possessed, or when, because it all depends on the god of a particular place. This localized and immanent Balinese ritual practice is based on the assumption that invisible (*niskala*) agents, who inhabit the same world, manifest themselves from time to time in a human body to convey their wishes. This important feature of Balinese rituals is eliminated from the official agenda of *agama Hindu*, because it contradicts the idea of a universal religion in more than one way. Not only are local gods related to specific places, and thus not part of a world religion, but, moreover, their spontaneous appearance can initiate new local forms of worship, including new sanctuaries and collective decisions. This implies a kind of immanent agency, creativity and innovation that would potentially threaten to supersede the authority of a doctrinal text (Hornbacher 2011).

On account of its relatively unpredictable character, there is a certain reluctance regarding possession among Balinese. And, indeed, many feel threatened or embarrassed by the often violent and uncontrollable behavior of the possessed, which contrasts sharply with the prevailing cultural ideal of emotional self-control.

Confronted with the unexpected possession of the priestess, the Balinese tour guide handled the incident quickly and effectively, by following the practice of Balinese ritual. He got some water from the *kund* and sprinkled it on her head, which brought her immediately back to consciousness—much as would have been the case in Bali, where the sprinkling of *tirtha* by a priest is the appropriate way to worship a deity and induce him or her to leave the body. And yet the otherwise eloquent tour guide had no little trouble interpreting the incident with reference to *agama Hindu* and its conception of a transcendent deity. Finally, however he did so, explaining that this should not irritate anyone, because God the Almighty (Sanghyang Widhi) had tried to communicate with the group.

But this explanation did not convince the Balinese participants, as they later told me. The priestess was possessed not only once, but several times in different circumstances. And, as her behavior indicated, these possessions were by different deities in different places. In one case, she was even possessed by a Chinese deity, who spoke in what the other participants identified as Chinese. They were puzzled because this could neither be linked to local Hindu gods nor to neo-Hindu monotheism, but rather to the Chinese ancestor gods who had already entered the priestess in southern Bali. The pilgrims were not sure how to interpret the case. But they were sure that *agama Hindu* as a transcendent monotheism was not helpful for explaining what was happening.

The trance medium herself had an interesting theory. She was convinced that her frequent possessions during the *tirtha yatra* were only possible because *agama Hindu* was in fact a world religion. But she explained this universality in terms that differed from those of reformist Hinduism. She assumed that local Indian deities had entered her because, as member of a global Hindu community, she was a spiritually fitting medium for their manifestation. She was all the more confident in her assessment as she felt many of the Indian sanctuaries were extremely spiritually vibrant (*sangat vibrasi*) dwelling places of local gods. For her, the possession experiences at sacred places in India were evidence of the universality of *agama Hindu*, even though possession along with the worship of place gods is in fact a feature of Bali's animist ontology and *adat*. This interpretation was shared by other pilgrims as well. This seemed to suggest that, to them, the universality of *agama Hindu* is not based on a universal doctrine, belief system or book, but rather on the fact that the perception of and interaction with *niskala* beings are possible in India as well as in Bali. Or, in other words, possession was seen to have proved the global validity of a Balinese world perception and cosmology in terms of a universal *agama Hindu*.

I am inclined to interpret this as an act that is at once creative and subversive, turning the normative and doctrinal agenda of *agama Hindu* inside out through reinterpretation. Here reformist Hinduism's politically powerful claim to universality has been adopted, while at the same time it is redefined in terms of a localized animist ontology. Ironically, the latter was formerly one of the aspects of Balinese *adat* that disqualified it from recognition by the state as a universal religion or *agama*. In this way, the idea of an enchanted being-in-the-world—which was formerly dismissed as a residue of Bali's backward animist *adat*—is now being actively extended to India as a redefinition of *agama Hindu* in terms of a Balinese world perception and immanent style of worship.

This brings us back to the uncontested highlight of the pilgrimage. The ritual immersion in the Ganges River represented the third—and, for the Balinese, by far the most important—experience of the true 'source' of *agama Hindu*. I have argued that the interreligious 'communitas' experience of this ritual bath was related to the shared experience with holy water that has different, but always important, implications in each of the different religions in play. The ritual engagement with the medium of water is in several respects remarkable. It shows how Indonesian pilgrims of different doctrinal backgrounds can ritually cooperate in immanent worship, thus avoiding what van der Veer and others have observed: the implementation of a modern concept of religion as a coherent doctrine creates in postcolonial states new exclusivist group identities, and eventually violent conflicts—for example, between Indian Muslims and Hindus (van der Veer 1996).

Whatever this ritual immersion might have meant to the Muslim, Christian and atheist members of the group, from the perspective of *agama Hindu* the Ganges River bath was not just a social experience of multi-religious harmony. It was, for them, the crucial ritual during the *tirtha yatra*. As the tour guide explained, the Hindu pilgrims would reach *moksa* and thus realize the highest goal of *agama Hindu*, once their sins were washed away after sixteen immersions in the Ganges.

The pilgrims, for their part, confirmed that in the Ganges they had found what they were looking for: the 'source' of their religion, *agama Hindu*. But, rather than emphasizing *moksa* as a personal motivation for the bath, they described the direct and unmediated immersion in holy water as a communion with *Ibu Gangga*, or 'Mother Ganges,' and as their strongest spiritual experience during the pilgrimage. If we take this explanation literally, it suggests that the bath was not just a means for the realization of a transcendent end—ultimate liberation, or *moksa* after death—but rather it was the real and direct connection with an immanent deity residing in a particular place in India.

Once again, rather than replacing their ideas of an enchanted world with a transcendent doctrine, the Balinese extended their engagement with it in the course of their pilgrimage to North India. In this respect, their idea of a *tirtha yatra* was not informed by the concept of ultimate liberation, as it had been taught to them by their tour guide, but rather by common Balinese ritual practice and its concept of *tirtha* as a medium of cosmological communion. This, however, raises a question as to the significance of *tirtha* in its transcultural usage.

As we have seen, the word *tirtha* is omnipresent in Bali. But it refers only to 'holy water,' which is essential for every ritual, despite being used in a variety of ways. It can be prepared by Brahmin priests (*pedanda*), who empower it with their *mantra*. But it is also a manifestation of divine presence in particular places in the natural environment and thus a manifestation of Bali's animist ontology.[10] Ritually important forms of *tirtha* are the water of the crater lake Batur and of spring sanctuaries, some of which are related to old kingdoms (e.g., Tampaksiring). But there is also water from the sea, as well as the runnel of dripping water on the top of the holy mountain Gunung Agung, the dwelling place of deified ancestors and gods. The water of young coconuts is similarly a ritually important form of holy water. The cosmological aspect of holy water is particularly obvious during big temple ceremonies when ritual delegations are sent to ask for holy water (*nunas tirtha*) from the most important water sanctuaries and temples of Bali. This water is carried back to their temple, where it is mixed with the holy waters of other places before it is sprinkled over the shrines and gods. Yet, in Bali, this ritual pilgrimage to water sanctuaries is not generally linked to the idea of *moksa*. Rather it is more commonly regarded as a communion with the powers of significant places in the world. Water is the visible medium of the invisible agency of divine presence in the Balinese cosmology.

Historically, *tirtha* is a term derived from Sanskrit, in which it has a somewhat different meaning—namely the crossing or ford of

---

[10] A priest in the old Balinese mountain village of Trunyan told me that the holy water (*tirtha*) in his temple was not 'made' by virtue of *mantra*, but directly taken from the crater lake, which is regarded both as a divinity and as the source of *tirtha*.

a river—where the water is shallow and easy to traverse from one side to the other. However, in the context of Indian pilgrimages, *tirtha* refers metaphorically to holy places in general and even to holy books as media—or easy crossings—between the material world and *moksa*. A *tirtha yatra* is therefore a procession to places, persons or objects that provide a passage from this world to *moksa*. But these are not necessarily related to water, even though this happens to be the case in pilgrimage places along holy rivers, such as Haridwar, and most obviously in Benares, which is the paradigmatic place to reach ultimate liberation—*moksa*.[11]

Concluding Remarks

These different ideas concerning the meaning and goal of a *tirtha yatra* represent in microcosm the different and rival conceptions of *agama Hindu* with which the Balinese pilgrims were grappling during their trip.

For its organizers, the *tirtha yatra* was clearly an instrument of ideological normalization and religious modernization—which ultimately involved rationalization, and therefore the disenchantment of human–environment relations. Notwithstanding the 'top-down' agenda of this entire event, the pilgrims developed their own, subversive ideas about the universality of *agama Hindu* during their journey. Their resistance to the official agenda was at least partly a result of the new political situation that emerged in the wake of Indonesian *Reformasi*, with its less restrictive politics of *agama*, which facilitated the emergence of new religious movements and revitalizations of local ideas and practices. One example is the reappropriation of *agama Hindu* in aid of environmental politics defending *adat* traditions. This would include, for instance, recent resistance movements against development plans around Lake Buyan and elsewhere. A similar tendency may be seen in the Balinese pilgrims' practical or performative realization of *agama Hindu* during their pilgrimage. Although they visited the origin places of their 'holy books,' they showed no interest in learning more about the *Bhagavadgita*. Instead, they discussed the 'vibrations' (*vibrasi*) of specific places in relation to trance possession. And while a bath in the Ganges was

---

[11] Moreover, in South Indian temples, *tirtham* is also given as part of a *puja* to the worshippers. Yet, notwithstanding such similarities, *tirtha* is not necessarily connected to water in the Indian context.

recommended as a means for liberation from the world, and thus as a distinctive ritual for *agama Hindu*, they practiced it as a multi-religiously integrative ritual of immanent worship—thus performing *agama Hindu* as a spontaneous revitalization of Indonesia's integrative ritual *adat*.

We may therefore say that the Balinese pilgrims performatively extended their animist ontology to India, rather than adopting a transcendent and rationalist reform Hindu paradigm of religion. They actually performed their pilgrimage as *nunas tirtha*, 'asking for holy water' from the Ganges, which they carried back home to mix it with holy water from other places in Bali in their local rituals. In this way, the Balinese pilgrims turned the political agenda of *tirtha yatra*, and for that matter of *agama Hindu*, inside out. For, rather than adopting *agama Hindu* as an abstract doctrine, they experienced India in terms of their Balinese ontology—which centers on the personal engagement with holy places imbued with the agency or *vibrasi* of immanent deities. In other words, it turned out during the pilgrimage—ostensibly to the 'real Indian source' of *agama Hindu*—that their immanent worship was no longer a matter of a backward Balinese custom, but rather the manifestation of a modern globalized Hinduism.

In the end, the pilgrims had dialectically appropriated the modern concept of 'religion' by using the political power of *agama Hindu*, while replacing its ontological implications—especially the idea of a disenchanted world—with their own world perception and immanent style of worship. However, since the latter had become a matter of universal Hinduism, they no longer thought of it as an expression merely of local tradition (*adat*). Instead, they used a modern and global buzzword—'*sepiritual*'—to describe their experience, which they thought of as the universal essence of religion. The *tirtha yatra* may have been intended to support a universal and modern reform Hinduism. But instead it confirmed the pilgrims' conviction that experiences of immanent spirituality were not limited to the island of Bali, but rather were universal. By the end of their journey, however, most of the pilgrims felt that the spiritual essence of *agama Hindu* was in fact more readily apparent in Bali than in India.

Such is my understanding of the words of one of the Balinese priests who echoed what others had said. To him, the pilgrimage was a wonderful experience, especially because of the Ganges. But he had come to the conclusion that—precisely in this respect—Bali was even 'more spiritual' (*lebih sepiritual*), and thus truly universal. And this was because

Balinese sanctuaries were more obviously connected with springs, trees and mountains—and thus with an environment inhabited by non-human agents. For him, Balinese sanctuaries support the experience of a divine presence, in places that can be perceived by everyone—even by tourists—as *sepiritual*, no matter in which religious doctrine he or she believes.[12]

References

Agamben, Giorgio. 1998. *Homo Sacer: Sovereign Power and Bare Life*. Stanford: Stanford University Press.

Assmann, Jan. 2000. *Religion Und Kulturelles Gedächtnis: Zehn Studien*. München: Beck.

Bakker, Frederik L. 1993. *The Struggle of the Hindu Balinese Intellectuals. Developments in Modern Hindu Thinking in Independent Indonesia*. Amsterdam: VU University Press.

Davidson, Jamie Seth, and David Henley. 2007. *The Revival of Tradition in Indonesian Politics: The Deployment of Adat from Colonialism to Indigenism*. London: Routledge.

Dihle, Albrecht. 1988. Heilig. In *Reallexikon für Antike und Christentum*, vol. 14, ed. E. Dassmann, 1–63. Stuttgart: Anton Hiersemann Verlag.

Fitzgerald, Timothy. 2000. *The Ideology of Religious Studies*. New York: Oxford University Press.

Geertz, Clifford. 1964. 'Internal conversion' in contemporary Bali. In *Malayan and Indonesian Studies: Essays presented to Sir Richard Winstedt on his eighty-fifth birthday*, ed. J.S. Bastin and R. Roolvink, 282–302. Oxford: Clarendon Press.

Gottowik, Volker. 2008. *Interagama*: Multireligiöse Rituale in Zentralindonesien. In *Zwischen Synkretismus und Orthodoxie. Zur religiösen Dynamik Südostasiens*, ed. V. Gottowik and A. Hornbacher. *Themenheft der Zeitschrift für Ethnologie* 133/1: 31–50.

Harnish, David D. 2014. "Balinese and Sasak Religious Trajectories in Lombok. Interactions, Tensions, and Performing Arts at the Lingsar Temple". In *Between Harmony and Discrimination: Negotiating Religious Identities within Majority-Minority Relationships in Bali and Lombok*, ed. B. Hauser-Schäublin and D.D. Harnish, 61-83. Leiden & Boston: Brill.

Hornbacher, Annette. 2011. The withdrawal of the gods: Remarks on ritual trance-possession and its decline in Bali. In *The Politics of Religion in Indonesia: Syncretism, orthodoxy, and religious contention in Java and Bali*, ed. M. Picard and R. Madinier, 167–191. London: Routledge.

---

[12] I want to thank my colleagues William Sax and Richard Fox for taking the time to improve the English of this essay.

Hornbacher, Annette. 2014. Contested *Moksa* in Balinese *Agama Hindu*. Balinese death rituals between ancestor worship and modern Hinduism. In *Dynamics of Religion in Southeast Asia. Magic and Modernity*, ed. V. Gottowik, 237–260. Chicago: The University of Chicago Press & Amsterdam: Amsterdam University Press.

Howe, Leo. 2004. Hinduism, identity and social conflict: The Sai Baba movement in Bali. In *Hinduism in Modern Indonesia: A minority religion between local, national, and global interests*, ed. M. Ramstedt, 264–280. London: RoutledgeCurzon.

http://whc.unesco.org/en/list/1194.

Kipp, Rita Smith, and Susan Rodgers. 1987. *Indonesian Religions in Transition*. Tucson: University of Arizona Press.

Picard, Michel. 2004. What's in a name? *Agama Hindu Bali* in the making. In *Hinduism in Modern Indonesia: A minority religion between local, national, and global interests*, ed. M. Ramstedt, 56–75. London: RoutledgeCurzon.

Picard, Michel. 2011a. Balinese religion in search of recognition: From *agama Hindu Bali* to *agama Hindu* (1945–1965). *Bijdragen tot de Taal-, Land- en Volkenkunde* 167 (4): 482–510.

Picard, Michel. 2011b. From *Agama Hindu Bali* to *Agama Hindu* and back. Toward a relocalization of the Balinese religion?. In *The Politics of Religion in Indonesia: Syncretism, orthodoxy, and religious contention in Java and Bali*, ed. M. Picard and R. Madinier, 117–141. London: Routledge.

Pitana, I Gde. 2010. Tri Hita Karana—The local wisdom of the Balinese in managing development. In *Trends and Issues in Global Tourism*, ed. R. Conrady and M. Buck, 139–150. Berlin Heidelberg: Springer.

Ramstedt, Martin. 2004. Negotiating identities—Indonesian 'Hindus' between local, national, and global interests. In *Hinduism in Modern Indonesia: A minority religion between local, national, and global interests*, ed. M. Ramstedt, 1–34. London: RoutledgeCurzon.

Reuter, Thomas. 2008. *Global Trends in Religion and the Reaffirmation of Hindu Identity in Bali*. Working Paper. Clayton: Monash University, Centre of Southeast Asian Studies.

Roth, Dik, and Gede Sedana. 2015. Reframing Tri Hita Karana: from 'Balinese culture' to politics. *The Asia Pacific Journal of Anthropology* 16 (2): 157–175.

Smith, Wilfred Cantwell. 1962. *The Meaning and End of religion. A New Approach to the Religious Traditions of Mankind*. New York: The Macmillan Company.

Somvir, Yadav. 2004. Cultural and religious interaction between modern India and Indonesia. In *Hinduism in Modern Indonesia: A minority religion between local, national, and global interests*, ed. M. Ramstedt, 255–263. London: RoutledgeCurzon.

Strauss, Sophie. 2015. Alliances across Ideologies: Networking with NGOs in a tourism dispute in northern Bali. *The Asia Pacific Journal of Anthropology* 16 (2): 123–140.
Turner, Victor. 1967. *The Forest of Symbols: Aspects of Ndembu Ritual.* Ithaca: Cornell University Press.
Van der Veer, Peter. 1981. Pilgrimage as a social process in Uttar Pradesh. Conference Paper at the SOAS, London.
Van der Veer, Peter. 1996. *Religious Nationalism. Hindus and Muslims in India.* Delhi: Oxford University Press.
Von Stietencron, Heinrich, and Vasudha Dalmia. 1995. *Representing Hinduism. The Construction of Religious Traditions and National Identity.* New Delhi: Sage.
Warren, Carol. 1998. Tanah Lot: The cultural and environmental politics of resort development in Bali. In *The Politics of Environment in Southeast Asia. Resources and Resistance*, ed. Ph. Hirsch and C. Warren, 229–261. London: Routledge.
Weber, Max. 1988. Die protestantische Ethik und der Geist des Kapitalismus. In *Gesammelte Aufsätze zur Religionssoziologie I.* Tübingen: Mohr.
Wirz, Paul. 1928. *Der Totenkult auf Bali.* Stuttgart: Strecker und Schröder.

Author Biography

Annette Hornbacher is Professor of Cultural Anthropology at the Institute of Anthropology, University of Heidelberg (Germany). Her main fields of research are Balinese ritual and its current transformation, intercultural ethics, and ecology. Her recent publications include "The withdrawal of the gods: remarks on ritual trance-possession and its decline in Bali", in M. Picard & R. Madinier (eds), *The Politics of Religion in Indonesia. Syncretism, Orthodoxy, and Religious Contention in Java and Bali* (2011), and "Contested *Moksa* in Balinese *Agama Hindu*. Balinese Death Rituals between Ancestor Worship and Modern Hinduism", in V. Gottowik (ed.), *Dynamics of Religion in Southeast Asia. Magic and Modernity* (2014). "The Body of Letters: Balinese *Aksara* as an Intersection between Script, Power and Knowledge", in A. Hornbacher & R. Fox (eds.), *The Materiality and Efficacy of Balinese Letters* (2016).

CHAPTER 7

A Wall, Even in Those Days! Encounters with Religions and What Became of the Tradition

Cécile Barraud

PREAMBLE[1]

The beginning of the seventeenth century saw the development of an intense rivalry among Dutch, English, and Portuguese traders competing all over the Moluccas, in Eastern Indonesia, for the control of the spice trade. The Banda Archipelago of the central Moluccas was once systematically visited by Chinese, Muslim Javanese and Malay traders, and its population's conversion to Islam began in the 1480s.

---

[1] As I was writing this paper, when I described the wall constructed in this village in the seventeenth century, my interlocutor exclaimed: 'A wall! Already back then?', hence the title of this chapter.

I would like to express my sincere thanks to Michel Picard for having attentively read this text numerous times, to Bénédicte Brac de la Perrière and to André Iteanu for their suggestions, to Dinah Fay for her idea, and to ChelsieYount-André thanks to whom this text became readable!

C. Barraud (✉)
Centre Asie du Sud-Est, CNRS-EHESS, Paris, France

The struggle between the Dutch and the British for the monopoly on nutmeg cultivation and trade in Banda became particularly fierce in the early 1600s (Reid 1993: 6–7)[2]. The Dutch considered the Bandanese unfaithful and treacherous, unwilling to follow any trade agreement. In 1621, the Dutch governor general of the V.O.C. (*Vereenigde Oost-Indische Compagnie*), J.P. Coen, decided to attack the Bandanese, which resulted in a massacre. Only a few Bandanese succeeded in escaping towards nearby islands of the Moluccas, Seram, in the north, and Kei and Aru in the south-east (15,000 dead, 1000 survivors). The Bandanese were then replaced by Javanese slaves who cultivated the plantations (Kaartinen 2010, Chap. 2; Aveling 1967; Hanna 1978).

This is where History ends and the story begins.

In the Kei Archipelago, in the Southeast Moluccas, the people of Tanebar-Evav—a tiny island south-west of the Kei Archipelago main islands, which are comprised of the Great Kei and Small Kei—recall that, long ago, Muslim refugees from Banda Island, fleeing the Dutch, asked for shelter. According to the elders who reported this story, which they cannot date, the refugees came before the islanders and persistently asked the people of Tanebar-Evav to convert to Islam. The latter refused firmly and decided to wage war against the refugees, saying that: 'our "tradition" (*adat*) goes with our land, the Sun-Moon God wants us to guard and protect it, our tradition has not been washed ashore from the sea like flotsam and jetsam to become our belief (*perca*) and to be worshipped, *adat* belongs to our land'. But the Banda people did not want to fight. Instead of war, they came to an agreement in the form of a mutual aid relationship called *baran ya'an war* ('elder-younger brothers'), involving mutual aid in all matters and the prohibition of intermarriage. The refugees went on to settle on the Great Kei and founded the village of Wadan-El (Banda-Ely), where they still live today. They do not speak Keiese, but a different language, close to Bandanese (Kaartinen 2010). Islam was thus rejected by the people of Tanebar-Evav, and as testament to this agreement with the Bandanese, a wall was constructed in front of Tanebar-Evav village in the bay used as

---

[2] The conflict between the Dutch and the British was settled in 1667 by the Treaty of Breda, in which the latter exchanged the tiny island of Run that they controlled in the Banda Islands for the island of Manhattan, controlled by the Dutch.

a harbour, which is left exposed at low tide. The wall, about two metres wide, one metre high, and fifty metres long, runs discontinuously from one side of the bay to the other. The bay narrows into a U-shape approximately a hundred metres from the village shore where the wall leaves open a wide entrance on its left side and a smaller one on the right side. On a picture taken in 1893 (Pleyte), two statues are visible on each side of this entrance. Although the wall has since collapsed, heaps of stones in a line and the entrance are still visible. The wall signified that Islam should never trespass this border it marked on the ground. An elderly man told me that the wall protected them from 'religion' (*agam*), specifically Islam, but Christianity as well. The entrance (called 'mouth') is still a place where women bathe for the first time after childbirth. The name of the wall translates literally to 'the wall that jingles and surrounds the village' (*lutur ngil rov oho*). It is said that at one time the wall made a clear sound at the approach of enemies, alerting and protecting inhabitants. It separates the land of the ancestors (inland, 'island mother') from the land beyond ('island child'). On the ancestors' side of the wall, *agam* should not enter, but beyond the wall, it is allowed. When a woman marries a man from another village, it is said that the wall is 'destroyed' (*lutur varaha*). A ritual must be held as a compensation for the society (*lór*)[3] lest, they explain, 'pigs will enter the gardens and take our food'.

This is the people of Tanebar-Evav's first known encounter with new beliefs and 'religion'.

The wall was not aimed at forbidding the arrival of foreigners nor at expelling them, as will become clear with the developments below. Neither was it meant to exclude refugees and newcomers. But rather, its open entrance or 'mouth', guarded by the two statues, was meant, on the contrary, to integrate and welcome them, on the condition that they refrain from bringing 'belief' in with them. It functions as a reminder that some events, thought to endanger the socio-cosmic order of the society or perceived as pertaining to a different order, could not enter (Fig. 7.1).

---

[3] The term *lór*, meaning 'society', will be discussed below.

Fig. 7.1 The wall (Pleyte 1893)

INTRODUCTION

The society studied here has been relatively isolated from the routes, trends, and movements that brought world religions to the region. In this context, world religions refer first to Islam, long ago introduced in the Moluccas by traders, and then Protestantism and Catholicism, established during colonial domination. These religions are called *agam* in the local language and are contrasted with *adat* ('tradition'). Apart from these, another religion was introduced more recently, *agama Hindu*, connected in some ways with Bali but which should not be confused with Hinduism. The word *agama* ('religion') is used in Indonesia to designate these different faiths, by those who practise a religion as well as by those who do not. That same word has also come to designate a Hinduized version of Balinese ritual practices and scriptures that is now called *agama Hindu*, or *Hindu Dharma*.[4]

---

[4] See Picard's chapter in this volume.

Until the 1980s, Tanebar-Evav[5] had only been slightly touched by Protestantism or Catholicism, while a small community of Muslims had long ago marginally settled on the island. But while these religious institutions were established relatively recently, foreign religious notions pertaining to Islam or Christianity have long been integrated into the socio-cosmic order of this society and its mythology, mainly through conceptual language, to the point that they became assimilated into expressions of tradition.

With the hindsight granted by carrying out fieldwork in the Kei Archipelago over a period of more than forty years, it is possible to trace how certain changes occurred and infer as to why others did not, in both discourse and practice, as well as to learn what values are attributed to these changes in terms of the socio-cosmic order. This essay attempts to untangle the diverse discourses found in people's comments about their views of tradition and religion, those of outsiders such as politicians or missionaries, and official definitions of *adat* and *agama* used by the Ministry of Religion.

My aim is to understand the distinctions local people make between *adat* and *agama*. Facing diverse flows of contact, this population has accepted some influences and rejected others, bringing its own original responses, which oblige scholars to reconsider the relationship between religion and tradition. The question is why and how the people coped with the coexistence of religion and tradition, and whether they perceive continuity or social change in this ongoing process. To examine this process, the chapter analyses ritual notions and practices, usually described as 'religion' or 'beliefs' by scholars, but which are called *adat* in Tanebar-Evav. Furthermore, it explains how four 'religions' have come to coexist in such a small village.

The picture is different in the rest of the Kei Archipelago, which, unlike Tanebar-Evav, was touched by Islam before the nineteenth century, while Christianity (Catholicism and Protestantism) was introduced at the beginning of the twentieth century. Nowadays, all villages in Kei are either Muslim, Protestant, or Catholic. Sometimes the confessions are mixed; in other cases, they are spatially separated, divided according to which neighbourhood has a mosque or a Protestant or Catholic church. Although the situation of Tanebar-Evav village figures as an exception, this does not mean that other villages rejected their traditions,

---

[5] Tanebar-Evav is the name of the island, the village, and of the society.

all the more so after the 1999–2000 events (detailed below). The interplay of *adat* and *agama*, not specific to the Moluccas (see, e.g. Aragon 2000), has been particularly noticeable since these events.

Indeed, these questions are part of an ongoing debate in Indonesia, where the combination of *agama* (religion) and *adat* (tradition)—as well as *budaya* (culture)—varies from one region to another. In some regions, religious celebrations are made in the name of tradition. In others, as is the case in Tana Toraja (Dana Rappoport, personal communication, 2016) and in Bali, *upacara adat* ('traditional ceremony') and *upacara agama* ('religious ceremony') appear interchangeable.

This chapter deals with the following questions: How do people who hold to ancestral traditions define religion? Do they differentiate it from their traditions? What are the implications of new beliefs? Is the idea of belief itself meaningful in a traditional context? Do those who practise a religion define religion in a way that differentiates it from traditional ritual practices and discourse (Ortigues 1999)?

My introduction to these debates, in the preamble, has already begun to work towards some answers to these questions. This chapter presents first a short historical account to introduce the contemporary religious context in the Kei Archipelago. Second, it describes social life in Tanebar-Evav village society and shows how villagers have incorporated new ideas into their world view. The third section studies the relationship between the religions present on the island and the village's original position towards them. These changes are then analysed through the lens of the Indonesian government's regional policies. Finally, this chapter attempts to delineate distinctions, if any exist, between that which pertains to religion and that which belongs to tradition in these varied discourses. It focuses on both ritual and everyday practices and attitudes in the relationship between the people as human beings and various categories of deities, spirits, or beings. The conclusion points to the ceaseless efforts and adjustments necessary to maintain a certain coherence while adapting to the world changing circumstances.

The Context

Before introducing the question of 'religions' in the society of Tanebar-Evav, a brief sketch of the complex contemporary socio-politico-religious context in the Kei Archipelago and Moluccas is in order. For this background description on the Kei islands, I rely on historical data, surveys,

Fig. 7.2 Map of the Kei Archipelago, southeast Moluccas

and publications on different regions of Kei. There are not many of these documents, and generalizations concerning the entire Archipelago are hazardous. Each village presents a particular case; the same reference myth appears in multiple versions, depending on what region it originates from. However, there remain certain common cultural features in Kei (Laksono 1990, Aritonang and Steenbrink 2008) (Fig. 7.2).

Before the first Catholic missionaries arrived in 1887, there was already a mosque in the main town of Tual on Small Kei, as testified by a drawing by H.G. Langen in 1885 (Langen 1888, 1902: 26). There are no data about the process of conversion or the progressive establishment of Islam in the region. Supposedly, the religion was brought by Makassarese, Bugis, Butonese[6], and Arab merchants, who remain

---

[6] From the islands of Buton and Selayar, south of Celebes.

very present in towns to this day. About 40% of the population in Kei is Muslim (depending on the figures, which are not very precise).

The Dutch local government encouraged Catholic missionaries to relocate to Kei through the intermediary of a German trader, A. Langen, the brother of H.G. Langen. They complained that their goals to 'civilize' the Keiese, bring them happiness, and make them serious workers were obstructed by Muslims who were too difficult to control. The Catholic (*Roman Katolik*) mission developed rapidly from the 1920s on, with churches, schools, and dispensaries. Its policy to rely on Keiese laymen to become school and religion teachers was extremely successful. The Catholic mission in Kei became the centre of Catholicism for the Moluccas and Papua, with a bishop until the 1960s, when the archbishopric was transferred to Ambon, the capital of the Moluccas province (Steenbrink 2003). The Catholic Church brought economic development; the Dutch sent funds for the mission and the circulation of money began.

It was Dutch policy to allow either Catholics or Protestants to settle in a region, but not both at the same time. At the turn of the twentieth century, the Protestant Church was well established in Ambon, but not yet in Kei, where the Catholics had been the first to obtain the authorization to develop a mission. The Protestants (*agama Kristen*) began to settle in the 1930s, in connection with the Protestant Church of the Moluccas (Gereja Protestan Maluku), and they were well established among civil servants, all the more so after Indonesia's independence. The schools built were, and still are, the property of the church or the mosque, but all children are welcomed, regardless of their confession. Nowadays, the teachers are government employees and the schools part of the public education system. Each school has a special teacher called *guru agama* who teaches the religion to which the school belongs.

Up to now, observers have noted that there is a fierce, but peaceful, competition, in social, political, and economic terms, between builders of churches and mosques in most tiny Keiese villages. Some of these builders have erected more than one mosque or church. As noted by Timo Kaartinen (2010), whereas there were once huge fortified walls surrounding villages, seen from very far away at sea, now churches and mosques are always bigger, always higher.

With the exception of Tanebar-Evav, a particular situation due to its recent conversions and the presence of *agama Hindu*, today all Keiese villagers and most Moluccans belong to one of these three religions. According to historical accounts, in the early twentieth century,

Protestant missionaries were very aggressive, destroying and burning ritual objects and statues in the far South-West Moluccas. Catholic missionaries, for their part, had a more educational approach when they finally received authorization from the Dutch colonial government to settle in Kei. This 'civilization' process was accompanied by a certain tolerance, which I witnessed in the 1970s when the bishop baptized entire villages but provided a written guarantee that traditional ceremonies could still be attended. This is still the case today, where traditional institutions such as houses (as social units) or villages relationships are intertwined with religious institutional ties. Traditional leaders work hand in hand with religious leaders. Religion and tradition each purportedly have its own task, although they often mix in practice. *Agama* is an individual or family choice; *adat* is not a choice.

In this context of multiple religious influences, one might expect to see significant changes to tradition. The brief fieldwork I carried out in the 1980s in the north of the Great Kei illustrated the contrary. Apart from separate settlements for the members of each of the three religions, the Protestant village head still ruled the village following Keiese tradition, together with *adat* elders, for all matters concerning houses relationships, gardens, marriages, traditional ceremonies, and so on. The statuses of noble, commoner, and dependant still play an important part in the religious configuration. As far as I was able to verify, the dependants practised the same religion as the noble to whom they were attached.

THE 1999–2000 CONFLICTS

While focused on the Kei Archipelago, this paper should make note of the extremely violent upheaval, labelled 'religious conflicts', that occurred throughout the Moluccas after the fall of President Suharto in 1998. The unrest continued sporadically until 2004–2005, mainly in the Central Moluccas. In 2007, the scene of destruction in the capital of Moluccas, Ambon, was depressing, despite numerous reconstruction sites. Beyond the 5000 victims and more than 10,000 refugees, villages in Ambon island, and elsewhere in the province, were destroyed, burnt and displaced. Mistrust was strong among people of different confessions, especially between Muslims and Christians (Böhm 2006, Kusumadewi 2005, Klinken 2001). During my latest visit in 2013, social relations were still tense. People often grouped themselves by religion rather than neighbourhood or profession, as had previously been the case.

Smaller conflicts spread over the Kei Archipelago, situated approximately 800 km south-east of Ambon. Fierce fights arose between Muslims and Protestants, later joined by Catholics. While the number of casualties is imprecise, we know that these often fatal conflicts also resulted in rapes, arson, refugees, and deportation (Laksono 2002a). As was the case in Ambon at that time, in 2007 the situation was disastrous, but in 2013, economic change was visible as a result of the flow of governmental and private funds. These transformations materialized in the form of luxury hotels, supermarkets, banks, new roads, air connections, and the development of external private enterprises exploiting Keiese marine resources including pearlshells or fish. Foreign NGOs and national development programs also appeared, as did new Churches missionaries and an influx of civil servants due to the recent policy of regionalization. These movements caused money to flow, a small part of which eventually reaching the poorest Keiese (Barraud 2012). But, as was the case in Ambon, interreligious relationships remain occasionally tense. Extremist or charismatic religious movements have appeared, which are often criticized. And yet, traditional collective actions are still organized.

For example, after the 1999 conflicts, all of Tanebar-Evav society, Hindus, Christians, and Muslims alike attended the consecration ceremony of a newly rebuilt Protestant church in another village on the Small Kei, in the name of the traditional alliance between the two villages. And recently, *adat* leaders from Keiese villages (converted or not) united to restore peace between members of different confessions in the name of *adat*, while Muslim, Catholic, and Protestant religious leaders supported them.

It is in this particular context that I conducted field research in 2007, 2009, 2011, and 2012–2013, a span of six years during which religion was a topic that roused great interest.

From the World Beyond: New Ideas and Agencies

Although they speak a language similar to that of other villages of the Kei Archipelago and are considered part of Keiese 'culture', the social lives of Tanebar-Evav villagers are in some respects distinct, as illustrated in the story of the wall. In the 1970s, Tanebar-Evav had the reputation of being the last stronghold of Keiese traditions, maintaining its social organization and practising its own rituals. The village of about 500 or 600 people is made of two parts. The upper village (*oho*, lit. 'village') is surrounded on four sides by a wall. Located on a cliff, it can only be accessed by a wooden ladder, some 20 m high. The upper village includes around thirty traditional houses, built on huge wooden posts. Roughly the same number of houses, these constructed of concrete and wood, have been progressively built underneath the upper village, at the foot of the cliff, forming a lower village (*tahat*, lit. 'sea water') close to the shore. One must cross the lower village to access the ladder to the upper village. The houses in the upper village are organized into named clusters located around small squares. The whole upper village is divided into three areas named after Keiese spirits. The three areas also divide the lower village. Elders are ritual officiants who rule the village life, particularly during the annual millet ritual cycle, which lasts about eight months and involves large and small rituals and offerings all over the island almost everyday. The explicit aim of the ritual is to 'feed' the island—the mountain Masbaït—so that it will provide food. Verbalized invocations ask the mountain Masbaït to bring 'life principles' from the four 'corners' of the world that will renew the land and its contents. The cycle begins with the ritual choice of where the gardens will be grown, a different spot each year, and then continues with rituals for clearing, burning, sowing, and weeding. Before the harvest, there is a boar hunt, followed by an offering of game caught to the spirits and the Sun-Moon God, the highest deity (*Duang Ler Vuan*). A large portion of the harvest is stored in a communal granary inside one of the houses. Ritual charges are inherited from father to son, the latter going through a kind of rebirth ritual before entering his function. The ritual, with only slight changes, is still held each year (Barraud 1979; 1990a, b; 1996) (Fig. 7.3).

We can now begin to explain the story of the wall.

The story describes something called a 'belief' (Keiese: *perca*, from Indonesian *kepercayaan*) that came from elsewhere and was related to a 'religion' (Keiese: *agam*), in this case Islam, which villagers refused to incorporate into their society. What is striking in the story is the emphasis on flotsam and jetsam, central notions related to the values of *lór*, 'the society in relation to the world beyond' (beyond the island territory proper), and *haratut*, 'the society in relation to the land, the territory, the inner organization' (houses, ancestors, etc.). The relationship between these two values, referring to different ideas, entities, and ritual

Fig. 7.3 The bay and the remnants of the wall at Tanebar-Evav, July 2009

practices, constitutes the overall ideological configuration underlying Tanebar-Evav social life. Central to the understanding of the values, particular attention should be given to the movements into and out of the island, in relation to the expression of the society as a boat and of the island as a human body.

Indeed, this society settled on a tiny island has the natural experience of sea currents bringing all sorts of things on the shore. Villagers are forbidden from collecting flotsam and jetsam without a ritual to welcome it (*yaf*) and 'muffle the sound of the conch'. This debris came unannounced from the sea, unknown to the people. The rituals to welcome them consist of offerings given to the spirits of *lór*. All that is washed ashore belongs to *lór*; it is uncontrolled, beyond people's will or action, subject to ritual precautions, and is valued negatively. Worse, if the rituals are not held, pests and vermin belonging to *lór* and pertaining to the world beyond will destroy the millet crop.

There is a difference between people and things that arrive or are requested by the people in the island, such as 'life principles' that renew the island during the millet ritual, and things that are washed by the sea, belonging to *lór* and distinguished in different categories (*lór mas*—'gold': canoes, bottles, etc.; *lór tomat*—'humans', or *yeya'an*—'shark's elder brother': tortoise, dolphin, whale, sea cow, human being; *lór balanun*—'poison': stranded waste, garbage, etc.). Things washed ashore should be ritually incorporated but cannot replace that which comes from the land.

There is thus a very sophisticated conceptual elaboration of flotsam and jetsam, according to which 'belief', such as that of Islam, is partly conceptualized, categorized alongside debris washed in from the sea. Following Hamayon (2005) and Lakoff and Johnson (1980), I label this a metaphorical structuration rather than a metaphor, in that it is indeed more than an image of the society. The organization and conceptualization of the society—houses, people, rituals, births, marriages, funerals, transgressions, and so on—are construed in various idioms related to the sea and to sailboats, their construction, steering, and progress at sea. The people of Tanebar-Evav are gardeners as well as fishermen, but they conceive of their social life as seafarers, sailing on the high seas under the command of their 'captains', i.e. leaders of the millet ritual. Hence, the pertinence of such a developed discourse about what washes in from the sea, and its destructive effect. 'Belief'(*perca*), pertaining to something called 'religion'(*agam*), destroys 'tradition' (*adat*) and is thus forbidden.

In contrast, one of the most striking features of this society is that so many foreign conceptual categories, particularly Arabic or Malay idioms transferred through Islam, penetrated the local language long ago and are perceived as pertaining to tradition, despite the fact that they are acknowledged to have come from elsewhere. To begin with, the word *adat* designates 'tradition' or 'customs' in Keiese and Indonesian languages. But the same word, which I write as Adat to mark the difference, is also the name of the highest deity in Keiese traditions, along side the God Sun-Moon. He is a founding spirit (*mitu*), also called Adat-Aturan, said to have arrived in the island with two other spirits, Hukum and Wilin. When evoked together, one speaks of Adat-Aturan, Hukum, and Wilin. In Indonesian, *aturan* means 'rule' and *hukum* means 'law'. *Wilin* is a Keiese word meaning a 'rudder'. Upon their arrival, the three spirits are said to have crossed the island from the south coast to the north, in the direction of the village, their itinerary marked by named spots on the land itself: paths, places, and directions. The story of the three spirits claims that they were asked to stay on the island and to protect 'the contents of the mountain' Vu'ar Masbaït, an expression referring to the island and all that it contains. The most important spirit, Adat, also called 'the Great Ancestor' (*Ubun Hila'a*), is honoured at the very centre of the village and plays the main role in the rituals. Hukum, the spirit related to *lór*, punishes all those who break prohibitions, including incest, murder, and adultery. These spirits have been welcomed and given the most important position among deities, besides ancestors, in order to rule the land and its contents. As spirits, Adat-Aturan and Hukum are clearly differentiated from the Indonesian notions expressed by these three words, although from an etic point of view the ideas associated with the spirits names and the meaning of the Indonesian words are close to one another. This is a good example of the loan of words and their transformation. Without their origin being known, the three spirits come from the world beyond and, once integrated, are fully constitutive of the society's socio-cosmic order. They play an important part in the main rituals and ceremonies held in the name of *lór* and *haratut*. The *adat* described in the preamble refers to 'tradition' which, despite the unknown origin of the spirit Adat (from whom it is not dissociated), clearly belongs to the land. *Adat* is part and parcel of the land, perceived as its foundation, as is the Sun-Moon God. This has not been the case with the terms *perca* or *agam*.

Beyond these important deities, local names, rituals, other spirits, precious goods, laws, and so on have been introduced into local culture in Tanebar-Evav. For instance, the important ritual function of the *orang kaya*, the person in charge of relations with the outside, i.e. other villages and societies, has been assigned to newcomers from another island in the Moluccas, whose story is known. The name of the *orang kaya* ritual function is an Indonesian language loan. Other foreign words and ideas have been integrated into the Keiese language, most often through the Malay language mixed with the Arabic and Javanese used by the merchants, and later through the Indonesian language during the Dutch

---

[7] For instance, the word *iman* ('faith' in Indonesian) lost this sense and in Kei refers to something like mind, consciousness, spirit (Indonesian *roh*), or the seat of feelings, as opposed to the body. It contrasts with *ralan*, the 'inside', the seat of love and afflictions, qualifying people relationships, and also with *mat-inya*, 'life principle' (from Indonesian *nyawa*, 'soul'). Another instance is the expression *reski-rahmat*, 'chance, good fortune'

colonization. These words and ideas of foreign origin became usual words of everyday and ritual discourse, with their original meaning transformed more or less in each case[7]. Mostly used in ritual context, these words do not connote any link to Muslim or Christian religious creeds. Although they are very close to 'religious' idioms, they refer only to traditional specifications, that is, to '*adat*'.

Clearly, that which comes from the world beyond can occupy diverse statuses: acknowledged as coming from without and at the same time from within; necessary in ritual circumstances to bring chance and good fortune (*reski-rahamat*) to the island; yet, also, rejected as in the case of certain debris from the sea, which are, however, collected and transformed by ritual; having a destructive effect, like pests, vermin, sicknesses, which are ritually thrown out as not being part of the island. 'Belief' and 'religion' belong to the last category, and the wall is there to remind the people of Tanebar-Evav of this. Indeed, 'religion' was refused long ago, in the terms of flotsam and jetsam, while many ideas related to the so-called religious field were integrated, but not through institutional or official agencies. And the notion that tradition could be linked to 'religion' never arose. This is to some extent no longer the case.

RELATIONSHIPS BETWEEN RELIGIONS AND NEW EVENTS

At present, one can distinguish four different confessions in Tanebar-Evav: Islam, Protestantism, Catholicism, and *agama Hindu*[8]. Muslims live apart in a small village in the northern part of the island of about twenty dwellings, which house less than a hundred inhabitants. Many

---

Footnote 7 (continued)
('mercy' in Indonesian), always used in the requests addressed to the Sun-Moon God, the deities and the ancestors, or to the world beyond during the millet ritual to bring in renewed life principles. Very close to the Indonesian 'science' is *ilmu*, 'knowledge', which gives the authority *tur-kwas* (Indonesian *kuasa*, 'power'); *tur, tur-kwas* is also to teach, to have authority, because knowledge gives authority and allows to teach; *kwas* is also the authority one has over somebody. Knowledge is related to religion in proverbs. The Indonesian *kesalahan* ('mistake, fault') became in Keiese *sa*, 'not true, wrong', together with *dos* 'doing wrong' (Indonesian *dosa*, 'sin'). And the angel Gabriel is also known as Jibrail, who, in some stories, guards Paradise's door (*surga*, as in Indonesian).

[8] To these four religions could be added the Baptist religion, to which one family recently converted.

are of Buginese or Butonese origin, descendants of traders who married into the village long ago. Their genealogies, which may be traced back at least five ascending generations, are linked to those of the main village houses; they also maintain strong ties with family members in the islands of Buton and Selayar, where they travel for trade purposes.

While still under Dutch rule in the 1930s, some village children went to town to receive an education in Protestant elementary schools. Back in the village, some of them converted to Protestantism and founded the Protestant community in the village. It seems that conflicts had already begun to appear at that time. An elementary school administered by the Protestant Church of the Moluccas was built in the 1950s, which is attended by all children of the village, who take religious classes according to the Indonesian government's rule. At Catholic and Muslim schools, the religious teachings are Catholic or Muslim. A church built in the 1960s sparked conflict when the elders were unable to reach an agreement regarding its location. It was ultimately built inside the lower village, an act forbidden according to the story of the wall. This led to many violent conflicts, followed by trials and jail sentences in the 1970s. These conflicts have continued sporadically and are particularly common during the most important moment of the millet ritual. Around 30% of families on the island are Protestant, and a permanent appointed Protestant minister lives on the island.

More recently, after the turn of this century, similar problems occurred surrounding the construction of the Catholic church. A small group of Catholics, mainly in the same family, have inhabited the island for roughly forty years. As their numbers increased, they decided to build a church five hundred metres from the lower village limits, on a land owned by a Catholic family. No permanent priest lives on the island. Conversions are mainly associated with schooling, marriages, or long stays in Tual, the main town of the Archipelago, or in the provincial capital, Ambon. These three religions are directed and financially supported by regional institutions, such as the Protestant Church of the Moluccas, the Catholic archbishopric of Ambon, and the mosque of Ambon.

When I began fieldwork in the 1970s, about 80% of the inhabitants had not converted to any of these three religions and instead practised their own rituals (*adat*) that I briefly described above. According to the Indonesian regional government, they were considered 'not yet religious' (*belum beragama*). Religious in this sense opposes 'religion' (*agama*) to 'beliefs, superstitions' (*kepercayaan*). The expression 'still

Hindu' (*masih Hindu*) was often used in the province to refer to traditional societies with no official religion, a label more or less equivalent to the term 'pagan' (*kafir*). Before the recent inception of the new 'Hindu religion' (see below), the term Hindu was not understood as referring to *agama*. Today, however, new ritual practices are called *agama Hindu* and are considered 'religious' practices, under political pressure from the government and the Indonesian Constitution, which stipulates that everyone must have a religion. Members of the *Hindu* confession make up more or less 40% of the population. There has been also a recent increase of both Protestants and Catholics. This transformation demonstrates that people who were formerly *Hindu* in the sense that they were 'not yet religious' are now described as having a religion, which is officially labelled *Hindu*. However, they do not call their traditional ritual practices *agama Hindu* but *adat*.

A Fourth Religion

Even before the 1990s, some Tanebar-Evav villagers had made contact with Balinese workers and civil servants in the Kei Archipelago, but the new Hindu religion and its connection to Bali are more recent. In their exchanges with the Balinese, some villagers came to progressively find concordances between Balinese practices and some Keiese stories and cults. Indeed, one of the founding myths common throughout the Archipelago is the basis of the law Hukum, called Lar-Vul Nga-Bal ('Red Blood and Spear from Bali'), which tells the story of the arrival of a princess from Bali who married a raja of Kei. On the basis of this story, some local people and Balinese attested that ancestors of Tanebar-Evav could trace their origins to Bali. They suggested, moreover, that Tanebar-Evav *adat* had common principles with *agama Hindu*, to the extent that part of the population was willing to welcome *agama Hindu* on their territory, while maintaining their own traditional ritual practices and ceremonies in the name of their *adat*. With the acknowledgement of the new Hindu religion, they decided to establish a place of worship for members of the *Hindu* cult in the village. In 2007, they obtained financial support from the Ministry of Religion (Kementerian Agama Republik Indonesia), the regional branch of the Hindu Council (Parisada Hindu Dharma Maluku Tenggara), fellow coreligionists, and the regional government, to construct a temple (*pura*) in the upper village, outside its walled limits but near the most traditional part of the village. The construction was almost finished when I was last there in 2013, and sculptors from Bali came to make statues and ornamentation that conformed to Balinese models. It was named the *Pura Masbaït* after the ritual centre of the island, *Vu'ar Masbaït*. It seems that a reference can be made here with the East Javanese kingdom of Majapahit, for there is a historical temple in Bali named Pura Maspait (also spelled Maospahit), but Tanebar-Evav villagers (even those convinced of the link with Bali) did not mention this possible link.

The advent of the new cult was made possible after meetings and discussions with the ritual leaders, who more or less willingly agreed with the construction of the *pura*. Although accepted by most non-Muslims and non-Christians, the new *Hindu* cult is not easily understood and opinions about it vary. Some elders say that the deities revered at the *pura*, mainly Sanghyang Widhi (the Supreme God of *agama Hindu*), are similar to and speak the same language as local spirits, others say that they are neither spirits nor ancestors. Some say that at the *pura* Hindus ask for good fortune (*reski-rahmat*) like one might at the mosque or in church. Others are suspicious of the new religion, saying that it is not their religion and they do not understand its ceremonial language, but are nonetheless tolerant overall. But some say that it is a mistake to have built this temple, because it is like a church, and thus forbidden on this ancestors' land. They warn that there will be dire consequences for this transgression. *Agama Hindu* is not presented as a new 'belief' (*perca*), like that described in the story of the wall, but for some people it raises questions regarding what society's rules allow regarding the ancestors' land. In fact, the main ritual elders do not attend the ceremonies at the *pura*, although their families do, as do most non-Muslims and non-Christians.

This is where the boundary between *agama* and *adat* blurs, because this *agama* and the new *Hindu* cult practised do not oppose the local *adat*, like other 'religions' do. On the contrary, the new cult purports to maintain and reinforce it. Indeed, the people who follow the new cult in the *pura* do not view it as conflicting with their traditions. Because of their common 'history', told in the Keiese myth of the Bali princess, Tanebar-Evav people argue that this cult identified as *agama Hindu* from Bali follows the main principles of their *adat* and all its traditional rituals. This is more or less also the case in other Indonesian societies affiliated with *agama Hindu*.

Although the *pura* is often described as similar to a mosque or to a church in that it is a worship place, the new cult itself is not generally compared to Islam or Christianity. The word *agama* used to describe it occurs mainly in official discourses. Followers of *agama Hindu* and traditional ritual elders describe the ceremonies held in the *pura*, as 'doing *adat*', referring not to Tanebar-Evav tradition, but to another tradition called also *adat* that they have appropriated. As those followers explain: this cult is close to their tradition and reinforces it, protects it, and prevents it from disappearing, whereas Protestantism and Catholicism threaten their *adat*. With regard to Islam, the discourse is less clear. Given that Islam was first introduced to the island so long ago, relations with Muslims in the northern part of the island are good. A number of families are part Muslim and part Hindu or Christian. There was one period of tension when violence broke out on the Kei Archipelago in 1999–2000. Although these conflicts did not touch Tanebar-Evav, which, on the contrary, welcomed many refugees from the main islands, some Muslims of Butonese and Selayar origin chose nonetheless to return to Buton or Selayar during this period.

Few on the island voice opposition to religion in general. Yet Tanebar-Evav people maintain that 'religion' (*agam*), a term whose meaning varies with context, its first iteration being Islam, should not enter what is considered the ancestors' land, which is located mainly on the southern half of the island and delimited by the wall. The northern part is not subject to these same prohibitions. In fact, if, like the mosque, the Protestant and Catholic churches had been built outside of the village, there would likely have been little opposition to their construction. Tensions surrounding the building of these religious spaces were more a question of land than a question of religion itself. This gives *agama Hindu*, treated both as a new religion and an older custom, a very particular position in that respect.

Indeed, as we have seen, the people who did not practice a 'religion' in Indonesia were called *Hindu* or *belum beragama*, meaning those who have only *kepercayaan* ('beliefs', 'superstitions'). This was the case with the people of Tanebar-Evav and their *adat*. It is noteworthy that the same people in Tanebar-Evav, influenced by the government policies towards religions, now describe themselves as having a religion: *agama Hindu*. The *pura*, which protects *adat*'s rules, contributed to the religion's new status. Unlike what happened earlier in Bali, where *agama Hindu* had to be demarcated theoretically from *adat Bali*, the new religion has been accepted in the name of tradition and is practised in parallel with *adat*.

Villagers mark a distinction between Islam, Protestantism, and Catholicism, on the one hand, and *agama Hindu*, on the other. Christians and Muslims are not allowed to be in charge of the traditional ritual functions. Some Protestants were obliged to renounce their religious practices when called on to replace their fathers as head of traditional ritual charges. Protestants or Catholics can sometimes act in specific ceremonies of the millet rituals in the name of the ritual function traditionally attributed to their house. But those followers of *adat* who adhere to *agama Hindu* carry out all ritual functions, given that the new religion is viewed as protecting tradition. Some traditional ritual leaders, however, refuse to join these new rituals.

This requires some explanation. Islam, Protestantism, and Catholicism render their followers part of communities that exist beyond the village society, which deny local traditions and are part of a universal religious order, in terms of partaking in the nation state and its institutions. The fourth religion officially recognized by the Ministry of Religion, *agama Hindu*, was not introduced by foreigners but 'reactivated' by the Balinese. This confession holds a distinct position in the eyes of Tanebar-Evav people, for it relates them, through their *adat*, to Bali, to which they refer in their own mythology. Although knowledge of its precepts is limited, it is believed to strengthen local tradition. Furthermore, as adherents of an *agama*, its followers participate in the nation state and in a universal order.

Whatever the conflicts and disputes, it is a fact that 'religion' is now integrated into the village life, each community practising its own religious celebrations. After the Moluccan conflicts in the early 2000s, villagers were proud to talk about the pacific coexistence of four religions in Tanebar-Evav. Religious leaders at the mosque and churches are respected and called upon when necessary for funerals or sicknesses. Like male nurses or school officials, they are considered 'elders with authority' (*itaten*). It might be noted that, as guests, they receive shares of the offerings and game hunted, but never act as ritual participants. This constitutes an important distinction from that which is labelled 'religion': Christians and Muslims never act in the traditional ceremonies and rituals, even if they sometimes participate as guests, whereas all followers of *agama Hindu* continue practising and acting in all traditional events.

As I noted earlier, this state of affairs does not prevent the maintenance of traditional ceremonies, like the millet ritual cycle, rites to establish new ritual leaders, or repair ceremonies. Ritual activity has been dense during my most recent trips to the field. But there is an ever-present threat that latent tension caused by the locations of the Protestant and Catholic churches spark new conflict.

Forty years ago people rarely discussed religion, but today, the word *agama* is frequently used, even to speak of the traditional rituals. To shed light on this transformation, the next section examines the relationship between 'religion' and the 'state'.

SIGNIFICANCE OF THE STATE'S ROLE IN RELIGION ON THE REGIONAL LEVEL

Unlike the introduction of Christianity in Papua New Guinea, described by André Iteanu in this volume (see also Robbins 2004, 2009; Comaroff 2009), the introduction of Islam in Tanebar-Evav took time and caused a shock at first, as illustrated by the wall, whereas in the case of Christianity, as far as I know, missionaries never came to the village to convert the people of Tanebar-Evav. Those who converted were children who attended school in town and then brought Protestantism and Catholicism back to the village.

Despite the presence of a few Protestant and Catholic families when I began doing fieldwork in the 1970s, the people of Tanebar-Evav society were often disparaged by government authorities for having no 'religion' and continuing to practise traditional rituals. For Keiese and Moluccan government officials, traditional rituals clearly did not constitute a religion. And at that time *adat* was considered an obstacle to development and education. My continued presence on the island studying villagers' customs has itself been considered strange, as my first visit was not that long after the traumas of 1965. Things have changed in forty years and particularly after the 1999 conflicts. *Adat* laws, which in a number of instances were called on to settle conflicts, are now acknowledged throughout Indonesia, despite their local and regional variation. This general tendency at the level of the national government coincided with an increase of autonomy granted to the regions[9].

---

[9] The 1999 Law on Regional Autonomy granted more authority to district (*kabupaten*) and municipal (*kota*) levels of government.

As noted by Indonesian anthropologist, P. M. Laksono, who studied the Kei islands after the conflicts: 'there were two models of community in Southeast Maluku. One shaped by Indonesia, which bound together religions through the distribution of patronage in the form of official appointments. This experienced melt-down and violence in 1999. As a consequence, people once more began to look to another model, one based on custom and local autonomy' (Laksono 2002b: 3). Villagers today elect the village chiefs themselves, selected from traditional elders, whereas government nominations were formerly the rule.

Regional traditions and cultures are now increasingly praised and promoted throughout Indonesia. The case of Tanebar-Evav is remarkable, however, for government officials today wish to attract tourism to far off archipelagos such as Kei, promoting what they call Keiese culture for that purpose. In the village, 'culture' (*budaya*) as defined by regional authorities is reduced to traditional wooden houses on posts, welcome dances performed wearing customary red costumes and ritual pig killings, which impress outside visitors. Their definition of culture certainly does not include the complex structure of the socio-ritual organization that people of Tanebar-Evav associate with their terms for 'society', *lór-haratut*. Villagers benefit from tourism, selling ordinary seashells at high price to the foreigners and tourists. But, if officials are concerned with maintaining traditional villages for tourism and other economic purposes, this does not suggest that they have any real interest in the culture and the traditions which they highlight in order to glorify the 'exotic' character of the village people still attached to their ritual practices, like providing offerings to the spirits and hunting wild pigs. The pride Tanebar-Evav people may have in taking an inclusive position towards four religions, with respect to the precepts of the nation state, and in maintaining some form of their millet ritual, does not continue past the boundaries of the island. Elsewhere in the Archipelago, Tanebar-Evav people are still disparaged for being poor and underdeveloped. The official aim to develop tourism does not prevent, but rather emphasizes the society's exoticism. What appears to be a laudable aim could also be a double-edged sword, paradoxically leading to the maintenance of the people's low status situation. Yet, no exotic villagers means no tourism. Most Christians and Muslims of the two main Kei islands know almost nothing about *agama Hindu*. Bali is a historical reference in the origin story of their law, but most know little about actual ritual practices in Bali, even if *agama Hindu* belongs to the state's officially recognized religions.

Although they have welcomed the new religion, the fact that Tanebar-Evav people continue to practise traditional rituals (*adat*) contributes to the exoticism or folklore of the society to the local government. The position of Tanebar-Evav in the Indonesian government's regional policies is ambiguous. Villagers tend to maintain *adat*, which is treated as *budaya* ('culture') by the administration, as highlighted by a photograph of the village's dancers that welcomes travellers at the local airport. The government provides the village with financial support to promote culture and thus tourism. It also financed not only the construction of the *pura*, illustrating that the village has religion, but also subsidizes the repair of traditional raised wooden houses in the upper village, to assure that they look presentable when visitors or officials come. The regional government is also concerned with economic development, electricity, roads, the marine environment, coastal preservation, and improvement of fishing practices, for which it puts forward new projects.

Within the Kei Archipelago, members of other villages, all either Protestant, Catholic, or Muslim, still maintain certain ritual practices, on the individual or family level: when building a house or a boat, opening a new garden in the forest, looking for the cause of a sickness, and so on. They also maintain multiple traditional social relationships through exchanges at marriages, funerals, etc. (Thorburn 2004). These practices are never understood as being contrary to their religion or unworthy. If you are a member of a religious community, pray regularly, and assume your responsibilities in common tasks, then all other rituals, even those honouring the dead, ancestors, or forest spirits, are considered acceptable as forms of *adat*. In that respect, *agama* is clearly distinguished from *adat*, by villagers and government officials alike.

Comparisons: Opening or Closing to 'Religion'. Tanebar-Evav Society's Relations to Deities and 'Religious' Concepts

At the beginning of this chapter, we saw how members of Tanebar-Evav society integrated people, things, and ideas from beyond into the socio-cosmic order of the society. Have then notions related to the 'religious' field been integrated in the socio-cosmic order and how?[10].

Although there exists significant overlap between their 'religious' and 'traditional' notions and attitudes, there are no loanwords between Indonesian and Keiese languages—except for general ideas like *agam* and *adat* (see above), and the special position of the word *perca* (see below)—and most of the religious notions are translatable in the Keiese language. The attitudes examined here are not only relevant to the context of worship but also in everyday life. These practices are still in use in this highly structured society, which corresponds with the spatial organization of its houses, its elders, its ranks, organized similarly to a sailboat, with its crew and captain. These attitudes are expressed in emic terms like 'authority' (*tur-kwas*), 'to command' or 'order' (*yangun*), 'knowledge' (*ilmu*), 'weighty words' (*ngarihi len*), 'to prohibit' (*fafelek*), 'to offer' (*sob*), 'to receive' (*vanat va'a*), 'to prostrate' (*jo*), 'to bow one's head' (*be*), 'to raise with one's hands' (*fasak*). This vocabulary of gestures and actions translates 'religious' notions such as 'the power of God', 'God's kingdom', 'wisdom', 'the Bible' (Hukum Taurat), 'the sacred', 'to pray', 'benediction', 'to bow in front of God', and 'to glorify God'.

But one also finds discontinuities between these attitudes towards worship. The ceremonial language required in the address of the Sun-Moon God, people's relationship to deities, and the meaning of offerings, illustrate that in emic terms there exists a substantial distinction from religion as understood in Western contexts. It points to certain interconnections between beings, which translate into social relations. For instance, speech addressed to the Sun-Moon God is marked, like kinship terms, by a pronominal suffix. In invocations, one addresses *duang*, 'my god', *duan*, 'his god'[11], and *duad*, 'our god', in contrast with the Christian God, called *duad*, 'our God', but Christian and Muslims never address *duang*, 'my God'.

---

[10] To this end, I used a Keiese translation of some texts of the Gospel from the four evangelists and a Protestant Indonesian Bible and discussed with the people of possible equivalences in Tanebar-Evav idioms, mainly about the relationship with God, the offerings, the worship behaviour, and the nature of human beings.

[11] *Duan* also designates a specific relationship between the inhabitants and the house, the gardener and his garden, the captain of a boat and the boat, etc. In general, it defines a relationship that qualifies both terms, which have no meaning outside of this relationship (Barraud 2010).

Continuity is also manifest in the relations between living human beings and deities, all of whom are perceived to be part of the same world, as *umat* ('beings' in Keiese)[12]. The Sun-Moon God represents a notable exception. The difference between humans and deities is expressed in terms of visibility and invisibility (*nelyoan/kavinin*)[13] and allows for a community of beings thought to share a common nature. This common nature is manifest through ritual offerings, whose objective is not simply to offer but to share offerings and game among the Sun-Moon God, other deities[14], and the villagers. Redistribution is the function of ritual leaders, called 'the ones who stand at the prow of the boat and share and distribute' (*dir'u ham wang*)[15], recalling the idiom of the society as a sailboat. The terms used to describe behaviour and actions considered 'right' (*ken*) again make reference to the sailboat, likening the society to the motion of the sailboat, moving straight ahead in the right direction (*in ba ken* or *nablo*), in opposition to *naskil*, 'to be twisted or curved' or 'wrong' (*sa*). *Ken/sa* also refers to 'even' and 'odd' numbers, as well as the right measures when building a boat or a house. Ritual invocations often end with the sentence: 'if too short, please make it longer, if wrong, please turn it upside down so it becomes right'. There is no idea of forgiveness, similar to that which is often present in Christian discourse for instance, but rather an idea of shared responsibility. This brings happiness, which is compared to the motion of the sailboat in a calm sea (*nablin*).

In this respect, one may insist upon the fact that there is no individual connection with the deities, be they spirits or the Sun-Moon God, as is present for example in the Christian perception of individuals' relation to God. A direct connection is absolutely irrelevant to the people's conceptualization of their socio-cosmic order, organized according to

---

[12] The same word *umat* exists in Indonesian, meaning 'people', 'congregation', or 'community'. In Keiese, this is not the case and *umat* designates only living beings, be they humans or spirits.

[13] This appears to be comparable to the contrast between *sekala* and *niskala* in Bali (see Hornbacher, this volume).

[14] Typical of this exchange, the share of the spirits is for instance called the 'bride price'; they receive the fat part of the pig, while human beings receive the leftovers.

[15] One can contrast this with Christian communion, in which redistribution is carried out within the community but not with God. Curiously, in Keiese, 'communion' is translated as *Jesus minan laran*, 'Jesus' fat and blood', an expression which, when used with the pronominal suffix—*ng*, means 'my offspring'.

the relationship of the values of *lór* and those of *haratut*. Even in the case of individual wrongdoings or transgressions such as incest or murder, the consequences always strike the society as a whole and 'repair' must thus be made on the society level, as the example in the introduction of the destruction of the wall illustrates. Completeness (*kinomón*) must be recovered, which was made clear after the 2000s conflicts, when the Kei Archipelago's *adat* and religious leaders called for the restoration of unity and peace in all villages (*lór*) under the banner of Hukum Lar Vul Nga Bal, considered to be their common law, rather than in the name of a specific community of believers. The continuity between beings and the lack of a clear-cut difference between the mundane world and that of deities accentuates the relational component of all beings, which together constitute a complete society. There exists no equivalent to this notion of completeness in 'religious' discourse.

Focusing on vocabulary rather than practices and attitudes, certain terms and ideas become particularly interesting to examine. *Kepercayaan*, in the Indonesian language, is used to mean superstition and in that sense is opposed to *agama*, 'religion'. In the story of the wall told by the villagers, the word 'belief' (*perca*) is associated with Islam, that is, *agama*. 'Belief', in the sense of *perca* in Keiese and as described in the story of the wall, is associated with religion rather than 'superstitions', i.e. *adat*. When questioned, villagers described *perca* as a loanword from Indonesian. Attempting to find an equivalent in the Keiese language, they translated this concept of 'belief' as an attitude in everyday life and in rituals, *wawat*, meaning literally 'to take into account', 'to respect', 'to be aware of', or 'to have confidence' in whatever is done or said. This shows how, transferred from one society and language to another, the meaning of the words can lead to misunderstandings and confusion. This is often the case with religious notions in this context.

In sum, there are many Islamic or Christian notions and idioms that correspond with the attitudes of belief present in the traditional ritual language and practice. This means that in villagers views there is no conceptual break between following the new *Hindu* religion and taking part in most *adat* rituals. This illustrates continuity in their language and actions, which allows the people to translate into their own terms many aspects of the 'religious' discourse. For them, continuity between beings (human and deities) is not in itself problematic, as would be in the eyes of 'religious' specialists or exegetes. Furthermore, the recent rise of *agama Hindu*, as we have seen, is linked to *adat*, mainly through the worship behaviours and certain precepts of *agama Hindu* which villagers compare to the rules of *adat*.

This does not mean, however, that *agama* can replace *adat*, except in the confusion of meanings brought in with *agama Hindu*.

Conclusion

This discussion appears to have led us far away from the story of the wall with which this chapter began. But this is true on the surface only. For all these comments are doors that leave open the communication between the socio-cosmological order and 'religions'. Far from closing and excluding, as many walls do, the wall in Tanebar-Evav functions more as a warning aimed at maintaining some sort of coherence. This social meaning remains significant, whatever the mixing of world religions in this single village society.

But up to what point is there coherence?

Coherence may be located in the social structure and lies in both ritual and everyday practices and attitudes. For instance, ranked social statuses continue to be relevant, although individuals avoid explicitly evoking them. But rank is clearly visible in the ways people address one another. Another instance of this coherence is in people's relationship to the sea and the sailboat, which structures everyday vocabulary, ritual language, rituals themselves, the building of houses and boats, gardening, etc.

While there is generally social consensus regarding how to conduct *adat* ceremonies, we have seen that there is no firm unanimity about the new cult of *agama Hindu* and 'religion'. There is no unified idea regarding what constitutes *agama* or *adat*. What then are the differences between definitions of 'religion' and 'tradition'? Villagers recognize differences between religions, since Christians and Muslims are not allowed to lead *adat* ceremonies, while followers of *agama Hindu* still do.

This leads us back to the ways members of Tanebar-Evav society manage objects that come from beyond the island. Things, like religious ideas, could be treated as coming from the outside and should thus be organized according to notions of *lór* as a value and islanders' conceptions of their relation to the world beyond the island. But *lór* can be considered a value only relative to ideas about *haratut*, in that value is ultimately located in the relationship between *lór* and *haratut*. Religion cannot be integrated into the socio-cosmic order at the level of *haratut*.

In contrast, people and things from the outside, like newcomers recognized as nobles and given a ritual charge, or precious goods entering the circle of exchanges, are all integrated at the level of *haratut* and take part in the society's renewal through participation in the millet ritual. In that respect, whatever the connections and overlap among most 'religious' precepts, the way they are used frames religion as completely distinct from tradition. Religion concerns communities that split the society into different branches: Protestants follow their own religious practices, as do Catholics. Muslims too have their own calendar and celebrations, in which non-Muslims in the village are not implicated. While villagers celebrate Christmas and the New Year like those in town, these feasts do not have religious connotation but are opportunities to drink and to dance to modern music projected on huge loudspeakers.

One must thus distinguish between religious institutions (churches or the mosque, and their complex and powerful political organizations) and practices that can be understood through the idiom of ritual attitudes, as is the case of the new *Hindu* cult. Formally called *agama*, it has not replaced *adat*, any more than Islam or Christian cults, as 'beliefs' took the place of traditional rituals. In that respect, I refer back to Roberte Hamayon's proposals about belief (2005), in which she neatly distinguishes between the act of believing, which treats all beliefs other than one's own as false, and the 'belief attitude', which does not imply a unique belief and allows for the inclusion of other ideas, as the 'opened' wall testifies (see also Pouillon 1979). The various interpretations and opinions demonstrate the openness or the flexibility of the society, although they also show some confusion.

The picture is different in regions that have been Christianized for decades, such as among the Toraja. According to Dana Rappoport (personal communication, 2016), Christianity invaded tradition and transformed it. There, the Indonesian word *agama* is rarely employed and 'religions' are defined in Toraja as *aluk*, 'ritual rule'. So Islam represents one *aluk* (*aluk kasallangan*) and Christianity another (*aluk kasaranian*), while traditional practices are called *aluk nene'*, meaning 'the ancestors' rule', which is hardly ever referred to nowadays. Although traditional ceremonies are maintained (funerals, rituals surrounding house building, etc.), they have been Christianized and communication with or offerings to ancestors are forbidden. Ritual language has also been replaced by Christian prayers, and a new kind of poetic speech borrowed from the traditional one. There is no Toraja word which translates the Indonesian *adat*. The Toraja word *ada'*, meaning 'teaching', comes close, although *adat* in the sense of *budaya* ('culture') is now increasingly heard. In Kei there is a sort of ambiguity with the word *adat*, used to mean both the 'rule' and to refer to any type of ritual action, which excludes the 'religious' ceremonies of Islam or Christianity, with the notable exception of the ceremonies held at the temple (*pura*), called *agama Hindu*, which are also sometimes described as 'doing *adat*'. Indonesian language also describes this as *budaya*, 'culture'. This also seems to be the case among Christian Toraja, who summarize their rituals, using Indonesian language, as *Tuhan hidup dalam kebudayaan* ('God lives in the culture').

To conclude, turning back to the title of this paper, despite the wall or perhaps because of it, in Tanebar-Evav, from an etic point of view, *agama* ('religion') is clearly distinguished from *adat* ('tradition'), in common usage and political meanings. But from an emic point of view, that of the language, practices, and attitudes of the local people, *adat* and *agama* both ultimately demonstrate a huge capacity to integrate many things from elsewhere.

A final remark, in agreement with Louis Dumont's teachings: 'Yet we should guard against the assumption that each culture has evolved in isolation: we may be sure that 'commerce' in the widest sense of the term has always gone on, and we should not close the door to hints of interaction' (Dumont 1975: 153).

REFERENCES

Aritonang, Jan Sihar, and Karel Steenbrink, eds. 2008. *A History of Christianity in Indonesia*. Leiden: Brill, Studies in Christian Mission 35.

Aragon, Lorraine V. 2000. *Fields of the Lord. Animism, Christian Minorities, and State Development in Indonesia*. Honolulu: University of Hawai'i Press.

Aveling, Harry. 1967. "Seventeenth century Bandanese society in fact and fiction: 'Tambera' assessed". *Bijdragen tot de Taal-, Land- en Volkenkunde* 123 (3): 347–365.

Barraud, Cécile. 1979. *Tanebar-Evav. Une société de maisons tournée vers le large*. Paris: Maison des Sciences de l'Homme & Cambridge: Cambridge University Press.

Barraud, Cécile, and Jos. D.M. Platenkamp. 1990. "Rituals and the Comparison of Societies". In *Rituals and Socio-Cosmic Order in Eastern Indonesian Societies, Part II: Maluku*, ed. C. Barraud and J.D.M. Platenkamp. Special

Anthropological Issue, *Bijdragen tot de Taal-, Land- en Volkenkunde* 146 (1): 103–123.

Barraud, Cécile. 1990. "Wife-givers as Ancestors and Ultimate Values in the Kei Islands". *Bijdragen tot de Taal-, Land- en Volkenkunde* 146 (2): 193–225.

Barraud, Cécile, and Cl. Friedberg-Berthe. 1996. "Life-giving Relationships in Bunaq and Kei Societies, Eastern Indonesia". In *For the Sake of Our Future: Sacrificing in Eastern Indonesia*, ed. S. Howell, 351–398. Leiden: CNWS, N° 42.

Barraud, Cécile. 2010. "De la résistance des mots. Propriété, possession, autorité dans des sociétés de l'Indo-Pacifique". In *La cohérence des sociétés. Mélanges en hommage à Daniel de Coppet*, ed. A. Iteanu, 83–146. Paris: Éditions de la Maison des Sciences de l'Homme.

Barraud, Cécile. 2012. "Notes sur la situation religieuse dans l'archipel de Kei aux Moluques". *Le Banian* 13: 81–100.

Böhm, C.J. MSC. 2006. *Brief Chronicle of the Unrest in the Moluccas, 1999–2006*. Crisis Centre Diocese of Amboina, Jl. Pattimura 32, Ambon 97124, Indonesia.

Comaroff, Jean. 2009. "Politics of Conviction". *Social Analysis* 53 (1): 17–38.

Dumont, Louis. 1975. "On the Comparative Understanding of Non-Modern Civilizations". *Daedalus* 104 (2): 153–172.

Hamayon, Roberte. 2005. "L'anthropologue et la dualité paradoxale du 'croire' occidental". *Théologiques* 13 (1): 15–41.

Hanna, Willard A. 1978. *Indonesian Banda. Colonialism and Its Aftermath in the Nutmeg Islands*. Philadelphia: Philadelphia Institute for the Study of Human Issues.

Kaartinen, Timo. 2010. *Songs of Travel, Stories of Place. Poetics of Absence in an Eastern Indonesian Society*. Helsinki: Academia Scientiarum Fennica.

Klinken, Gerry van. 2001. "The Maluku Wars: Bringing Society Back In". *Indonesia* 71: 1–26.

Kusumadewi, L.R. 2005. *Pour la vie ou la religion: La conversion forcée à l'Islam dans le conflit des Moluques (2000-2001)*. Mémoire de DEA en Sociologie, EHESS, Paris.

Lakoff, George, and Mark Johnson. 1980. *Metaphors We Live By*. Chicago: The University of Chicago Press.

Laksono, Paschalis Maria. 1990. *Wuut Ainmehe Nifun, Manut Ainmehe Tilor (Eggs From One Fish and One Bird): a Study of the Maintenance of Social Boundaries in the Kei Islands*. Ph.D. Dissertation, Cornell University, Ithaca.

Laksono, Paschalis Maria. 2002a. *The Common Ground in the Kei Islands (Eggs from One Fish and One Bird)*. Yogyakarta: Galang Press.

Laksono, Paschalis Maria. 2002b. "We are all one. How custom overcame religious rivalry in Southeast Maluku". *Inside Indonesia* 70. http://www.insideindonesia.org/we-are-all-one-3.

Langen, H.G. 1888. *The Key, or Ké, Islands*. In *Proceedings of the Royal Geographical Society and Monthly Record of Geography*, 10 (12): 764–779, Published by: on behalf of Wiley Royal Geographical Society (with the Institute of British Geographers).
Langen, H.G. 1902. *Die Key- oder Kii-Inseln des O.I. Archipelago aus dem Tagebuche eines Colonisten*. Wien: Druck und Commissionsverslag von Carl Gerold's Sohn.
Ortigues, Edmond. 1999. *Le monothéisme*. Paris: Hatier.
Pleyte, C.M. 1893. *Ethnographische Atlas van de Zuidwester- en Zuidooster-Eilanden meer bepaaldelijk der Eilanden Wetar, Leti, Babar en Dama, alsmede der Tanimber-, Timorlaut- en Kei-Eilanden*. Leiden: E.J. Brill.
Pouillon, Jean. 1979. "Remarques sur le verbe 'croire'". In *La fonction symbolique; essais d'anthropologie*, ed. M. Izard and P. Smith, 43–51. Paris: Gallimard.
Reid, Anthony. 1993. *Southeast Asia in the Age of Commerce 1450–1680*, volume 2: *Expansion and Crisis*. New Haven: Yale University Press.
Robbins, Joel. 2004. *Becoming Sinners: Christianity and Moral Torment in a Papua New Guinea Society*. Berkeley, Los Angeles and London: University of California Press.
Robbins, Joel. 2009. "Conversion, Hierarchy, and Cultural Change. Value and Syncretism in the Globalization of Pentecostal and Charismatic Christianity". In *Hierarchy. Persistence and Transformation in Social Formations*, ed. K.M. Rio and O.H. Smedal, 65–88. New York: Berghahn Books.
Steenbrink, Karel. 2003. *Catholics in Indonesia, 1808–1942. A documented history*, vol. 1. Leiden: KITLV Press.
Thorburn, Craig. 2004. "*Musibah*: Governance, intercommunal violence and reinventing tradition in the Kei Islands, Southeast Maluku". Working Paper 125, Centre of Southeast Asian Studies, Monash Asia Institute, Monash University, Victoria, Australia.

Author Biography

Cécile Barraud is a retired senior researcher at the French National Center for Scientific Research (CNRS) and a member of the Center for Southeast Asian Studies in Paris. She has conducted extensive fieldwork in the Southeast Moluccas, Eastern Indonesia, since 1971. Her research focused initially on understanding 'houses' as social groups (*Tanebar-Evav*, 1979), then on rituals, exchanges and the comparison of ideologies (co-edition of *Rituals and Socio-Cosmic Order in Eastern Indonesian Societies*, 1990) and on kinship, gender and sex distinction (co-direction of *Sexe relatif ou sexe absolu?* 2001). She has published an essay on the notion of property in Austronesian languages and in the Indo-Pacific area (2010).

CHAPTER 8

Encounters with Christianity in the North Moluccas (Sixteenth–Nineteenth Centuries)

Jos. D. M. Platenkamp

INTRODUCTION

The North Moluccas has had the dubious privilege of being among the first Asian regions to draw the attention of the early modern European expansionists. Lured by the prospect of a direct access to the sources of exotic spices that until then had reached Europe through an Indian, Arab and Ottoman-Venetian conducted trade only, and seduced by the perspective of fabulous market profits, Portuguese and Spanish military merchant ships reached the area in the early 1500s. The ships not only carried renowned navigators dispatched by their Iberian monarchs to discover new worlds but also Jesuits following the Papal command to spread the Roman Catholic faith worldwide. Then, in the beginning of the seventeenth century, the Dutch United East India Company (*Vereenigde Oostindische Compagnie*, VOC)—the first globally operating shareholder company born in the Republic of the United Provinces—chased both the Iberian merchants and the Jesuit and Augustinian priests from the region in order to establish the militarily enforced trade

J.D.M. Platenkamp (✉)
Westfaelische Wilhelms-Universitaet Muenster, Institut Fuer Ethnologie, Muenster, Germany

© The Author(s) 2017
M. Picard (ed.), *The Appropriation of Religion in Southeast Asia and Beyond*, DOI 10.1007/978-3-319-56230-8_8

monopoly that laid the foundation for the Dutch colonial empire in the centuries to come. For when in 1799 the VOC went bankrupt the Dutch State took over its debts and established the Netherlands East Indies under the direct supervision of the Crown.

During all these years the perception of the North Moluccan societies had been a Euro-centric one. Not that the facts reported were the outcome of a mere fantastic imagination, but their selection and interpretation were steered by the paradigms that governed the ideologies of the early modern Iberian and Netherlands societies. Largely absent from these historical reports is an understanding of the ways in which the North Moluccan societies themselves perceived the representatives of European societies who appeared in their midst. This indigenous perception and valuation of the European 'other' must concern social anthropology as the comparative science *par excellence*. But before embarking on an anthropological journey into history a brief note on the history of anthropology is due so as to outline the theoretical perspective adopted here. Scholars of comparative Indonesian studies of Leiden University were the first outside France to put the seminal analysis of Émile Durkheim and Marcel Mauss (1903) of the pertinence of cosmology for understanding social and political structures to the empirical test in series of comparative analyses of Indonesian societies (e.g. van Ossenbruggen 1977 [1918]; Duyvendak 1926; Pigeaud 1977 [1928]). In 1935, J.P.B. de Josseling de Jong, inspired by his student Frans van Wouden's comparative research of eastern Indonesian societies (van Wouden 1968 [1935]), first attempted to isolate the basic socio-cosmological principles that provided the numerous societies in this vast Archipelago with the common properties of a 'field of ethnological study'. By now this is history, too, and much in this approach has been criticised, amended and refined since (e.g. P.E. de Josselin de Jong 1977a, b; Fox 1980; Barnes 1985; Platenkamp 1990; Oosten 2006; Prager unpubl.). But one of the so-called core elements that J.P.B. de Josselin de Jong considered characteristic of this field of study still deserves our close attention. It is the propensity of the societies in question to incorporate foreign influences in particular manners, transforming their meaning and value in the process—a phenomenon that only diachronic analyses may identify. I aim to analyse the representations that steered the North Moluccan encounters with the Iberians and the Dutch and the denominations of Christianity they introduced. Drawing upon reports on the North and Central Moluccas from the sixteenth to the twentieth century as well as on

8 ENCOUNTERS WITH CHRISTIANITY IN THE NORTH MOLUCCAS ... 219

fieldwork data and indigenous mythologies I shall try to identify certain structural patterns of a *longue durée* governing the 'foreign' provenance

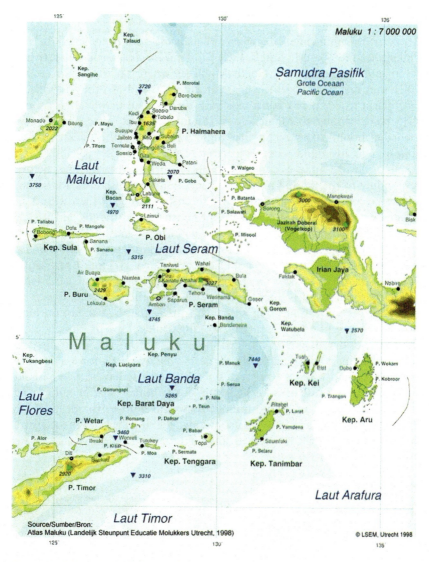

Fig. 8.1 Map of the Moluccas, 1998

of people and ideas as a constitutive part of overall socio-cosmological orders (Fig. 8.1).[1]

First Encounters

After their commander Magellan (Magalhães) had been killed in the Philippines the Spanish vessels *Victoria* and *Trinidad* sailed on, arriving seven months later in the North Moluccas where on the 8 November 1521 they cast anchor off the coast of Tidore Island. To the Tidore sultan their arrival did not come as a surprise. He had dreamt that "some ships were coming to Maluco from distant countries" and had "examined the moon" to ascertain that these were indeed the ones that had appeared in his mind's eye (Pigafetta [c. 1524] 1874: 124). Having come on board in the company of his court dignitaries and before responding to the trading proposals made by the Spanish crew the sultan addressed a different issue first. He assured the Spanish "that he and all his people were well content to be the most faithful friends and vassals of the King of Spain; that he received us in his island as his own sons; that we might go ashore and remain there as [if] in our own houses; and that his island for the future should not be named T[i]dore but Castile, in proof of the great love he bore to the King our master" (*loc. cit.*). Thereupon the Spanish offered fine cloths and other valuable objects to the sultan and his retinue. The sultan lamented "that he had got nothing worthy to be sent as a present to our king, unless he sent himself, now that he considered him as his lord" (*op. cit.*: 125).[2] The next day, the sultan elaborated his remarkable request: "He asked us for a signature of the king and a royal standard, since he desired that both his island of T[i]dore, and also that of [Ternate] [...] should become subject to the King of Spain, for whose honour he would fight to the death". He implored the Spaniards to leave some men behind "who would always keep alive his recollection of us and of our King, as he would more

---

[1] I am indebted to the late Prof. Jarich Oosten for his inspiring comments and Mr. Jan Hermans, Librarian of the Koninklijke Bibliotheek The Hague, for his assistance in locating relevant sources.

[2] In another edition of Pigafetta's report it reads "he had nothing else except his own life to send to the king his sovereign" (Pigafetta 1995: 84). Other crewmembers' reports largely corroborated Pigafetta's on the Tidore sultan's discourse (Alderley 1874).

esteem having some of us with him than our merchandise, which would not last him a long time" (*op. cit.*: 126).

The question arises why before taking up the trade proposed by the Spaniards the sultan should first surrender his sovereignty to the Spanish monarch. Why did he declare himself his vassal, re-name his realm "after Castile" and ask for the insignia of the Spanish monarchy? And why should he pose as a destitute person with only his life to offer, while by the same token declare himself the "father" of the Spanish crew? A common sense interpretation would seek the answer to these questions in the sultan's political interests. Indeed, in soliciting the support of the Spanish the Tidore sultan stood not alone. Also before the arrival of the Europeans, continuous strife among the sultanates of the Four Mountains of Maluku (*Maluku kie raha*) had haunted their interrelationships and the sultanates of Tidore and Ternate in particular had been entangled in an ongoing struggle for political supremacy in the region. And since from 1514 onwards the rulers of Ternate, Jailolo and Makian—the other three Moluccan sultanates—had sent letters offering *their* vassalage to the King of Portugal (Abdurrachman 1978: 171), would it not stand to reason that Tidore's submission to the King of Spain was a mere strategic move to acquire a superior military ally (cp. Henley 2002)? Keeping in mind, however, that "one cannot do good history, not even contemporary history, without regard for ideas, actions, and ontologies that are not and never were our own" (Sahlins 1995: 14), I suggest that the encounter between the Tidore sultan and the Spanish makes us witness of a confrontation between the different ways in which relations with 'strangers' were valued in terms of contrasting models, each subordinating the 'short-term' trade transactions to those 'long-term' exchange relations (Parry and Bloch 1989), the enactment of which constituted the Iberian and the North Moluccan societies as two differently conceived socio-cosmological wholes (Barraud and Platenkamp 1990).

Iberian Ventures

The Iberian global explorations from the mid-fifteenth century onwards had been authorised by a series of Papal bulls issued between 1456 and 1514. By the Treaty of Tordesillas of 1494 Pope Alexander VI exercising his universal sovereignty had assigned to the Crown of Portugal the task of *Padroado Real*, the patronage of the Roman Catholic mission in all lands East of the demarcation line 370 miles west of the Cape Verde Islands; to the Spanish Crown was assigned the *Patronato Real* over the lands to the West of that line.[3] The bulls stipulated that whatever military and commercial endeavours were to be undertaken they should serve the dissemination of the Roman Catholic faith. That in the notion of *padroado* "mediaeval-theocratic conceptions appeared to have merged with vague reminiscences of the classical idea of colonisation" (Wils 1960: 313[4]) is illustrated by the letter sent in 1591 by the Venetian Jesuit António Marta to the Spanish Governor in the Philippines urging him to conquer the Moluccas: "Your Lordship will gain more than 200,000 souls for God [... and] have a burning flambeau in this world to light and lead you to heaven [...] it will perpetuate your name with a title equal to that of such Roman commanders as Germanicus, Africanus and others like them" (cited in Jacobs 1980: 304). The Portuguese policy of expansion accordingly aimed at *"feitora* (trading), *fortaleza* (military dominance) and *e igreja* (the gospel)" (Abdurrachman 1978: 170). These objectives were hierarchically ordered—the preaching of the gospel being assigned the highest value[5]—so that in Iberian perspective the interests in global trade should be subordinated in value to the religious efforts ensuring that the explorations of foreign lands ultimately serve the transcending spiritual destiny of their inhabitants. In the wake of the Counter-Reformation this aim was pursued in the Moluccas in an increasingly ruthless manner (Meilink Roelofsz [1962] 2001: 236; van Fraassen 1981: 19). The moral state of the 'heathens' was deemed to warrant this task, were they not "[...] intriguers, treacherous, malicious, untruthful, and ungrateful: they have all the evils. When one

---

[3] A congress convening on the Spanish–Portuguese border in 1524 to decide jointly on the actual geographical location of the Moluccas and hence on the title to its possession failed to reach an agreement (Villiers 2004: 135).

[4] The English translation of this and all subsequent Dutch language quotations is mine, J.P.

[5] Apart from the Portuguese need for new food resources and the Renaissance intellectual curiosity of new discoveries, "[u]ndoubtedly the main intellectual and ideological reason for Portuguese overseas expansion was the idea of spreading the Christian faith. This was seen as a continuation of the Crusades and received explicit recognition in the Papal Bull *Romanus Pontifex* (January 1455)" (Abdurrachman 1978: 167; cp. Boxer 1969: 18–19). Thus when an emissary of Vasco da Gama arriving in Calicut (India) in 1498 was asked what it was that the Portuguese searched for so far away from home he answered: "we look for Christians and spices" (Tiele 1875: 212).

makes them reproaches about that, they answer that this is the Moluccan [...] custom. This is what the Holy Scripture confirms for us, saying that the lands along the sea will be fruitful and its people very malicious" (António Galvão (c. 1544), in Jacobs 1971: 71).[6] The politico-economic exploitation of the North Moluccan markets therefore went hand in hand with an intense missionary activity conducted above all by Portuguese and Spanish Jesuit priests.

Tidore Perceptions

The Tidore sultan perceived his encounter with the Spaniards in quite different terms. He interpreted the appearance of the Spanish vessels on the horizon as governed by a cosmic order of which the planets and stars served as main indicators. In the North Moluccas an astronomical model prevailed well into the twentieth century that governed all social, economic and ritual activities. According to this model the Pleiades emerging 'from the ocean' above the northern horizon in early November were perceived as 'stars' (Ternate, Galela (Tobelo) *wonge-wonge(mi)*) into which the primeval ancestors (*wonge(mi)*) of the domains (Ternate, Galela *soa*, Tobelo *hoana*, Tobaru *soana*) had turned once these had vanished from the people's collective memory (Platenkamp 2015). If it was this model that the Tidore sultan—"a very great astrologer" himself (Pigafetta 1874: 126)—had consulted, then the Spanish ships' arrival coincided with the re-appearance of these 'ancestral' Pleiades. Rather than perceived as a historical contingency the Spanish arrival appears to have been deemed embedded in, hence predicted in terms of, this overall circulation of people, ancestors and stars at a vast socio-cosmic scale.[7] At first glance this would signal a remarkable contradiction. For if the

---

[6] Even though condemning the brutality with which both Portuguese and Spanish pursued their political dominance in the Moluccas, the Spanish priest Argensola (1601) judged the indigenous people to be "savages, without law, without king, without towns, living in the wilderness [...] false, brutish and pusillanimous people", while Muslims were an "abominable sect" (cited in Villiers 2004: 144).

[7] Galvão's (c. 1544) observation of a system of "worship of the sun, the moon and the stars" prevailing in the North Moluccas (Jacobs 1971: 76) appears to confirm this. The analogy with the Hawaiian perception of James Cook's arrival almost three centuries later is noteworthy. The Hawaiians at Maui "were already on the look-out for [the deity] Lono" when Cook arrived in 26 November 1778, "a week after the Pleiades had appeared on the horizon at sunset" (Sahlins 1995: 36).

Spanish were indeed perceived as ancestors re-emerging from social oblivion, then they qualified both as 'strangers' coming from afar and as 'progeny' of the Tidore sultan returning to their autochthonous origins. The sultan's discourse actually expressed these dual origins. For whereas the Spanish were hailed as representatives of a foreign monarch whom the sultan pledged to acknowledge as his sovereign, they should also consider themselves as his 'sons' enjoying the shelter of the 'houses' in his domain, that is, as sharing in his own line of descent. This model of differential—foreign *and* autochthonous—origins, in terms of which the Tidore sultan perceived his relations with the foreigners, was articulated in a particular mode of exchange. On the one hand, his submission to the Spanish sovereign should entitle him not only to the valuable cloth and other gifts which the Spanish so lavishly bestowed upon him, but also to the flags, insignia, seals, coinage and the very name of the realm Castile—gifts in which this foreign sovereignty was objectified. The very reception of these gifts connecting him to this foreign origin would have a transitive bearing upon the political legitimacy of his own rule: they would authorise him to proclaim his own sovereignty vis-à-vis other competing sultanates in the region. The sultan, on the other hand, posited himself as the giver of a quite different gift, and one of inferior value at that: he had "nothing to give but his own life" in return.

The model of differential origins was articulated in other sultanates as well. Around 1540 the Ternate sultan told the Portuguese that some hundred years earlier one of his ancestors had brought from a court of Java his own title of *kolano*[8] along with titles bestowed on his subordinate officials (such as *sangaji, menteri*). The Javanese ruler, so he said, had "made them Muslims and introduced coinage to their country, as well as the gong, the *serunai* [reed instrument], ivory, the *kris*

---

[8] The fourteenth-century Javanese mythological figure of *kalana* represents "a wandering adventurer of noble birth from abroad" (Zoetmulder 1982/I: 771) who "attaches himself to the community and as a sophisticated and righteous ruler creates order and prosperity" (van Fraassen 2005: 56). The figure is still known as *ratu adil*, "righteous ruler". Along with the Javanese lexeme *kalana* the North Moluccan rulers (*kolano*) adopted this very association of ideas. Here it is of interest that the *Nāgarakretāgama*—the great mid-fourteenth-century epic eulogy on its ruler Hayam Wuruk—listed 'Wandan Maloko' among the vassalages paying tribute to the Majapahit Kingdom (Brandes 1902: 8–9; Cp. Sahlins 2008).

[ceremonial dagger], and the law, and all the other good things they have" (António Galvão, cited in Jacobs 1971: 105).[9]

In these instances foreign courts—be they of Java or Castile—were valued not merely as the origins of political sovereignty of the North Moluccan realms but as sources of their societal order as such. Thence originated the institution of kingship, the system of political and religious offices, law, coinage and 'court culture' and—in the case of Java—Islam.[10] These origin relationships were transitive in nature. They authorised the local rulers not only to proclaim supremacy over the competing polities in the region but also to act as *roi civilisateur* vis-à-vis the peoples inhabiting their own dependencies proper. These models display a remarkable historical tenacity. For example, until the early twentieth century the Tidore sultan in return for the tribute brought to him still performed such transfers of royal gifts and titles to his Biak-Nomfur dependency in Papua, authorising the political rule of those local chiefs who had received these gifts in his court (Kamma 1982).

Competing Sixteenth-Century Perspectives

Whereas in sixteenth-century Iberian perspective the Catholic Church represented the long-term cosmological order, to which the short-term trading transactions with the Moluccan peoples should be subordinated, the Tidore and Ternate sultans did not require the Iberians to convert to Islam as a precondition of trade. Neither did the sultans deem the Catholic faith of the Iberian kings an impediment to accept them as their foreign sovereigns. In 1512, 9 years before the Spanish arrived in Tidore, the Ternate sultan invited the Portuguese under Francisco Serrão

---

[9] That Majapahit was an unlikely source of the Muslim conversion of the Ternate sultans is underlined by Galvão: "I have been in Java, and according to what they [the Javanese] told me, the Moluccan people became Muslims before them" (in: Jacobs 1971: 105). Yet one should not judge the Ternatan statement to that effect as to its historical accuracy. It reflects the ideological message that the 'civilised order' originates from 'abroad', and apparently in sixteenth-century Ternate, Java figured as such and Islam was merely presented as part of a set of indices of such 'civilised order', as were the titles, court culture, etc.

[10] Islam was and still is a major identifier of the North Moluccan sultans' office. As 'Lord of the Believers' (Arabic *amir-ul-mu'minin*) the Ternate sultan was head of the *Ummat Islam* of Ternate and the Muslim communities in its overseas dependencies (van Fraassen 1987/I: 344).

to Ternate, and "[a]lthough they were Muslims, the rulers of Ternate eagerly declared themselves loyal vassals of their Lord, the Christian king of Portugal" (Jacobs 1974: 3). The distinction between Islam and Christianity was apparently not conceived as one between 'true' and 'false' 'religions' but as one reflecting the complementary origin relationships. Hence, whereas for the North Moluccan sultans Christianity was an attribute of the Iberian sovereignty, it did not constitute a superior cosmology pertaining to foreign and autochthonous peoples alike—as the Iberians themselves conceived of it. In the sultans' perception, therefore, submitting themselves to the Iberian monarchs did not require their conversion to Catholicism. On the contrary, at that encompassing level the very distinction between Christianity of foreign origin and Islam— 'originating from Java' but in relation to the Iberian Christianity an attribute of the sultans' indigenous identity—lost its meaning. In analogy to the dual nature of supreme Deities in other eastern Indonesian societies,[11] at the highest level of cosmology the contrast between Christianity and Islam was merged into the notion of an encompassing cosmological order itself.[12] Hence the declaration of the Ternate sultan Hairun before Portuguese Jesuits that "[...] Christians and Muslims have the same God, and at some point in time all of us will be one".[13]

In the course of the sixteenth century local rulers in some cases declared themselves prepared to adopt Christianity—perceived as

---

[11] Cp. Barnes 1974, Barraud 1979, Geirnaert-Martin 1992, Lewis 1988, Renard-Clamagirand 1982, Schulte Nordholt 1971.

[12] In the South and Central Moluccas the cosmological duality recurred in a social organisation of contrasting confederations of 'five' and of 'nine' domains (e.g. *ulilima/ulisiwa; patalima/patasiwa*), associated with foreign and indigenous origins. Europeans were classified according to this basic paradigm. When in 1537 the Portuguese had been expelled from the *ulilima* villages in Ambon-Hitu they were welcomed by the *ulisiwa* village of Hatiwe. Since its inhabitants had been converted to Catholicism by Xaverius the duality of 'five'/'nine' began to encompass that of Islam/*lima* and Christianity/*siwa* (Van Fraassen 2005: 58). Here, too, the distinction between Islam and Christianity thus was encompassed by a cosmologically grounded dual order of society as a whole.

[13] [...] *diziéndome que christianos y moros teníamos un Dios común, y que en algún tiempo todos seríamos unos* [...] (Jacobs 1974: 40; I owe this translation to Mr. Joseba Estévez MA). Five hundred years later this statement was still incomprehensible to the Catholic mind. Hubert Jacobs S. J., the learned editor of the voluminous sixteenth-century Jesuit correspondence from the Moluccas, commented: "Quite surely, Hairun did not think in this way from an ecumenical spirit *avant-la-lettre*, but out of a deep-rooted religious indifferentism" (Jacobs 1974: 40, Note 39).

attribute of their vassalage to the foreign Iberian sovereign—if this would enable them to gain precedence over their political adversaries. They were equally willing to forsake their Christian faith again. But for the same reason the North Moluccan sultans vehemently opposed the conversions made by Portuguese Jesuits in their dependencies of Morotia and Morotai in North-east Halmahera. They did so not because their inhabitants had forsaken Islam in favour of Christianity—the Moro people had never adopted Islam—but because their conversion signalled the Moro rejecting the sultans' suzerainty. Until then, they had paid the Ternate and Tidore sultans their tribute in spices, food crops, cattle, labour and military service.[14] The fact that Portuguese priests not only baptised them but also supplied them with abundant gifts of Portuguese clothing (Schurhammer 1963: 756–757)—a gift of eminent symbolic value as we saw—must have signalled to the sultans that the Moro had adopted the Portuguese king as their new sovereign. The mere fact that once converted the Moro no longer sent the tribute due to Ternate but provided the Portuguese garrisons with food instead (Tiele 1879: 53; Villiers 1983: 280) can only have strengthened the sultans in this conviction. From 1536 onwards warriors in the service of the sultans of Tidore, Ternate and Jailolo repeatedly attacked the Moro settlements, culminating in their final defeat in 1627 (Wessels 1935: 54; Schurhammer 1963: 775).

It is instructive to examine how these historical events have been mythically transmitted—and how they were fundamentally transformed in the process. A Tobelo myth about the fate of Moro society recorded in 1980 and analysed elsewhere in detail (Platenkamp 1993) fully ignores the Portuguese military and missionary interventions. It identifies as the final cause of the Moro defeat the disloyalty of the Ternate sultan towards them. Instead of fulfilling his part in the exchange of gifts of foreign origin against those of autochthonous provenance the sultan violently re-appropriates those valuable objects that he himself had transferred to them in the past. This renunciation of the diarchic relationship between the foreign ruler and the indigenous people not merely results in the latter's military defeat; in their perception it deprives them of their social condition altogether.[15] The myth recounts how "walking backwards

---

[14]Letter of 1536 from Captain Lionel de Lima to the Portuguese King (in Villiers 1983: 280; cp. Villiers 1983: 287).

[15]That the sultan's renunciation of his socialising relationship immediately devalues the autochthonous fertility is signified by the Moro sending a gift of excrements instead of food to the Ternate sultan (Fortgens 1911: 114).

into the forest" they are transformed into invisible beings, living as spirits (Tobelo *mor'oka*, literally "beings localised in Moro") in the forest, the skies and the deep sea—timeless cosmological domains that envelop the social domains of villages and garden territories. In this mythical articulation of the fundamental relationship between autochthonous forms of existence and the socialising agency of foreign rulers, neither Islam nor Christianity is assigned any significance.

Seventeenth-Century Dutch Perceptions

We have observed how the Iberian global commercial explorations in the sixteenth century were subordinated to the task, assigned by the Popes to the Portuguese and Spanish Crowns, to incorporate the inhabitants in the hemispheres under their respective patronage into the universal Catholic Church. The actions of the Dutch United East India Company (VOC), established in 1602 and swiftly replacing the Iberians as the dominant foreign power in the North Moluccas, displayed a very different ideological configuration. The Dutch Republic of the Seven United Provinces, born in 1581 from a protracted war of secession from the Spanish Crown, had secured the Dutch Reformed Protestant Church its position of State religion while allowing for a certain measure of freedom of religious conscience and without actively persecuting other forms of worship (Frijhoff and Spies 1990: 179–182, 351ff.; Schutte 2002a: 15). Not only in the Netherlands itself this policy of de facto religious tolerance[16] resulted in recurring tensions between the Reformed Church and the Republic's government. The second VOC Charter of 1622 granting the Company a global monopoly in the spice trade specified the "preservation of the public faith" as one of its tasks (Schutte 2002b: 47). Yet the VOC derived from this monopoly the right to strictly curtail the activities of the Protestant Church in the East Indian Archipelago

---

[16] In the mid-seventeenth century the religious tolerance of the 'Reformed theocracy' of the Dutch Republic, allowing Lutherans, Huguenots, Presbyterians, Jews and Catholics to practice their religion (Schutte 2002a: 15), "was not yet an ideological principle founded on philosophical arguments but rather a matter of municipal policies [responding to the necessity] of civil order and civic unity, combined with the acknowledgement that religious diversity was an inevitable fact and freedom of conscience an inviolable good" (Frijhoff and Spies 1990: 181).

(Boetzelaer 1906: 18–19) so as to prevent it from jeopardising its commercial interests. And whereas the Amsterdam Church Council in 1599 had condemned the VOC' pursuit of trade monopoly, arguing that "only free trade is in accordance to the Word of God" (*op. cit.*: 31, Note 1), the VOC articulated this relationship between global trade and the Protestant Christian values in a quite different manner. It had commissioned the learned scholar Hugo Grotius (Hugo de Groot) with the task to conceptualise a legal foundation of its claim to gain access to the global markets still largely controlled by the Iberian powers. This had resulted in a remarkable treatise in which the Iberian ventures and their Papal authorisation were sharply criticised.

In his *Mare Liberum* of 1609[17] Grotius construed a hierarchy of values of universal application. At the highest level he placed the category of Natural Law. Deriving from Divine Providence this law is valid for Humankind whose members share the same "race" and "origin" and are united in a "natural social bond and kinship" (Feenstra (ed.) 2009: 7). Natural Law transcends the distinctions between single nations, for its imperatives are "implanted" in each individual's "mind" irrespective of the nation to which he belongs, the ruler to which he is subject, or the religious creed to which he subscribes (*op. cit.*: 19). God has supplied these nations with different resources and has willed them to exchange these with one another so as to satisfy each other's needs. This Divine imperative of exchange is the foundation of universal sociality: whoever "abolishes this system of exchange abolishes also the highly prized fellowship in which humanity is united [...] in short, he does violence to nature itself". Therefore this "law of human fellowship" is "absolutely just" (*op. cit.*: 27–29). This supreme status ascribed to Natural Law enabled Grotius to incisively criticise the Popes' decision to assign to the Iberian kings the suzerainty over the world's hemispheres. Since "Christ the Lord renounced all earthly sovereignty [...] in his human form he certainly did not possess dominion of the entire world". Hence "[...] the Pope is not the civil or temporal lord of the whole earth [...] he has no power at all over infidel peoples, since they are not members of the Church" (*op. cit.*: 41). And whereas this very fact had motivated the Popes to delegate the "patronage" over the non-European peoples to the Iberian

---

[17] *Mare Liberum, sive de Iure quod Batavis Competit ad Indicana Commercia Dissertatio.* Leiden 1609. All subsequent quotations in English are from Feenstra (ed.) 2009.

kings, for Grotius the distinction between different religious creeds did not justify the claims made by Christian rulers at taking the property of newly "discovered" "pagan" peoples. For even though the "natives of the East Indies" were "in part idolaters, in part Mohammedans, and sunk in grievous sin", they "nevertheless enjoyed public and private ownership of their own property and possessions, an attribute which could not be taken from them without just cause" (*op. cit.*: 35). Grotius maintained that "Christians, whether laymen or clerics, may not deprive infidels of their civil power and sovereignty merely on the ground that the latter are infidels [...] for the factor of religious faith, as Thomas [Aquinas] rightly observes, does not cancel the natural or human law from which ownership has been derived" (*op. cit.*: 35–36). And since the indigenous peoples of the Orient are "neither insane nor irrational but clever and sagacious [...] not even in that respect can a pretext for their subjugation be found" (*op. cit.*: 37).

In Grotius' view the Papal bulls thus constituted a twofold transgression. On the one hand, the bulls testified to the Popes' illegitimate claim at the spiritual authority over peoples that were not part of the Holy Catholic Church; on the other hand, they bore witness of the Popes' equally illegitimate assumption of secular power justifying the alienation of property rights of indigenous peoples and the granting of monopoly rights of maritime navigation to the Iberian rulers—both being inalienable under the terms of Natural Law. In neither case had the Pope the "authority to commit acts repugnant to the law of nature" (*op. cit.*: 97, quoting Prierias 1596[18]). Solely the right to exchange resources among nations—Christian and non-Christian alike—expressive of the "fellowship" and "sociality" of Humankind, was justifiable under the terms of permanent, immutable and universal Natural Law. And since "the principle of exchange (*metablètikè*[19]) in itself is derived from nature" (*op. cit.*: 129), the Dutch cause, refuting the Portuguese monopoly of maritime trade "[...] is more just than that of such a competitor, inasmuch as their own profit in this case is bound up with profit to the entire human race, a universal benefit which the Portuguese are attempting to destroy"

---

[18] Sylvester Prierias, *Sylvestrinae Summae, Verbo Papa*. 2 vols. Antverpiae 1596
[19] Aristotle, *Politica* Book I.

(*op. cit.*: 143).[20] Thus, instead of valuing the differences between the nations on earth in Biblical reference to different religious beliefs and moralities (as the Iberians had done earlier), the VOC followed Grotius in assessing them in terms of their different and unequally distributed resources. Free trade as the only means to create economic equity would be in accordance with God's universal order and the Natural Law common among all peoples. In this perspective the religious identity of potential trading partners was of no particular concern. An efficient conduct of the highly profitable monopolised spice trade being its prime objective, the VOC administration "[…] knew better than to endanger it through the preaching of [the Protestant] doctrine, and the Reformed Church in [the East Indies] was too dependent on the [VOC] to display much fervency in its missionary work" (Meilink Roelofsz (1962) 2001: 236). Hence the interest in converting the adherents of other religions in the East Indies to Protestant Christianity (as insisted upon by successive Church Synods in the early 1600s and confirmed in the *Confessio Belgica* of 1619[21] (Boetzelaer 1906: 19)) was to be firmly subordinated to this—surprisingly modern—economic ideology.

IMPLEMENTATION IN THE NORTH MOLUCCAS

With the expulsion by the VOC of the Spanish and Portuguese merchants and priests from the North Moluccas, a major source of ethnographic information about the indigenous peoples had dried up. This

---

[20] In the negotiations resulting in the Treaty of Westphalia (Münster 1648), this legal argument indeed enabled the Dutch to successfully challenge the Iberian trade monopoly in the West and East Indies (Frijhoff and Spies 1990: 40).

[21] Article 36 states that "[…] our gracious God […] hath invested the magistracy with the sword, for the punishment of evil doers, and for the praise of them that do well. And their office is […] that they protect the sacred ministry, and thus may remove and prevent all idolatry and false worship; that the kingdom of antichrist may be thus destroyed, and the kingdom of Christ promoted" (*Christian Classics Ethereal Library* http://www.ccel.org/ccel/schaff/creeds3.iv.viii.html#fnf_iv.viii-p7.1906). This call remained unanswered, for in 1614 the Church Council of the City of Delft reproached the VOC for being "only interested in its riches, not in the salvation of souls, and that its support of the [Christian] religion only serves to establish its trade and to bind the natives by the tie of religion to our people" (Boetzelaer 1906: 62). And in 1618 the Synod of Dordrecht, lamenting the "great disorder in matters of religion" in the East Indies, implored the States General of the Republic to adamantly devote itself to the conversion of the "heathens" (*op. cit.*: 46–47).

stands to reason, for in line with the VOC's objectives virtually all seventeenth-century Dutch documents on the North Moluccas are concerned with the trade conditions imposed on the sultans. Whereas these texts tell us next to nothing about the indigenous perceptions of this newly arrived foreign power, they do offer us an illuminating view on how in VOC perspective Dutch Protestant Christianity was to be valued relative to Iberian Catholicism on the one side and to North Moluccan Islam on the other. The initial appearance of the VOC in the North Moluccas was indigenously perceived in terms of the diarchic order discussed earlier. From submitting themselves to a new foreign sovereign the sultans expected the benefit of acquiring an authority superior both to other foreign powers and to the competing sultanates in the region itself. Thus it was on the initiative of the Ternate sultan wishing to expel the Spanish from his realm that the VOC admiral Cornelis Matelief in 1607 sailed to the North Moluccas. But while the Iberians had kept record of the ceremonial exchanges marking their first encounters, the VOC representatives immediately proceeded to consolidate their politico-economic relationships with the sultans in the form of legal contracts. These contracts reflect the hierarchy of values as advocated by Grotius, subordinating the distinctions between nations, their respective 'positive laws' and religious creeds to the supreme significance of exchange as the foundation of universal Humankind's sociality. However, in blatant contradiction to Grotius' thesis condemning—under the terms of Natural Law—single nations monopolising global exchanges, the VOC immediately imposed these very conditions on the North Moluccan sultans.

The first of such contracts was concluded in 1609 between admiral Matelief on behalf of the Lords States General of the United Netherlands Provinces and the "King of Ternate and his council", the latter acknowledging the former as his "protector" (Corpus 1907: 52[22]). It obliged the sultan to accept the conditions of trade monopoly: no other "nation or people" would be allowed access to indigenous produce of the land, and the VOC would be entitled to purchase the spices at a fixed price. The imperative that such interactions be conducted by partners sharing the *same* ideology—whether of the Catholic-monarchic type of the

---

[22] I am indebted to Dr. W. M. A. Henneke for her philological advice on these seventeenth-century Dutch texts. This and all subsequent translations of quotations from the contracts are mine.

Iberian *padroado* or of the diarchic type of the North Moluccan sultans—was explicitly rejected. The partners' socio-cosmological representations other than those legally defined were to be kept strictly separate. While Article 12 of the contract, stipulating that "[i]n matters of religion no one shall deride or obstruct the other, but everyone shall live as he wishes to be responsible to God" (*op. cit.*: 53), at first glance reflected the Dutch domestic *Realpolitik* of religious tolerance, Article 13 erected insurmountable barriers between the respective religious creeds of the trading partners: "If someone of the Dutch should defect to the Ternatans [i.e. convert to Islam], he shall be delivered again by the Ternatans, likewise someone of the Ternatans who would come to the Dutch shall be delivered by them [to the Ternatans] again" (ibid.).

In July 1609 vice-admiral François Wittert confirmed the contract with the Ternate sultan. While the radical boundaries between the trading partners' religious faiths were asserted once more[23], also Grotius' thesis that only trade constitute the common foundation of universal 'human fellowship' was now explicitly articulated as a value transcending this contrast between Protestant Christianity and Islam. The relationship between the Dutch and the Ternatans was to be valued as an "eternal connection (*eeuwige verbintenisse*) of friendship, conversation, trade and commerce" (*op. cit.*: 65). Indeed, the terms of the contract were to be sanctioned by "the obligation of loyalty, honour and word, which we both owe to God and our fellow humans" (ibid.).

Whereas a common supreme Deity ("our God") was invoked to encompass the contrast between the VOC and the sultans and their respective subjects, all being connected in "eternal friendship", the Catholic God of the Iberians was now excluded from this unification. The contract, for instance, concluded with the sultans of Bacan and Ternate later that year stipulated that "[…] the new Christians […] who by serious request wish to become Muslims" shall not be prevented to do so (*op. cit.*: 76–77). Since the term "new Christians" referred to those inhabitants of the Bacan sultanate whom Iberian Jesuits had converted earlier to Catholicism, their re-conversion either to Islam or to Protestant Christianity would signal a renunciation of their assumed

---

[23] "When some Hollanders, Zeelanders etcetera would want to take the Muslim faith (*Moorsch geloff*) they shall be delivered in the hands of the Hollanders and Zeelanders justice" and vice versa (*op. cit.*: 64).

allegiance to the Iberian Crowns. And since the latter were deemed the archenemies of the sultans and the VOC alike, the contract concluded "to honour God, to serve the augmentation and observation of the mutual friendship between the subjects of both royal majesties", should lead to "the ruin and destruction of the Portuguese and Spaniards and their associates [...]" (*op. cit.*: 77–78). Thus the barrier erected earlier between Islam and Christianity was replaced by one between Dutch Protestantism and Iberian Catholicism. This propensity to treat religious identity as an attribute of politico-economic loyalty would justify the brutal persecutions, performed in the 1650s by the Ternate sultan's troops on the instigation of the VOC, in parts of Sulawesi still inhabited by Catholic converts (Wessels 1935: 60).

That in VOC perspective the legal framework of the relations between the sultans and the VOC indeed transcended the religious contrast between Protestantism and Islam is evident from the practice to have the contracts sealed by oaths to God and to Allah. The first of such contracts was concluded in 1651 with the rulers (*sangaji*) of Makian and Motir Islands. It made the contractual parties swear "to behave as pious and loyal subjects [...] on the Moor book of law or Moesaphij" (Corpus 1931: 11), a reference to the Pentateuch, the Psalter, the Gospel and the Qur'an alike (cp. Hammer-Purgstall 1827: 626).

The contracts concluded from 1657 onwards all confirmed the pledge that Muslims and Protestant Christians will be free—but shall not be forced—to convert to each other's religion. Let "each act in such manner, as he deems to be of benefit for his own salvation" (*op. cit.*: 103). The VOC' argument that trade be conducted among "loyal friends" was thus morally grounded in the idea value of universal "human fellowship" obeying laws "common to all peoples" on earth—each of them "free" to subscribe to their own religious beliefs as long as these did not convey a loyalty to other politico-economic powers (as Catholicism was perceived to do). The VOC was more than willing to grant the sultanates their freedom to practice Islam, and even to put Islam on a legal par with Protestant Christianity, if this secured it the sultans' compliance with the rules of trade imposed upon them. Religious 'freedom' was the price it was prepared to pay for its profitable monopolised trade (Fig. 8.2).

Fig. 8.2 Map Allain Manesson Mallet, 1683

Introducing Protestant Christianity in the Nineteenth Century

The VOC had largely refrained from intervening directly in the North Moluccan sultans' dependencies. As the sultans adhered to the terms of the contracts that secured it the trade monopoly such interventions were redundant. For neither did the VOC heed the call from the Dutch Churches to spread the Calvinist creed nor would a direct trade with the dependencies have brought it significant additional profits. Sanctioned by oaths sworn on any religious agency—save that of the Roman Catholic Church—the contracts sealed the sultans' de facto surrender of political sovereignty to the VOC but they did not affect their status as 'foreign' sovereigns in their own overseas domains. It therefore stood to reason that in the perspective of these local societies it was not the VOC but the sultans who continued to be valued as the foreign sources of social order.

After in the early nineteenth century the Dutch Netherlands East Indies government had replaced the VOC as the ruling colonial power and the Protestant mission in the 1860s had gained access to the North Moluccas, this configuration of relationships began to shift. By that time the dependencies of the Tidore sultanate in South and Central Halmahera encompassed the domains of Weda, Maba, Patani and Bicoli, all of their inhabitants being Muslims. To the Ternate dependencies in North Halmahera belonged the domains of Tobelo, Galela, Tobaru, Loloda, Sahu, Madole, Tololiku, Pagu and Tugutil. In these domains only the Ternatan sultan's representatives and a few immigrant merchants living along the coast professed Islam; by far the majority of the inhabitants adhered to their own ancestral orders of belief and ritual action. In the North Moluccas as a whole the number of Christians was negligible. A few hundred Christians of European and 'native' descent constituted a single parish (*gemeente*) in Ternate (Tobias [1857] 1980: 78), whereas in Bacan Island only the village of Labu(hu) had preserved its Christian identity, presumably originating from the Iberian conversions of the sixteenth century (*op. cit.*: 89).

The colonial government had not significantly changed the policy pursued by the VOC during the previous 200 years regarding the political status granted Islam and Christianity. As this policy was predicated on the sultans' "complete dependence of the rulers on the Netherlands Government paired with a possibly minimal interference from the side of the [Dutch] overlord in the [sultans'] internal administration" (*op. cit.*: 4), the government proclaimed itself "neutral in relation to Islam" (Tip 1918: 13). Since it was deemed "[...] expedient that the government in the eyes of the people takes as much as possible an impartial stance in matters of religion (*godsdienstzaken*)" (Palmer van den Broek 1915: 10), it also carefully refrained from interfering in the sultans' overseas dependencies in this respect. But it did support initially the tributary relations prevailing between the sultans and their dependencies: it militarily assisted in the Tidore sultan's punitive expeditions (Tidoran/Ternatan *hongi*) to New Guinea and in the Ternate sultan's one to Seram, yet it did not hesitate to depose a sultan in favour of a more cooperative candidate either (Bosscher 1859: 108–109). In its pursuit of maintaining political 'order' the government kept its distance from 'religious' interests—Islamic, Christian and 'heathen' alike.

This did not imply, however, that it valued all these religious creeds equally. For, notwithstanding their proclaimed political neutrality in matters of 'religion', the colonial officials (*residenten*) in charge of the *Residentie* Ternate perceived the local populations through the lenses of the contemporary European paradigm of universal evolutionary history. This paradigm classified Christianity as a major indicator of a superior stage of civilisation and morality. In reporting on the state of affairs in the North Moluccan territories under their jurisdiction successive officials assigned to Muslims in particular a civilisatory status inferior to both Christians and indigenous 'Alfurs'. By the mid-nineteenth century they had come to depreciate the sultans' rule as a hindrance on the road to "development of enlightenment and civilisation [...] and exploitation of natural resources", not in the least because these rulers "cling to old decayed principles, religious bigotry [...] and are repelled by all that is new" (*op. cit.*: 6–7). As a result, a "regression in the moral and material sense" (Bosscher [1859] 1980: 100) characterised the social condition in Muslim Ternate. The Muslims living in Halmahera were judged likewise—in this case relative to the non-Muslim indigenous people. In North Halmahera the latter lived in "clean" settlements in the interior, whereas the "Muslims from Ternate and elsewhere" who had settled along the coast were "arrogant", lived in "pitiful houses" and in settlements that were "collections of filth and garbage, making a disgusting impression on the European" (Tobias [1857] 1980: 30).

Following the general liberalisation of missionary activity in the Netherlands East Indies, the Utrecht Missionary Association (*Utrechtsche Zendingsvereeniging*) in 1865 dispatched the missionary Hendrik van Dijken to preach the Dutch Reformed Protestant faith in North Halmahera. The Ternate sultan ordered him to live in coastal Galela village under the watchful eyes of his Muslim representatives, but after the intervention of the Dutch *resident* permitted him to settle along the shore of Lake Galela in the interior. In spite of the fact that in the following years fellow missionaries were stationed in other Ternatan dependencies in North Halmahera, in the early 1900s the missionaries had not yet succeeded in converting significant numbers of people. In 1899, Duma—the first Christian village founded by van Dijken in Galela territory and by that time still the only entirely Christian village in North Halmahera—counted 65 church members and 105 baptised children (van Baarda 1905: 98). The colonial government estimated the number of Christians in the whole of the North Moluccas at "a few thousand" (Roos 1909: 5) at an overall population of 107,500 (James 1918: 11).

The missionaries blamed the allegedly moral and cognitive deficiencies of the local population for their lack of success. Like the colonial officials they valued the Muslims and 'Alfurs' according to the prevailing paradigm of global human development. The Muslim inhabitants of coastal Galela were deemed "morally completely degenerated, inert, dumb and ignorant. [...] It is evident that they stand far beneath the Alfurs of the Lake [Galela]; these are a sturdy people, much more original" (BUZ 1866: 174). For whereas the "superstitious" beliefs of the "Alfurs" marked them as "original" peoples, Muslims had "degenerated" into a state of "atheism" (BUZ 1871: 64). In their "original" state of humanity the "Alfurs" lacked any attributes that might be qualified as "religious". They were "heathens in the full meaning of the word, for they are totally insensitive [...] to the salvation of their soul". For "since the people stand on a very low level, they have no spirituals needs" (BUZ 1887: 119) and "no or little conception (*denkbeeld*) of Divine worship (*Godsvereering*)" either. "They do have many customs, morals and habits but one absolutely cannot place them with any certainty in the domain of their religion" (BUZ 1869: 55; cp. Platenkamp 2015: 83–84). The missionaries searched the Galela and Tobelo languages in vain for lexemes approximately signifying their own Christian conception of 'religion' (van Baarda 1895; Hueting 1908).

More perceptive was the account that van Baarda, van Dijken's successor in Galela, presented of the state of affairs. He recognised the Galela propensity to associate the presence of the missionaries with the political leverage that the Dutch colonial government had with the

Ternate sultan, and to assess the power of the Christian God relative both to the Muslim identity of the sultan's office and to indigenous spiritual agency. Indeed, had not in the very beginning of the Galela mission the Ternatan sultan's representatives put the Christian God's protective power to the test when they selected "with satanic cleverness" the very plot for van Dijken to build his house where the "giant spirit *tumadoa*" had inflicted the epidemic disease that had killed or chased away all inhabitants (van Baarda 1905: 13)? Numerous were the missionaries' complaints that people sought their interventions whenever they were hit by drought, floods or other catastrophic events, only to turn their back on them after the threat had passed (e.g. BUZ 1874: 53–58).

This tendency to engage Christian notions as a potential source of superior power prevailed in the region even before the first missionaries had arrived. At least since the mid-nineteenth century local peoples in North and Central Halmahera had evidently carefully monitored the Dutch political interventions in the sultans' realms and interpreted these in terms of their own socio-cosmological ideology. In North Halmaheran societies one basic ideological tenet stipulates that the faculty to wield violence, and the warrior's renown this generates, must be ritually induced into the warrior's 'consciousness' (Tobelo *ma hininga*, Galela *ma sininga*). It derives from, is authorised by and 'belongs to' (Tobelo *ma dutu*, Galela *ma duhutu*) the domain's founding ancestor of immigrant origin (Galela *wonge*, Tobelo *wongemi*; Platenkamp 1988). Applying this tenet, one apparently deduced that the military power enabling the Dutch to intervene in the sultans' political affairs must have originated in, and be authorised by, a Christian Deity. Notwithstanding the political neutrality in matters of religion proclaimed by the colonial government, the latter's own Christian faith thus was perceived locally as a source of power that could be wielded in any competition for political supremacy. Being merged into a single representation of 'ownership' (*ma du(hu)tu*), the notions of 'religion', 'power', 'authority' and 'origin' could not be dissociated from one another.

One case may serve as an example. The rich pearl fishing grounds of Kau Bay of old were exploited as part of the relationship between the Tobelo-Boëng of Kau and the Ternate sultan. The pearls harvested were a tribute due to the sultan, whereas gifts of white cloth, head clothes and swords were to be received in return (Bosscher [1859] 1980: 161). But when the *anachoda* Abdulla—the sultan's representative supervising the fishing industry in Kau—refused to respect these reciprocal obligations any longer and implemented a market exploitation of the marine resources and human labour he provoked a rebellion. Its leader, by the name of Gaw-Gaw, proclaimed himself 'son of Christ' and promised to liberate all Tobelo from the yoke of Ternate (*op. cit*.: 154). The Ternate sultan sent a punitive expedition and many of the rebels were killed, but the Dutch *resident* examining the case found the grievances legitimate and intervened with the sultan to have the original tributary relationship in Kau re-instated. To the *resident*, the matter was one of political concern only and his interventions aimed at the restoration of the political order. But while in his report he devoted not a single word to the presumed 'blasphemy' of Gaw-Gaw's proclamation, for the latter it was this Christian 'Divine descent' that both authorised his violent actions and his claim at a power superior to that of the Muslim sultan.

After the first years of missionary presence, however, this indigenous tendency to assess the meaning and value of the Christian religion propagated as an instrument to oppose superior powers ('political' and 'spiritual' alike) began to lose its significance. The longer the missionaries were active, the more the people became disappointed in their "excessive expectations of political or supernatural powers" ascribed to them (van Baarda 1905: 77, 86), so that the mission in North Halmahera remained largely ineffective in the decennia to come.

Towards the end of the nineteenth century the colonial government began to assess its policy of non-interference in the sultans' internal affairs as being "harmful to the development of these regions" (Verbeke 1917: 77). This eventually led to a radical re-definition of the diarchic relationship between the sultans and the autochthonous people and its tributary exchanges. Two events accelerated this process. In 1876, local resistance in Jailolo district in North-west Halmahera against the 'extortions' by Ternatan representatives erupted in a revolt. After the revolt had been suppressed, the colonial government no longer aimed at re-instating the conventional tributary relationships but abolished them in Galela, Tobelo, Gane, Maba, Weda and Kau altogether, replacing them by a tax-per-capita of 4 guilders for a married and 2 guilders for an unmarried man (Roos 1909: 7). The revenues were to be shared between the sultan (in addition to his annuity of 45,000 guilders) and the colonial government (Gerrits 1912: 27). In 1903, in each district a Dutch *controleur* was appointed to supervise the tax collection (Verbeke 1917: 77). The sultan's relatives (collectively labelled *dano*, 'grandchild') of old had been charged with collecting—and taking their share of—the tributary payments in Halmahera. Under the new taxation they were no longer entitled to do so, so that the categorical contrast between them as the sultan's Muslim representatives and the 'Alfur' local population had been superseded by a legally defined equality manifest in the uniform tax-per-capita imposed on Muslims and 'Alfurs' alike. This created a profound resentment. So when in 1912 the tax-per-capita was replaced by a tax on "entrepreneurial and other revenues" (*bedrijfs- en andere inkomsten*), it led to a second revolt in 1914 during which the Ternatan inhabitants of Tuada-Todowongi village killed the Dutch *controleur* named Agerbeek. The Ternate sultan and his sons being charged with complicity were exiled, and Halmahera was placed under military rule (*op. cit.*: 79; Palmer van den Broek 1915: 70). It appears that in local perception these events led to an essential realignment of relationships, substituting the Dutch colonial government for the Ternate sultanate as the external source of power. Letting themselves "[...] no longer be intimidated by the [Ternatan] *dano*-with-their-head cloths", the local people now "[...] call themselves *orang Kompenia*" (Roos 1909: 15), so as to express their allegiance to the new political authority. And yet, in the early twentieth century most Galela and Tobelo were still not prepared to heed the missionaries' call to forsake their rituals of initiation, marriage and death (Platenkamp 1988), presumably because conversion to Christianity would turn them into 'Company people' themselves (BUZ 1908: 21). This inability to value Christian 'religion' as a system of belief and ritual action in its own right, independent of the diarchic relationship between their own society and the foreign source of political power and authority[24], much annoyed the missionaries. They judged the people being "totally indifferent concerning anything resembling religion (*alles wat naar godsdienst zweemt*), they do not hate Christianity at all, no, it just has no attraction for them. If tomorrow the Government would issue an order that all must go to church on Sunday, be baptised

---

[24]The missionary Fortgens observed in Jailolo district that "in their minds the natives fully identify the [colonial] administration with the mission, or rather they see in the foreign rule only one body, that of the 'Kompani'". And as a 'Kompani person' (*Kompanimensch*) one should be entitled to the missionary's assistance in chasing 'evil spirits' from the village (Fortgens 1917: 48, 49). Tobelo of Kau district conceptualised the politico-spiritual power ascribed to the missionaries in terms of their 'soul stuff' (*zielestof*, presumably referring to (Tobelo) *ma gurumini*), in which they sought to partake by collecting the water in which the missionary had bathed (Ellen 1920: 9–10).

and become Christian, this would be heard just like an order that 'the [Dutch] Resident is approaching, all must go to the beach' [...] When we discuss this they say: 'but, sir, you did not order us'" (BUZ 1880: 57; Platenkamp 2015: 89). But what in missionary perspective was an inadmissible confusion of 'religion' and political authority the colonial government perceived as advantageous to the colonial polity as a whole. As one official observed, once being converted to Christianity people experience a greater proximity to the colonial administration "than the Muhammedans or heathens. They more than once demonstrate their loyalty to and sense of unity with the Dutch government. This is the sunny side of the mission" (Karsen 1918: 16).

The conjunction of Dutch colonial and Christian missionary interests would eventually mark the beginning of a comprehensive transformation of the local societies of North Halmahera, involving the relocation of villages, the reduction of extended family to nuclear family houses, the introduction of cash crop plantations, the establishment of primary village schools and, last but not least, the replacement of village temples dedicated to the founding ancestors by Protestant churches. In 1917, the outgoing *resident* expressed his satisfaction with this course of events: "The Alfurs now stay in new [villages] and begin to cultivate coconut plantations everywhere. One has gained self-confidence, increasingly feels equivalent vis-à-vis Ternatans and Tidorese, since one knows to be supported by [Dutch] protection" (Verbeke 1917: 31).

Conclusion

In the course of history, representatives of various European societies have perceived the North Moluccan societies through different ideological lenses. Although they all appeared on the scene in search of spices, their commercial ventures were embedded in different models of universal order. The Iberians' economic pursuits were subject to a Divine command to incorporate indigenous peoples into the Catholic Church, providing them with a universal cosmological identity and securing them the eternal salvation of their 'souls'. The Dutch ascribed to the local societies a common identity derived from the legal tenets of Natural Law and a shared humanity of 'eternal fellowship' conceptualised above all in economic terms. Rather than letting the indigenous societies share in the blessings of the Protestant faith—as the Churches at home urged it to do—the VOC ideologically justified its short-term trading ventures by a long-term perspective of an eventual 'God-willed' levelling out of economic inequalities. After the Netherlands East Indies government had replaced the VOC, it pursued a similar policy, refusing to let the missionary interests propagated by the Churches in the Netherlands interfere with its policy of non-intervention in the sultans' domestic rule.

Neither the Iberians nor the Dutch appear to have grasped through which lenses they themselves and the 'religions' they propagated were being perceived. Assigning to them a position of *roi civilisateur* within a system of differential origins, the North Moluccan sultans tapped into the foreign sources of sovereignty so as to articulate transitively their own position vis-à-vis their local competitors and their dependencies alike. Relative to the foreigners they had "nothing to give but their own life", but in the local societies under their suzerainty they radiated the very civilising agency that was objectified in the signs and valuables obtained from abroad. And since Islam and Christianity were perceived as attributes of one of the differential origins only, the idea that such contrasting identities should be unified under the aegis of either one of these religions exclusively—let alone be subjected to a universally valid Natural Law—would have called into question their very relational foundation.

When Dutch missionaries began to preach the Protestant creed in North Halmahera the people perceived its significance—in accordance with this diarchic model—as an alternative foreign source of cosmological power to be wielded against both political and spiritual domestic oppression. It stands to reason, therefore, that people remained aloof as long as the missionaries insisted that the Protestant 'religion' represent a universally valid corpus of thought and action that—instead of serving colonial and indigenous political interests—should lead the convert towards a 'civilised' state of being in his life and the salvation of his 'soul' afterwards. Only after the colonial government had begun to appreciate the political merits of an indigenous ideology that identified Christianity with the superior political authority of the *kompeni*, it began to endorse conversion as a means of generating political loyalty. In the early twentieth century the missionary and colonial interests began to converge, initiating a comprehensive transformation of the societies of North Halmahera.

References

Abdurrachman, P.R. 1978. Moluccan responses to the first intrusions of the West. In *Dynamics of Indonesian History*, ed. H. Soebadio, and C.H. du Marchie Sarvaas, 161–188. Amsterdam: North-Holland Publishing Company.

Alderley, Lord Stanley. 1874. *The first voyage around the world by Magellan*. Translated from the accounts of Pigafetta, and other contemporary writers. The Hakluyt Society, First Series, No. LII. New York: Burt Franklin Publisher.

Baarda, M.J. van. 1895. *Woordenlijst Galèlareesch-Hollandsch; met ethnologische aantekeningen op de woorden die daartoe aanleiding geven*. Den Haag: Martinus Nijhoff.

Baarda, M.J. van. 1905. *Zendeling H. van Dijken. Zijn leven en arbeid op Halmahera*. Nijmegen: P. J. Milborn.

Barnes, R.H. 1974. *Kédang: A study of the collective thought of an eastern Indonesian people*. Oxford: Oxford University Press.

Barnes, R.H. 1985. The Leiden version of the comparative method in Southeast Asia. *Journal of the Anthropological Society of Oxford* 16 (2): 87–110.

Barraud, C. 1979. *Tanebar-Evav. Une société de maisons tournée vers le large*. Paris: École des Hautes Études en Sciences Sociales & Cambridge: Cambridge University Press.

Barraud, C., and J.D.M. Platenkamp. 1990. Rituals and the Comparison of societies. In *Rituals and Socio-Cosmic Order in Eastern Indonesian Societies, Part II: Maluku*, ed. C. Barraud, and J.D. M. Platenkamp. Special Anthropological Issue, *Bijdragen tot de Taal-, Land- en Volkenkunde* 146 (1): 103–123.

Boetzelaer van Asperen [en Dubbeldam], C.W. Th. Van. 1906. *De Gereformeerde Kerken in Nederland en de Zending in Oost-Indië*. PhD dissertation. Utrecht: P. Den Boer.

Bosscher, C. 1859. *Memorie van Overgave van het bestuur der Residentie Ternate van den aftredenden Resident C. Bosscher aan den benoemden Resident C. I. Bosch*. Reprinted as: Penerbitan Sumber-sumber Sejarah No. 11, 98–249. Jakarta 1980, Arsip Nasional Republik Indonesia.

Boxer, C.R. 1969. *The Portuguese Seaborne Empire: 1415–1825*. New York: Alfred A. Knopf.

Brandes, J. (ed.). 1902. Någarakretâgama. Lofdicht van Prapantja op koning Rasadjanagara, Hajam Wuruk, van Madjapahit. *Verhandelingen van het Bataviaasch Genootschap* LIV, 1e stuk, 70 pp.

BUZ (Berigten van de Utrechtsche Zendingsvereeniging). 1866. Almaheira, *Berigten van de Utrechtsche Zendingsvereeniging* Deel 7: 169–174.

BUZ (Berigten van de Utrechtsche Zendingsvereeniging). 1869. Almaheira, *Berigten van de Utrechtsche Zendingsvereeniging* Deel 10: 33–42, 49–58, 137–151.

BUZ (Berigten van de Utrechtsche Zendingsvereeniging). 1871. Almaheira, *Berigten van de Utrechtsche Zendingsvereeniging* Deel 12: 53–68.
BUZ (Berigten van de Utrechtsche Zendingsvereeniging). 1874. Almaheira, *Berigten van de Utrechtsche Zendingsvereeniging* Deel 15: 49–61, 65–79, 133–143, 181–191.
BUZ (Berigten van de Utrechtsche Zendingsvereeniging). 1880. Almaheira, *Berigten van de Utrechtsche Zendingsvereeniging* Deel 21: 49–61, 69–77, 151–159.
BUZ (Berigten van de Utrechtsche Zendingsvereeniging). 1887. Almaheira, *Berigten van de Utrechtsche Zendingsvereeniging* Deel 28: 33–43, 65–79,117–125, 197.
BUZ (Berigten van de Utrechtsche Zendingsvereeniging). 1908. *Berichten van de Utrechtsche Zendingsvereeniging* Nieuwe Serie. Deel 21: 2–146.
Corpus Diplomaticum Neerlando-Indicum. 1907. Verzameling van Politieke contracten en verdere Verdragen door de Nederlanders in het Oosten gesloten, van Privilegebrieven, aan hen verleend, enz, ed. J. E. Heeres. Eerste Deel (1596–1650), *Bijdragen tot de Taal-, Land- en Volkenkunde van Nederlandsch-Indië* 54.
Corpus Diplomaticum Neerlando-Indicum. 1931. Verzameling van Politieke contracten en verdere Verdragen door de Nederlanders in het Oosten gesloten, van Privilegebrieven, aan hen verleend, enz, ed. J. E. Heeres. Tweede Deel (1650–1675), *Bijdragen tot de Taal-, Land- en Volkenkunde van Nederlandsch-Indië* 87.
Durkheim, E., and M. Mauss. 1903. De quelques formes primitives de classification. *Année sociologique* 6: 1–72.
Duyvendak, J.P. 1926. *Het Kakean-Genootschap van Seran*. Almelo: N.V.W. Hilarius WZN.
Ellen, G.J. 1920. *Uit mijne ervaring*. Oegstgeest: Zendingsbuerau.
Feenstra, R. (ed.). 2009. *Hugo Grotius' Mare Liberum 1609–2009*. Original Latin text (1609) and modern English translation. Leiden: E.J. Brill.
Fortgens, J. 1911. Bijdrage tot de kennis van de naamgeving onder de Tobelo. *Bijdragen tot de Taal-, Land- en Volkenkunde* 68: 88–116.
Fortgens, J. 1917. Zending en bestuur in de Onderafdeeling Djailolo. *Mededeelingen van het Nederlandsch Zendingsgenootschap* 61: 47–77.
Fox, J.J. 1980. Models and metaphors. Comparative research in Eastern Indonesia. In *The Flow of Life. Essays on Eastern Indonesia*, ed. J.J. Fox, 327–333. Cambridge: Cambridge University Press.
Fraassen, Ch. F. van. 1981. Historical introduction. In *The North Moluccas. An annotated bibliography*, ed. K. Polman, 1–38. The Hague: Martinus Nijhoff.
Fraassen, Ch. F. van. 1987. Ternate, de Molukken en de Indonesische Archipel. Van soa-organisatie en vierdeling: een studie van traditionele samenleving en cultuur in Indonesië, 2 vols., PhD dissertation. Leiden: Leiden University.

Fraassen, Ch. F. van. 2005. Dynamiek in een gespleten wereld. In *Een vakkracht in het koninkrijk. Kerk- en zendingshistorische opstellen*, ed. Chr. G.F. de Jong, 54–66. Heereveen: Groen.
Frijhoff, W., and M. Spies. 1990. *1650. Bevochten eendracht*. Den Haag: Sdu.
Geirnaert-Martin, D. 1992. *The Woven Land of Laboya. Socio-Cosmic Ideas and Values in West Sumba, Eastern Indonesia*. Leiden: Centre for Non-Western Studies.
Gerrits, E.J. 1912. *Memorie van Overgave van de Residentie Ternate*. The Hague: Nationaal Archief, Collectie Ministerie van Koloniën, 59, microfiche nr. 322.
Grotius, H. [Hugo de Groot]. 1609. *Mare Liberum, sive de iure quod Batavis competit ad Indicana commercia dissertatio*. Leiden: Elzevier.
Hammer-Purgstall, J. von. 1827. *Geschichte des osmanischen Reichs*. Pest: C. A. Harleben.
Henley, D. 2002. *Jealousy and Justice. The indigenous roots of colonial rule in Northern Sulawesi*. Amsterdam: Free University Press.
Hueting, A. 1908. *Tobeloreesch-Hollandsch woordenboek*. Den Haag: Martinus Nijhoff.
Jacobs, S.J., H. 1971. *A Treatise on the Moluccas (c. 1544). Probably the preliminary version of António Galvão's lost História das Moluccas*. Edited, annotated and translated into English from the Portuguese manuscript in the Archivo General de Indias, Seville. Sources and Studies for the History of the Jesuits, Vol. III. Rome: Jesuit Historical Institute.
Jacobs, S.J., H. 1974. *Documenta Malucensia* Vol. I (1542–1577). Rome: Institutum Historicum Societatis Iesu.
Jacobs, S.J., H. 1980. *Documenta Malucensia* Vol. II (1577–1606). Rome: Jesuit Historical Institute.
James, K.A. 1918. *Vervolg Memorie van Overgave van de Residentie Ternate*. The Hague: Nationaal Archief, Collectie Ministerie van Koloniën, 59, microfiche nr. 325.
Josselin de Jong, J.P.B. 1977a. The Malay Archipelago as a field of ethnological studys. In *Structural Anthropology in the Netherlands*, ed. P.E. de Josselin de Jong, 164–182. The Hague: Martinus Nijhoff [1935].
Josselin de Jong, P.E. de. 1977b. Introduction: Structural anthropology in the Netherlands: creature of circumstance. In *Structural Anthropology in the Netherlands*, ed. P.E. de Josselin de Jong, 1–29. The Hague: Martinus Nijhoff.
Kamma, F.C. 1982. The incorporation of foreign culture elements and complexes by ritual enclosure among the Biak-Nomfurese. In *Symbolic Anthropology in the Netherlands*, ed. P.E. de Josselin de Jong, and E. Schwimmer, 543–584. The Hague: Martinus Nijhoff.

Karsen, K.M.H. 1918. *Memorie van Overgave van Onderafdeling Tobelo*. The Hague: Nationaal Archief, Collectie Ministerie van Koloniën, 59, microfiche nr. 1245.

Lewis, E.D. 1988. *People of the Source. The social and ceremonial order of Tana Wai Brama on Flores*. Dordrecht: Foris Publications.

Meilink Roelofsz, M.A.P. 1962. *Asian Trade and European Influence in the Indonesian Archipelago between 1500 and about 1630*. The Hague: Martinus Nijhoff, pp. 173–206 and 272–383; Reprinted as *The coming of the Northern Europeans to the Malay-Indonesian Archipelago*, in Paul H. Kratoska, ed. 2001, *South East Asia. Colonial History*, 229–268. London: Routledge.

Oosten, Jarich G. 2006. 'A privileged field of study': Marcel Mauss and structural anthropology in Leiden. *Inuit Studies* 30 (2): 51–71.

Ossenbruggen, F.D.E. van. 1977. Java's *monca-pat*: Origins of a primitive classification system. In *Structural Anthropology in the Netherlands*, ed. P. E. de Josselin de Jong, 32–63. The Hague: Martinus Nijhoff [1918].

Palmer van den Broek, Ch. L.J. 1915. *Memorie van Overgave van de Residentie Ternate*. The Hague: Nationaal Archief, Collectie Ministerie van Koloniën, 59, microfiche nr. 323.

Parry, J., and M. Bloch. 1989. Introduction. In *Money and the morality of exchange*, ed. J. Parry, and M. Bloch, 1–32. New York: Cambridge University Press.

Pigafetta, A. 1874. Navigation et Descouvrement de la Indie Superieure faicte par moy Anthoyne Pigapheta, Vincentin, Chevalier de Rhodes. In Lord Stanley of Alderley, *The first voyage around the world by Magellan. Translated from the accounts of Pigafetta, and other contemporary writers*. The Hakluyt Society, First Series, No. LII. New York: Burt Franklin Publisher [1524].

Pigafetta, A. 1995. *The First Voyage Around the World (1519–1522). An account of Magellan's expedition*, ed. J. Cachey Jr. New York: Marsilio Publishers [1522].

Pigeaud, Th. G. Th. 1977. Javanese divination and classification. In *Structural Anthropology in the Netherlands*, ed. P.E. de Josselin de Jong, 64–82. The Hague: Martinus Nijhoff [1928].

Platenkamp, J.D.M. 1988. *Tobelo. Ideas and values of a North Moluccan society*. Leiden: Repro Psychologie.

Platenkamp, J.D.M. 1990. *North Halmahera: Non-Austronesian languages, Austronesian cultures?* Selected Lecture published by Het Oosters Genootschap in Nederland. Leiden: E.J.Brill.

Platenkamp, J.D.M. 1993. Tobelo, Moro, Ternate. The cosmological valorization of historical events. *Cakalele* 4: 61–89.

Platenkamp, J.D.M. 2013. Sovereignty in the North Moluccas: Historical transformations. *History and Anthropology* 24 (2): 206–232.

Platenkamp, J.D.M. 2015. On the confrontation between perennial models in 19th-century Halmahera. In *Representing the Future. Zur kulturellen Logik der Zukunft*, ed. A. Hartmann, and O. Murawska, 61–98. Bielefeld: Transcript Verlag.
Prager, M. (unpublished). Strukturale Anthropologie in Leiden, 1916–1982. Ursprung und Entwicklung eines wissenschaftlichen Forschungsprogramms. PhD dissertation. University of Heidelberg.
Prierias, S. 1596. *Sylvestrinae Summae*, Verbo Papa. 2 vols. Antwerpiae.
Renard-Clamagirand, B. 1982. *Marobo, une société ema de Timor*. Paris: Selaf.
Roos, K.H.F. 1909. *Memorie van Overgave van de Residentie Ternate*. The Hague: Nationaal Archief, Collectie Ministerie van Koloniën, 59, microfiche nr. 322.
Sahlins, M. 1995. *How "Natives" Think. About Captain Cook, for example*. Chicago: University of Chicago Press.
Sahlins, M. 2008. The stranger-king, or elementary forms of the politics of life. *Indonesia and the Malay world* 36 (105): 177–199.
Schulte Nordholt, H.G. 1971. *The Political System of the Atoni of Timor*. The Hague: Martinus Nijhoff.
Schurhammer, S.J.G. 1963. *Franz Xavier, sein Leben und seine Zeit, Vol. 2, Part.1, Indien und Indonesien 1541–1547*. Freiburg: Herder Verlag.
Schutte, G.J. 2002a. De Gereformeerde kerk in de Republiek. In *Het Indisch Sion. De Gereformeerde Kerk onder de Verenigde Oost-Indische Compagnie*, ed. G.J. Schutte, 15–23. Hilversum: Verloren.
Schutte, G.J. 2002b. De kerk onder de Compagnie. In *Het Indisch Sion. De Gereformeerde Kerk onder de Verenigde Oost-Indische Compagnie*, ed. G.J. Schutte, 43–64. Hilversum: Verloren.
Tiele, P.A. 1875. De vestiging der Portugeezen in Indië. *De Gids* 13: 177–238.
Tiele, P.A. 1879. De Europeërs in den Maleischen Archipel, Deel. 2, 1529–1540. *Bijdragen tot de Taal-, Land- en Volkenkunde van Nederlandsch-Indië* 26: 1–69.
Tip, L. 1918. *Memorie van Overgave van de Residentie Ternate*, The Hague: Nationaal Archief, Collectie Ministerie van Koloniën, 59, microfiche nr. 326.
Tobias, J.H. 1980. *Memorie van Overgave van het bestuur van de Residentie Ternate van den aftredenden Resident J.H. Tobias aan den benoemden Resident C. Bosscher 1857*. Penerbitan Sumber-sumber Sejarah No. 11, 1–97. Jakarta: Arsip Nasional Republik Indonesia.
Verbeke, E. 1917. *Memorie van Overgave van de Residentie Ternate*. The Hague: Nationaal Archief, Collectie Ministerie van Koloniën, 59, microfiche nr. 324.
Villiers, J. 1983. The Jesuit mission in Moro 1546–1571. In *Halmahera dan Raja Ampat sebagai kesatuan majemuk: Studi-studi terhadap suatu daerah transisi*, ed. E.K.M. Masinambow, 277–288. Jakarta: Leknas-Lipi.

Villiers, J. 2004. 'A truthful pen and an impartial spirit': Bartolomé Leonarda de Argensola and the Conquista de las Islas Malucas. In *Asian Travel in the Renaissance*, ed. Daniel Carey, 124–148. London: Blackwell.

Wessels, C. 1935. De katholieke missie in de Molukken, Noord Celebes en de Sanghir eilanden, gedurende de Spaanse bestuursperiode 1606–1677, *Historisch Tijdschrift*, Serie Studies No. 3. Tilburg: Bergmans.

Wils, J. 1960. Het werk der missie. In *Balans van beleid. Terugblik op de laatste eeuw van Nederlands-Indië*, ed. H. Baudet and I.-J. Brugmans, 311–328. Assen: Van Gorcum.

Wouden, F.A.E. 1968. *Types of Social Structure in Eastern Indonesia*. The Hague: Martinus Nijhoff [1935].

Zoetmulder, P.J. 1982. *Old Javanese-English Dictionary*, 2 Vols. s-Gravenhage: Martinus Nijhoff.

AUTHOR BIOGRAPHY

Jos. D. M. Platenkamp is Professor of Social Anthropology at the Institut für Ethnologie, Westfälische Wilhelms-Universität Münster, Germany. He conducted field researches in the North Moluccas and Laos. His recent publications include: "Money alive and money dead," in C. Haselgrove & S. Krmnicek (eds.), *The Archaeology of Money* (2016); "On the confrontation between perennial models in 19th Century Halmahera," in A. Hartmann & O. Murawska (eds.), *Representing the Future. ZurkulturellenLogik der Zukunft* (2015); "Sovereignty in the North Moluccas: Historical transformations," *History and Anthropology* (2013); "Political change and ritual tenacity: The New Year's ritual of Luang Prabang, Laos," in A. Iteanu (ed.), *La cohérence des sociétés* (2010).

CHAPTER 9

Continuity and Breaches in Religion and Globalization, a Melanesian Point of View

André Iteanu

Melanesian religiosity, or at least, something which the ethnography allows us to imagine as such,[1] does not possess the homogeneity or the cosmological status which Asians usually attribute to Islam, Hinduism or Buddhism. Instead, these characteristics are reputedly present in Christianity, the religion that has recently spread across the Pacific. This sharp discrepancy between the 'old' Melanesian forms of devotion and Christianity is clearly visible in the fact that the countless evangelists of all denominations who have worked in Melanesia have always fallen short of finding local words that could render our term religion. Consequently, they usually stuck with the English words 'Church' or 'religion' that

[1] In Melanesia historical records are very shallow.

This paper owes much to the sympathetic readings of Michel Picard, Cécile Barraud and Annelin Eriksen. I want to thank them. I am also grateful to Chelsie Yount-André who greatly improved my broken English.

A. Iteanu (✉)
Centre Asie du Sud-Est, CNRS-EHESS, Paris, France

© The Author(s) 2017
M. Picard (ed.), *The Appropriation of Religion in Southeast Asia and Beyond*, DOI 10.1007/978-3-319-56230-8_9

most Melanesian languages still employ today. These terms have even now gained Melanesian authenticity in opposition to the pidgin word *kastom*,[2] which designates everything which is not Christian religion, politics and more generally the Euro-American way of living (see, for example, Lindstrom and White 1994, Rio 2002). The appearance all through the Pacific of this opposition between new and old, and within the new, between religion, politics and business, whereas nothing of the sort previously existed, can be interpreted as a 'disembeddedness' in the sense that Karl Polanyi (2001) gave to this term in the context of the emergence in Euro-America of the Economy out of Politics. This means that whereas Melanesia was formerly a civilization in which social phenomenon of the kind Mauss called 'total social fact' played a central role, it is now crosscut by a number of distinctions which recall those that Euro-American societies make. Today, most Melanesianists consider this change, and the appearance of the notion of religion, as critical and acknowledge that it has provoked considerable social disruption.

This is also the position advocated by Joel Robbins, one of the most prominent scholars in what is now called the anthropology of Christianity. In his book *Becoming Sinners* (2004a), he claims that the advent of Christianity among the Urapmin, with whom he worked, has not only produced a usual historical change, but a most radical transformation, that must be considered as an extreme form of historical revolution:

"... people take on an entirely new culture on its own terms, forgoing any conscious effort to work its elements into the categories of their traditional understandings. Although Sahlins discusses this as a model of modernization, I would argue it can also apply to changes other than modernizing ones and hence requires a different name. One might be tempted to call it a model of replacement, but since the new culture does not necessarily replace the old, I will call it one of adoption; the image here being one that emphasizes the taking on of something new without prejudging what happens to what was there before" (Robbins 2004a: 10–11).

And indeed, Robbins' ethnography shows that the Urapmin consider Christianity to be utterly incompatible with that which they previously

---

[2] Although the terms religion, Church and *kastom* are widespread in Melanesia, I am not sure that every language uses them. My use of these terms does not therefore claim to be universally valid.

lived by and they now call *kastom*. Every time they indulge in the latter, they feel that they have betrayed the former to become sinners. Therefore, Robbins convincingly concludes that, among the Urapmin, individualism, the value associated with Christianity, has overthrown relationality, the value which, he claims, is generally associated with customary Melanesian life.[3]

However, the distinction between religion and *kastom* is not everywhere so radical. Annelin Eriksen (2008) reports that, due to a different colonial history, the changes produced by the advent of Christianity were less dramatic in Vanuatu than among the Urapmin. Here, Christianity is intimately merged with *kastom*. Eriksen, however, simultaneously admits that in Vanuatu a major value inversion also occurred: the unmatched value earlier accorded to male grade societies (a complex form of initiation) was surpassed now by Christian values, essentially represented in women's activities and church-related practices. Although Eriksen does not stress it, this inversion appears as quite considerable because gender distinction is most important in Vanuatu, and because it triggers a reappraisal of several other important ideas and practices like healing and the notion of the person. In the end, we are left with the impression that the sharpness of the distinction between religion and *kastom* may, after all, not be the appropriate scale to evaluate whether the changes that occurred in Vanuatu after Christianization were shallower than the Urapmin's, or the other way around.

As I mentioned earlier, Robbins argues that the radical transformation that affected the Urapmin is characterized by the rise of individualism and the consequent weakening of the value of relatedness, formerly so prevalent in Melanesian conceptions and practices of agonistic exchange, for example. For the author, this shift is concomitant with the replacement of the 'dividual person'[4] (Strathern 1988) by a different form of a person presenting certain characteristics generally associated with the

---

[3] Robbins' use of these notions is inspired by Dumont (for example 1986). By individualism he means, I believe, a social configuration in which a notion of the person that Euro-Americans call the individual, characterized by its freedom, equality and autonomy, is attributed the highest social value. By contrast, he claims that Melanesian social configurations consider relations as their highest value. Hence, each person is not an individual, but an emanation of the relations he or she creates and maintains with others.

[4] Following Schneider and Wagner, Marilyn Strathern uses the expression dividual person to designate the specific Melanesian person made of relations. This notion has lately become dominant among Melanesianists and Americanists.

Euro-American individual. In short, a person constituted by relations was replaced by another person, self-sufficient, autonomous and alone responsible for her or his own salvation. Eriksen also notes that such an individually defined person has appeared in Vanuatu. This connection between conversion and the emergence of an individual goes along with Louis Dumont's insights who saw in Western Christianity the origin of modern individualism (Dumont 1986).

However, more recently, the link between the advent of Christianity and individualism has been questioned on Melanesian grounds. Marc Mosko, for example, argues against Robbins that the person that Christianity promotes since the first centuries is not the individual, but a dividual person, exemplified in the Christ, and not altogether so different from the Melanesian one. For him, the individual which is present today both in Euro-America and in Melanesia only emerged much later, in association with the notion of ownership that characterized the advent of modern capitalism (Mosko 2015). Therefore, he calls that kind of person 'the possessive individual.'

In spite of their hardly reconcilable points of view, all these authors agree upon the fact that today's Melanesian conceptions of the world and of the person are radically different from what they were earlier. This conclusion seems only normal as it makes sense to think that small peripheral societies may well be profoundly disrupted by the combined advent of Christianity, capitalism, globalization and so forth. In Melanesia, this was also the ideas that the colonialists held around the turn of the century. Against these certitudes, however, F.E. Williams, who was appointed as a government anthropologist from 1922 to 1942 in Papua, proposed a different interpretation. Although he served the colonial authorities, he was a sharp ethnographer who bitterly fought to 'deconstruct' many prejudices then commonly held against the Melanesians and more widely against all 'natives' around the world. In his introduction to *Orokaiva Magic*, published in 1928, he takes to task the firmly entrenched Western contention that the 'natives' are very conservative, hardly ever willing to modify their ideas and practices, and all the more so in the realm of religion. He writes:

> "The Vailala Madness and the Taro cult[5] have each in their time and place made a veritable conquest, a kind of bloodless victory in which

---

[5] Both these cults have appeared in the wake of colonization and are today classified as Cargo cults.

innovation has met with welcome rather than resistance. It is indeed subject for remark that the native whom our despairing philanthropist, with his rejected gifts and suggestions, always calls an ultra-conservative, should leap forward to embrace anything so extremely new-fangled as the Vailala Madness or the Taro cult. So general has been the adoption of the Taro cult by the Orokaiva people that no little confusion now exists between new and old; and the investigator is constantly perplexed in his endeavours to disentangle one from the other. To do so completely is impossible" (Williams 1928: 5).

Then, he provides an explanation to account for this situation:

"When in regard to this and all the other new cults of Papua we observe the suddenness of their beginning and the rapidity of their spread, we may be assailed by a doubt concerning one of the assumptions of anthropology. We only know of those cults which have come into being since our acquaintance with the native. We are apt to assume that they are all in some manner the result of a clash between high civilization and low, in which the latter has had its head a little turned. That assumption may be in the main correct. But when we consider the manner in which the Taro cult and the others have come into being, the easy and obvious way in which the first step is taken, and the rapidly increasing momentum and wave-like progress of the new movement, we may well enough suspect that similar wide changes have swept over native civilizations before our own coming. The almost absolute stability of native custom has been practically a maxim of anthropology. New religious cults such as these may do something to shake our faith in it" (*ibid.*: 5–6).

This passage, as many others in F.E. Williams work, is strikingly modern. The author shreds here to pieces our belief that the 'introduction' of a new cult might have caused a thorough revolution in Melanesian thought. His argument stems from two main ideas. The first one makes sense of the fact that elements (ideas or behaviors) belonging to recently invented cults are often gradually incorporated into regularly practiced rituals, like marriage, initiation or mortuary ceremonies. This, Williams argues, proves that the Melanesians do not consider that there is a radical difference between the older practices and the newer ones. The second idea is that the advent of a new cult is never treated in Melanesia as an unmatched event, no matter how original or exceptional it may be, but on the contrary, as a new instance of a formerly known type of event. This is why those who receive a new cult, instead of resisting it because they are firmly attached to 'their own' traditions, welcome it as a precious opportunity to obtain new ideas, new things and to meet new people. Williams' position about the unproblematic adoption of new religions therefore also implies that the idea that Melanesians would oppose resistance to Christianity so as to preserve their ancestral traditions is but a Euro-American power fantasy. Except in certain remarkable cases, like among the Urapmin (Robbins 2004a) that I previously mentioned, Williams' analysis accounts much better than the radical difference positions for the way in which Melanesians enthusiastically welcomed Christianity and converted to it unanimously, while continuing to perform the rituals they practiced previously.

The present paper intends to substantiate F.E. Williams' twofold idea and to develop its implications. It is very likely that his argument could fit many Melanesian societies, in spite of their baffling variety. However, to demonstrate it would be a daunting task. Here, therefore, I only focus on Papua New Guinea (PNG).[6] When detailed ethnography is needed, I use the Orokaiva case, which I know best. Taking a historical view, I first summarize what we know about pre-Christian, pre-colonial circulating cults that regularly appeared and then disappeared in certain regions of Melanesia. Building on the ethnography, I argue that these cults constituted one form, among others, of a regional exchange system. Then, I reconstruct the particular and gradual encounter of most Melanesians with Christianity. I argue that many of them, and especially Papua New Guineans who live on the largest island, gained familiarity with it long before they ever met any administrator, gold digger or missionary. I then briefly decode, from as far back as historical records take us, the dynamic nature of what we generally perceive as Melanesian religion, a domain that we can often sum up as a cluster of rituals. To enter into ethnographic detail, I shortly describe how Christianity has established itself among the Orokaiva, the largest population of the Oro Province of Papua New Guinea. My conclusion is here that Melanesians primarily understood the original Christian Churches as new circulating cults,

---

[6] Melanesia is so diverse and its Christianization has been achieved over such a long period of time that no generalization can represent each and every case. I hope nonetheless that my wider argument, as well as some of its intermediary conclusions, applies to a significant number of cases. When I think that my analysis may be widely valid, I use the terms Melanesia or Melanesians in relation to it.

roughly similar to those they had witnessed earlier in their vicinity. Finally, I extend this argument to the most recent emergence of numerous Charismatic Churches and to their probable replacement nowadays by a new form of local Christian movement. I finally argue that this succession of appearances and disappearances of new denominations and repeated conversion to them indicate that the temporality of older circulating cults has persisted to this day. The paper closes on a brief conclusion that presents a most recent political incident which happened in Port Moresby, the capital of PNG. This case reinforces the impression that, due to their dynamic social conceptions, it is almost impossible to predict in the short term whether Christianity has introduced a major irreversible change or whether a form of cult is still at work among the Melanesians.

From Circulating Cults to Mystic Regional Systems

When the colonizers first settled in PNG, they witnessed the appearance of a number of prophetic cults sweeping through some of the few regions they were in contact with. Fragments of old ethnography, patrol officers' reports, old informants' recollections and biographies written by Melanesians or missionaries involved in these cults in one way or another inform us on what they might have been. In what is now the Gulf, the Central Province, the Oro Province (Williams 1923 and 1928) and some of the outer islands (New Britain, New Ireland, Bougainville), for the best-known cults, the villagers participated in meetings led by prophets who preached the observance of all kinds of strange rituals and prohibitions. As many of their prophecies included troubling allusions to the colonizers and to the Christian missionaries, the Whites construed them, in F.E. Williams' words, as "all in some manner the result of a clash between high civilization and low, in which the latter has had its head a little turned" (*op. cit.*: 5) and identified them as a corrupted form of what they thought was 'true' Melanesian religion. All this led them to suspect that the locals had invented these cults to organize resistance against their penetration. In consequence, they regularly used force to suppress them.

After WWII, the appearance and disappearance of cults continued, but now some of them displayed new themes. The most famous of these was directly linked to what the Melanesians had experienced during the conflict. In 1942, American, Australian and Japanese soldiers established bases and waged war against each other in several parts of Melanesia. The local people helped them greatly. So, when the war ended, they presented them with everything they had left and promised to send back more gifts from home. Some locals took this oath more literally than others. In certain seashore areas, for example, the villagers collectively destroyed their houses, killed and ate their pigs, stopped planting gardens and settled on the beach, waiting for their gifts to be delivered by ship. In other places, they constructed homemade landing strips and air-control towers, to host the planes that were to bring the goods. Much data were collected on these post-war cults that were later named 'Cargo cults,' in view of their most spectacular forms (Trompf 1991: 188–210). Once again, they were interpreted as reactions to the presence of the white soldiers and administrators to whom they supposedly manifested either 'religious' deference or violent resistance (see Burridge 1960, Lawrence 1964, Worsley 1968).

Later, however, when more ethnographic material became available, some scholars, among whom the first Papua New Guinean anthropologist, John Waiko (Waiko 1984, Trompf 1977), drew attention to the fact that although the specific contents and aspects of these Cargo cults were obviously original, their structure resembled very much that of the older circulating cults, which traversed entire regions from earlier times on, before the arrival of the Whites. Their interpretation was that Cargo cults were in fact the form that the circulating cults had taken in post-WWII times.

Indeed, both old circulating cults and Cargo cults share many operating rules in spite of their apparent diversity. To start with, as Williams explained, every Melanesian society that had such cults considered them to be of foreign origin. However, the practices and ideas they carried did not remain alien for long, because over time bits and pieces were integrated into local ritual practice (initiation, marriage, funerals, magic, etc.)[7] and oral history.

Then, a vast majority of these cults were built around some sort of prophecy, in a broad sense of the term. The prophet was a woman or a man who had been struck by a vision that granted her or him the power to produce what Christians would call miracles: unusual crop growth,

---

[7] Among the most visible ones is the replacement, in many places, of the initiation ritual by birthday parties.

spectacular hunts, curing of the sick, revival of the dead or multiplication of wealth. She or he subsequently imparted these powers to disciples who thereby acquired equivalent skills. Expanding in the form of a tree structure, these cults developed rapidly and widely.

To mobilize the prophet's powers, the cultists adopted specific dressing codes and bodily attitudes that constituted the cult's trademark. For example, some of the participants to the famous Orokaiva Baigona cult (from about 1925 to 1955) entered, during séances, a sort of trance manifested by intense body shaking.[8] These séances were complemented by the collective performance of a specific song repertoire accompanied with drums beaten in a sitting position (*kasamba*).[9] Participation in these events did not demand faith in any supernatural beings. Only the miraculous nature of what was achieved maintained these cults alive. When it wore out, they disappeared.

To obtain the expected results, the followers had to offer contributions (of food or valuables) to the prophet and/or to the disciples, and partake in gift-giving feasts where food was exchanged and consumed. Over time, these gatherings produced a reconfiguration and an intensification of relations between neighbors and kin, and new networks of exchange were created that reached beyond the usual circle of local solidarity maintained by marriage and life-stage rituals. This is why I argue here (see infra) that these cults created temporary regional networks of relations.

Cults usually developed a new vocabulary, if not a new language, including expressions that did not exist previously. The meanings of these new words or sentences were either revealed to the prophet, for example in dreams, or deemed to pertain to a foreign language. Their meaning was often obscure or unknown. So was also the case of most of the texts that were sung during the séances or the invocations made. Sometimes, words or expressions were also given totally new revealed meanings.

Their particular temporality was a crucial feature of these cults. Williams notes that they transformed rapidly as new disciples joined in and, after acquiring cult knowledge, added their personal vision to the

---

[8] This can be found in several other places in Melanesia, either in cults or in rituals like initiation or divination.

[9] In contrast to usual rituals where drums are always beaten while dancing.

cult. The original prophet's visions were thus massively challenged by those of their disciples. Conversely, through the members' action, salient features of the cult soon started to be included in stages of life or magic rituals over large regions: for example, among the Orokaiva and many other neighboring societies, the sitting drumming performance, mentioned earlier, was included in many other sorts of rituals. The cult's original features were thus rapidly trivialized, and the cult itself then withered away. Because cults circulated regularly in certain regions, Melanesians were familiar with their particular form of temporality: the cults appeared, then reached a peak when their activity was most intense, their followers most numerous, and their expansion regional, and then they disappeared.[10]

The available data suggest that the circulating cults were endemic to, at least, parts of Melanesia, and nurtured the societies they swiped through new ideas and practices that were often integrated into local rituals. However, due to their specific temporality, these cults did not promote cultural homogeneity, but on the contrary, reshuffled the ritual features of each society, producing in the end even more diversity.[11]

On top of being 'religious,' these circulating cults also generated regional systems of relations (Iteanu 2015), of which many other forms are known in Melanesia, including the Kula exchange classically described by Malinowski (1922), the Moka exchange that links large sections of the Highlands of Papua New Guinea (A. Strathern 1971), the regional systems delineated by circulating rituals in other parts of the Highlands (Schneider 2011), the dance exchange complex among the Arapesh (Mead 1938), the intricate head hunting systems portrayed by C.G. Wheeler between Mono and Alu (Monnerie 1996), the regionally ordered grade societies on Ambrym Island in Vanuatu and many others. Unlike several of these forms that maintained permanent regional systems, like the Kula Ring, circulating cults created only transient systems of relations that had to be rebuilt each time a new cult reappeared.

The old forms that circulating cults took (producing an unusually successful hunt, or harvest, or bringing about Cargo, etc.) now have more

---

[10] I mean, extending beyond a village or a cluster of villages.

[11] Marilyn Strathern (1991) discusses this question of the persistence of local diversity from a different point of view oriented on the construction of the person. The two arguments seem to me complementary.

or less disappeared. However, new social phenomena have emerged that bear the same sort of temporality, but have a different content. In Melanesia, prophetical announcements continue to be numerous and enthusiastically welcomed by the population. Their realm of action is now typically business, politics and religion, that is, all major domains that are primarily cited as opposite to the category of *kastom*.

Concerning business, new prophets regularly raise money from villagers to be invested in foreign companies where it will multiply by thousands in no time. They then rapidly disappear with the money, for ever. At least among the Orokaiva, these 'business opportunities' scams are less and less successful with the villagers as time goes by.

In politics, like everywhere else, prophecies are numerous. For example, in the 2007 general election, during his campaign, one of the Oro Province candidates claimed that he had talked with God and promised that in less than three months he would bring about highways, supermarkets, television, electricity, mobile phones and a hundredfold increase in the price of commercial crops (Iteanu and Kapon 2007). He was promptly elected governor of the province.

In religion, among the Orokaiva, many have announced, in recent years, the Second Coming of Jesus or the return of the dead on board a tourist ship. However, these are only minor phenomena as the bulk of religious cultism lies in Christianity.

CHRISTIANITY WITHOUT CHRISTIANS

From 1874 onward, a handful of missionaries of various denominations settled along the coasts of Papua New Guinea.[12] Those who landed closest to the Orokaiva, with whom I work, were Anglicans. They initially founded their mission station in 1891 in Dogura, close to today's town of Alotao, some 250 km southeast of the Orokaiva. Their mission slowly grew in size, and almost fifty years later, in 1939, they erected a large cathedral.

---

[12] Christianity was introduced at least fifty years earlier in the outer islands that belong now to PNG. However, I have no clue whether the news was then spread in mainland PNG. A wealth of information on the Anglican Church in Melanesia can be found in the Canterbury Project, http://www.anglicanhistory.org/, and bibliographical references and information on religion in Melanesia in Trompf 1991 and 2006.

When these first missionaries arrived, at the outset of the twentieth century, there were no roads leading inland, so they did not travel much, except around their settlement. When they wanted to go further upcountry, administrators, priests and gold miners carried out most of their explorations by boat along the major rivers. In turn, most of the Melanesians who lived inland never ventured out to visit a mission if they did not have a very good reason for it. Thus, some of the Orokaiva had to wait until the late 1940s to be visited by missionaries for the first time.

However, everyone in this region, and probably in the whole island, regardless of how far inside the bush she or he dwelled, was constantly informed by kin or neighbors from adjacent or distant villages of what the white people who lived in the mission stations both nearby and far away did and said, long before (sometimes up to eighty years) they would actually see a minister or a white person with their own eyes. Thus, for decades, the majority of Papua New Guineans relentlessly debated the information they obtained from other Melanesians concerning the missionaries' activities, attempting to understand who these new and strange newcomers were.[13]

Most of the Orokaiva live deep inland Papua New Guinea. Those from whom they got their information, at that time, were friends or kin that seldom, if ever, possessed first-hand knowledge. Most often, the news about the missionaries they circulated had travelled to them across the country, retold and modified several times, often also translated from one language to another, as it moved from a culture to the next, something that happens quite often in Papua New Guinea.[14] One can imagine that the reports one heard in a small village at the foot of the Mount Lamington, far away from the coast, had little to do with what the eyewitness who first told the story had actually seen, sometimes years before.

Each community, each village or each cluster of villages, thus received, through various channels, very diverse and often contradictory versions of what the Christians were saying and doing. As a result, the structure and form of the narratives about Christianity and colonization that circulated resembled the rest of the oral literature produced by the Melanesians. These stories therefore felt familiar to those who heard them and in line with what they already knew, despite the fact that what

---

[13] This of course does not apply to much smaller islands where everyone had a chance to see the missionaries as soon as they settled.

[14] Papua New Guinea is known to have more than 800 hundred different languages.

they described might have been unheard of before. For example, drawing on their own culture, the Orokaiva interpreted Christianity as a ritual practice bestowed on the Whites by their ancestors, just as their own rituals had been given to them by theirs. As such, this practice did not strike them as particularly outstanding.

Soon, however, the narratives about Christianity circulated through rumors began to seriously contradict one another. So much so that the Orokaiva started wondering whether they misunderstood what was told, were misled by dishonest informants, or whether the whole thing was simply untrue. This uncertainty has not ceased up to now. Discussing religious matters is still a common evening activity, in both villages and towns. These endless debates often revolve around hard to define notions, like faith, sin, sacredness or prayer. They regularly consist in attempting to translate unfamiliar foreign religious terms into expressions belonging to the vernacular language or languages of those who are present. At least in Orokaiva and Aeka, the only Melanesian vernacular languages that I understand, this process of translation usually moves the meaning of the term nearer to local views. For example, 'holy' was translated in Orokaiva as *otohu*, a term that otherwise designates a familiar most valued paraphernalia used during initiation. Translation thus functions here as an assimilating process and constitutes a further reason why the Papua New Guineans were not terribly destabilized by the advent of Christianity. Rendered in 'their terms,' the Christian Gospel and practices substantially resembled the cults they had seen earlier circulating through their regions. Because implanting Christianity in any Melanesian society always requires a form or another of translation, it is difficult for me to grasp what Robbins has in mind when he states, "people take on an entirely new culture on its own terms" (*op. cit.*: 10).[15]

Exposed to intense gossip about the missionaries and more widely about the Whites, the inhabitants of the village of Jajau, where I work, spent decades reflecting on the meanings of Christianity before they ever had a chance to decide for themselves if they wanted to convert to it or not. Therefore, those who embraced the Anglican faith when the first missionaries arrived did not do it naively, but enacted a conclusion they had slowly matured. They became, in turn, enthusiastic Christians, full

---

[15] This is of course different when conversion occurred centuries ago, like in South America.

of good will and strongly determined to enjoy its benefits. Making an earnest attempt at fulfilling Christianity's mandates, many scrupulously respected for years its prescribed practices, like hiding one's genitals, refraining from cannibalism and praying regularly with one's eyes closed.

However, even if deeply involved in Christianity, few Melanesians contemplate giving up their previous beliefs or rituals, including those related to their ancestors.[16] This is so because, as Williams has argued regarding the circulating cults, Melanesians see continuity between Christianity and customary practices. Therefore, they often claim that Christian priests promote ancestral worship when they insist on establishing permanent graveyards and erecting cement tombs that preserve the ancestors' memory much longer than do most traditional Melanesian forms of disposing of the corpse.

This perceived continuity was also instrumental in the rapid conversion that took place in the vast majority of cases. In Melanesia, Christianity was everywhere adopted so fully that, in contrast to Africa or South America, where Christianization is much older, there are no 'pagans' left whatsoever. Total conversion also suggests that, despite the individualistic appearance of Melanesian societies[17] and notwithstanding the strongly individualistic leanings of Christianity,[18] decisions about conversion were not made individually, but collectively according to the customary division of social groups. In short, the process that led to unanimous conversion was representative of local social practices and thus further reinforced the idea of continuity between Christianity and ritual customary practices.[19]

Given this evidence, I have extended Williams' argument, assessing the lack of radical difference in Melanesia between cult and local

---

[16] This is not the case of the Urapmin (Robbins 2004a).

[17] Since most Melanesian societies lack organizing features like unilinear descent, social hierarchies, chiefs, priests, they appeared to many anthropologists to be highly individualistic.

[18] As I mentioned earlier, whether Melanesian societies were originally individualistic or not and whether Christianity construes a dividual person or not are ongoing discussions concerning which I do not take position in this paper. My point is only to stress the highly socialized nature of conversion.

[19] In certain cases, the treatment of Christianity as a cult may fail. This was the case among the Urapmin, who immersed themselves in the most radical form of Christianity, rejecting almost all previously practiced cults and customs.

ritual practices, beyond circulating and Cargo cults, to the advent of Christianity. My point is that rather than accepting Christianity in its own terms, most Papua New Guineans, and surely the Orokaiva, have treated it in the same way they have previously dealt with pre-Christian cults, including those that are now known as Cargo cults. For them, Christianity was merely another cult to sweep through their region. Therefore, in line with the way in which these older cults worked, following its enthusiastic adoption and its peak activity stage, a period of disappointment began, during which Christian elements, among which ritual commensality, were gradually incorporated into tradition. Then eventually, the historical Churches were more or less abandoned.

As Williams suggested for the circulating cults, the resulting mixture of Christianity and tradition is now so intimate that it has become almost impossible to distinguish one from the other (Iteanu and Kapon 2007, Vevehupa 2013). However, most missionaries did not consider acceptable this sort of amalgamation, where Christian elements are included into tradition. Against it they advocated that incorporation must only work the other way around. From the 1960s on, through inculturation, they therefore attempted to put their ideas into practice, integrating customary elements, like drums and dances, into the Christian rituals (Johnston 2003).

The dynamic through which Christianity was incorporated into Melanesian cultures may seem unremarkable if one reads it only as the consequence of the pressure exerted by what the Euro-Americans view as a powerful universal religion over small local cultures. However, the Orokaiva interpretation evades this understanding. As I hope I have shown, Christianity is not for them an absolute ever-lasting religion, but only a further time-bound circulating cult, the best elements of which they can eagerly incorporate into their own customary life. As I have shown, this dynamic understanding of all new cults permits each group 'clan' or village to continue assimilating new ideas, practices, objects and people, without losing the distinctiveness that has characterized their social organization from immemorial time on. This sounds like a surprising perversion of the notion of religion, but results simply from a shift in the dimension that its definition privileges. While anthropologists and other social scientists base their opposition between religion and custom on the contrast between generality (or universality) and particularity, Melanesians draw theirs on the opposition between stability over time (*kastom*) and perishability (any cult, or religion, in our terms).[20] If this shift is taken seriously, one can reasonably conclude that the Orokaiva, and many other Melanesians, judge *kastom* to be universal while considering Christianity as particular.

The Orokaiva and the Original Anglican Church

F.E. Williams argued that the Melanesians perceived similarity between circulating cults and 'their own religion.' Having extended this argument to Christianity, I now aim to investigate the basis of this interpretation. Since, for lack of space, I cannot offer here a proper history of Melanesian conversion, I limit my argument to Orokaiva ethnography, but I insist on the dimensions that are, in my view, common to many Melanesian cases.

As stated earlier, the Anglican Church first established itself in the Orokaiva region, some sixty years ago.[21] Conversion was then rapid and unanimous. According to my analysis, this was so because, from the beginning, the Orokaiva thought that Christianity temporality closely matched that which characterized their circulating cults. Like these cults, it appeared suddenly, brought by foreigners and expanded very widely and quickly. And they knew it would wither away at some point.

However, this was not all. The more they were given to know about Christianity, the more they were convinced it resembled their circulating cults. Like them, Christianity was centered around a prophet, Jesus, who performed miracles: food multiplication, healing and resuscitation, very similar to those produced by the cults. For example, an older Orokaiva man told me that the colonial authorities arrested him, alongside the main Baigona prophet, for practicing the resuscitation rituals of that cult. While in jail, in contact with the Whites, he finally understood why they so desperately wanted to put an end to their activity. Jesus, he told me, only resuscitated a single person, whereas they did it several times a day. To stop this uneven competition, in which they were totally outdone, the Whites used force against the cultists.

---

[20] This applies as well to politicians and businessmen, whose importance comes and goes at a fast pace.

[21] The establishment of the Anglican Church was a long process in the Oro Province. In the Asigi region where I work, it dates back to the mid-1950s.

Orokaiva Christianity stresses efficiency, just as the old circulating cults did. Even today, most Christian believers bitterly complain that although they pray to God continually, they never receive anything in return. To defeat this argument and demonstrate that God responds to everyone who prays, Lucian Vevehupa, the most popular local Anglican priest, recently published an autobiography (Vevehupa 2013). Using his life story as testimony, he claims that God's efficiency is comparable, but less visible, to that of the Orokaiva ancestors. For most Orokaiva, this confirms a widely spread local creed that God is not new to the Melanesians, but was earlier present in their ancestors.

Furthermore, Christian dualism between body and soul was rapidly made to fit with Orokaiva's categories. In Orokaiva initiation, the outer social visible 'skin' of the person (*hamo*)[22] is manipulated so as to envelop and control its hidden 'inside' (*jo*), where all kinds of forces, both good and evil, reside. Using the same pattern, the Orokaiva construed the Christian pomp—robes, crosses, songs, books, rituals and churches—to be an outer skin, equivalent to initiatory paraphernalia, fit to control the hidden ambivalent soul of the Christian individual so as to promote personal salvation. Therefore, participation in services is said to efficiently diminish men's inner violent outbursts against their wives.[23]

Finally, Christianity posed and still poses linguistic problems similar to those that arose in the context of previous circulating cults. In both cases, a specific vocabulary had to be learned and translated and new terms and new grammatical formulations added to Orokaiva language. Today the linguistic situation remains unclear. Both vernacular-modified terms and English words are used to designate specific Christian notions. Yet, most people still feel that they do not understand either of them fully.

As Christianity came to be considered a sort of local phenomenon, changes had to be undertaken to reflect this reality. This was accomplished through the integration of the Whites into genealogies, myths and rituals (Iteanu 2008). In Orokaiva view, the Whites did not reach Papua New Guinea at random, but they returned to a place where their

---

[22] This skin is ritually constituted to include all paraphernalia attributed in initiation (Iteanu 1998).

[23] Nonetheless, Papua New Guinea has one of the highest violence rate against women.

ancestors formerly lived. The Orokaiva therefore rewrote their history to reintegrate their white kin (and their offspring) into the relations and rights they earlier held, but which had been forgotten and neglected for numerous generations (Iteanu 2008). The same method was applied as well by the state of Papua New Guinea, that inscribed Christianity in its Constitution, at independence, in 1975.

In sum, the introduction of Christianity in Papua New Guinea was a gradual process, although conversion itself was immediate and unanimous. This gave the Melanesians and certainly the Orokaiva time to determine that many Christian themes, practices and prohibitions closely resembled those that had previously characterized circulating cults. Therefore, the Orokaiva adopted Christianity very confidently, although they simultaneously confess that they did not understand it at all. This relative serenity misled the Christian religious authorities. They soon believed that their work was over and that the sweeping conversion they had achieved was never to be undone. They were, however, wrong because they overlooked a difference, which was then difficult to see for them, but which our analysis has unearthed: while the missionaries considered Christianity the ultimate religion, which could only be threatened by free-thinking individuals, the Melanesians saw it as a transient circulating cult that would be replaced as soon as its specificity wore off.[24]

THE CHARISMATIC TIME

I hope that, so far, the hypothesis that Christianity is perceived in part of Melanesia as a circulating cult has become tangible. I will try now to reinforce this claim by showing the direction in which Melanesian Christianity has more recently evolved. Two further steps concern us here: firstly, a majority of believers abandoned their historical Churches (Anglican, Catholic and Methodist) to adhere to various Evangelical or micro-Evangelical denominations, and secondly, more recently, they appear to have taken a new direction by joining substantially larger, locally organized, independent Christian Churches.

Although the Melanesian Catholic, Anglican and Methodist Churches were determined to keep their position in Melanesia until Jesus returned,

---

[24] However, Marcel Gauchet (1985) considers Christianity to be the religion with inevitably brings forth 'the end of religion.'

numerous Charismatic Evangelical denominations have rapidly supplanted them. Among the Orokaiva, this happened only 20 to 30 years after the original conversion. Much has been said and written about this transformation (for a comprehensive review see Robbins 2004b), so I will not deal here with the phenomenon as a whole, but concentrate on the points that plead, I believe, for the idea that Evangelical Churches have replaced 'historical' denominations in the same way new circulating cults had been replacing older ones.

Let us note from the start that most Orokaiva people have not only switched Christian religious affiliation once, but they have done it successively at different period intervals. Each time, they say they changed denomination because their former Church has deceived them, failing to deliver the modernity (*development*) that its promoters (missionaries) have promised. This blame closely recalls those addressed to circulating cults once they have lost their efficiency, along their dissolving process. It is also an argument that evangelists rise when attempting to convince villagers to join their Church.

The advent of Evangelism in Melanesia, which appears from afar as a homogeneous social movement, can in fact be divided into three quite distinct periods. Initially, foreign missionaries introduced and promoted a limited number of Charismatic Churches, sometimes according to what seemed, at that time, very modern methods, like preaching with electric guitars on the back platform of a truck. Some of these evangelists then made promises that appeared very appealing to the Orokaiva, like saving their Church members with a helicopter during Armageddon in the year 2000, or establishing bank accounts for them in foreign countries, in which money would multiply miraculously.[25] These denominations rapidly gained momentum and managed to appropriate a large proportion of believers from previously established Churches. However, after a while the Orokaiva turned away from them as their promises remained unfulfilled.

---

[25] During the same period, 'traditional' knowledge also sustained similar promises. In the region surrounding the village where I work, a man presented himself as Totoïma, a famous mythical character. He asked everyone to chip in money, which he promised to invest in order to pay them back, with considerable interest. Everyone did. The man was never seen again and those who gave money felt stupid. Recalling this story, I recently told my friends about what happened in America with Madoff.

Consequently, some years later, these large foreign Evangelical denominations were massively deserted in favor of countless micro-Churches established by local people in their own village. The creation of one such denomination would typically follow a standard pattern: a man pays a visit to a big city, for the Orokaiva, Port Moresby or Lae, to work or just spend time with kin. While there, he attends one of the neighboring Evangelical Churches and learns about the cult it offers. After receiving a vision, he returns home and becomes the promoter and the minister of a new Church and builds an edifice next to his house. Subsequently, only his close kin and friends attend his services. The sermons delivered in such churches usually emphasize personal salvation and proper social behavior in the family and the community, instead of miraculous developments, as former denominations did.

Finally, the third stage consists of the depletion of the former smaller Churches and the appearance of much larger religious movements, modeled on influential Churches (like the Catholic or the Anglican), but independent from their organization and hierarchy. These movements, promoted by local influential men, also often play an important role in politics, local and national. For example, in the Oro Province, several of these Churches (or ministries[26]) regularly back up political candidates for elections. They are also very supportive of inculturation,[27] in contrast to former Evangelical Churches, which often prohibited deep-rooted customary practices, like dancing, eating pork or chewing betel nut.

In Orokaiva view, each new Church, big or small, is to be understood in relation to previous Christian denominations or in relation to former circulating cults. Therefore, the largest of these third-stage ministries claims to represent the 'true original Anglican Church,' whereas the official Anglican Church considers it a Cargo cult. Newly created denominations are thus placed in a continuous line with former local or Christian cults.

On the one hand, historical Christian Churches require their priests to go through a long apprenticeship, usually away from home. Thus, almost all Anglican ministers who are based among the Orokaiva come

---

[26] For certain Orokaiva, a ministry is a branch of a larger Church. In the Oxford dictionary, the term appears as: "The body of men set apart for spiritual functions in the Christian Church or in any religious community."

[27] In Christian official contexts and especially in Catholicism, this term designates the adaptation of the Christian faith and ritual to local cultures.

from other cultures and are rarely proficient in the local language. Communication with the villagers thus remains limited, especially on complex religious issues, as most Orokaiva do not speak pidgin well. In contrast, as it is often argued, part of the success of Evangelical Churches is due to their inclusive approach, permitting common villagers to become ministers without any apprenticeship. Therefore, those who have established their own little Church or founded an extension of larger Evangelical denominations are common Orokaiva villagers standing in good position to attract new recruits. However, their fellow villagers often say that in contrast to earlier priests, their knowledge of the Christian doctrine is very limited. Given these combined circumstances, the Orokaiva regularly deplore that they never managed to obtain reliable information on what Christianity is all about.

This is why the third-stage Churches claim that they will correct this shortcoming and bring 'light' to the worshipers. Furthermore, they ceaselessly repeat that they are 'the last ministry' or the 'last Church.' In their mouths, this expression refers both to the proximity of Jesus's return and to the will to put an end to the ceaseless appearance and disappearance of successive cults. In my view, this claim may constitute the first serious attempt to differentiate Melanesian Christianity from former circulating cults and to bring it in line with the universal notion of religion preached by foreign Christian Churches. To ease the shock produced by this important re-evaluation, the very same Churches propose to render manifest, through inculturation, continuity between Christianity and *kastom* at a different, more superficial, level: a 'Euro-American Church in Melanesian costume.' Today these Churches are very successful, but it is still impossible to evaluate whether they will later evolve into the next generation of circulating cults sweeping through Papua New Guinea or into the first Churches to achieve radical distinction between Christianity and Melanesian circulating cults.

Conclusion

In 1928, F.E. Williams convincingly argued that the cults that were active, in his time, in Papua New Guinea stood in a relation of continuity with what was then called traditional Melanesian religion, the former regularly feeding the latter new ideas and new rituals. In such circumstances, nothing was steady: the cults were randomly appearing and disappearing, and 'traditional Melanesian religion' was ever changing under their repeated influence. However, the system constituted by the relation that linked these two institutions formed a steady dynamic to which the Melanesians were accustomed.[28]

In adopting Williams' analysis, my goal was here to show that when Christianity arrived in Melanesia, it harmoniously entered this dynamic in the position earlier occupied by the cults, which persisted under various forms alongside Christianity. To demonstrate this, I first described the inherently circulating nature of the old Melanesian cults. In my view, these cults constituted one form, among many others, of circulating regional systems well known all over Melanesia. Seeing these cults in this fashion that one could call Durkheimian allowed my analysis to relativize the cumbersome notion of religion in order to bring my subject into the anthropological realm.

I then attempted to show that in most parts of Melanesia, and surely in the Oro Province, Christianity did not arrive at once as a shock, but that the villagers had a great deal of time to become accustomed to its ideas and to reflect on them in their own way. Later on, when these villagers were finally given the opportunity to become Christians, they eagerly converted, having earlier determined, through collective reflection, that Christianity was one of their usual circulating cults.

Then, I investigated what brought the Melanesians to consider that Christianity was much alike a circulating cult. Two consequences of this assimilation are worth restating here. The first one is that, in line with the older circulating cults, Christianity was above all asked to prove its efficacy, a task which Melanesians judged it did not perform well. The second is that Christianity was expected to slowly blend into 'custom,' as previous cults had. Because of these two characteristics, I ventured to say that, thus far, in Melanesia, custom is considered universal and Christianity particular.

Finally, I showed through a rapid examination of subsequent developments toward Evangelism and, today, toward large independent Churches, that Christianity has retained, in the eyes of Melanesians, the specific form of temporality that formerly characterized circulating cults:

---

[28] This is, in spirit, very similar to what Margaret Mead described ten years later among the Arapesh (1938).

followers join a Church, assimilate some of its principles into their customs and then abandon it to convert to a different denomination.[29]

The transformation that the Melanesians I dealt with here imposed on Christianity, by converting it into a non-permanent cult, regularly expecting its replacement, offers, I think, a new case to be added to the long list of studies about Christianization and, more widely, about contact between cultures. In its particularity, it brings to light a methodological point to which I wish to draw attention.

In the realm of religion, as elsewhere, acculturation often operates reciprocally. Here, the appropriation of Christianity did not only affect its visible reality (rituals, definitions of religious concepts and so forth), but its very nature according to the place Melanesians offered it into their own society. In many Melanesian societies, Christianity was considered a form of circulating cult and the Whites who conveyed it were treated as former kin who had left long ago. Even God was pictured as akin to the ancestors. Christianity was in this fashion deprived of its universal attribute and turned into a variant of a local cult.

All this seems to imply that Melanesians have a high sense of stability that blinds them to actual changes, which anthropological observation nonetheless reveals. Indeed, during my many years among the Orokaiva, I witnessed several such changes that one could consider as directly linked to the incorporation of Christianity into local life: for example, commensality has become a prominent feature in rituals, whereas previously taking the food home was the universal practice, or again personal names were partially replaced by family names, and so forth.

The Orokaiva do not negate the novelty of these practices, but see them as part of a wider phenomenon. For them, incorporation of new elements is the very way in which *kastom* thrives. It then becomes difficult if not impossible, as Williams argues, to distinguish the new from the old. This is why their *kastom* always remains true to itself, no matter how much Christianity they know it has absorbed. As Marilyn Strathern (1991) suggested from another standpoint, Melanesians thus bypass the unifying nature of Christianity to preserve the diversity inherent in '*kastom*.'

---

[29] For a similar situation in a different society, see Handman (2015), for example pp. 7–9.

However, Papua New Guinea is today subject to new currents. In 2014, the Speaker of Parliament took it upon himself to chop up with a bush knife a gigantic carved board decorating the pediment of the Parliament House in Port Moresby (Geismar 2014). This board had been installed in 1975, after independence, to glorify the nation's diversity. It was made by diverse male sculptors, each from a different region of the country, who were asked to contribute to the piece by depicting a subject of particular importance to their culture. Most of them represented ancestral or mythical characters. Forty years later, in an interview with the press, the Speaker considers that he was entitled to destroy these ancestral figures because Papua New Guinea has inscribed Christianity in its Constitution. He added that he knew that the presence of these sacrilegious characters on the National Parliament House motivated God to refrain from helping Papua New Guinea become a modern and affluent country.

Fig. 9.1 Map of Papua New Guinea

This story seems to show that despite my allegation that in Melanesia religion has not succeeded in uprooting local ideology, elements of inversions crop up in which Christianity is presented as universal and exclusive. However, simultaneously, the Speaker's assertion that a sacrilege has again inhibited the country's modernization matches perfectly similar declarations made by earlier Cargo cults' prophets in the late 1940s. It remains therefore impossible to foresee whether the Parliament Speaker will end up, in the short run, inverting former religious practices or creating a new circulating cult. If this latter case proves true, the religious movement that he represents will then probably gradually vanish as its elements are slowly integrated into Papua New Guinea's national culture (Fig. 9.1).

REFERENCES

Burridge, Kenelm. 1960. *Mambu: A Study of Melanesian Cargo Movements and their Social and Ideological Background*. New York: Harper and Row.

Dumont, Louis. 1986 [1983]. *Essays On Individualism : Modern ideology in anthropological perspective*. Chicago: The University of Chicago Press.

Eriksen, Annelin. 2008. *Gender, Christianity and Change in Vanuatu: An analysis of social movements in North Ambrym*. Bergen: University of Bergen.

Gauchet, Marcel. 1985. *Le Désenchantement du monde, Une histoire politique de la religion*. Paris: Gallimard.

Geismar, Haidy. 2014. http://www.materialworldblog.com/2014/02/a-new-government-breaks-with-the-past-in-the-papua-new-guinea-parliaments-haustambaran/.

Handman, Courtney. 2015. *Critical Christianity : Translation and denominational conflict in Papua New Guinea*. Oakland: University of California Press.

Iteanu, André. 1998. Corps et décor. In *La Production des corps*, ed. M. Godelier, and M. Panoff, 115–139. Amsterdam: Édition des Archives Contemporaines—Overseas Publishers Association.

Iteanu, André. 2008. La mondialisation par le petit bout de la lorgnette. *Anthropologica* 50 (1): 87–101.

Iteanu, André. 2015. Recycling Values: Perspectives from Melanesia. *Hau* 5 (1): 137–150.

Iteanu, André, and Eytan Kapon. 2007. *Come Back Tomorrow*, documentary film, 71 minutes, distribution: Iteanu and Kapon.

Johnston, Elin. 2003. *Bishop George : Man of two worlds*. Melbourne: Currency Communications.

Lawrence, Peter. 1964. *Road Belong Cargo: A Study of the Cargo Movement in the Southern Madang District, New Guinea*. Manchester: Manchester University Press.

Lindstrom, Lamont, and Geoffrey M. White (eds.). 1994. *Culture, Kastom, Tradition: Developing cultural policy in Melanesia*. Suva: Institute of Pacific Studies, University of the South Pacific.

Malinowski, Bronislaw. 1922. *Argonauts of the Western Pacific*. London: George Routledge and Sons.

Mead, Margaret. 1938. *The Mountain Arapesh*. New York: The American Museum of Natural History.

Monnerie, Denis. 1996. *Nitu. Les vivants, les morts et le cosmos selon la société de Mono-Alu (Iles Salomon)*. Leiden: Research School CNWS.

Mosko, Marc. 2015. Unbecoming individuals: The partible character of the Christian person. *Hau* 5 (1): 361–393.

Polanyi, Karl. 2001 [1944]. *The Great Transformation: The political and economic origins of our time*. Boston: Beacon Press.

Rio, Knut M. 2002. The sorcerer as an absented third person. Formations of fear and anger in Vanuatu. *Social Analysis* 46: 129–154.

Robbins, Joel. 2004a. *Becoming Sinners: Christianity and moral torment in a Papua New Guinea society*. Berkeley, Los Angeles and London: University of California Press.

Robbins, Joel. 2004b. The Globalization of Pentecostal and Charismatic Christianity. *Annual Review of Anthropology* 33: 117–143.

Schneider, Almut. 2011. *La vie qui vient d'ailleurs: mouvement, échanges et rituel dans les Hautes-Terres de la Papouasie-Nouvelle-Guinée*. Paris: EHESS.

Strathern, Andrew. 1971. *The Rope of Moka: Big-men and ceremonial exchange in Mount Hagen, New Guinea*. Cambridge: Cambridge University Press.

Strathern, Marilyn. 1988. *The Gender of the Gift*. Berkeley: University of California Press.

Strathern, Marilyn. 1991. *Partial Connections*. Walnut Creek, CA.: AltaMira Press.

Trompf, Gary (ed.). 1977. *Prophets of Melanesia*. Port Moresby: The Institute of Papua New Guinea Studies.

Trompf, Gary. 1991. *Melanesian Religion*. Cambridge: Cambridge University Press.

Trompf, Gary. 2006. *Religions of Melanesia. A Bibliographic Survey*. Westport: Praeger Publishers.

Vevehupa, Lucian. 2013. *The Man Who Would Not Die. Autobiography of an Orokaiva* (bilingual Orokaiva-English, translation André Iteanu). Port Moresby: University of Papua New Guinea Press.

Waiko, John. 1984. *The Binandere People of Papua New Guinea*. Bathurst, N.S.W.: Robert Brown.

Williams, F.E. 1978 (1923). *The Vailala Madness and the Destruction of Native Ceremonies in the Gulf Division*. New York: AMS Press.
Williams, F.E. 1928. *Orokaiva Magic*. Oxford: The Clarendon Press.
Worsley, Peter. 1968. *The Trumpet Shall Sound: A Study of "Cargo" Cults in Melanesia*. New York: Schocken Books.

Author Biography

André Iteanu is a social anthropologist. He is Directeur de recherche and a member of the Center for Southeast Asian Studies (CASE, CNRS-EHESS) in Paris at the French National Center for Scientific Research and Professor (DE) at the École Pratique des Hautes Études (Paris). He has carried out research among the Orokaiva of Papua New Guinea and among marginalized youngsters in the northern suburbs of Paris. Among his latest publications are "Comparison made radical: Dumont's anthropology of value today" (*Hau*, 2015), *Lucian Vevehupa, The man who would not die. Autobiography of an Orokaiva man* (2013), and *La cohérence des sociétés* (A. Iteanu, ed., 2010).

Index

A
Abhidhamma, 79, 80
Abrahamic religions, 5, 22
Adat, 25–29, 128, 129, 135–137, 139, 140, 147, 155, 158, 159, 169, 170, 186, 197, 198, 200, 201, 203, 204, 210, 211, 213
Agama
  agama Hindu, 25–27, 29, 124, 130, 134, 137, 139, 140, 142–144, 146–148, 154, 155, 157–162, 164, 165, 168, 170, 171, 173–177, 179, 180, 192, 201, 203, 204, 211, 213
Akshardham Mandir, 166, 174
Anak tā, 75, 82, 85
Ancestors, 25, 27, 29, 82, 98, 103–105, 107, 109, 110, 112–118, 129, 136, 138, 142, 155–158, 170, 174, 175, 178, 187, 195, 198, 201–203, 207, 212, 223, 224, 242, 263, 264, 267, 268, 273
Aṅg Cănd (King), 75
Aṅg Ḍuoṅ (King), 71, 72
Anglican, 28, 261, 263, 266–268, 270
Animism, animist, 24, 27, 95, 99, 100, 103, 108, 110, 113, 115, 138, 153, 155, 159, 174, 177, 180
Apotropaic, 83, 85, 91
Appropriation, 4, 8, 19, 22, 30, 109, 159, 179, 273
Arya Samaj, 163, 166, 171
Asian traditions, 6, 7, 22

B
Balineseness (*Kebalian*), 135
Balinese religion, 25, 26, 124, 133, 136–138, 140, 142, 143, 146, 147, 157
Batha (P. *basha*), 40, 44–46, 56, 58, 62, 63
Belief, 2–4, 16, 18, 25, 28–30, 42, 44, 58, 69, 79, 85, 124, 128, 129, 136, 137, 139, 140, 153–158, 164, 176, 186, 187, 189, 190, 195, 197, 199, 200, 202, 203, 210, 212, 231, 234, 236, 241, 255, 264
Bhagavadgita, 157, 159, 162, 163, 179

Bhishma Kund, 162, 166, 175
Brahmana, 130, 132, 133, 144, 147
Brahmanism, Brahmanist, 24, 47, 68,
    71, 75–77, 91, 103
Buddha, 13–17, 22, 40–43, 46, 48,
    50, 60, 62, 63, 87, 89, 174
Buddhasāsanā, 23, 24, 68–71, 75, 78,
    82, 84, 86, 87, 90, 91
Buddhism, Buddhist, Buddhicization
    Hīnayāna Buddhism, 48
    Mahāyāna Buddhism, 14, 48
    Theravāda Buddhism, 14–16, 22,
        41, 48, 49, 71, 85
    Vajrayāna Buddhism, 14
Burma, Burmese, 22, 23, 39, 41, 43,
    45, 47, 48, 50, 58, 83
Buth Savong, 80

C

Cakkavattin, 89, 92
Cambodia, Cambodian, 22–25, 48,
    67–75, 77–81, 83, 87–91, 103
Canon, canonical, 6, 8, 11, 14, 17, 23,
    50, 71–73, 141
Cargo cult, 258, 265, 270
Catholic, Catholicism, 4, 14, 27, 28,
    140, 173, 188, 189, 191–194,
    199–201, 203–205, 207, 212,
    217, 221, 222, 225, 226, 228,
    230, 232–234, 236, 242, 268,
    270
Ceylon, 14–17, 73
Christian, Christianity,
    Christianization, 3–11, 15,
    16, 18, 22, 23, 25–28, 45,
    102, 123, 128, 133, 135, 137,
    139–143, 151, 169, 170, 177,
    187, 189, 194, 199, 202–206,
    209, 210, 212, 213, 218, 228,
    268, 271
Chuon Nath, 73, 80, 83, 85, 88

Circulating cult, 28, 29, 256–258,
    260, 264–271
Colonial, colonialism, 5–8, 10, 12,
    15–18, 20, 22, 23, 28, 43, 45,
    51, 52, 55, 71, 79, 83, 123, 129,
    132–134, 139, 188, 218, 236–
    238, 240–243, 253, 254, 256
Commoners (jaba), 136, 137, 144
Communist party, 75
Conflict, 68, 136, 145, 147, 158, 164,
    169, 171, 177, 193, 194, 200,
    203–206, 210, 257
Cosmic, 21, 25, 28–30, 89, 96, 108,
    128, 187, 189, 198, 207, 209,
    211, 223
Cosmos, 9, 72, 111
Crawfurd, John, 130
Culture, 2, 4, 7, 11, 18, 19, 42, 49,
    68, 73, 76, 88, 98, 100, 102,
    115, 160, 164, 198, 206, 252,
    262, 263, 265, 271
Custom, 5, 8, 20, 29, 60, 69, 73, 84,
    128, 135, 136, 155, 180, 203,
    205, 223, 255, 265

D

Deities, 175, 176, 180, 190, 198,
    202, 207, 209, 210, 226
Dhamma, 22–24, 40, 74, 78–81, 83,
    90–92
Dhammayuttika, 72, 74, 83
Dharma, 9–12, 127, 128, 132, 146,
    147, 148, 159, 165
Dialogic, 8, 18–20, 30
Diaspora, 69, 79, 84, 90
Disenchantment, 29, 158, 159, 179
Doctrine, 3, 4, 6, 11, 13, 18, 20,
    22, 23, 29, 63, 73, 78, 79, 128,
    155–158, 165, 166, 171, 177,
    181, 271
Donation (dāna), 81, 83

Dutch, 28, 124, 129–135, 138, 139, 185, 186, 192, 193, 198, 200, 217, 218, 228, 230, 232–234, 236, 238–243

E
Elders, 48, 186, 193, 195, 200, 202–204, 208
Elite, 11, 15, 22, 124, 136, 158
Enlightenment, 4, 6, 166, 237
Ethnic, ethnicity, 6, 8, 9, 20, 24, 27, 43, 46, 53, 56, 70, 88, 99–101, 107, 109, 113, 115–117, 129, 135, 140, 142, 143, 146, 150, 170

F
Flotsam and jetsam, 186, 195, 197, 199
French Protectorate, 80
Friederich, Rudolf, 131

G
Galela, 223, 236, 238–241
Galvão, António, 223, 225
Ganges, 26, 27, 162, 166, 171–173, 177, 179, 180
Globalization, 19, 20, 26, 67, 147, 254
Grotius, Hugo, 229

H
Halmahera, 28, 227, 236–243
Haratut, 195, 198, 206, 210–212
Haridwar, 26, 161, 162, 166, 170–172, 174, 179
Hindu, Hinduism, Hinduization, 7–14, 18, 22, 25, 27, 29, 123, 124, 130, 131, 133, 137, 138, 141–143, 146–148, 154, 156–159, 163, 165, 173, 180, 201, 203, 210, 251
Houses, 104, 106, 109, 112, 113, 115, 193, 195, 197, 200, 206–208, 220, 237, 242, 258
Hukum, 129, 197, 198, 201, 210
Huot Tat, 73, 80

I
Identity, 1, 17, 20, 23, 24, 26, 46, 49–52, 56, 67, 72, 98, 105, 107, 114, 115, 117, 133–135, 139, 144–146, 169, 170, 231, 234, 239, 242
Immanent, 8, 27, 153–159, 171, 175, 177, 178, 180
Independence, 23, 26, 49, 52, 53, 88, 139, 144, 192, 268
India, Indian, 8, 9, 11, 12, 14, 16, 17, 26–28, 61, 71, 72, 81, 123, 126, 127, 130, 132, 133, 137, 138, 141–143, 145, 147, 154, 156, 159–162, 165, 166, 168–170, 173–177, 179, 217
Individual, individualism, individualistic, 2, 10, 57, 62, 75, 81, 83, 91, 106, 193, 207, 211, 229, 253, 254, 264
Indonesia, Indonesian, 25–29, 123–126, 128, 129, 133, 134, 138–141, 143–146, 153–155, 157, 159–161, 164, 165, 168, 169, 172, 177, 185, 188, 197, 198, 200, 203, 207, 210, 212, 226
Intelligentsia, 11, 124, 134, 137, 146
Islam, Islamic, Islamization, 7–9, 11, 22, 25, 26, 29, 123, 124, 126, 129, 130, 133–135, 138, 139,

141, 143, 144, 147, 155, 168, 173, 188, 191, 197, 203, 205, 212, 227, 228, 233, 236, 243

J
Jailolo, 221, 227, 240
Jāti, 73, 83, 89
Java, Javanese, 123, 126, 127, 130, 131, 133, 138, 143, 161, 162, 164, 165, 170, 172, 186, 202, 224, 225
Jesuits, 217, 226, 227, 233
Jru', 24, 25, 96, 100–104, 107–110, 112–117

K
Kaba Aye council, 49, 50
Kamma, kammatic, 82, 85, 91, 92
Kastom, 29, 252, 253, 261, 266, 271, 273
Kerauhan *(possession)*, 175
Khleang Muang, 75–77, 91
Khmer, Khmerness, 25, 67–76, 79, 81–85, 88–90, 101
Kurukshetra, 162, 163, 166, 173

L
Laity, 15, 17, 43, 51
Language, 9, 11, 16, 22, 69, 71, 73, 79, 81, 99, 115, 124, 127, 129, 131, 132, 134, 186, 188, 189, 194, 197, 202, 208, 210, 212, 213, 238, 252, 259, 263, 271
Lao, Laos, 22, 24, 25, 48, 67, 97–103, 107, 109, 113, 116
Law, 9, 10, 19, 28, 54, 126, 128, 131, 132, 198, 206, 229, 232, 242
Ledi (abbot of), 46
Localization, 19, 22, 25, 30, 50

Lór, 187, 195–198, 210, 211
Loven. *See Jru'*

M
Ma Ba Tha, 41, 46, 53, 56, 62, 63
Mahanikaya sect, 72, 74, 81
Majapahit, 130, 136, 172, 224
Majelis Ulama Indonesia (MUI), 164, 165
Malay, 127, 129, 132, 134, 135, 149, 185, 197, 198
Meditation, 15, 162, 170
Merits, 48, 53, 77, 81, 82, 92, 243
Millet, 195–197, 200, 204–206, 212
Missionaries, 5, 7, 8, 10, 12, 15, 17, 22, 23, 28, 44, 45, 123, 133, 189, 205, 238, 239, 241, 243, 257, 262
Modernity, modernization, 6, 20, 74, 124, 153, 154, 159, 160, 179, 252, 269
Moksa, 27, 157, 162, 174, 177–179
Moluccas, 25, 185, 188, 190, 192, 193, 200, 217, 219, 220, 222, 223, 232, 236
Monastery, monasteries, 56, 69, 74–76, 79–89, 92
Monastic, 15, 22, 43, 47, 49, 52–54, 69, 74, 88
Monk, 17, 23, 24, 43, 47–50, 52–55, 62, 69, 73–76, 92, 103, 108, 110, 111, 116
Monotheism, monotheistic, 4, 11, 26, 140, 147, 155, 174, 176
Moro, 227
Mortuary rituals, 105, 111, 114, 115
Muslim, 9–12, 22, 23, 26, 28, 29, 41, 44, 53, 56, 68, 123, 128, 136, 138–140, 143, 161, 164, 165, 167, 169, 170, 172, 177, 185, 186, 189, 193, 194, 199, 200,

202–204, 207, 211, 234, 237, 238, 241

N
National League for Democracy (NLD), 54, 57
National, nationalist, 8, 11, 13, 23, 46, 47, 49, 50, 52–54, 68, 70, 73–75, 88, 91, 129, 139, 146, 154, 160, 168, 205
Natural Law, 229, 231, 232, 243
Neo-Hinduism, 13, 142
Netherlands East Indies, 218, 236, 243
Ne Win, 23, 53
Nibbāna, 87, 91
Niskala, 156, 175, 176
Nobility (*triwangsa*), 136
Nu (Prime Minister), 49, 53, 58

O
Offering, 72, 77, 81, 104, 106, 107, 111, 112, 115, 156, 195, 196, 204, 206, 209, 212, 221
Orientalism, Orientalist, 7, 8, 11, 13–18, 23, 47, 71, 123, 130–133
Orthodoxy, 3, 8, 49, 136, 154, 158
Orthopraxy, 3, 8, 136, 154, 158

P
Padroado Real, 221
Pali
  Pali canon. *See Tipitaka*
  Pali Text Society, 71, 73
Pancasila, 139, 155
Panca Sraddha, 157
Paṅsukūl, 77, 82
Parisada
  Parisada Besakih, 146
Parisada Campuan, 146
Parisada Hindu Dharma, 142, 144, 201
Parisada Dharma Hindu Bali, 141, 142, 147
Parisada Hindu Dharma Indonesia, 143, 144, 147–149, 159
Patronage, 54, 83, 92, 148, 206, 221, 228, 229
Patronato Real, 222
Patrons, 53, 92, 141
Pedanda, 130, 132, 145, 146, 178
Pigafetta, António, 220, 223
Pilgrim, pilgrimage, 26, 27, 145, 147, 148, 154, 159–163, 165, 167–169, 171, 173–177
Protestant, Protestantism, 4, 11, 14–16, 193, 199, 200, 203–205, 229, 233, 234, 242
Purification, 23, 53, 74, 83, 88, 98, 172, 173
Pursat, 69, 80
Pwe, 59, 60, 62, 102

R
Raffles, Thomas Stamford, 131
Rationalization, 8, 22, 153, 155, 179
Reformation, 4, 6, 222
Reform, reformer, reformist, 136, 138, 139, 145, 159, 162, 163, 166, 168, 173, 174, 176, 177, 180
Relics, 87
Religion
  Local Religion, 102
  national religion, 72, 130
  National Religion, 71
  state religion, 53, 155, 228
  world religion, 5, 6, 8, 9, 13, 15, 16, 19–21, 24–26, 29, 30, 90, 95, 102, 116, 125, 157, 159, 176, 211

Religionization, 18, 21, 23, 41, 42, 63, 75, 98, 124
Renunciation, 47, 48, 55, 62, 227, 233
Revival, 15, 16, 49, 73, 78, 144, 259
Rice, 89, 107, 110, 155
Rishikesh, 162, 166, 171
Ritual, ritualist, ritualistic, ritualization, 3, 9, 15, 16, 19, 20, 23, 24, 26, 57–62, 81, 82, 196, 197, 199, 205, 209, 210, 212, 213, 236, 256, 260, 264, 267
Roi civilisateur, 225, 243

S

Sacrifice, 104, 110, 111, 113, 115
Saffron revolution, 52, 53
Sailboat, 197, 208, 209, 211
Sampradaya, 144–146
Sangha
 Sangha Maha Nayaka Ahpwe, 53–55
Sanskrit, 9, 10, 25, 27, 72, 125–128, 131, 136, 155, 163, 178
Sasana, sāsana, sāsanā, 127, 132
Secularization, 4, 8, 22, 45
Sekala, 156
Sermons, 69, 79, 80, 82, 165, 270
Shiva, 127, 161
Siam, Siamese, 72–75
Sīla, 76
Social space, 23, 46, 56, 58
Socio-cosmic order, 21, 208
Somvir, Yadav, 163, 166, 171
Spirit
 spirit cults, 20, 42, 74, 82, 87
 spirit possession, 57, 58, 60
 spirit religion, 24, 96, 100, 102, 111
 spirit worship, 23, 44, 56, 62
Spiritual, 2, 15, 43, 74, 81–83, 91, 109, 164, 166, 170–172, 177, 180, 222, 230, 238–240, 243

State Law and Order Restoration Council (SLORC), 54
State Peace and Development Council (SPDC), 39
Statue, 77, 83, 87, 160, 174, 175, 187, 193, 202
Sun-Moon God, 186, 195, 198, 208, 209
Superstition, 3, 6, 8, 15, 19, 20, 99, 128, 129, 132, 200, 203, 210

T

Teaching, 15–17, 22, 50, 73, 80, 89, 91, 128, 156, 166, 171, 200, 213
Temporality, 257, 259–261, 266
Ternate, 28, 221, 223–227, 232, 233, 236–238
Thathana (P. *sāsana*), 40
Theosophical Society, 15
Tidore, 28, 220, 221, 223–225, 227, 236, 237
Tipitaka *(Three Baskets)*, 47, 71
Tirtha
 tirtha yatra, 145, 154, 159–168, 170, 171, 173, 176–180
 tirtha yatra, 159, 167
Titib, I Made, 160, 166
Tobaru, 223
Tobelo, 223, 227, 228, 238–241
Tradition
 local tradition, 8, 9, 19–21, 24, 26, 30, 95, 102, 136, 180, 204
Trance possession, 179
Two religions thesis, 58

U

Universalism, 25, 47, 144
Utrechtsche Zendingsvereeniging, 237

V

Value, 28, 30, 41, 55, 82, 97, 98, 113, 117, 135, 189, 195, 210, 211, 222, 253
van Baarda, M.J., 238–240
van Dijken, Hendrik, 237, 238
van Hoëvell, Wolter Robert Baron, 131
Veda, 11, 145, 157, 159
Vereenigde Oostindische Compagnie (VOC), 217
Vietnam, Vietnamese, 68, 75, 83, 89, 101, 109
Vinaya (monastic rule), 47

W

Warga, 144–146
Water, 173, 175, 177–179
World Hindu Federation, 148
World Hindu Parisad, 148
Worship, 5, 6, 12, 27, 30, 56, 58, 60, 82, 128, 131, 132, 153–155, 228, 264

Y

Yoga, 164–166, 169, 170
Yoya, 60

Printed by Printforce, the Netherlands